GCSE
Applied Business
FOR OCR

DOUBLE AWARD

Carol Carysforth
Mike Neild

OCR
RECOGNISING ACHIEVEMENT

Heinemann

Heinemann Educational Publishers,
Halley Court, Jordan Hill, Oxford OX2 8EJ
A division of Harcourt Education Ltd

Heinemann is a registered trademark of Harcourt Education Limited

OXFORD MELBOURNE AUCKLAND JOHANNESBURG BLANTYRE
GABORONE IBADAN PORTSMOUTH NH (USA) CHICAGO

© Carol Carysforth, Mike Neild 2002

First published 2002

07 06 05 04 03 02
10 9 8 7 6 5 4 3 2 1

British Library Cataloguing in Publication Data is available from the British Library on request.

ISBN 0 435 44746 7

Copyright notice
All rights reserved. No part of this publication may be reproduced in any form or by any means (including photocopying or storing it in any medium by electronic means and whether or not transiently or incidentally to some other use of this publication) without the written permission of the copyright owner, except in accordance with the provision of the Copyright, Designs and Patents Act 1988 or under the terms of a licence issued by the Copyright Licensing Agency, 90 Tottenham Court Road, London W1T 4LP. Applications for the copyright owner's written permission should be addressed to the publisher.

Designed by Artistix

Typeset by J&L Composition

Original illustrations © Harcourt Education Limited, 2002

Printed in Spain by Edelvives

Cover design: Artistix

Cover photo: © Arcblue

Acknowledgements
Every effort has been made to contact copyright holders of material reproduced in this book. Any omissions will be rectified in subsequent printings if notice is given to the publishers.

Websites
There are links to relevant websites in this book. In order to ensure that the links are up to date, that the links work, and that the sites are not inadvertently linked to sites that could be considered offensive, we have made the links available on the Heinemann website at *www.heinemann.co.uk/hotlinks*. When you access the site, the express code is 7467P.

Tel: 01865 888058
www.heinemann.co.uk

Contents

Acknowledgements — iv
Introduction — vii

Unit 1 Investigating business — 1

Chapter 1	Aims and objectives of businesses	2
Chapter 2	Business ownership	11
Chapter 3	Business location	29
Chapter 4	Business activity	37
Chapter 5	Functional areas within business	54
Chapter 6	Business communications	101
Chapter 7	External influences on business	112

Portfolio evidence for Unit 1 — 137

Unit 2 People and business — 147

Chapter 8	Stakeholders	149
Chapter 9	Investigating job roles	163
Chapter 10	Working arrangements	186
Chapter 11	Rights of employers and employees	203
Chapter 12	Resolving disagreements	224
Chapter 13	Recruitment	235
Chapter 14	Personal job applications	246
Chapter 15	Staff development and training	259
Chapter 16	Customer service	269

Portfolio evidence for Unit 2 — 285

Unit 3 Business finance — 293

Chapter 17	Investigating the flow of financial documents used to make a business purchase	295
Chapter 18	Investigating methods of making and receiving payments	321
Chapter 19	Covering the costs of a new product or service	332
Chapter 20	Using a cash-flow forecast	337
Chapter 21	Using a budget	350
Chapter 22	Calculating the break-even point	357
Chapter 23	Calculating the profit or loss of a business	366
Chapter 24	Understanding a balance sheet	371
Chapter 25	The importance of business accounts	378
Chapter 26	Sources of business finance	385
Chapter 27	Financial planning	397

The external test for Unit 3 — 405

Appendix 1: Getting the most out of work experience — 408

Appendix 2: Photocopiable documents for use with activities in Unit 3, Chapter 17 — 412

Index — 419

Acknowledgements

The authors would like to record their thanks and gratitude to all those who so freely gave of their time and expertise to help in the writing and production of this book and the associated tutor resource file and the Richer Sounds StudentZone.

Especial thanks are due to Catherine Carysforth, LLB; Joanna McGowan, MA, BA (Hons), GIPD and Maureen Rawlinson, LID for their specialist assistance in relation to employment law, consumer law and human resources. Our gratitude is also due to David Williams and Paul Carysforth – both experienced IT practitioners – for their advice and assistance on IT, e-business and e-marketing; to Matt Neild for his expert help with environmental issues in relation to motor vehicle developments and to Carolyn Briggs, a local employer, for her advice on work experience placements. We would also like to thank Sarah Garbett for converting our original, rather basic PowerPoint slides into works of art – and also our team who helped with the index – Matt, Roger Neild and Frances Russell.

We also owe a great debt to the Directors and colleagues at Richer Sounds plc, who prepared the StudentZone on their website, to provide the opportunity for GCSE students reading this book to investigate their business online. Firstly, we would like to thank them for believing in and supporting the original idea, secondly for their continual encouragement and assistance as the project took shape, and thirdly for inspiring us by proving that it is possible to run a large, successful and ethical business that consistently places care for its employees and its customers at the top of its agenda. If only a handful of all the students who read this book each year internalise those ideals and put them into practice in business, the project will have been more than worthwhile.

Particular thanks are due to Julian Richer, the owner and founder – for his vision and ideals – and his ability to 'grow' a company without losing sight of either; and David Robinson, the MD – for his inspirational decision-making and ongoing support and help. We are also grateful to Gemma Baker, David's PA, for her consistently cheerful and friendly approach as she undertook the difficult job of being our main channel of communication and pulling the whole project together. Many Directors and colleagues in the company provided invaluable help by patiently answering our questions and finding the time to clarify our queries. Especial thanks are due to Jez Avens, Deputy MD and Store Operations Director for lending us a helping hand so cheerfully on so many occasions; many thanks, too, to John Currier, Financial Director; John Clayton, Training Director; Tracey Armstrong, Colleague Support Manage (for her friendly support to us, too!); Claudia Vernon, Marketing Director and Dan Burnham, Marketing Manager; Nick Halliday, Purchasing Director; Darren Woodward, IT Manager; Perry Sillett, Repairs and Servicing Manager; Lee Lynane, Property Manager and Solomon Essah Essel,

Distribution Director. Thanks are also due to all the colleagues who prepared colleague profiles – Lee Nelson, Field Sales Manager; Clive Lambert, Store Manager/AD; Andrea Day, Sales Assistant; Lol Lecanu, Marketing Manager and James Donnan, Cost Control Manager. Thanks are also due to all the IT staff both at Richer Sounds and Heinemann who were involved in the StudentZone.

As ever, thanks are also owed to all our colleagues at Heinemann – particularly Susan Ross, who edited the typescript, for her meticulous attention to detail and Anna Fabrizio, our editor, who coped with numerous requests and problems with her customary good humour and positive approach. Finally, no book of ours would be complete without thanks being given to our friend and development editor, Margaret Berriman, for her continual support, encouragement and inspiration throughout each new project we attempt.

The authors and publishers would also like to thank the following individuals and organisations for permission to reproduce photographs and other copyright material:

ACAS page 230; Alvey & Towers Picture Library pages 41, 208, 270, 295; Amnesty International page 156; Courtesy of Apple page 93; Bluewater page 33; BMW group Press Club page 73; Carphone Warehouse page 18; CBI page 156; CEC Mark Boulton pages 115, 192, 259, 324; Club 18–30 page 117; Corbis/JFPI Studios Inc. page 105; Haddon Davies page 217; Empics/John Marsh page 30; Empics/Neal Simpson page 39; Eyewire page 71; Hamley's plc page 7; Health and Safety Executive/Crown copyright page 212; HJ Heinz & Co page 84; Hulton Archive page 126; Imparta Ltd page 261; Investors in People page 265; John Walmsley Education Photos pages 149, 192, 246, 259; KidSmart page 156; Marks and Spencer pages 278, 375; National Training Awards page 265; PA Photos/Johnny Green page 153; PA/Chris Ison page 231; Photodisc pages 174, 205, 217, 348; The Prince's Trust page 389; Red Letter Days page 20; Rex Features/Ray Tang page 122; Richer Sounds page 11; Roger Scruton page 22; Seabrook Crisps Ltd page 80; Seaward Electronic Ltd page 273; Shell Livewire 160; Shelter page 156; SPL/Martin Bond page 130; SPL/Mauro Fermariello page 15; Stone/Mark Douet page 98; Stone/Jon Gray page 86; Stone/Sean Murphy page 49; Stone/Bob Thomas page 74; Stone/Terry Vine page 61; Tesco pages 33, 46; UCLH page 155; Woodfall Wild Images page 130.

Carol Carysforth and Mike Neild
August 2002

Dedication

To Paul and Caroline

May your future together be filled with hugs and kisses, love and laughter, obedient dogs and MU wins!

Introduction

Welcome to **GCSE Applied Business**. This book has been written to help you enjoy and *understand* business today, so that you will achieve the best grades you can for this award.

Special features

The following features have been included to help you.

- An overview at the start of each chapter, to tell you about the topics you will learn.
- Regular Spot checks so that you can check that you understand a topic.
- Snapshots which give up-to-date examples from real businesses.
- Fact files to help you to understand important points.
- What can go wrong sections, which identify problems businesses may encounter. These will help you when you write about your investigations into a real business and need to analyse or explain a situation.
- It makes you think and Over to you activities – which give you problems to think about or tasks to do, either on your own or in a group.
- Case studies and Integrated activities – so that you can apply your knowledge to real situations.
- A section review and practice, at the end of each chapter – to test your own knowledge and understanding. Your tutor will tell you if you should do the red flag or the green flag questions.

Help with your portfolio evidence

- Portfolio evidence sections at the end of Unit 1 and Unit 2 help you to identify the evidence you need and explain clearly what you need to do to obtain a good grade from your awarding body.
- The work experience section helps you to get the most out of work experience. This is very important if you are also obtaining evidence for your portfolio from your work experience placement.
- The external test section at the end of Unit 3 explains how to prepare for the test and achieve the best mark possible.

Chapter 1 — Aims and objectives of business

What you will learn
Linking business aims and objectives
'SMART' objectives
Monitoring performance

Overview: business aims and objectives

Why do businesses exist?

All businesses exist for a reason or purpose – either to make a product or to offer a service, and in some cases to do both. To survive, a business needs income from selling its goods or services, so it has to offer something that consumers or industry want and will pay to obtain.

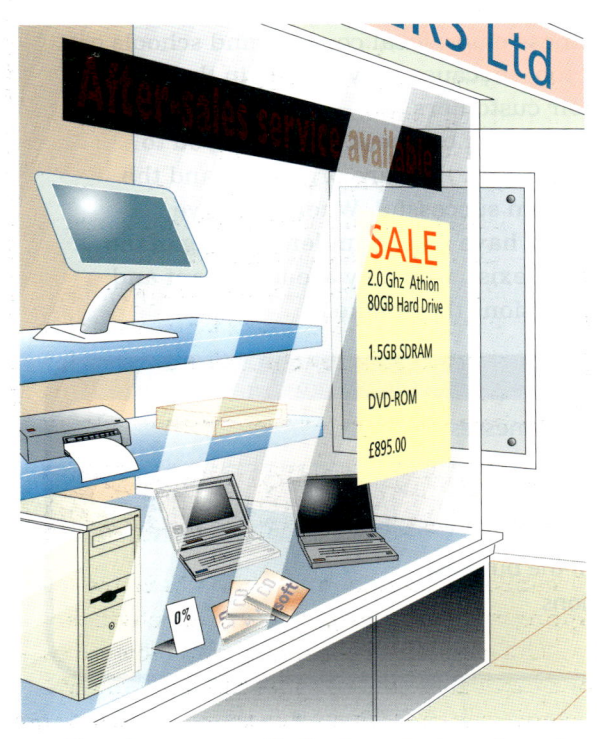

Many businesses offer both products and services

Fact file

All organisations in the **private sector** need to make a profit to survive in the long term. These are business enterprises owned and controlled by companies and private individuals. Their revenue – or income – from sales must be greater than the costs of running the business. Examples of private sector businesses range from corner shops to large enterprises such as the supermarket chain Tesco.

Institutions owned or controlled by the government or local authority are in the **public sector**. Their revenue comes mostly through government grants and funding. Although they may not have to make a profit, there are strict controls over how they spend their money. Examples include the police and the National Health Service.

Business aims

An **aim** is a goal the business wants to achieve. A business may have one aim or several:

- In the private sector, businesses aim to make a profit. Public sector businesses aim to make a profit if possible and meet strict expenditure targets (costs must not exceed grants and income).
- All businesses aim to provide goods and/or services, either to their local community (such as a newsagent) or to the wider community (such as Ford cars).
- When times are difficult, some businesses may simply aim to survive.
- Some businesses aim to grow larger – to expand.
- Often businesses aim to maximise sales. This means selling as much as they can. Or they may choose to improve the quality of their products.
- Some businesses aim to provide a highly

competitive service, so that they will do more business than their competitors.
- Some businesses focus instead on providing a charitable or voluntary service, such as the NSPCC or the Samaritans.
- Today, many businesses also aim to be environmentally friendly.

Although a business may have more than one aim, most tend to focus on just two or three. This allows them to target their efforts more effectively.

Business objectives

We all have aims. For example, you may aim to pass all your exams, or to get fitter, or to save up for something you really want. To achieve your aims you will need to take specific steps towards them. First, you have to decide what these steps are (the easy bit!), then you have to keep on doing them (which is much harder). You also need some way of measuring your progress so that you know whether you are 'on target' to achieve your aims.

Businesses also need to decide what steps to take to achieve their aims and to set targets or **objectives** along the way. For instance, a business may try to:

- sell more products than its competitors
- provide more services than in the previous year
- produce new goods or provide a new service
- improve a product or service.

It then has to work out how to achieve its objectives. It also needs to know *when* it has achieved them and it can do this only if it can measure its progress.

This is achieved by having **measurable objectives**. Therefore, instead of simply saying you will 'save more', you set yourself a target or objective – 'I will save £5 a month', for example. It is then much easier to see if you are succeeding or not. In a business, this means deciding exactly what will be done and by when, for example 'We will introduce six new products over the next 12 months'. The best objectives are SMART objectives, as you will see on page 6.

Snapshot

Going for organic growth

Research by the supermarket chain Tesco showed that 63 per cent of its customers would like to buy more organic products. In response, Tesco, which already offers 1000 organic items, revised its aims and objectives. It now wants to increase sales of organic products to £1 billion by 2006 and intends to do this by increasing the range available and cutting prices, which are currently about 20 per cent higher than other goods. It also hopes to supply more organic British products. At present about 80 per cent of its organic range is imported.

The largest supermarket supplier of organic produce is currently Sainsbury's, which sells about £235 million worth a year against Tesco's sales, in 2001, of £200 million. Tesco aims to become a major supplier in this area.

Spot check

Write down your answers to the following questions:

1. What is an aim?
2. Identify one personal aim you have.
3. If you started your own business, what would be your major aim?
4. What is an objective?
5. Decide one objective which would help you to achieve your personal aim.
6. Adams Childrenswear wants to grow by 20 per cent over the next five years. Is this a measurable objective? Give a reason for your answer.

Linking aims and objectives

Organisations select only aims which are appropriate to their purpose and activities.

Once an aim has been agreed, objectives – or practical steps – are identified to help to achieve the aim. These are then converted into measurable targets. From this, you can see customers away from each other. Superstores also tempt customers with other products and services, such as loyalty cards, family parking bays, coffee shops and cash machines. Tesco offers loans, travel insurance and car insurance as well as home shopping via the Internet.

If the aim is to be highly competitive, objectives will be set to enable the organisation to be one step ahead of its rivals. This may involve developing new products or facilities or identifying where further price cuts can be made.

Aiming to provide charitable or voluntary services

There are many large charities in Britain which are run like business organisations. Instead of sales revenue, their income comes mainly from donations which are used to support special causes or provide a particular service. Well-known examples include the NSPCC, Oxfam and Shelter. Voluntary services, such as the Samaritans, take on unpaid helpers to provide a service in addition to asking for donations.

Charitable and voluntary organisations do not aim to make a profit, although they may make a **surplus**. From the money they obtain through fund-raising events, charity shops and donations they deduct the costs of running the service. Any remaining money is the surplus they can use to support their aims. In 2000–2001, the NSPCC spent £8.23 million on administration and support costs. While this may seem a lot, it amounted to only 10 per cent of its total expenditure. The remainder was spent on activities to end child cruelty and on campaigning and educating the public. Future objectives focus on ways in which they can increase their surplus and target those in need even more effectively.

Aiming to be environmentally friendly

All organisations have to comply with environmental legislation (see pages 128–131) but many go much further. They want to be respected for having positive policies on issues such as pollution, waste disposal, recycling, packaging and energy use. Some organisations, such as The Body Shop, have built their reputation on being 'environmentally friendly'. The Body Shop was the first cosmetics producer to advertise that none of its products had been tested on animals, to sell them in reusable bottles and to identify specific company environmental aims.

Today, many other companies have similar aims and objectives. Sainsbury's has opened a revolutionary store in Greenwich, south-east London, partly powered by wind turbines and with an environmentally friendly combined heat and power system.

'SMART' objectives

The best type of objectives are said to be SMART. This means they are

S – specific
M – measurable
A – agreed
R – realistic
T – time constrained.

In the snapshot on page 3, you saw that Tesco wants to increase sales of organic products to £1 billion by 2006. This is a specific objective. It is also measurable and is time constrained (it must be achieved by 2006). Given customer interest in organic produce, it is also realistic. If this objective has also been agreed with suppliers and store managers, then it is a SMART objective. If Tesco had merely said it wanted 'to increase sales of organic produce', then this is not SMART – and also cannot be measured easily.

Objectives should be agreed with the people who have to achieve them. You know yourself that if you *agree* to complete some work by a given date, you feel more committed towards doing this than if the decision is made by someone else and imposed upon you. Managers and employees feel the same way. They are more likely to work hard on achieving an objective when they have been involved in setting it in the first place.

> **What can go wrong?**
>
> Organisations may fail to meet their stated aims and objectives because of **external factors** (which may be outside their influence or control) or **internal factors** (which may be within their control).

External factors

These can include:

- unforeseen events – such as the terrorist attacks on the USA on 11 September 2001 which affected the travel and tourism industries and many other organisations
- unexpected falls in customer demand – e.g. through economic problems, new trends or more competition
- changes in technology.

Internal factors

These can include:

- over-ambitious aims or objectives which cannot be met
- production problems or service delivery problems which affect sales
- failure to anticipate customer needs accurately.

Monitoring performance

Many organisations set aims and objectives and then have problems meeting them. This is because, in a rapidly changing world, it is not always possible to predict future events. It is also possible that the aims set one year may not be appropriate the next.

All organisations monitor their progress towards meeting goals – and take action if things are going wrong. Computers make this easy. Retail store managers, for example, receive daily print-outs of sales performance so that they can see which product lines are selling well – and which are not. They can also compare sales figures between stores and over different time periods. Corrective action, such as reducing prices, increasing advertising or selling off unwanted stock at discount prices, can then be taken if there are problems.

The flow chart below shows the way in which aims and objectives are reviewed by organisations. Remember that this should not be done once a month or once a year but should be continuous. Unless organisations continually adapt and change they are unlikely to survive in today's business world.

```
Decide aims
    ↓
Agree measurable objectives
    ↓
Work towards objectives
    ↓
Check performance regularly
    ↓
if unsatisfactory
    ↓
Take corrective action
    ↓
Review and adjust objectives where necessary
    ↓
Review and change aims where necessary
```

How organisations review aims and objectives

> **It makes you think!**
>
> In your group, discuss how you might become more environmentally friendly.
>
> a   Decide what actions each of you could take to achieve this aim.
> b   Agree a statement which summarises the main aims of your group.
> c   Write down three SMART objectives which will help you to achieve this aim.
> d   Suggest how you could monitor your progress.
>
> Compare your suggestions with other groups.

Case study

Hamleys

One of Hamleys' attractions is that it is unique – what makes it unique?

Simon Burke used to work for Virgin Entertainment, where he ran cinemas and megastores. In 1999 he took on the challenge of running Hamleys, the well-known toy store in London's Regent Street. Hamleys was struggling, despite its claim to be 'the finest toyshop in the world'. Profits were down to an all-time low; customers were dismayed at the poor service and complained about the limited range of toys which they also thought were over-priced. Unless urgent action was taken by the new chairman, the company was unlikely to survive.

By 2001, the picture was very different. Profits had increased from £27,000 to £3.9 million, the store had been modernised to include a new 'cyber zone' for computer games and interactive toys, and a direct mail catalogue, online and phone service – Hamleys Direct – was fully operational. Unprofitable businesses, such as a joint venture in Singapore, had been closed and the old Toystack stores had been converted to Bear Factory stores where customers could buy their own customised teddy bear.

However, Simon Burke is adamant that the company will never open any branches, either in the UK or abroad. He considers that one of Hamleys' main attractions is the fact that it is unique and this feature would be lost if there were Hamleys stores all over the country.

You can find out more about the business at www.heinemann.co.uk/hotlinks.

▶ 1 Who is Simon Burke?
  2 How long has he worked at Hamleys?
  3 What was Simon Burke's main aim when he started at Hamleys?
  4 Why did he have this aim?
  5 Identify two actions Simon Burke has taken to achieve this aim.
  6 What do you think Simon Burke will want to continue to do?
  7 Why does Simon Burke think the store is 'unique'?
  8 Do you think Simon Burke's aims have been met? Give a reason for your answer.

▶ 1 Identify Simon Burke's main aim when he first started at Hamleys.
  2 State three objectives which were identified to help to achieve this aim.
  3 What did customers think of Hamleys in 1999?
  4 Did Simon Burke take any notice of customer views when he decided upon his aims and objectives? Give a reason for your answer.
  5 What do you think Simon Burke's aims are now? Give a reason for your choice(s).
  6 Identify the one aim Simon Burke does not have, and say why he has made this decision.
  7 To what extent do you think organisations should adjust their aims to take into account current business performance and new sales opportunities, and why?

Chapter review and practice questions

▶

1. Decide which of the aims below would be most appropriate for each organisation in the list. Some aims will apply to more than one organisation.
    a. Aim for high-quality performance at all times.
    b. Maximise sales by keeping prices low.
    c. Provide a service to the local community.
    d. Develop products that are more environmentally friendly.
    e. Expand by opening more outlets.

   Vet
   Supermarket
   Car manufacturer
   Football club
   Video/DVD store

2. Each of the aims in the chart has an *incorrect* objective alongside. Match each objective with an appropriate aim.

Objective	Aim
Improve existing product	Expand
Introduce a free counselling service	Maximise sales
Only use recycled paper	Provide a highly competitive service
Open longer hours than nearest competitor	Improve quality
Open more stores	Provide a charitable or voluntary service
Lower prices	Be environmentally friendly

3. Develop the following aims so that each becomes a measurable objective:
    a. Open more stores.
    b. Lower prices.
    c. Produce new products.

4. The high street retailer W H Smith intends to open 120 new shops in the UK by December 2004. This is expected to cost £120 million and will create 3000 jobs.
    a. Explain whether this is an aim or an objective. Give your reasons.
    b. Suggest how this target could be monitored.

▶

1. All organisations set aims which link with their priorities (e.g. high quality versus low price) and their scale of operations. Suggest one appropriate aim for each of the following business organisations:
    a. Oxfam
    b. Woolworths
    c. Burger King
    d. Blockbuster
    e. Ford
    f. Armani
    g. Kwik-Fit
    h. your local chemist
    i. Nokia
    j. PC World.

2. Each of the organisations below has an aim, but has not yet decided on any objectives. For each aim, suggest two SMART objectives. To help, the first one is done for you.
    a. Chang's Chinese restaurant wants to be more competitive. *Objectives:* Open longer hours and offer takeaway delivery service, i.e. stay open two hours longer on Friday and Saturday evenings and offer free delivery on all orders over £10. Do both for trial period of 3 months.
    b. A charity shop wants to maximise sales.
    c. Your school wants to be more environmentally friendly.
    d. A graphic design company wants to expand and offer its services to the wider community.
    e. A clothes manufacturer wants to improve the quality of its products.

- **f** A sandwich shop wants to survive during a difficult period when road works outside the shop have prevented parking and reduced the number of customers coming to the shop.
- **g** A new health and fitness club wants to make a profit as quickly as possible.

3 For any two of the businesses in question 2, identify:

- **a** how you would measure whether the objectives were being met
- **b** how often you would check this
- **c** what action you would take if there was a problem.

4 In the late 1990s Mothercare decided to sell more goods from large, out-of-town stores and close its town centre shops. It is developing Mothercare World outlets and improving baby and toddler clothing and home, travel and toy products. Four new Mothercare World stores will open in 2002. But costly problems occurred when it changed to a new warehouse in August 2001. Stock was wrongly located and the right items weren't sent to stores. Low stocks promptly affected sales.

- **a** Identify Mothercare's main aim.
- **b** Identify Mothercare's objectives to achieve this aim.
- **c** Have recent problems affected its aims and objectives? Give a reason for your decision.
- **d** Suggest how the achievement of all its objectives may be monitored in future.

Chapter 2: Business ownership

What you will learn
- Private enterprises
- The public sector

Overview: business ownership

Privately owned enterprises

Many people own and operate their own small, private business. These businesses include hairdressers, corner shops, plumbers. The individuals who run these businesses are called sole traders.

Some people own a business in partnership with others. The partners are responsible for all aspects of running and controlling the business. Examples of partnerships are firms of solicitors and accountants.

Other people own and run a company. If the company is large, then the owners may be different people from the directors who are paid to run the company as is the case with organisations such as Vodafone and Dixons.

There are other types of privately owned businesses. The manager of your local Pizza Hut or Benetton may also own the business but as a franchisee. In this case, the manager makes the daily decisions but must comply with certain conditions set by the larger company.

Where a group of people set up in business together and share everything – there is no overall boss or leader in control – this is known as a co-operative. The Co-op is the most famous example of this.

There is one common feature about all these businesses. The owners will always want to make a **profit**. This is the reward for individuals who are prepared to start a business and take the risk of investing – and possibly losing – their own money. Another word for such an individual is **entrepreneur**. If the business is successful, the owners can keep all the profit after paying the business's expenses and any tax due.

Fact file

There are four main types of privately owned enterprises:

- **sole traders** – owned and run by one individual
- **partnerships** – owned and run by two or more people
- **private limited companies** – often a family-run business with the protection of limited liability (see page 12)
- **public limited companies** – large organisations whose shares are traded on the Stock Exchange.

In addition, there are two other types:

- **co-operatives** – where a group of people run the enterprise together and share the profits or losses
- **franchises** – where a large organisation allows a person to sell its products and use its name in exchange for a fee and a share of the profits.

Julian Richer, one of the UK's top entrepreneurs and owner of Richer Sounds

In other ways, the organisations are very different:

- The owners will have different responsibilities and involvement in the business.
- There are different benefits and drawbacks for the owner(s).
- Some types are more suitable for small businesses whereas others are more appropriate for large-scale enterprises.
- They raise money to run the business in different ways.
- Their ability to develop and expand varies.
- They have different legal responsibilities.
- They are likely to use and distribute their profits differently.

> **Fact file**
>
> All privately owned enterprises can be divided into two types:
>
> - those with **unlimited liability** – sole traders and partnerships
> - those with **limited liability** – all companies, some franchises, some co-operatives.
>
> Unlimited liability means that the owners are responsible for all the debts. If the business struggles, then the owners may have to sell personal possessions to pay the debts. If they cannot do this, they are declared **bankrupt**.
>
> Limited liability restricts this responsibility. The owners are liable to pay debts only up to the limit of their investment. They would not usually have to sell their personal possessions.

Publicly owned organisations

In Britain some organisations are publicly owned. This means they are owned and controlled by the state on behalf of the people. Such organisations are monitored by the government and are said to be in the **public sector**. They include:

- central government departments, such as the Department of Health, which runs the National Health Service
- local authorities, such as your local council
- public corporations – large enterprises owned by the government, such as the BBC.

In all these cases, the finance to run the enterprise comes mainly from the government and is raised by taxation.

The number of public corporations in Britain has fallen in the last 20 years as governments today prefer private ownership. Several public sector organisations have been **privatised**, that is, moved from the public to the private sector. Examples include the coal mining industry, the railways and the British Airports Authority.

You may wonder why the government wants to own or run anything at all! There are several good reasons, which are described on page 27.

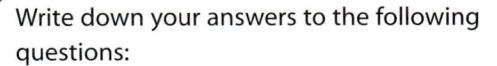

> **Spot check**
>
> Write down your answers to the following questions:
>
> 1. Identify three types of privately owned enterprises.
> 2. Why do entrepreneurs start up in business?
> 3. A sole trader is responsible for paying all the expenses of the business, even if it is necessary to sell personal possessions to meet any debts. What is this called?
> 4. Who keeps the profit in a privately owned enterprise?
> 5. Who owns enterprises in the public sector?
> 6. Give one example of a publicly owned enterprise.
> 7. Why is it considered beneficial for some enterprises to be publicly owned?

Private enterprises

Sole traders

Fact file

The money used to start up a business is called **capital**. Most sole traders have to use their own savings or borrow from friends or relatives.

The profit made *before* business expenses are paid is called **gross profit**. After expenses have been paid, the amount left is the **net profit**. It is on the net profit that the owner is taxed.

Examples of sole traders include newsagents, plumbers, hairdressers, beauticians, small retail shops, market traders and small catering outlets such as Chinese takeaway restaurants.

Benefits of being a sole trader

- It is easy to start in business. There are no complicated procedures to follow especially if the sole trader is using his or her own name.

Snapshot

Joanne Williams, florist

Joanne Williams trained as a florist and then opened her own business. She used her savings to rent a shop, buy the items needed to equip it, pay for advertising and buy stock. Any profits will be her reward for starting the business. However, she is responsible for paying all the business expenses and must also pay national insurance and income tax on her profits to the Inland Revenue.

If she is unsuccessful and makes a loss, then the business will close. If she owes money, then she is personally responsible for paying her debts. She could have to sell her personal possessions to do this and even be made bankrupt. This is because all sole traders have unlimited liability.

As a sole trader, Joanne makes all the decisions as to how the business is run. She must also keep accounts which show how much profit or loss has been made over the year.

Sole traders run a variety of businesses. Next time you visit your local high street, see how many sole trader businesses you can spot

Chapter 2 — Business ownership

- The sole trader is his or her own boss and doesn't have to take instructions from anyone else.
- The opening hours and days worked can be flexible.
- Other staff can be employed to help at busy times.
- Quick decisions can be made – there is no one else to consult.
- A personal service can be offered to customers.
- Bad (unpaid) debts can usually be avoided as customers are normally known to the owner and most purchases are paid for immediately.
- Paperwork is easy – unless the business is registered for value added tax (VAT) when special accounts must be kept.
- The financial affairs and accounts of the sole trader are private, only the Inland Revenue must be informed.

Drawbacks of being a sole trader

- Long working hours may be necessary for the business to be a success.
- Illness and sickness can create problems. If the business is closed, then expenses continue but no money is being made.
- Success is dependent on the skills of the owner.
- It can be difficult to raise capital to start up or expand the business.
- The sole trader has unlimited liability for all debts.
- The owner may have no experience of running a business or have any business skills, e.g. in completing accounts, paying wages, managing staff.

Other important facts

- A sole trader is **self-employed**. He or she must register the business with the Inland Revenue and is responsible for keeping accurate business accounts and completing an annual self-assessment tax form.
- In law, the *sole trader and the business are the same thing*. If you fell in Joanne's shop because the floor was wet, and broke your ankle, you would sue the owner – Joanne.
- If the owner dies, then the business ceases to exist.

- Money for expansion often comes from ploughing back the profits. This means the owner reinvests some or all the profits into the business to expand, but this reduces the amount the owner receives as a reward.
- The biggest risk taken by a sole trader relates to unlimited liability. If debts are likely to be few, and very small, then the risk is worth taking. If debts may be higher and buying stock would be very expensive, it is advisable for the owner to form a company and gain limited liability (see pages 16 and 17).

Partnerships

Snapshot

Mark Fox and Phil Eddington, M & P Motor Engineers

Mark Fox and Phil Eddington both trained as motor mechanics and have decided to open their own workshop. They will specialise in car repairs and MOT tests.

Mark is a good salesman and a skilled mechanic. Phil is the technical wizard and can also repair bodywork. This extends the range of services they can offer. Neither of them is good at accounts, so they will employ Mark's sister to do this. She will work for them three mornings a week, making sure all the bills are paid on time.

Mark and Phil will pool their savings and borrow some money from Phil's mum. They will operate a partnership and will share the profits that they make. However, Phil's mum makes the loan conditional on them taking out a Deed of Partnership. This is a legal document which sets out the details of their agreement, such as the salary of each partner, the share of the profits each will receive and the procedure to follow if there is a dispute. This is good sense, as it may save any arguments later.

Fact file

Phil's mum is lending money to increase their start-up capital. An alternative would be for her to invest money in the partnership and become a partner herself. However, whereas Mark and Phil are **active partners** because they work every day in the business, she would be a **sleeping partner** because she would not take an active part in the business. She would still be entitled to a share in the profits, but would normally receive a smaller amount than the active partners.

Most partnerships are relatively small scale. They include accountants, dentists and estate agents. Many partnerships exist in professions where the professional body insists that members are personally responsible for their actions, such as accountants, solicitors and doctors.

A few larger organisations are run on a partnership basis where the employees become partners when they join the company. The largest company of this type in Britain is the John Lewis Partnership, where all 54,000 staff who work for John Lewis and Waitrose supermarkets are classed as partners and receive a share of the profits as a bonus each year.

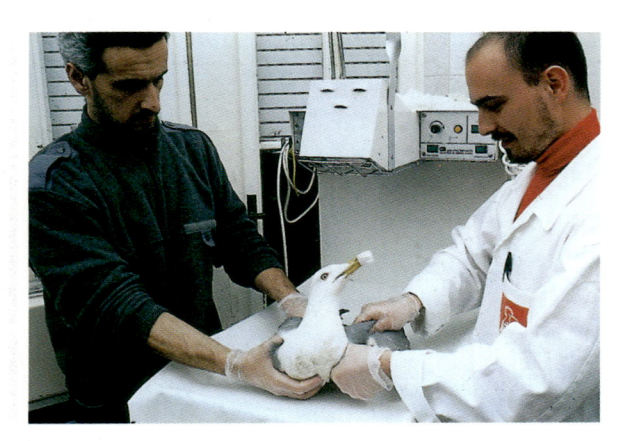

Vets often form partnerships

Benefits of being in a partnership

- Any problems or worries can be shared and discussed.
- Between them, the partners have more skills and ideas than a single person.
- More capital can be raised as all the partners contribute.
- Partners with different skills can specialise in their own areas and increase the range of services they offer to customers.

Drawbacks of being in a partnership

- The partners may not always agree and some may work harder than others, which can cause problems.
- The profits must be shared.
- All the partners must be consulted before a decision is made.
- The partners have unlimited liability for all the debts.
- An action or decision made by one partner is binding on all the other partners.
- The death of a partner means that his or her share must be taken out of the business and paid into the partner's estate. Because this can cause serious problems, each partner usually has a life assurance policy to cover this amount. The insurance company then pays this money into the estate if the partner dies.

Other important facts

- The minimum number of people required to set up a partnership is two and the maximum allowed is normally 20.
- The partners are self-employed, like sole traders, so must register their business with the Inland Revenue, keep accurate accounts and complete self-assessment tax forms.
- In law, partners are 'jointly and severally' liable for the actions of each other. This means, for instance, that if one partner ran up large debts and then disappeared, the remaining partners would be responsible!
- All partnerships are governed by the **Partnership Act 1890**. This assumes that all the partners are equally liable for the debts and receive an equal share of the profits unless a Deed of Partnership has been drawn up with different terms. Often partners share the profits equally, but not always. In some organisations, such as solicitors, there may be senior partners (who receive a larger share) and junior

partners. All partners must pay national insurance and income tax on the money they receive.

- Obtaining start-up capital and raising money for expansion is easier for a partnership as all the partners contribute.
- All the partners have **unlimited liability** for the debts but the accounts are still private. From 6 April 2001, it has been possible to form a *new* type of enterprise in the UK – a limited liability partnership (LLP). The regulations relating to the formation of an LLP and their accounts are similar to those for a company (see pages 17–18), but in other respects the business can operate as a partnership.

Snapshot

Knowing me, knowing you

Some partnerships are very famous and go down in history, such as the collaboration between Charles Rolls and Henry Royce which led to the formation of Rolls-Royce. Others start as partnerships but are now only associated with one person. Sir Richard Branson, Chairman of the Virgin Group, co-founded his original enterprise with Nik Powell, a childhood friend. Bill Gates, founder of Microsoft, started out with a partner called Paul Allen. Some famous entertainers have had business partners, and then fallen out with them, for example Elton John whose split with his former manager, John Reid, cost him £8 million in legal fees.

Many partnerships start out with good intentions, but are rarely permanent because partners can cease to agree on how they see either their own future or that of the business. Experts say that the more partners know about each other at the start and the more they have worked out the business details of their arrangements, the less chance of arguments later.

Spot check

Write down your answers to the following questions:

1. What is a sole trader?
2. Identify two advantages and two disadvantages of being a sole trader.
3. List three differences between a sole trader and a partnership.
4. Identify two benefits of going into partnership, rather than running a business as a sole trader.
5. Identify two examples of typical sole trader businesses and two examples of partnerships.
6. What is the difference between an active partner and a sleeping partner?
7. Clearly explain the term 'limited liability'.

Private limited companies

Snapshot

Website Designs Ltd

Nikki, Jamil and Rob all studied IT and worked in new media companies. Nikki was a website graphic designer, Jamil a programmer and Rob was both an IT and a marketing expert. Between them they decided to form their own website production company to design and create websites for other businesses.

Rob suggested that they should form a small company rather than a partnership. His reasons were these:

- A company would help them to obtain capital more easily – they would need expensive IT equipment and software. Banks and other financial institutions are normally more willing to lend to companies.
- A company would improve their own financial security. Because they would have limited liability each one of them could lose only the amount they invested in the business. If the business failed, then the company would go into liquidation, but as owners, they could not be made bankrupt.

- A company would provide a better 'image' to its customers, who would see the letters 'Ltd' after its name and consider they had greater financial security (whether they had or not!).
- A company would mean fewer problems if one of them left the business. This is because the company is <u>legally separate</u> from the owners and would still continue until it was legally 'wound up'.

Rob told them they must choose a name for the company and decide how much each of them would invest in the business. They would then visit a company registration organisation to draw up the <u>Memorandum of Association</u>, which sets out the structure of the company, and the <u>Articles of Association</u>, which set out how it will operate. They would then receive a <u>Certificate of Incorporation</u>. In effect, this is the company's 'birth certificate'.

Each of them would receive shares in the company, in relation to the amount they had invested. Each share would equal one vote. The company would then employ each of them and pay them. They would be <u>directors</u> of the company, because they ran it, and also <u>shareholders</u>, because they had shares in the company.

There are many examples of private companies in your own area, such as garages, caterers, garden centres, small manufacturing companies, recruitment consultants and building firms. Look through your local *Yellow Pages* and you will find examples of company names which end in the word 'Ltd'.

Benefits of forming a private limited company

- The business can still remain small. Many private companies are family firms where the family members are the only shareholders. Under European law, one person can set up a private company on his or her own.
- All the shareholders have the protection of limited liability and can lose only the amount they have invested no matter how much money is owed.
- Because the owners, or shareholders, work in the business they know it well and have a vested interest in its success.
- Banks are more willing to lend money to limited companies, both for start-up capital and for expansion.
- The accounts are still private between the owners, their accountants and the Inland Revenue.
- Setting up a private company is quite easy and there is no fixed amount which has to be invested. In some cases, owners may invest only £100 or £200 each at the outset.
- Shares cannot be transferred to other people unless all the shareholders agree, and cannot be bought by members of the public. This gives the owners direct control of the business.

Drawbacks of forming a private limited company

- Limited companies have to comply with more regulations than sole traders or partnerships. They have to register with the Registrar of Companies and large companies must have their accounts audited (checked) by an accountant.
- The owners must decide on the structure of the company and other details before formation can be agreed and the documents completed. There are also costs involved, usually about £200.
- The owners must not choose a name which is the same as an existing company if this would cause confusion to suppliers or customers.
- The company must comply with all the requirements of various Companies Acts. For instance, they must have an annual general meeting (AGM) once a year.
- Because one share equals one vote, a shareholder with more shares than all the others would always have control by out-voting the rest. Therefore, the proportions of the shares need to be carefully thought out.

Other important facts

- The company has a *separate legal identity* from the owners. This means that it:

- owns property, hires and pays staff, not the owners
- continues after the death of the owners until it is formally 'wound up'
- can be sold by its owners, simply by selling the shares
- can take legal action in its own name, and have legal action taken against it. If you broke your ankle because you fell on a slippery floor on the company's premises, you would sue the company not the owners.
• The company pays corporation tax on its profits to the Inland Revenue. The company also pays the directors and staff a salary on which *they* pay income tax as employees.
• All the profit after tax belongs to the shareholders. This is usually distributed according to the proportion of shares held but it is usual to keep some back as reserves for financing future developments.
• There are more sources of finance available to companies, particularly those with a good track record. Sources can include local authorities (which control certain funds, such as European grants for development areas), specialist finance houses, investment banks and venture capitalists (see Unit 3, Chapter 10).
• Additional capital can also be raised by selling shares to family members, friends or employees.

Public limited companies

Carphone Warehouse is just one example of a public limited company. Originally, it was a private limited company until it was 'floated' on the London Stock Exchange. This is the term used for launching a public limited company, the largest type of private enterprise in the UK. These enterprises are easily identified because they have the initials 'plc' after their name.

It makes you think!

Within your group, imagine that you are going into business together, then discuss the following issues:

a Decide on how many people you think would be a sensible number to run the business and justify your choice.

b Decide whether you want to form a partnership or a private limited company, and identify the advantages and disadvantages of *both* types of enterprise before coming to a conclusion.

c In either case, you will need to reach an agreement on profit sharing and how decisions are made. If you all share everything equally, then how will a 'leader' be rewarded? If you have a leader, will this person receive more? If you have no leader, what happens if you cannot agree? Discuss how you would solve this problem.

Compare your answers with other groups.

Carphone Warehouse is a public limited company, or plc

In common with many other organisations, Carphone Warehouse was floated to raise more money. The existing shareholders knew that the mobile phone business was growing and wanted to expand rapidly. If a plc is floated, then many more shares are issued and can be bought by the general public such as private individuals and large organisational investors. The directors run the company as salaried employees and can choose whether to own shares or not. The shareholders own shares, but have nothing to do with the day-to-day operation of the company.

A plc must have more than £50,000 in paid-up share capital before it can be floated on the Stock Exchange and also needs a good financial track record. However, not all plcs choose to have a listing on the Stock Exchange. In this case, they are known as **unlisted plcs**.

Public limited companies are all the famous names you regularly hear about, such as Marks & Spencer and Barclays Bank. Their share prices are quoted every day in the financial pages of most national newspapers. Obtain a copy of a list from a newspaper and see how many names you recognise!

Benefits of forming a public limited company

- The amount of capital for expansion and development is greatly increased because there are thousands of shareholders.
- If the company is successful, then the value of the shares increases. This increases the overall value of the company.
- A public company can remain a small enterprise. The minimum is two directors and two shareholders.
- A large public company can achieve savings which smaller companies cannot. For instance, they can mass produce goods for sale and buy in bulk to save money.
- Additional finance can be raised in several ways. The company can borrow from a range of financial institutions, issue additional shares or ask for special loans, called **debentures**.

Drawbacks to forming a public limited company

- A public limited company is registered as such with the Registrar of Companies and must comply with many external regulations.
- The financial affairs of the company and the discussions and votes at the annual general meeting are often reported in the media. If a company is having problems or financial difficulties, this quickly becomes public knowledge.
- Shareholders expect to receive a **dividend** in return for their investment and will also want the shares to increase in value. If the company is in difficulties and share values fall, then many shareholders may sell, which will lower the price further. This can make the company vulnerable to a take-over bid.
- The shareholders often have different aims from the directors. The shareholders want quick results so that the share value increases, whereas the directors may be looking at the long-term prospects of the company. Most shareholders are institutional investors who hold large blocks of shares and can easily outvote smaller shareholders.
- The original owners will lose much of their control over the company, even if they retain some shares. This has led to some entrepreneurs, such as Richard Branson, buying back the company at a later date!

Other important facts

- Legally, the shareholders own the company. As shares are constantly being traded on the Stock Exchange, the actual 'ownership' is constantly changing.
- All public limited companies must comply with the requirements of the Companies Acts and all listed plcs must also abide by the rules of the Stock Exchange.
- The net profit (after tax) is usually divided between paying a dividend to shareholders and keeping back a proportion as **reserves**. Deciding this balance can be critical, especially when profits are low. If the dividend is low, shareholders may sell their shares (depressing the price). If too little is kept in reserves, there may be insufficient money for reinvestment, e.g. to replace outdated equipment.

Spot check

Write down your answers to the following questions:

1. State how you could tell *immediately* whether a company is a private limited company or a public limited company.
2. What is the main advantage of forming a limited company?
3. Who employs the directors of a limited company?
4. What is the difference between income tax and corporation tax?
5. Identify two important differences between private limited companies and public limited companies.
6. In a public limited company:
   a. who are the owners
   b. who runs the company?

It makes you think!

Imagine that the members of your group are the directors of a private limited company. There are six shareholders. Four senior directors hold 20 per cent of the shares each, two junior directors have 10 per cent each. Your accountant informs you that the company's profit this year (before tax) is £720,000. Assume that you will pay corporation tax at 20 per cent.

a. What will be your profit after tax?
b. How will you distribute this, assuming that you want to upgrade your computer facilities this year?

Co-operatives

Alpha Communications Ltd, in Durham, is a graphic design company. It is also a co-operative because each of its workers jointly owns and controls the company. Their profits are jointly shared. In addition, the owner directors believe in co-operative values of honesty, caring for the community and the environment.

Snapshot

A profitable experience!

Until 1989, Rachel Elnaugh was a tax consultant, but wanted to form her own company to develop a gift idea she had – packaging 'experiences'. She joined with a friend and they both started working part time in Rachel's spare room, with Rachel continuing in her job while the business got off the ground.

An important decision was the company name. Another friend suggested Red Letter Days – as the name signifies an important occasion – and red packaging to match. In the first year the company took only £10,000 but the breakthrough came at Christmas 1990 after a magazine promotion. At that point, Rachel left her job and raised £10,000 from family and friends in return for 20 per cent of the shares.

Today, Rachel's company is an unlisted plc, which offers 300 experiences, employs 140 staff and has a turnover of £14 million. In 2000–2002, the company sold over 120,000 experiences – from sky diving to a day at a health spa. Rachel has one further ambition and one regret. She wants to float the company, not for additional finance but as a career achievement. But she regrets giving away 20 per cent of the company for extra finance all those years ago, especially given the amount it is worth today!

A typical Red Letter Day experience

You can find out more about the experiences on offer at www.heinemann.co.uk/hotlinks.

A graphic design company may not be the first thought you had when you read the word 'co-operative'. Most people think about retail co-operatives instead. However, all types of co-operatives – retail, worker and housing, and so on – have the same aim: they are run by the owners *or* the members for the benefit of all.

Co-operatives have traditionally been more successful in Europe than in the UK, but more is being done to encourage the formation of worker co-operatives in Britain, including special types of finance for start-up capital and guidance services.

Benefits of forming a co-operative

- Each worker/owner has an equal share in the business and one vote each.
- Each person also has an equal share of the profits.
- A worker co-operative can also be a limited company, such as Alpha Communications Ltd, and have the protection of limited liability.
- Decisions are made jointly by the owners and in the collective interests of everyone.
- Jobs can be rotated so people can extend their skills and the least popular jobs can be shared.
- Because the workers own and work in their own business, they are committed to its success.
- Workers are not forced to be owners. Each worker can make an independent decision.

Drawbacks of forming a co-operative

- Traditional financial organisations, such as banks, are often wary of lending money to co-operatives because there is no recognised leader.
- Suppliers may be reluctant to provide goods on credit for the same reason.
- Decision making can take a long time if everyone is involved.
- Hard business decisions may conflict with members' social beliefs, such as sacking a worker even if this would be in the best interests of the business.
- Members often lack financial and business skills.
- A good leader may become impatient and feel unable to operate effectively.
- Job rotation may not work effectively – some people may not be sufficiently competent to do certain jobs.

Other important facts

- The largest **consumer co-operative** is The Co-op Group, which comprises the Co-operative Wholesale Society, the Co-operative Retail Society, the Co-operative Bank, the CIS (Co-operative Insurance Society), as well as funeral services, dairies, Travelcare and other businesses. In 2001, the group was valued at £9 billion. It employs more than 55,000 employees, runs over 5,000 shops and 44 superstores with annual sales across the group of £4.7 billion. In this case, the customers own the society, not the employees. Originally, each member was paid a dividend each year in relation to the amount they had spent on goods. Following a review of the society in February 2001, there were proposals to reintroduce this and pay a 10 per cent minimum dividend to members each year.
- **Workers' co-operatives** can often be the result of a worker buyout when a company is failing. In this case, rather than lose their jobs, the workers get together to raise the money to buy and run the enterprise themselves.
- Other types of co-operatives include housing and producer co-operatives. **Housing co-operatives** operate to give all the members a voice in decisions relating to their estate or area. In **producer co-operatives**, producers join together to help to sell and market their products. An example is the Milk Marque, a dairy farmers' co-operative which buys milk from farmers and sells it to the dairy industry.
- All co-operatives share ethical values and principles and aim to be socially responsible. Co-operative retail stores are anti-pesticide, pro-organic and won an award for their support for fair trade. The Co-op's Fairtrade Mark guarantees a fair price for Third World growers and producers.

Snapshot

Lucky thirteen!

Pilling is a village about 10 miles from Blackpool. It has few employers. In 1984, the largest employer was Tayban Precast which made pre-cast concrete products but there were problems at the company. The owner decided his only option was to relocate to Bolton, several miles away. The existing workers were faced with redundancy.

A member of staff, Jim Stamper, proposed instead that the workers bought the business and ran it as a workers' co-operative. Thirteen founder members invested £17,500 and persuaded a bank to match this amount. They also obtained financial support from Lancashire Enterprises. In January 1985, the co-operative started trading as North West Precast Ltd.

Today, the company employs over 40 people and is the major employer in Pilling. It has done much better than Tayban, which went into liquidation in Bolton not long after its formation.

Two well-known franchises – look out for franchise businesses in your area

Franchises

If you like pizza, you may well have visited Pizza Hut as there are about 300 restaurants and 130 takeaways around the country. But who owns and runs all these restaurants – Pizza Hut, the manager or someone else?

The company Pizza Hut is owned and controlled by Whitbread (the former brewery), together with Tricon Global Restaurants, but many of the outlets are often franchise operations. This means that there is an owner/manager in charge who operates the business with the agreement of Pizza Hut.

In common with many organisations, Pizza Hut has used franchising as one way to enable it to grow faster, and more cheaply, than buying all the restaurants itself. The restaurant owners benefit because they are using a well-known name which is promoted nationally, obtain advice on how to run the business and usually have exclusive rights to operate in a certain geographical area.

Fact file

The owner/manager of a franchise outlet is called a **franchisee**. The company which lends its name and expertise is called the **franchisor**. The franchisee must raise most of the capital and pay an initial franchise fee to the franchisor. The owner also has to pay royalty payments or a management service fee each year, normally based on a percentage of the sales.

Benefits of owning a franchise

- When the name is well known, franchises have a higher success rate than other small businesses.
- In addition to advice, guidance and expertise from the franchisor, the franchisee can benefit from national advertising campaigns.
- There are fewer decisions to make in relation to operating the business and problems can be discussed with the franchisor.

- Most of the profit is retained by the owner.
- It is easier to raise capital from a bank to start a franchise than to start other small businesses.
- Franchise operations in Britain are overseen by the British Franchise Association (BFA) which operates a code of conduct for its members.

Drawbacks of owning a franchise

- Some of the profit must be paid to the franchisor.
- The owner does not have the freedom to make all the decisions, particularly in relation to the product range or sale prices which may be controlled by the franchisor.
- Only the franchisor's product(s) or service(s) can be sold.
- The terms of the franchise agreement are drawn up by the franchisor. They are likely to restrict the sale of the business and may include 'performance' terms. This means that if target sales are not met, the agreement may be terminated.
- The franchisee is largely dependent on the popularity of the franchisor's product or service and the amount of advertising and promotion activities undertaken by the franchisor.
- Business success is still dependent on the skill of the franchisee and also the dependability of the franchisor. If these qualities are lacking, the business may fail.

Other important facts

- Over 665 business franchises operated in the UK in 2000 with an annual sales turnover of £9.3 billion. Many are household names, such as Benetton, Wimpy, KFC and The Body Shop, and employed 316,000 people. Ninety-five per cent of franchisees reported they were profitable and 85 per cent considered their relationship with the franchisor was satisfactory (NatWest/BFA franchise survey, 2001).
- Franchising costs money which the franchisee needs to borrow or save. The initial fee can range from £5,000 to £100,000 for a well-known name. Franchisees also often need to pay for equipment and stock and to rent premises.
- The franchisor normally charges 6–8 per cent of sales turnover a year in fees.
- Banks offer special loan packages to franchisees which are more generous than normal start-up loans.
- Franchisors provide initial training and ongoing advice and support to franchisees.
- There are risks in buying a franchise from an unknown organisation. A few disreputable organisations may offer unfavourable terms, ask for large initial fees and then leave the franchisee with little or no support.

Snapshot

Copying can be a good idea

The Young Entrepreneur scholarship scheme is just one of many incentives offered to franchisees by Prontaprint, the largest provider of digital design, print and copy services in the UK. Other support includes guidance on obtaining start-up capital, a comprehensive franchisee 'package' and continued training and support. Existing franchisees are also eligible for a range of awards such as Franchisee of the Year and prizes for achieving top sales.

Prontaprint is a successful organisation. It has grown from one outlet in Newcastle in 1971 to over 200 all over the UK. Its success is due to its good reputation, technical expertise, its team of dedicated sales people who continuously promote the business and also because of the enthusiasm and commitment of its franchisees.

Find out more at www.heinemann.co.uk/hotlinks.

Spot check

Write down your answers to the following questions:

1. Who are the owners of a worker's co-operative?
2. What is meant by the term ethical values? Give an example of an ethical value held by The Co-op retail organisation.
3. Identify two advantages and two disadvantages of operating a co-operative.
4. What is meant by the term franchisee?
5. Who, or what, is a franchisor?
6. Identify two benefits and two drawbacks of being a franchisee.
7. You are a franchisee with a sales turnover of £40,000 after tax. Your franchise agreement states you must pay the franchisor 7 per cent of sales each year. Your profit after tax is £22,000. How much will you each receive that year?

It makes you think!

Your friend has inherited £15,000 and wants to set up in business. She cannot decide whether to be a sole trader or start a franchise business. She has completed a business course and is used to working in the retail trade. Within your group, summarise the advantages and disadvantages of both courses of action and decide which you would recommend, and why.

The public sector

Anna is an administrator in the National Health Service (NHS). Katya works at the local Job Centre. Suhail, who was always good with figures, is a trainee at the Inland Revenue and Jason works in the housing department at the town hall. What do these friends have in common? They are all employed in the public sector. This means they are either employed by the government, another public authority, such as the local council, or a public corporation.

Central government departments

There are a large number of government departments, all of which deal with different matters at a national level. They oversee public services provided across the nation – from education, health care and social security benefits, to defence (such as the army), the police and prison service, and motorway building and maintenance.

Each department is overseen by a government minister and has its own budget. Ministers bid for money each year from the Treasury, the government department which manages the government's money. The amount which is agreed forms part of the main government budget, which is raised from taxes.

It makes you think!

Ten government departments are listed below. Within your group, decide what the main functions of each one is likely to be.

- Ministry of Defence
- Home Office
- Department for Education and Skills
- Department of Environment, Food and Rural Affairs
- Department of Transport, Local Government and the Regions
- Department of Trade and Industry
- Foreign and Commonwealth Office
- Department of Health
- Department of Culture, Media and Sport
- Inland Revenue.

You can find out about individual government departments through the government's website at www.heinemann.co.uk/hotlinks.

Local authorities

Local authorities provide services within the local community. Needs for these can vary, depending upon the area. For instance, those of a rural community are very different from those of an inner city.

In most areas of the country, there is a two-tier system. **County councils** offer services across a large area and **district councils** run specific services for smaller communities. For example, social services would be overseen by the county council but refuse collection would be undertaken by the district council. In 1993, some authorities such as Blackpool bid for unitary status. These authorities are no longer responsible to the county council for the services they provide.

Councils receive money from the government through the **Revenue Support Grant** and also charge householders **council tax** and levy a **business rate** on all businesses (see page 31). Other income comes from loans, council house rents and the sale of council services such as leisure centre charges. They spend the money on providing a range of services, as shown in the diagram below.

Some of the services provided by local authorities

Each year a council must publish its budget and send a copy to every council tax payer in the area.

Public corporations and the privatisation issue

The public sector is a very large employer in Britain, but it used to be even bigger. This was because the state *used* to own a large number of public corporations – businesses controlled by the government. Examples included British Airways, British Telecom, British Gas and British Steel. In the 1980s, it was decided that these organisations should no longer be publicly owned and most were sold or privatised, that is, 'moved' from the public to the private sector. Today, there are few public corporations. The main organisations still owned by the state are:

- the Bank of England
- the BBC
- British Nuclear Fuels (which the government plans to privatise)
- Royal Mail Group (which runs post offices and the Royal Mail).

Many services undertaken by government departments and local authorities have also been partly privatised because this is considered more efficient. For instance:

- Refuse collection, meals on wheels and home helps in your area are likely to be undertaken by private companies under contract to your local authority to provide these services.
- Your local hospital will probably subcontract its cleaning requirements to a private organisation.
- The computer systems in the income tax, social security and driving licence offices are operated by private companies.

Public and private together

Public–private partnership (PPP) and **private finance initiative** (PFI) refer to occasions when a privately owned organisation links with the public sector to set up and/or run an enterprise, such as when a private company builds a new school or hospital and may also manage it as part of the contract.

PPP is being used to improve the London Underground. Some people are in favour of

Chapter 2 — Business ownership

this because private money will help improve the service. Others think it will not work, as private organisations are interested in profit only, rather than services or safety.

What can go wrong?

In the 1980s, those against public ownership argued that it was inefficient. Most of the public corporations had a **monopoly** which meant they were the sole supplier. For instance, you could rent a telephone line only from British Telecom and buy gas only from British Gas. Because customers had no choice, prices could be high and service poor. In addition, public corporations were not expected to make a profit, only to break even – income and spending to be the same – year after year. If they made a loss, they were given a subsidy from the government. This money was largely raised from taxpayers, so problems with public corporations were apt to lead to a rise in taxes.

The government was also concerned that the costs of public services were too high and many local authorities and government departments were considered inefficient. Local authorities were told to put services out to **tender**. This means private companies compete to obtain the contract.

Why not privatise everything?

Many people consider that state ownership is still beneficial in some cases:

- When a socially desirable or essential service would not make a profit so would not be operated by a private business. Health care, education and social services are freely available for everyone, regardless of income.
- When it is difficult to charge people for individual use, such as police, the fire service, the legal service and defence.
- When it is in the national interest to keep the service in the hands of the state. The Bank of England is the government's bank and is responsible for England's bank notes. The government wouldn't want to lose control of what the Bank does, nor would it want the Bank to be taken over by foreign interests.

Spot check

Write down your answers to the following questions:

1. Name two government departments and state what they do.
2. List three services provided by your local authority.
3. How are public services paid for?
4. What is a public corporation?
5. State two ways in which a public corporation *differs* from a public limited company.

Case study

Who should own the railways?

Until 1996, the railways in Britain, in common with most of Europe, were owned by the state. However, British Rail was considered inefficient and costly. Government grants and subsidies were frequently required – in 1992, British Rail had losses of about £250 million and received grants of £1 billion. In addition, investment in replacing old track was forecast to cost a further £1.6 billion. This would mean further costs for taxpayers.

To avoid this, the railways were privatised. Train operating companies (TOCs) would run the trains. These are companies such as Virgin and Connex. Another company, Railtrack, would be responsible for the track, stations, signals, bridges, tunnels and level crossings. Railtrack was 'floated' as a public limited company and many institutional and private investors bought shares in the company. Each share cost £3.80, but the value increased so that by 1998 the shares were worth £18 each.

Serious accidents at Southall, Paddington and Hatfield resulted in the scheduling of major improvements to safety systems and tracks, which would cost Railtrack billions of pounds. By mid-2001, Railtrack had serious financial problems. In April it had requested £1.5 billion of subsidies from the government and by autumn said it would need even more.

The government refused. The Transport Secretary declared Railtrack insolvent because it could no longer pay its debts. By November, the shares were virtually worthless. This angered shareholders who were concerned they could lose all their money.

Others argued that Railtrack's payments of large shareholder dividends had been partly to blame, as this money should have been used to modernise the railway system. They claimed that the railways are successful in France, Germany and Spain because these governments have made large investments in modern rail systems. They said this should be the same in Britain.

By late 2001, the government had four choices: to create a 'not for profit' company to run the railways; to put the railways back into state ownership (renationalise them); to let the train companies own and run their own tracks; to sell Railtrack to the highest private bidder.

▷ 1 Who owned the railway system in Britain before 1996?
  2 What was Railtrack?
  3 What does the term floating a company mean?
  4 Who owned Railtrack?
  5 What does insolvent mean?
  6 Why did the government decide Railtrack was insolvent?
  7 Identify one benefit and one drawback of state ownership of the railways.
  8 Do you think the railways should be owned by the state or by a private company? Give a reason for your opinion and then find out what actually happened.

▷ 1 Who owns the railway systems in Europe?
  2 How did the ownership of the railways change in Britain between 1995 and 2001?
  3 For what aspects of the railway network was Railtrack responsible?
  4 Why did Railtrack need extra money in 2001?
  5 Why do you think the government insisted Railtrack was insolvent rather than paying the subsidy?
  6 Which group of people were annoyed by this decision, and why?
  7 Identify two reasons why some people think the railways should be renationalised.
  8 Evaluate each of the ownership choices faced by the government. Explain, with reasons, which one you think would be the most appropriate for the railways, then find out what the government actually decided to do.

Chapter 2 — Business ownership

Chapter review and practice questions

▶

1 Match up the types of business organisation shown in the chart to the most appropriate description.

Type of business	Description
Sole trader	Large supermarket chain
Partnership	Benefits Office
Private limited company	Plumber working on his own
Public limited company	Four friends who run a nursery school between them with no one as overall boss
Franchise	Jeweller who owns three shops
Workers' co-operative	Veterinary practice with three vets
State owned	Car valeting company which wants to expand rapidly by appointing owner-managers

2 A sole trader is considering taking a partner. Suggest two benefits and two drawbacks of doing this.

3
   a What are the benefits of having limited liability?
   b How would an entrepreneur obtain this?

4 Decide whether each of the statements below is true or false. Then correct all the 'false' statements.
   a The public can own shares in a private company.
   b In a consumer co-operative the customers are the owners.
   c State ownership of industry has decreased in Britain.
   d A franchisee can keep all the profits.
   e Public limited companies are the largest type of private enterprise.
   f In a partnership, there is no one who acts as the boss.

▶

1 Decide which type of business enterprise would be most appropriate in each of the following cases:
   a A husband and wife who decide to open a sandwich shop.
   b A group of ten workers who, when threatened with redundancy, decide to take over a clothing company and run the business between them.
   c A business which makes uPVC windows and doors.
   d A young graphic designer who decides to work for himself after inheriting £15,000.
   e A chain of hire shops which wants to expand nationally as quickly and cheaply as possible.
   f A mobile library in a rural area.
   g A large pharmaceuticals company.

2 A sole trader needs additional capital and cannot decide whether to take a partner or to form a private limited company. Explain the benefits and drawbacks of *both* courses of action.

3 Your friend works for a firm of accountants, but is thinking of changing her job. She has been for an interview at an organisation which operates as a workers' co-operative. She is unsure what this means.
   a In two or three sentences, explain how a workers' co-operative operates.
   b What differences do you think your friend will find if she starts work there?

4 In three or four sentences, clearly explain the difference between private and public ownership.

Chapter 3 Business location

What you will learn

- The availability of a skilled workforce and the cost of labour
- The cost of premises
- Local government charges
- Financial help
- Transport links for supplies and distribution
- Where the customers are
- History and tradition
- Sales techniques

Overview: business location

A place for everything . . .

Most people take for granted the businesses they see on their way to work, when they are shopping or when they are travelling down a motorway. They never question why large shopping complexes are next to a motorway, why solicitors' offices are grouped together in one area of the town and why their local newsagent is on a main road.

They may know that their own area is famous for a particular industry such as steel in Sheffield or pottery in Stoke-on-Trent, but without thinking about why these industries started there in the first place and how these industries have affected the businesses they see around them today.

In many cases there are definite benefits for a business to be situated in a particular location, and you will learn about these in this chapter.

Today, the location of business is starting to matter less in some cases because of the advances in ICT (information and communications technology). For example, a media company which designs websites and offers its services over the Internet could be located anywhere in the country, providing it can keep its customers happy. But this is the exception. For the majority of businesses, the right location can still mean the difference between success and failure.

Key reasons for location

All businesses need:

- people to work for them – in some cases, the workforce must have particular skills
- supplies to sell or raw materials to produce their products
- customers to buy the goods or service
- to keep their operating costs as low as possible.

These factors will influence a business's choice of location. In some cases, one factor may conflict with another. For instance, it is impossible to locate near to both suppliers and customers if supplies come from Scotland and customers are in London! The business will need to decide which are the most important factors in relation to its operations.

When you investigate the location of businesses in your own area, you will find that sometimes there is a very logical reason for location but in other cases there is not. This is often because several locations would be appropriate so the owner of the business has simply chosen the one he or she prefers! Sometimes location may be because of history and tradition and there may still be benefits to operating in the same place.

It makes you think!

Within your group, identify whether your region is well known for any particular types of industry or business. If so, discuss the reasons for this.

The choice of business location can depend on some or all of the factors outlined below.

The availability of a skilled workforce and the cost of labour

All businesses need workers so it is usually important to locate a business in a populated area. Those which locate in remote areas have to pay more to transport their staff. Motorway service stations have to do this, and usually operate their own transport service. So, too, do oil and gas producers who have to transport skilled workers to oil rigs and gas platforms at sea. This adds an extra cost which most businesses can avoid by ensuring there is a ready supply of workers nearby.

Most businesses concentrate on two factors:

- the skills they need
- the cost of labour in a particular area.

Skilled workers

Skilled workers are those who are experts in a particular trade, such as electronics or film production. When an area becomes known for an industry (like Cambridge and biotechnology), people who have the required skills are attracted to the area. It therefore makes sense for other businesses in the same industry to locate nearby. So most motor racing organisations are near Silverstone, film production in England is concentrated north of London and other industries are clustered together across the country.

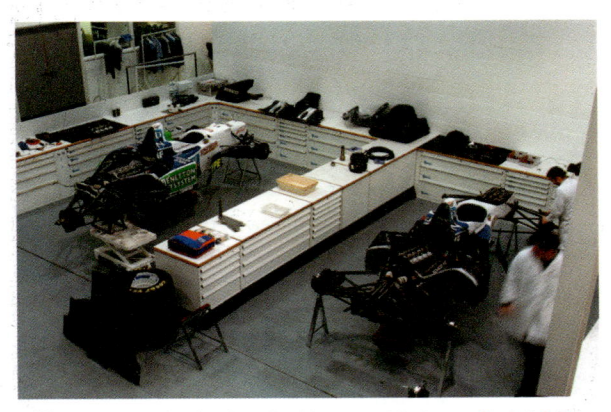

The Benetton workshop in Oxfordshire attracts a skilled workforce

Cost of labour

The cost of labour is influenced by the number of available workers in an area and by the type of skills required. Where labour is scarce, the cost is likely to be higher. This is why businesses prefer to locate where they are likely to have large numbers of suitable applicants for every job. It is also the reason why wage rates are normally lower in areas with high unemployment (where there is a surplus of workers) and higher in cities, where demand for workers is greater.

Fact file

Some businesses are **labour intensive** – they need a large number of workers, for example a hospital. Others are **capital intensive** – machines and/or technology do most of the work, as in an electricity generating plant.

The cost of labour will always be more important to a labour intensive business.

Snapshot

Silicon patches!

Silicon Valley in California is famous for its computer and software houses. It was the birthplace of the Apple Mac. But the USA isn't the only place in the world with such a name tag. In Britain, the area around the M4 has been named Silicon Corridor because this is where companies such as Microsoft, Oracle and Motorola have located. Technology and Internet companies have moved to Berkshire in their dozens, attracted to an area where the workforce is renowned for its skills in e-commerce, computers and communications.

In Scotland, the area between Glasgow and Edinburgh, with a high concentration of electronics businesses, is known as Silicon Glen, and around Cambridge, where high-tech and scientific skills are concentrated, the area is called Silicon Fen.

The cost of premises

Like labour, the cost of premises is determined by demand and supply. In the case of retail shops, it is also influenced by location – busy areas which attract lots of customers are in greater demand – which again affects the price. Conversely, the greater the number of available premises, or the quieter the area, the lower the cost. This is why the owners of offices and shops in large cities pay very high rents, particularly if they locate on a main road. Premises on secondary roads are cheaper, towns are cheaper than cities and industrial sites on the edge of town are the cheapest of all.

This is reflected in the type of buildings. In city areas, with limited space, you will find high-rise office blocks and multi-storey department stores. Out-of-town sites will be more sprawling, with low-level industrial units and large, often single-storey retail parks. This is because the land and rents are cheaper, so businesses can afford to have more space.

Local government charges

A business rate is charged on all business premises except those in Enterprise Zones (see page 32). This is paid to the local authority as the business's contribution towards local services such as road repairs, refuse collection and improvements to the area. Each property has a rateable value, which is linked to the amount of rent it would attract. For this reason, large premises in a desirable location have a high rateable value.

The amount paid depends upon the national rate in the pound. This is the same for all areas except for the City of London. In 2001–2 the national rate was 43p in the pound. The amount paid is calculated by multiplying this figure by the rateable value. So, if the rateable value for a shop was £5,000, then the business rate payable that year would be:

$$£5,000 \times £0.43 = £2,150.$$

Each local authority collects the rate and pays it to the government. The money is then reallocated to local authorities according to the population of their area. This helps to spread the benefit so that all areas gain according to their needs.

For small businesses in particular, the business rate can seriously influence location. This is because the amount paid in rates *as a proportion* of overall expenditure is much higher. Research by the Department of Trade and Industry in 1995 showed that small businesses with a sales turnover of less than £100,000 a year were paying more than 30 per cent of their profits in rates. This was twice as much as larger companies and ten times as much as companies with a sales turnover of more than £1 billion.

In 2001, the government announced plans to reform the business rate system. This would allow local authorities to vary the business rates in their own area, so enabling councils to be more responsive to local business needs.

Spot check

Write down your answers to the following questions:

1. All businesses have specific needs which influence their choice of location. Name two of these needs.
2. Why is a skilled worker usually more expensive to hire than an unskilled worker?
3. A distribution company which employs dozens of packers decides to locate in an area of high unemployment. Identify one benefit of doing this.
4. Oxford Street in London has some of the highest rents in the country. Why is this?
5. A shop premises is advertised in the local paper. It has a rateable value of £4,300. If the national rate in the pound is 50p, how much would the owner pay in rates each year?
6. Why do businesses have to pay business rates?

Financial help

Financial help is available for many businesses but the amount available and the source – at local, national or European level – will vary, depending upon the location.

Local help is available from the economic development departments of many local authorities who provide assistance packages for business. These may include:

- job creation grants
- financial assistance
- rent-free periods
- help with finding business premises.

The type and amount of financial assistance will depend upon the business proposal and the proposed location. In some cases special packages are available to certain types of ownership, for example workers' co-operatives.

In addition, **Business Link** organisations operate in many areas of Britain, offering both support and advice to small and medium-sized companies. They can advise, for instance, on the cost of similar premises in an area.

Nationally, the government offers financial assistance to companies in areas of greatest need – designated as **assisted areas**. This is targeted at promoting business opportunities and is promoted by the nine Regional Development Agencies in England. The schemes include:

- **Regional Selective Assistance** for business projects costing more than £500,000. The amount of the grant varies, depending upon the number of jobs likely to be created or protected
- **Regional Enterprise Grants** for small and medium-sized companies (employing under 250 employees) with investment projects under £50,000
- **Enterprise Zones** where companies gain specific tax benefits, such as paying no business rates and/or obtaining rent-free periods
- **Single Regeneration Budget** for schemes which will improve employment prospects and help the growth of local economies.

European Union finance is also available for business:

- The **European Regional Development Fund** gives financial assistance to development projects in specific regions, known as Objective areas. Objective 1 areas attract the most funding and include Merseyside, South Yorkshire, Cornwall and Wales. Objective 2 areas include many other areas of Britain.
- The **European Social Fund** provides financial help for training and job creation schemes.
- The **European Investment Bank** helps to finance large-scale projects, providing these link to European social and economic aims.

The variety of financial opportunities means that businesses may want to consider carefully where they will locate, to attract the best funding. The British government is also keen to attract foreign businesses to Britain and offers a range of incentives, and guidance on location, to help them to make an appropriate choice.

Transport links for supplies and distribution

Next time you are on a motorway, look for large distribution warehouses by the side of the road, normally near a junction. If you are travelling by train, try to spot the types of business which locate near a railway line and the loads carried by freight trains. In Britain, the majority of goods are transported by road, but heavy bulk items such as chemicals or cement are still transported by rail. Producers of these goods will site their factories near a railway line and often have their own sidings.

Because many businesses rely on road transport, nearness to a motorway may be an important factor in the choice of location. Businesses which are highly dependent upon the road network such as large manufacturers or distribution warehouses are often located close to a motorway junction. Superstores such as B&Q, Comet and Sainsbury's have several large depots around the country where they hold bulk supplies for breaking down into deliveries for local stores.

Good transport links are essential for supermarket distribution centres

Businesses which store items for transporting overseas, or which distribute imported goods, often locate near seaports, airports or the Channel Tunnel. Here you will find freight forwarding companies or cargo handling agents.

Where the customers are

For many businesses, where their customers are is an important factor in their location. Those which rely on passing trade such as shops, garden centres and petrol stations are usually found on main roads. Doctors and dentists locate within a community, small shops are to be found on housing estates and in other populated areas and retailers tend to group together in a town centre area or local market. On a larger scale, this is also why many companies prefer to locate in the south-east of England, because this is the largest consumer market in the country, as well as being near to the south coast ports to the Continent.

Customers may also be other businesses. A company which is dependent upon one type of industry for trade will locate close to its main customers. For example, suppliers of car parts are usually located near major car plants, and in Yorkshire, dyers and finishers of woollen cloth can be found near textile producers.

Shopping malls and retail parks are usually located outside towns and cities where land is cheaper. Superstores locate there as a group and have facilities such as large, free car parks, restaurants, coffee shops and even cinemas to attract customers.

Out-of-town shopping malls benefit from cheap land and tempt customers to come to them

History and tradition

Some industries are traditionally associated with an area. Historically, the location would have been chosen for geographical reasons, either because certain raw materials were available locally or because local climatic conditions were just right. Below are some examples:

- The steel industry of Sheffield was located there because it was near to coal, iron ore and limestone deposits, all of which are needed to make iron, from which steel is manufactured.
- The woollen industry thrived in Yorkshire because of large numbers of sheep and dry weather conditions.
- The cotton industry prospered in Lancashire because cotton needs damp conditions, and cotton from the USA was imported into Liverpool.
- The cider industry of Somerset has developed because the climate there favours apple growing.
- Cement companies are always found near natural deposits of limestone or chalk, such as in Yorkshire, Sussex and Dorset.

Case study

Location, location, location . . .

Martin ran the family jewellery business in a small town, like his father before him. His small shop was situated next to the entrance of the daily market. His main competitors, including national jewellery chains such as H Samuel, were located in the main shopping complex a few minutes' walk away. Anyone walking from the complex to the market passed Martin's shop – and business was good.

Last year all business premises were revalued by the council. As a result, Martin discovered that his rates would increase by 20 per cent. He thought this would be too costly so looked for an alternative location nearby. Premises in the shopping complex were even more expensive, so Martin chose a location just outside the complex. Parking was difficult but the shop was more spacious, so he could stock more items. Martin publicised the move in the local paper and made sure all his 'regular' customers knew about it.

Unfortunately for Martin, few customers followed him. Within 12 months the business had closed.

1 Martin's original shop was near the market. Why was this a good location?
2 Where were other jewellery shops in the town located? Give one reason why this type of location is popular.
3 Why do businesses have to pay business rates?
4 How were the business rates for Martin's shop changing?
5 Why were shops in the complex likely to be more expensive?
6 Give one advantage and one disadvantage of the shop's new location.
7 What action did Martin take to try to encourage his regular customers to 'move' with him?
8 Suggest one reason why Martin's new location was not a success.

1 Identify three advantages of Martin's original location.
2 Explain why business rates are charged and why the amount charged is so important for small businesses.
3 What is meant by a 'revaluation' and how would it affect Martin?
4 Why did Martin think that relocating the shop would be a success?
5 To what extent do you think Martin was dependent upon 'passing trade'? Give a reason for your answer.
6 What would you have done if you had been Martin? Give a reason for your answer.
7 Evaluate each of Martin's choices and assess the importance of location to retail businesses such as Martin's. Then state, with reasons, the action you think he should have taken.

- Paper manufacturers locate near water, because water is an essential ingredient in paper production.

If the original reasons for locating the business change, the industry may die. For example, cheap foreign imports of cotton virtually wiped out the cotton trade in Lancashire. However, in other cases, the industry continues to thrive. Lincolnshire, for instance, is renowned for horticultural businesses because the land is fertile and the climate good. It is also near ports such as Felixstowe where flowers and bulbs are imported from the Continent. Even though the conditions for cultivating plants can now be simulated in greenhouses across the country, Lincolnshire remains a major horticultural centre.

Another reason for industries remaining in a particular area is because they may benefit from working near similar organisations. Specialist labour will be cheaper. They will have built up associations and supportive links. Local colleges and universities may run courses which relate to the needs of the industry. Specialist suppliers will have been attracted to the area. For example, the East Midlands – around Coventry and Derby – is traditionally a major centre for engineering and car production. Because of local expertise these types of businesses are still attracted to the area, for example Rolls-Royce Aero Engineering, Toyota, Peugeot and Triumph Motorcycles. Another example is the City of London, where financial organisations benefit from their nearness to each other.

> **Fact file**
>
> Some industries are **bulk increasing**, that is they receive small components and assemble them into a larger product, for example refrigerators or computers. They benefit from good transport links and being near to customers.
>
> Other industries are **bulk reducing**, that is they receive large, heavy materials and break them down before distributing them (such as slate, coal and scrap metal). In this case, the business will be close to its source of supply, as it is cheaper to transport the goods after processing.

Sales techniques

The way in which companies interact with their customers also affects their location. A company which does its business mainly using ICT or even traditional mail services can locate almost anywhere, as in the following examples:

- **Call centres** are used by business organisations such as banks, insurance companies, the travel industry and the government to process enquiries and transactions. If you ring your bank or building society, your call could be answered in Scotland, Sunderland or Southend-on-Sea! Call centres specialising in offering these services are growing at the rate of about 10 per cent a year in the UK, and over half a million people in the UK work in such places.

- **Internet selling** is another example where location may be less critical. A company selling CDs, books or computers over the Internet will still need good transport links and skilled staff but, apart from that, can choose the region in which it wants to locate.

- **Mail order** companies may sell goods by mail only (such as Presents by Post), or by mail and through the Internet (such as Red Letter Days) or may have an Internet, mail order and high street presence (such as Hamleys or Tesco). A mail order company needs a good delivery service, but apart from this, it can locate almost anywhere. Its major task is to ensure that prospective customers receive catalogues and that orders are fulfilled accurately and promptly.

- A variation on the mail order company is a **fulfilment house**, which handles your application if you send off for a special offer on a packet of cornflakes! Because these organisations never need personal contact with the customer and fulfil all their orders by mail, their location is relatively unimportant.

> **Snapshot**
>
> *The benefits of togetherness!*
>
> *Call centres are the growth industry of the twenty-first century. In the future, they may be known as contact centres, handling emails, telephone enquiries and faxes. Just like the industries of old, they are grouping together in certain areas of the country, mainly the South East, North East and Scotland. In all these areas colleges and universities run training courses for staff and managers. Skilled staff can be obtained more easily. Subsidiary industries, such as IT suppliers and disaster recovery companies (to help if the system crashes), are attracted to the area. The only disadvantage for businesses is that wage rates are increasing as staff become more skilled and in greater demand!*

What can go wrong?

If location is important for a business, then changes in an area can have a devastating effect, particularly on small organisations. For example:

- a petrol station locates on a main road through town, a bypass opens five miles away – as a result, the volume of traffic falls by over 50 per cent
- a new out-of-town shopping complex attracts customers away from the town centre – local businesses suffer
- the council paints double yellow lines on both sides of a main road – shops relying on passing trade lose most of their business.

Even temporary changes, such as road works and diversions, can cause serious problems if these mean customers cannot reach the business's premises easily.

Chapter review and practice questions

1. Identify two major factors influencing the location of each of the following organisations:
   - **a** a haulage and distribution company
   - **b** a hospital
   - **c** a scientific research establishment
   - **d** a frozen fish producer
   - **e** a newsagent.

2. Many small businesses locate close to where the majority of customers will be found. Match each of these businesses with a suitable location from the list below: solicitor; taxi company; shoe shop; pizza restaurant; stationery and book shop; superstore.
   - **a** Major junction on a town's ring road
   - **b** Next to the train station
   - **c** Next to the cinema
   - **d** Near to the law courts and police station
   - **e** Near the local college
   - **f** In the town shopping centre.

3. A major video/DVD rental chain is opening an outlet in your area. There are three choices of location. List the advantages and disadvantages of each option and decide which would be the best, and why.
   - **a** On the high street in the centre of town
   - **b** In a small retail park one mile from the town centre
   - **c** In a large retail park on the outskirts of town near the motorway.

1. Identify two major factors influencing the location of each of the following businesses:
   - **a** a motel
   - **b** a leisure centre
   - **c** a brick manufacturer
   - **d** an international bank
   - **e** an estate agent
   - **f** a washing machine manufacturer.

2. Some people argue location is less important nowadays because of ICT. Others say location will always be important.
   - **a** Identify two types of business where location is very important.
   - **b** Identify two types of business where location is less important and say why this is.
   - **c** Identify four benefits to a business which locates near to others in the same industry.

3. Wages and premises costs are generally less in the north of England than the south.
   - **a** Why is this?
   - **b** Can you think of any exceptions, where wages and premises would be quite high in the north of England?
   - **c** If costs are lower in the north, why do many businesses still prefer to locate in south-east England?

Chapter 4: Business activity

What you will learn

- Identifying business activities
- Identifying trends
- Why changes occur
- Key facts and trends in activities related to producing raw goods
- Key facts and trends in manufacturing activities
- Trends in the sales of goods
- Trends in services activities

Overview: business activity

What is business activity?

Business activity refers to the operations carried out by a particular organisation – the type of goods it produces, the services it offers, whether it provides only goods or only services, or both.

Many organisations are involved in more than one activity, but the main one is known as its **core business**. This is the activity on which everything else depends. You need to be able to identify the core business activity as well as any other activities in which a business is involved.

Main types of activity

The main types of business activity include:

- producing raw goods
- manufacturing of goods
- sales of goods
- client services
- other services.

The flow chart gives examples of these.

Producing raw goods
The Forestry Commission produces raw goods for the timber industry – it plants trees, then cuts them down when they are grown

Manufacturing of goods
- Furniture producers use timber to manufacture furniture
- Paper manufacturers use wood pulp to produce paper
- Paper is used by printing companies to manufacture books

Sales of goods
- Furniture is sold by retailers in shops
- Books are sold in book shops and over the Internet

Client services
- Internet booksellers require a website and Internet access – specialist businesses provide these client services
- Customers pay by credit card and the payments are processed through the banking system – a client service

Other services, e.g. transport and distribution
- Books are distributed to the customer from the Internet bookseller's warehouse
- Furniture is transported from the manufacturer to retailers

How the main business activities link

Trends and business activities

The number of businesses involved in different activities constantly changes. This is because businesses are attracted *towards* profitable business activities and *away* from unprofitable activities.

Business activities also change over time for a variety of reasons:

- Customer tastes and preferences change, which affects what people buy.
- The number of people employed in a business activity will vary. This is affected by the overall requirement for workers in that area and changes in the way the work is done.

- The value of different goods and services can change. For example, in 1967, when colour televisions were introduced, they cost £350 – the equivalent of about £4,000 today! They were a luxury item, available only to wealthier people. Since then, their relative value has fallen, so now they are accessible to many more people.
- Technology changes, which affects what products are made, how they are made and how goods and services are sold. It can also affect the price and value of goods.

When you start to investigate business activities you will see that some general trends affect all businesses. For example, the increase in mobile phone ownership was widespread and benefited many businesses – from manufacturers to suppliers. Now that demand for new phones has fallen, this has affected all the businesses involved in this activity.

Other trends are more varied and only affect some businesses. For example, demand for transatlantic travel fell after the terrorist attacks on New York on 11 September 2001. But budget airlines concentrating on Europe still did well, especially when they cut prices to tempt passengers back.

It is important to find out *both* the general trend *and* whether any business you are investigating is affected.

Spot check

Write down your answers to the following questions:

1. What is meant by 'producing raw goods'? Give an example.
2. Glass is made from sand and other materials and produced by glass-makers such as Pilkington. How would you describe the activity in which Pilkington is involved?
3. State two methods of selling goods to consumers.
4. You visit a travel agent to book a holiday. In which of the following activities is this company involved?
   a producing raw goods
   b manufacturing goods
   c providing a service to clients.
5. Give one reason why business activities change.
6. Is the following statement true or false? Give a reason for your answer.

   'If demand for a type of goods falls, this always affects every business involved in that activity.'

Identifying business activities

Grouping business activities by sector is very common. There are three main groupings

- the **primary sector** – includes businesses that produce raw goods, e.g. farming, agriculture, fishing, mining, forestry and oil and gas drilling
- the **secondary sector** – includes manufacturers of consumer and industrial goods, e.g. makers of carpets, ships, computers and cranes; producers of electricity and gas; and builders of roads, buildings and bridges
- the **services sector** – includes providers of services to businesses and to individuals.

The services sector can be subdivided into:

- **wholesalers** and **retailers** – wholesalers buy in bulk and sell to the retail trade; retailers sell goods to the general public
- **other services**, including:
  - **client services**, such as health care, education, banks, insurance companies, accountants, hairdressers, travel agents, leisure centres, hotels, where the business provides a service directly to a client
  - **non-client services**, such as haulage companies, communications

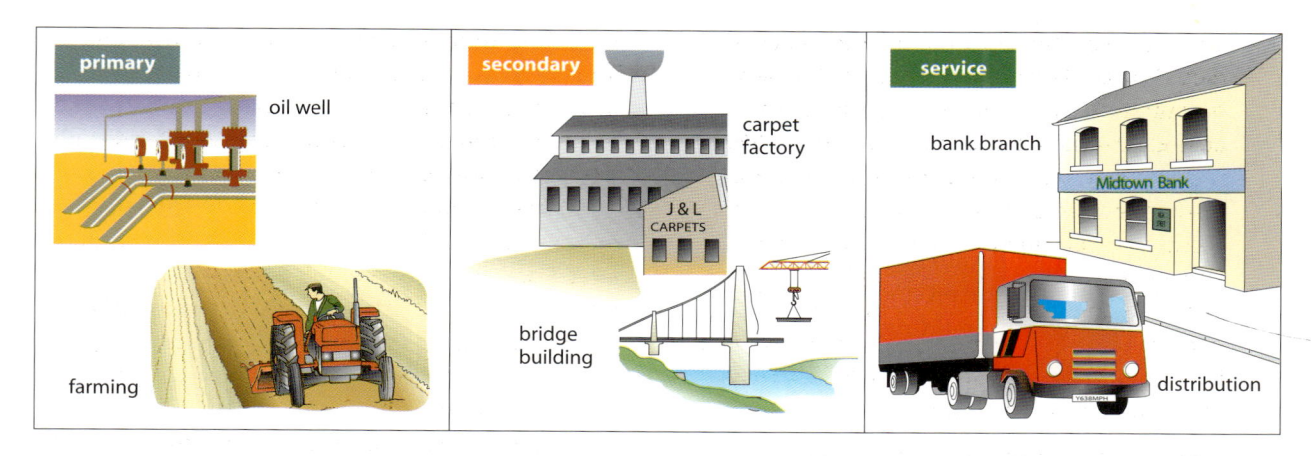

providers, radio and television companies, where a service is provided but it is not usually face to face with a client.

The Office for National Statistics collects data on business activities but does not divide services in the way described above. Instead, it uses nine main categories, some of which contain a mixture of client and non-client services (see page 48).

- manufacturers of windows and conservatories which sell direct to the public.

Identifying the core business activity

The core business is the key activity on which a business depends. It may *not* be the most profitable! Manchester United, for example, makes more money from selling merchandise than from gate receipts, but if there was no football team, there would be no business. Therefore, its core activity is playing football and, unless it does this well, everything else may suffer.

Sometimes, when a business has problems, it decides to concentrate on its core business. This is because additional activities may not prove very profitable or may be too costly to maintain.

Identifying the range of business activities

In some cases, a business organisation will be involved in one activity only, such as a garden centre which sells gardening products. Here the business is involved in retailing. If the centre *also* offers a landscape gardening service, it is involved in *two* activities.

Other examples of multiple activity businesses include:

- football clubs, such as Manchester United, which sells football strips and other merchandise
- retail stores, such as Tesco, which offer financial services such as savings accounts, loans and insurance
- oil companies, such as BP, which are involved in extracting oil, processing it into petrol and selling fuel in their own petrol outlets
- retailers, such as Boots, which manufacture their own products.
- farmers, who also sell goods direct to the public at farmers' markets or in farm shops

The core business activity of the England football team is playing football

Identifying trends

General sector trends

Sectors can change – some expand while others decline. One hundred years ago, the UK led the world in manufacturing. Today, it imports most manufactured goods. In the 1950s, coal mining, shipbuilding and steel production were booming in the UK. Now, there are more people employed in fast-food restaurants than in all these areas combined.

Employment and the number of businesses

All businesses need people and, usually, there is a relationship between the number of people employed and the number of businesses which exist. If the number of jobs in an activity is increasing, this is often because it is an expanding area – and the reverse if employment is decreasing. The only time this would not be true is if more work is being done by machines.

Look at the chart of employment by sector, below. It shows that, between 1981 and 2001, employment:

- fell in the primary and secondary sectors
- rose in the services sector.

Employment by sector

Year	Primary sector	Secondary sector	Service sector
1981	4.9%	30.9%	64.2%
1986	4.0%	26.9%	69.1%
1991	3.1%	23.5%	73.4%
1996	2.2%	21.4%	76.4%
2001	1.8%	19.7%	78.4%

Sector output

All businesses produce output. A farmer's output is measured by the quantity of crops he or she grows. A manufacturer's output is measured by the number of items made, a retailer's in the number of items sold, and so on.

Consumer demand was high during 2002

You may think that output would match employment, but this isn't always true. If a better, or quicker, method of producing goods is found, then output may rise even though there are fewer people employed in an activity.

As an example, today's farmers use modern methods to produce crops so output per farm has increased, even though employment has fallen.

Why changes occur

Changes occur because consumer demand for goods and services varies. Technological developments also affect how business activities are carried out.

The main reasons for change are listed below. You need to know these before you look at recent trends and changes so that you can identify the main factors which have affected different activities.

Changes in consumer demand

When consumer demand increases, retailers will want to supply more goods and they will demand more from manufacturers. The manufacturers, in turn, will need more raw materials. So one change can affect many activities in different sectors of production. For example, as computers have become more commonplace at work and at home, demand for paper (for print-outs) has increased. This has meant that more paper is made by manufacturers and there is a greater demand for the raw materials which make paper.

Manufacturers increased output to meet consumer demand for mobile phones

These are the main factors which affect what people buy:

- **Tastes and preferences** – your own personal tastes and preferences are personal to you, but will usually be affected by fashion trends. You may also be influenced by advertising and the use of brand names and designer labels.
- **Lifestyle** – the way you live affects the products you buy. Today, increasingly, people like to keep fit and eat a healthy diet. This has affected membership of gyms, food served by restaurants and the number of health conscious foods available in supermarkets. People also work quite long hours and lead busy lives so the demand for fast-food and takeaway meals has increased.
- **Population trends** – people are living longer. This has affected the demand for health care and retirement activities and services. There are also more working mothers, which means that more nursery places are required, and also that demand has increased for household appliances such as freezers and tumble dryers and for ready meals.
- **Seasonal factors** – Christmas is worth £12.5 billion to the retail trade, with increased sales of clothes, footwear, gifts, toys, alcohol, tobacco, food and electrical goods, plus increased spending in hotels and restaurants. The weather also affects our activities. The warm autumn of 2001, for example, lengthened the season for ice-cream sales. Cold and rain depress retail sales and, in the summer, may adversely affect tourism business in Britain.
- **Value for money** – normally, we choose a product which we think is good value for money. So, if three similar magazines are the same price, you would be more likely to buy the one which is the largest and which contains the most interesting articles. Expensive items, such as cars or foreign holidays, are usually compared more carefully than cheaper items, such as baked beans, because of the amount of money involved.
- **Income and wealth** – the amount of money you have to spend will affect what you buy and what you do in your leisure time.
- **Technological developments** – these not only affect consumers' preferences but also mean that some products become obsolete; for example typewriters have largely been replaced by computers. Technological development speeds up the rate of replacement of items such as DVD players replacing video recorders. In business, technology also affects the way in which people work and how products are made. Greater automation can increase the output of goods or a service and decrease the number of people employed in that activity at the same time.

The difference between success and failure is often linked to the ability of a business to spot a trend ahead of anyone else and to accurately forecast a change in buying habits. This skill is especially important in the fashion business.

Buying the wrong sort of item or too many of a fashion item can be a disaster for a business if it is unable to sell its stock. It is also essential to stay in touch with what consumers want.

Spot check

Write down your answers to the following questions:

1. Give two examples of a client service.
2. Tesco sells mobile phones. Is this its main business activity? Give a reason for your answer.
3. What is meant by the term 'output'?
4. Employment in an activity can sometimes be falling while output is rising. Under what circumstances would this happen?
5. Give three reasons why demand for items changes.
6. Below is a list of items bought by consumers. Some go out of date more quickly than others so a retailer could be left with unsold stock. Rearrange the list so that the most rapidly changing item is at the top and the longest lasting at the bottom.
   a. a household freezer
   b. a pair of designer label trainers
   c. a laptop computer
   d. a computer game
   e. a jug kettle
   f. a top ten single.

Special Note

Part of your GCSE will involve you in finding out about the different business factors – what they do and how they have changed. Refer to the rest of this chapter when you are investigating a particular business. It will help you with background and understanding. You don't need to read everything now – but you will need to read the appropriate sections as you do your research.

It makes you think!

Every year, the Office for National Statistics produces a list of goods in the average shopping basket, mainly obtained from its Family Expenditure Survey. But over time, tastes and fashions change. The list below shows several products which were included for the first time in the average shopping basket during each of the last seven decades.

Products:
a. Frozen ready-meals, low-alcohol lager, microwave ovens, CDs
b. Canned fruit, camera film, televisions
c. Satellite dishes, camcorders, foreign holidays, replica football strips
d. Condensed milk, sewing machines, wireless sets
e. Electric hairdryers, yoghurt, wine, duvets
f. Energy drinks, baseball caps, mayonnaise, cereal snacks
g. Sliced bread, crisps, jeans, eating out

Within your group, match the products to each of the following decades: 1940s, 1950s, 1960s, 1970s, 1980s, 1990s, 2001. Remember, you are not trying to guess when items were first invented but when they were being bought by the majority of the population.

In case you give up, the answers are given on page 44, but don't be tempted to cheat! If you need help, ask older friends and relatives.

Key facts and trends in activities related to producing raw goods

Output, employment and trends in activities related to producing raw goods, 2000

Activity area	Output	Employment
Agriculture, forestry, fishing	1.3%	1.4%
Mining and quarrying	2.2%	0.3%
Total share of British output/employment	3.5%	1.7%

Overall trend: Employment in primary activities has consistently fallen. Output has changed and the general trend is downwards, but by less than you would expect because of mechanisation.

Agriculture, forestry, fishing

In agriculture, output has increased. Today, farmers have better crop yields because of improved seeds, and are looking to new technology to produce cheaper, healthier food. These include computer-controlled greenhouses and computer-monitored fields to calculate maximum sowing densities, fertiliser and pesticide levels. Britain is now more self-sufficient in food than ever before. Three-quarters of all food eaten in the UK is produced here and the industry contributes £6.6 billion a year to the economy.

Although Britain grows only about 15 per cent of the timber products used in the UK, both the overall woodland area and the volume of softwood produced in Great Britain have increased in the past ten years. In 2000, this amounted to 9.3 million cubic metres of timber – 7.5 per cent higher than in 1999 and 17 per cent more than the average between 1994 and 1998. Most of Britain's wood is processed by 300 sawmills, with almost half being sawn by the 13 largest mills.

The UK still has a substantial fishing fleet and landed over 748,000 tonnes of fish in 2000. There are about 540 fish processing businesses, employing 22,000 people, and 1,400 fishmongers. However, limits on catches to conserve fish stocks have affected the fishing industry and fishing in some ports has been severely affected. The fishing industry also includes salmon farms and trout hatcheries.

Mining and quarrying

The largest coal producer in Britain is UK Coal, which operated 13 pits in 2001. However, the survival of these was in doubt despite an increase in the amount of coal being used at Britain's power stations. Output has fallen, costs have risen and the company is losing money. Employment is likely to fall still further as more staff are laid off. Many of the problems are related to difficulties at deep mines, so that the increased consumption of coal in Britain is being met entirely by imports.

Large-scale companies undertaking quarrying, such as Redland and Tarmac, are mainly involved in obtaining aggregates for road building. Companies such as Blue Circle obtain clay and limestone to make cement. Smaller quarries exist where distinctive stone is found, as in the Cotswolds.

Key facts and trends in manufacturing activities

Output and employment in manufacturing activities, 2000

Activity area	Output	Employment
Energy production	2.2%	0.6%
Manufacturing	19.0%	16.3%
Construction	5.3%	4.9%
Total share of British output/employment	26.5%	21.8%

Overall trend: Employment has fallen in all these areas. However, in energy production and construction, output has fallen by less because of increases in automation and different methods of working. Overall manufacturing output has fallen considerably (from nearly 24 per cent in 1985), but this trend is not consistent across all types of manufacturers, as the chart on page 45 shows.

Energy production

Supplies of North Sea oil and gas will decline in the twenty-first century as resources dwindle. However, oil and gas companies invest large amounts in identifying new fields and bringing these into production.

Other forms of energy production include hydro-electric power, nuclear fuel and wind farming. The government has a preference for gas-fired electricity stations because they are cheaper and cleaner and wants to see the amount of fuel obtained from renewable energy forces increase by 7 per cent over the next nine years (see case study on page 44). Output declined between 1985 and 1999 but has since started to increase.

Case study

Wind power

Renewable energy is 'clean' energy which does not deplete world resources. The government aims to provide 10 per cent of Britain's electricity from renewable sources by 2010, compared to less than 3 per cent at present.

Britain is Europe's windiest country, but currently has only 61 wind farms. The aim is to more than double Britain's renewable energy capacity by building the largest onshore wind farm near Stornoway on the island of Lewis. It is hoped that tidal and wave power stations will follow, reducing the need for more nuclear power stations which are far more expensive to run and considered hazardous by many people. The islanders are pleased at the prospect of more skilled jobs. Fish farming, tourism and agriculture have been the main activities on the island, together with the production of Harris Tweed, but many young people have left to work on the mainland as these activities have declined.

The idea has been suggested before, but there was always a problem of how to connect offshore islands to the national grid. The idea now is to run an underwater cable to England or Wales, rather than strengthening power lines in Scotland and northern England. Because the cable could be used by other renewable energy companies, this should attract them to the area, too.

▶ 1 What were the traditional activities on Lewis?
2 Are these flourishing or declining? Give a reason for your answer.
3 What is renewable energy?
4 Identify two benefits of producing electricity using renewable energy rather than nuclear power.
5 a   What were the technical problems involved for developers?
   b   How will these be overcome?
6 How will islanders benefit if the project goes ahead?

▶ 1 a   How have activities on Lewis changed over the years?
   b   How has this affected the population?
2 What do you think is the view of environmentalists on the proposed plan, and why?
3 Why do you think Britain wants to increase its supplies of renewable energy? Give as many reasons as you can.
4 How have technological developments helped the plan?
5 Assess the advantages and disadvantages for the islanders if the plan goes ahead.

Manufacturing

Manufacturing includes the production of two types of goods:

- **Consumer goods** are fast-moving items (known as FMCGs) such as over-the-counter medicines, toiletries and groceries. Some consumer goods, such as stationery and raw materials, are also bought by businesses.
- **Capital goods** last much longer. They include domestic appliances, furniture and cars. In business, they include machinery, equipment, tools and vehicles. Technological developments can influence the rate at which capital goods, for example computers, are replaced.

Manufacturing output and employment in Britain has been declining for several years. Traditional industries, such as shipbuilding and textiles, have virtually disappeared, unable to compete with cheap foreign

Answers to **It makes you think!** on page 42

a	1980s	e	1970s
b	1950s	f	2001
c	1990s	g	1960s
d	1940s		

industries. Textiles output shrank by 43 per cent in the UK between 1979 and 1999.

After 1999, there were hopes of an improvement in British manufacturing as more high-tech manufacturers located in Britain, making telecommunications equipment, electronic components and computers. However, economic problems across the world badly affected these manufacturers.

At the end of 2001, the Confederation of British Industry (CBI) forecast a further contraction in output of about 1 per cent in 2002. However, it forecast that by 2003–4 output would be growing by up to 2.5 per cent a year.

Not all manufacturers have experienced problems – it depends very much upon the type of products they make. The chart below shows the winners and losers in 2001.

Construction

The construction industry includes road builders like Alfred McAlpine and house builders like Barratt. The industry is heavily dependent upon demand for new roads, housing, hospitals, offices, schools, special projects and so on. Overall the output in these areas was unchanged between 2000 and 2001, but by the end of 2001 there was a increase in orders for infrastructure projects (such as town centre redevelopment), private housing and private commercial property developments which more than offset falls in other areas such as private industrial developments and public housing.

Trends in the sales of goods

Output and employment in activities related to the sale of goods, 2000

Activity area	Output	Employment
Wholesaling and retailing	13%	17%
Total share of British output/employment	13%	17%

Overall trend: Both wholesaling and retailing are buoyant areas. Sales have risen in both areas and growth is forecast to continue. Retail sales more than doubled in value between 1985 and 2000 to over £200 billion.

Sustaining this growth does, however, depend on consumer demand, and how much of their income people are prepared to spend. To encourage spending, retailers offer a variety of buying methods – shop outlet, mail

Manufacturing in 2001

Rising output	
Category	**Product examples**
Electrical and optical equipment	Office machinery, computers, videos
Paper and publishing	Paper, books, videos, computer media
Transport equipment	Cars, caravans, motorcycles, aircraft
Chemicals and man-made fibres	Plastics, paints, detergents, pharmaceuticals
Rubber and plastic products	Rubber tyres, plastic tubes, packaging
Other manufacturing	Furniture, jewellery, sports goods, toys
Food, drink and tobacco	Meat, poultry, cereals, pet food, bread, wine
Falling output	
Wood products (excluding furniture)	Wooden containers, doors, veneer
Non-metallic mineral products	Glass and glass products, bricks, cement
Basic metals and fabricated products	Iron and steel tubes, radiators, cutlery, tools
Textiles and leather products	Clothes, carpets, handbags, luggage, footwear
Machinery and equipment	Tractors, machine tools, domestic appliances

order and the Internet. This is an important trend affecting most retailers.

Wholesaling

Wholesalers supply goods to customers all over the country, from food and household appliances to machinery and live animals. Most are small businesses. Trade with retailers accounts for nearly 75 per cent of sales. Other customers are industry and other wholesalers.

The wholesale trade has a higher sales turnover per year than the retail trade. In 1999 about 125,000 businesses sold £350 billion of goods.

Most wholesalers offer cash and carry services, where customers collect their goods. This occurs particularly in the grocery trade. A few combine wholesaling and distribution and specialise in the storage and transportation of very large, specialist or perishable items. They offer an invaluable service, especially to small retailers.

Retailing

There are nearly 250,000 retail businesses in Britain from department stores to local greengrocers. In 1999, the retail trade sold £208 billion worth of goods.

Retailing depends upon consumer demand for goods and this can be divided into two types:

- **Consumer needs** – necessities such as food and clothing
- **Consumer wants** – non-essential or luxury items, such as DVDs.

Verdict Research forecasts that by 2004, only 40 per cent of consumer income will be spent on necessities. Retailing will become more competitive as individual shops have to work harder to attract customers. Small shops may fail, as larger stores will be able to offer cheaper prices.

In the 1990s, many large out-of-town shopping complexes opened, such as Bluewater, Trafford Park and Meadowhall. However, traffic congestion around some of these complexes is becoming so bad it is affecting business. This, plus efforts by planners to attract stores back to town centres, could mean that far fewer of these complexes are opened in future.

Trends in selling methods – mail order and the Internet

One way in which retailers can become more competitive is to offer a greater range of selling methods. Most are opting for a 'clicks and mortar' presence where the retailer has both a shop and a website. Supermarket chains such as Tesco have increased business by offering customers the option of buying groceries online. In 2001, Tesco reported that it had one million Internet customers with an increase of £300 million in sales. Other products with the greatest potential for online sales include books, music, software, video and electrical goods. Clothing is less easy to sell in this way, given customers cannot do the 'touch test' online.

The latest trend in grocery shopping – buy online and have your shopping delivered to your door

Direct catalogues are also increasing in popularity. Many retailers such as Next, Harrods and Debenhams offer customers the opportunity to buy from the store or from a catalogue. Smaller retailers can substantially increase their sales by offering customers different methods of purchasing. Thornton's Chocolates, for example, sells its products through its shops, by mail order and on the Internet. Verdict Research forecasts Internet sales to increase – 0.3 per cent of goods were bought online in 1999, and this is expected to reach 3 per cent by 2004.

> **Snapshot**
>
> *Pet needs rapidly supplied*
>
> Centaur Services Ltd was formed in 1964 by a group of veterinary surgeons to supply vets' practices with a wide range of items as quickly as possible. More than 8,500 lines – from worming tablets to diet food – are stocked in its warehouse. A specialist buying team can access a further 20,000 items almost immediately. Customers can order by computer, telephone or fax and orders placed by 6.30 pm are delivered the following day by one of Centaur's own fleet of vehicles. Its lorries drive to redistribution depots so that local deliveries can be despatched in small vans.
>
> The aim is to provide a fast service offering a wide range of choice at competitive prices. Given the growth of Centaur since 1964, it appears to be succeeding!

Trends in services activities

The chart below includes all services (client and non-client).

Output and employment service activities, 2000

Activity area	Output	Employment
Hotels and restaurants	3.1%	5.8%
Transport and storage	5.4%	4.0%
Communications	3.1%	2.1%
Financial services	5.5%	4.1%
Real estate, renting and business activities	18.6%	14.5%
Public administration and defence	4.8%	6.0%
Education	5.2%	8.0%
Health and social work	6.2%	10.4%
Other personal services	5.1%	4.8%
Total share of British output/employment	57.0%	59.5%

Overall trend: The service sector has steadily increased in size (see the chart on page 40). Overall output and employment have steadily increased for many years although the two are not always directly related. In banking, for instance, many jobs have been lost because of automation and changes in working practices (see page 48).

> **It makes you think!**
>
> There are many service activities. Before you start to look at trends in this area, it is helpful to understand how they are grouped together.
>
> Within your group, suggest some services people might want. (Turn back to pages 38 and 39 if you need some clues!) Then look at the headings below. Put your ideas under the heading you think would be the most appropriate. You might have some more ideas when you read the headings!
>
> - Hotels and restaurants
> - Transport and storage
> - Communication
> - Financial services
> - Real estate, renting and business activities
> - Public administration and defence
> - Education
> - Health
> - Other personal services.
>
> Check your ideas against the chart on page 48, which lists the main services in each category. Make sure you understand what is meant by each activity. If not, check with your tutor.
>
> Some of these areas offer only client services. Others offer a mixture of client and non-client services. Within your group, identify which are which. Check your ideas with your tutor.

Chapter 5: Functional areas within business

What you will learn

- The human resources function
- The finance function
- The administration and ICT support function
- The operations function
- The marketing and sales function
- The customer service function
- The research and development function
- The use of ICT in business

Overview: functional areas

Key functions that support business aims and objectives

All businesses need to be well organised to achieve their aims and objectives. Certain tasks, or **functions**, must be done regularly and these are usually grouped into specific types of activities. Each person is then responsible for a particular area of work. For example, in a supermarket some staff work as checkout operators, others fill shelves, and so on. Unless all the key functions are carried out, the business will not operate efficiently. (You will learn more about the different functions of individual members of staff in Unit 2.)

Functional areas that support business aims and objectives

In a large organisation, people work together in **functional areas**. These areas undertake key functions which must be carried out within the business. Each has a specific purpose. Below are the main functional areas:

- **Human resources** – relates to the people who work for the organisation. You would contact the human resources (sometimes referred to as personnel) department of a business if you were applying for a job there.

- **Finance** – responsible for checking the money going in and out of a business. If there are problems, action must be taken swiftly. Computers and IT mean that financial transactions can be recorded immediately and analysed.

- **Administration and IT support** – all businesses receive information daily, in many different ways. This must be dealt with quickly so that customers and suppliers receive prompt answers. Each business also generates its own paperwork which must be stored safely in case it is needed again. Computers are an essential part of many businesses as they are used for many administrative tasks. For this reason, many organisations have a section responsible for maintaining the IT system.

- **Operations** – responsible for producing goods and services by making the best use of resources (e.g. people and equipment). In a manufacturing company, it may be known as the production, manufacturing or works department. In a business providing a service, the operations manager is responsible for making sure that all activities run smoothly.

- **Marketing and sales** – responsible for making sure customers know about the business. This may include market research, advertising and sales promotions, the creation and development of a website or web store (although its maintenance may be undertaken by IT support staff). The sales department is responsible for selling the items to the customer and keeping sales records.

- **Customer service** – provides information, advice and after-sales service, and deals with customers' complaints. Staff need to know about consumer laws which are designed to protect customers' rights.

- **Research and development** – concerned with technological and scientific developments which can improve the product in the future. This is important in many industries, such as cars and pharmaceuticals.

The main functional areas

Key functions within a business:
- Customer services
- Operations
- Administration and IT support
- Finance
- Research and development
- Marketing and sales
- Human resources

Differences in the organisation of functional areas

Many businesses call their functional areas **departments**, for example the finance department. In some cases, a function may be divided between several departments or sections. In many businesses, administrators can be found in each department – there is no separate administration department. Sometimes two functions are linked together such as operations and research and development.

When you are investigating business organisations, you many find that sections or departments have different names from the functional areas given above. Rarely are two businesses identical because they are involved in different activities. Each organisation will organise itself in the best way to meet its aims and objectives.

Links between functional areas

Each functional area exists to support the business's aims and objectives. However, it is very important that they communicate with each other. There must be close links between people, especially when their activities overlap. Communication between functional areas is covered on page 101.

Spot check

Write down your answers to the following questions:

1. Why is it important that businesses are well organised?
2. a What is the main function of a checkout operator?
   b How does this function help to achieve a supermarket's aims and objectives?
3. State two functional areas you would find in a large organisation.
4. Why are businesses organised in different ways?
5. Identify three functions carried out in your school or college which are essential for it to meet its aims and objectives.

Fact file

In business, you will often hear the term **resources**. An organisation needs the following types of resources:

- **land and buildings**, e.g. offices, farmland
- **equipment**, e.g. machinery, computers
- **people** with different skills
- **materials** – includes raw materials which are converted into goods to be sold and items of stock which are being sold in a retail store.

You will learn more about these resources on pages 74–78. **Capital** (money) is another essential resource and you will learn about this in Unit 3.

The different functional areas of a business are now covered in detail:

- human resources
- finance
- administration and ICT
- operations
- marketing and sales
- customer service
- research and development.

You don't need to read everything now. Rather, before you go out to investigate a particular

Chapter 5 Functional areas within business

department in a local business, use this as a reference resource so you can read up in detail and understand the sort of tasks that the department undertakes. This will help you ask the right questions and understand the answers.

The human resources function

The purpose of human resources

All organisations need to employ people to carry out essential activities. Employees are one type of resource.

The purpose of the human resources function is to recruit the employees needed by the businesses and to try to meet their needs once they are employed. Human resources is involved in the following areas:

- **Recruitment, retention and dismissal**. Human resources aims to attract and retain high-quality staff. However, if staff have to be dismissed, human resources must make certain that this is done legally as there are many laws which relate to employing and dismissing staff.
- **Working conditions**. High-quality staff will be more attracted to an organisation which has good working conditions than one which has not. This relates to more than just salary, as you will see below.
- **Training, development and promotion**. These are key areas because most staff want to develop their skills and improve their career prospects.
- **Employee organisations and unions**. Staff like to think their views are being taken into consideration if there are major changes and developments planned within the business. They also need advice if they have a serious problem. This is often the role of an employee organisation such as a staff association or a trade union, which will discuss matters with the human resources manager.
- **Health and safety**. All employees have the right to work in a safe environment. Human resources must ensure that the organisation operates within health and safety laws.

All these areas are discussed in more detail below. The role of human resources in ensuring the fair treatment of all staff and protecting them against victimisation, harassment, discrimination and unfair dismissal is covered in Unit 2.

Recruitment, retention and dismissal

These relate to people starting jobs, staying in jobs and leaving jobs either through dismissal or redundancy.

Recruitment

All businesses want to recruit the best employees. This means that they need recruitment procedures and trained staff who can:

- identify the vacancy
- decide where to advertise it
- decide which applicants should be interviewed
- interview candidates (or arrange interviews)
- select the most appropriate candidate
- notify unsuccessful candidates.

Human resources staff are usually involved in all stages of this process. You will learn more about this in Unit 2.

Retention

All businesses want to keep good staff, otherwise they have to hire and retrain someone else and this costs money. Human

The main responsibilities of the human resources function

resources staff are often responsible for checking and analysing **staff turnover** – the rate at which people leave the organisation. Reasons for leaving may be unconnected with the workplace, such as someone moving to another part of the country. However, if many people are leaving because they are dissatisfied or because there are no promotion prospects, then this will be investigated, particularly if too many good staff are leaving.

People are more likely to stay in an organisation if they are interested and happy in their work and have the opportunity for promotion. To help retain staff, businesses usually provide the following:

- An **induction programme** to help new staff settle in quickly. The new employee spends a short time learning about the business, touring the premises and meeting colleagues (see Unit 2, pages 260 and 262).
- Fair and competitive **terms and conditions of employment**. This means that staff are paid a fair rate for the job, holiday entitlement and sick pay are reasonable and similar to those offered by other employers.
- Good **working conditions** (see opposite).
- An opportunity for employees to talk regularly to their manager about their performance and future prospects. These are often called **appraisal interviews** (see Unit 2, page 262–263).

There are other factors which contribute towards people being happy at work, for example you may work in a pleasant, well-equipped office, but if you are bored and your boss treats you badly, this counts for very little.

It isn't easy to make every job interesting, for example packing or simple assembly work. You may be surprised to learn that some people aren't bothered and prefer to have a routine job that they don't have to think about – providing they are earning enough money.

In business, however, most jobs *are* interesting and challenging. Whether you work in marketing, IT, human resources, administration or finance, the jobs are usually different each day and you have your own area of responsibility. However, this does not mean that *all* jobs are interesting *all* the time! Most people accept this, and managers often try to extend jobs to make them more interesting.

Dismissal

Staff may leave an organisation voluntarily or they might be dismissed. Staff who leave voluntarily have to give notice. This means they have to notify their employer formally, in advance, to give the company time to obtain a replacement. The required length of notice is stated in the employee's contract of employment (see Unit 2, page 187).

Employees may also be dismissed. This means the employee has to leave, whether he or she wants to or not. There may be different reasons for this. You will learn about the different types of dismissal in Unit 2 (page 227).

Working conditions

When applicants are interviewed, they should be told about their conditions of employment *and* their working conditions.

The terms and conditions of employment are stated in the contract of employment (see Unit 2, page 186). They relate to the location of the organisation, hours of work, pay, holiday entitlement, sick pay, pension rights and how much notice must be given if the employee wants to leave.

Working conditions relate to:

- physical environment – lighting and ventilation, furnishings and equipment, heating, space available, level of noise
- job content
- promotion prospects within the organisation
- training opportunities
- welfare policies, such as loans to employees, stress counselling and medical checks.

Training, development and promotion

Most people want to continue to develop their skills and abilities after they have started work. This helps them to apply for jobs with more responsibility and better pay. Usually, staff are eligible for promotion only if they can prove they have done well in their current job, kept up to date with technology and have continued to develop themselves.

It makes you think!

A famous study of motivation was done by Frederick Herzberg. He investigated the factors that contribute to job satisfaction. He concluded that factors related to the content of the job and undertaking more challenging work help to increase people's motivation. He called these motivators.

Other factors which relate to the facilities and conditions of employment cause dissatisfaction if they are not present but, on their own, don't make people happy in their work. Herzberg called these hygiene factors.

1. Below are some of the factors Herzberg considered. Within your group, discuss each of the factors and decide whether it is a motivator or a hygiene factor. As a clue, there are four in each list. (The answers are given on page 60, but don't refer to these until you've tried to do the activity!)

   - Salary
   - Working conditions
   - Interesting work
   - Being praised for doing a good job
   - Having responsibility
   - Facilities available, e.g. staff restaurant, equipment, etc.
   - The way the company is organised
   - Being able to achieve

2. List all the factors which would be important to you, and which would make you decide to stay with an organisation. Rank each factor out of ten and then put the factors in order of importance for your group. Then compare your answer with those given by other groups.

Training

Training relates to specific opportunities to learn a new skill or extend previous skills or knowledge. It may be undertaken at work or elsewhere such as at a college or specialist training centre. You will learn about training in detail in Unit 2.

A large organisation may have its own training facilities and run many of its own training courses and events. Its human resources department may have a training officer or even a separate training section.

All human resources departments will be involved in keeping staff training records, overseeing the procedures for applying for training and monitoring the training budget, that is the amount of money allocated for training (see Unit 2, page 260).

Normally, an application is made by the employee and agreed by that person's line manager before it is accepted. After a company training event, staff are often asked for feedback. This ensures that popular events are noted – and probably repeated – whereas unpopular ones are reviewed and improved.

Development

Development relates to the personal development of the person which is not the same as learning new skills. This is why you may often hear the phrase 'staff development', rather than 'staff training'.

Most companies expect their employees to take an active role in their own training *and* self-development. There is usually an opportunity for staff to discuss this with their manager during their appraisal interview (see Unit 2, pages 262–263).

Many companies will pay for staff development activities and may run them in the workplace. These include activities such as how to work effectively in a team, time management to enable staff to work more efficiently, presentation skills, and so on.

Promotion

Most people want to progress in their career. In a large organisation there are likely to be several different grades of jobs, so promotion opportunities enable staff to progress within the company. In a small organisation this is less likely, so they may have to seek opportunities elsewhere.

Staff seeking promotion have to prove that they:

- can do their current job well
- are committed, interested and willing to help out whenever necessary
- work well with other people
- have developed their skills and abilities since joining the organisation
- are capable of coping with a more responsible job.

This may seem a lot to ask, but in many cases companies will advertise promotional vacancies both within and outside the company. This means internal applicants have to compete with external applicants.

Employee organisations and unions

When you go to work, you can reasonably expect to be treated fairly and for your legal rights to be observed by your employer. In return, you have to fulfil your legal responsibilities. You will learn about these in Unit 2.

What would you do, however, if you felt you were being treated unfairly, or if you worked in a company where there were rumours of redundancy? You may say you would simply leave and work somewhere else, but this may be difficult if jobs are scarce.

In such situations, you might seek help and advice from an employee organisation or a trade union which represents employees in discussions with management. Their role is to protect employee rights and try to improve working conditions and job security.

Employee organisations

Sometimes referred to as the **staff association**, **staff forum**, **professional association** or **works association**, employee organisations are run by experienced staff, normally from a range of different jobs in the organisation. In some cases, employee representatives are nominated and elected by staff themselves.

The employee organisation will usually be consulted about major issues which may affect staff such as business trends that will affect employment and proposed future changes. It must also be consulted in any redundancy discussions which would affect more than 20 jobs.

Where organisations consult with their employee organisation, and work together to find solutions to problems, there is a usually a greater atmosphere of trust between staff and management, and employees are more likely to accept the results of a decision in which they have been involved.

The main advantage is that employee associations give 'a voice' to employees and can help to protect them in negotiations with management. The disadvantage is that they may have little formal power in an organisation and may consist of representatives who are inexperienced at negotiating and do not have any legal knowledge or access to specialist advice.

Trade unions

A trade union is an association of employees formed to represent the workers in an industry, especially on pay and conditions. At the end of 2000, there were 76 unions in Britain representing 6.9 million workers. These unions are affiliated to the Trades Union Congress (TUC) which represents all unions on a national basis. It lobbies the government on issues relating to workers in general – from health and safety to working hours – and provides its unions with information and advice to help them to advise their members.

Joining a union is voluntary and involves the payment of a subscription or membership fee. The union individuals join depends on the type of work they do and where they work. The largest union in Britain is UNISON, which represents public sector employees, with over 1.25 million members.

Union representatives take part in a range of activities:

- They negotiate pay rates and pay rises for staff with management and recommend improvements at work.
- They are involved in health and safety issues and improvements in the workplace.
- They take part in any discussions relating to redundancy to ensure a fair policy.
- They give advice and support to individual employees involved in a dispute at work, and accompany them to any disciplinary or grievance interviews (see Unit 2).

- They give advice about work-based training (see Snapshot on page 62).
- They provide advice and information on employees' legal rights; industrial benefits if an employee is involved in an accident; and financial services, such as insurance and personal loans.

It is the role of a senior member of the human resources staff, often the human resources manager, to negotiate with trade unions on behalf of management.

> Answers to **It makes you think!** on page 58
>
> *Motivators:* interesting work, being praised for doing a good job, having responsibility, being able to achieve.
>
> *Hygiene factors:* salary, working conditions, facilities available, the way the company is organised.

Health and safety

A safe environment at work is a legal requirement throughout Europe. Both employers and employees have to abide by the **Health and Safety at Work Act** and the various regulations which have followed this Act. Under the law, the responsibility for safety is that of each line manager and, ultimately, the chief executive or head of the organisation. However, the human resources department is also often involved to provide information and support to managers on health and safety issues.

Large organisations will usually have a **health and safety officer** who has overall responsibility for health and safety policies and training. In others, there may also be a **safety committee**, made up of representatives from management and employees. This group is responsible for checking that legal requirements are being met. Many businesses also have **safety representatives** who attend meetings of the safety committee. These

It makes you think!

Union membership fell between 1979 and 1998, but has since started to rise. It is forecast to increase from its current level of just under 7 million because, under the Employment Relations Act 2000, if a union can prove that a majority of the workforce supports it, it has a legal right to apply to be formally recognised.

However, the trend for membership of young workers has not followed this upward pattern. In 1984, 44 per cent of workers aged 18–29 were union members. In 2000, this had fallen to 17 per cent.

Below are seven statements made by young people. Within your group, discuss:

a   which statements you agree with, or have heard mentioned by other people

b   which statements are true, and which are not

c   if you ran a union, what you would do to persuade young workers to join.

- Unions are just for blue-collar workers, such as those who work in trades like manufacturing and shipbuilding.
- Union members are always going on strike and causing trouble.
- Unions help to protect pension rights – but pensions don't matter when you're young.
- Unions are involved in health and safety – but this doesn't apply to my job.
- I don't need a union to help me obtain good pay. I'll just change jobs when necessary.
- I don't believe in trade unions. They cause problems for employers.
- If I had a problem at work, I'd leave. At my age, I can do plenty of jobs.

> **Over to you!**
>
> You can find out much more about unions on the Internet. The TUC site (www.heinemann.co.uk/hotlinks) has a section for students and an excellent link to the student BizEd site. Here you can find out the answers to almost anything you want to know about the TUC and unions, as well as information on your own rights as an employee. In addition, many unions have excellent websites with useful information which can be accessed by non-members.
>
> 1   Access the TUC and BizEd websites and find out:
>   a   how long the TUC has been in existence
>   b   its role
>   c   why unions belong to the TUC
>   d   the current campaigns the TUC is involved with
>   e   the five most important reasons why people join trade unions.
>
> 2   Working in a small group, investigate a trade union website of your choice and find out:
>   a   the type of workers it represents
>   b   the services it offers to members.
>
> Then compare your answers with the information obtained by other groups on other websites. Links to the following trade union websites are available at www.heinemann.co.uk/hotlinks
>
> - Broadcasting, Entertainment, Cinematograph and Theatre Union (BECTU)
> - Communications Workers Union
> - GMB
> - MSF
> - Transport and General Workers' Union
> - UNISON
> - Union of Shop, Distributive and Allied Workers

representatives are appointed by recognised trade unions and elected by union members, not by the employer. (Health and safety law and the people who work in this area are covered in Unit 2.)

The role of human resources staff is generally to support all the specialists involved in this area, for example by:

- keeping and storing Health & Safety Executive advisory documents and health and safety reference materials, including codes of practice which give advice on how companies can comply with the law
- helping to draw up and distribute the organisation's safety policy – a legal requirement for organisations with five or more employees
- helping to put together and update company codes of practice – these state the procedures all employees must follow in the event of an emergency, such as a fire or gas leak
- updating and issuing lists of first aiders, arranging first aid training and issuing first aid information to staff
- keeping accident records – all organisations must record accidents and those with more than ten employees must keep an accident book and accident records for at least three years
- compiling accident statistics – which show the number of accidents (and 'near-misses'), and the types of injury
- keeping staff absence records and checking the reasons for absence against health and safety issues such as stress or back pain through lifting
- arranging health and safety training for staff at the request of the safety committee or health and safety officer.

Trade union safety representatives have helped to reduce the number of accidents in the workplace

Chapter 5   Functional areas within business

Snapshot

Union safety representatives

The role of the trade union safety representative is broadening. Many representatives have taken advanced training to obtain professional health and safety status. They can now become worker safety advisers and be selected by their unions to visit non-union workplaces and advise on how workforce participation can help to improve safety standards. This idea was based on a successful Swedish scheme where roving safety advisers visit other organisations.

From Australia comes another initiative, that of safety reps issuing formal warnings to employers who ignore safety warnings. Since November 2001, British workplace safety reps have been allowed to issue a Union Inspection Notice (UIN) to employers who have repeatedly ignored a safety issue and who are breaking the law. If the employer ignores the UIN, the matter is passed on to the Health & Safety Executive or local authority inspectors (see Unit 2).

There are 200,000 union safety reps in Britain and figures show they are successful in reducing accidents, as there are twice as many serious injuries in workplaces which do not have a safety rep.

The finance function

The purpose of finance

The finance department keeps track of all the money being earned and spent by the organisation and knows exactly how much profit (or loss) is being made for each item or service sold. Many business people consider finance to be the most important function of all. Financial information enables critical and rapid decisions to be made about the business, which can make the difference between financial success and failure.

Most businesses control finances through a **budget** system. Each manager or department is allocated a budget which identifies planned income and spending. The finance department regularly checks that managers are on target and investigates the situation if they are not.

The use of IT and computers has revolutionised financial operations. Spreadsheets are used to analyse income and expenditure. Large organisations have special accounting software and management information systems – often known as MIS. The benefit of computerised systems is that they provide accurate and in-depth financial information more quickly. This helps businesses to monitor and meet their financial aims and objectives.

Spot check

Write down your answers to the following questions:

1. Why do organisations prefer to retain staff?
2. Explain briefly how the human resources department is involved in recruitment of new employees.
3. A friend is changing his job and tells you his new working conditions will be much better. What does he mean?
4. Explain three ways in which the human resources department would be involved in providing training for staff.
5. a Why do many employees hope to be promoted?
   b Identify three qualities a person would need to be worthy of promotion.
6. What is the main benefit of having a staff association in an organisation?
7. State two reasons why employers are keen to promote health and safety in the workplace.
8. Identify three tasks which could be undertaken by human resources staff in relation to health and safety.

The finance function is also very important for the staff since it is through this department that wages and salaries are paid. All employees have a legal right to be paid and to receive an itemised pay statement.

Another responsibility of finance is to prepare the organisation's accounts, which is a legal requirement for most businesses. Even a small business has to calculate its profit, because the Inland Revenue needs this figure to calculate how much tax the owner must pay. Expenses must be accurately recorded as this will reduce the amount of tax which is due. A business which is registered for value added tax (VAT) also has to submit VAT returns regularly and on time, otherwise the business is fined.

Finally, the business may need to obtain additional capital to pay for additional raw materials, newer equipment or to buy new premises or even another company. Obtaining this money in the most economical way is the task of senior finance staff.

The activities of the finance function can be grouped into three main areas:

- preparing accounts – this includes keeping the financial records required by the organisation, listing receipts and payments and preparing accounts that are required for managers (called **management accounting**) and by law (called **financial accounting**)
- paying wages and salaries to staff
- obtaining capital and resources.

The main activities of the finance function

Financial staff will also be involved in:

- checking the income and expenditure of different departments against their budgets
- providing continuous, up-to-date financial information to managers and others
- controlling the level of debts owed to the company
- advising senior managers on the financial implications of any major decision they make.

Snapshot

Instant data = instant action

A management information system (MIS) in a chain of department stores captures and processes all the data the organisation needs. Reports are then produced which identify key information, for example sales figures for individual departments.

The store's cash registers are linked to the computer system. Every purchase is recorded as a sale. Every night a report is produced by the computer which analyses the sales at the store by area. Products which are selling well are highlighted – and so are those which are not. This report is on the manager's desk every morning, and on the desk of executives in head office.

Decisions can now be made to move stock from one store to another (e.g. if umbrellas are selling better in Manchester than in Brighton), to order additional stock (e.g. if DVDs are selling well everywhere) or stop ordering a particular line (e.g. if few people are buying sandwich toasters). These decisions can be made rapidly and in response to customer behaviour <u>because</u> of the computer system. This has a direct effect on profits.

Providing up-to-the minute financial information is the task of the **management accountant** who is a specialist in deciding the type of information which is required, how this should be analysed and what decisions should be made as a result.

Preparing accounts

Millions of financial transactions take place in Britain every day. Money is received by organisations and these businesses have to pay their own bills. For example, a company selling office equipment and stationery has the types of transactions shown below.

Receipts

- Cash, debit or credit card payments or cheques from buyers who have purchased goods and paid for them at the same time.
- Standing order or direct debit payments from individuals who have bought goods on credit – that is, buy now, pay over several months. In this case the money is automatically transferred from the individual's bank account to the supplier each month. (There is more about these in Unit 3.)
- Cheques from businesses who have bought goods on credit. Most businesses expect to be able to buy goods and pay for them some time later, usually after 28 days. This relationship involves an element of trust, so finance staff will check the creditworthiness of new customers by obtaining a credit reference from an agency or the customer's bank. This will help to decide how much credit that customer should be allowed.

Payments

- Payments for supplies and raw materials. These goods will usually be bought on credit and the supplier will issue an invoice and a statement at the end of each month. This will state the total amount due to that supplier. Most payments are made by cheque, but some may be sent electronically.
- Payments for minor items, such as milk or stamps. These items are paid for at the time of purchase through the petty cash system, but the total amounts must be calculated.

Activities of finance staff include:

- checking and recording *all* the amounts received and paid out and entering these into the correct accounts
- making sure that all monies are banked as soon as possible
- checking all the accounts at the end of the month and highlighting those where payments are still due
- sending statements to customers who have bought on credit
- reminding anyone with an overdue account that this must be paid
- checking invoices for goods received to make sure these match the actual delivery and the agreed price
- making out cheques to suppliers
- recording all payments in the correct accounts
- checking all banking documents (such as the bank statement) and transferring any surplus money so that it will earn interest, where possible.

Today, many of these operations are computerised. As incoming or outgoing amounts are entered, the accounts are automatically adjusted. As money is banked, the banking records are updated.

At the end of the year, the accounts information must be brought together into the correct format required for the official or **statutory** accounts (these are accounts which companies are required by law to produce). All companies *must* provide a profit and loss account and a balance sheet. Many companies produce a cash flow statement as well. (There is more about these in Unit 3.)

A public limited company will employ a financial accountant to supervise this work and its accounts will be made public. The main points may even be highlighted in the media. A private company will have to notify its shareholders and send a copy to the Registrar at Companies House, but it does not have to publicise its results. A small business is likely to employ a firm of registered chartered accountants to do this work, and send it all the financial data at the end of the year. Chartered accountants prepare financial accounts for local businesses which would not find it cost-effective to employ someone full time to do this work.

Paying wages and salaries

This task may be part of the financial function, or it may be **outsourced** to a specialist agency. Specialist agencies will calculate and supervise the payment of wages and salaries in any organisation for a fee.

> **Fact file**
>
> When a service can be provided more cheaply by an individual or company outside the organisation, this is known as **outsourcing**.

Today, this operation is normally undertaken by computer, using a payroll software package. Most organisations pay their staff monthly, by credit transfer, whereby the money is transferred from an organisation's bank account to the employee's bank account.

Payroll records are kept for each employee. These show how much each person earned as basic salary and in overtime or bonus payments, how much tax and National Insurance was deducted and the net amount which must be paid to him or her. Employees may make other payments, such as to a company pension scheme or a trade union subscription.

Some payroll records rarely change, unless the employee moves house, changes his or her bank or obtains promotion. Someone on a monthly salary with no special payments or deductions would be entered once into the system, together with his or her tax code, which is decided by the Inland Revenue. The computer then makes all the necessary calculations. Other individuals may be paid variable amounts and in these cases the payroll staff have to make the correct entries each month.

Other changes which may need to be recorded include:

- the tax code, because of a change in an employee's personal circumstances
- sick pay, because a person is ill
- maternity pay, because a woman is on maternity leave.

If temporary staff are employed, then individual records must be created for them for the duration of their employment.

Once the entries have been made, the payroll staff must check them carefully before sending the instructions to the bank, to ensure there are no errors. They also need to ensure that each employee will receive an itemised pay slip showing all the current payments and deductions and giving a running total for that tax year.

Finally, at the end of each tax year (5 April), the payroll staff must produce end-of-year payroll summaries for the Inland Revenue and issue P60s, which detail the year's earnings and tax paid, to all staff.

Obtaining capital and resources

Start-up capital is the amount of money the owner invests in the business at the outset. This buys all the essential requirements, such as paying for a lease or buying premises, purchasing a company vehicle, buying stock, fitting out the premises and obtaining essential items such as a cash register, telephone and computer system (see also Unit 3, Chapter 3).

Once a company is trading and, hopefully, making a profit, then some of this money will be kept in **reserves** to finance future developments. However, there may not be enough in the reserve account to pay for the improvements or expansion required. In this case, the company may need to borrow the extra money or to raise it in some other way. The source of funds will depend mainly upon:

- the type of organisation, its size and previous history
- the type of development being considered
- the amount of money required.
- the type of **security** the business can offer. For example, a company worth £5 million can usually offer greater security than a firm valued at only £200,000. The lender looks for the assets which can be converted into cash if the money cannot be repaid.

Generally, a company will want to borrow at the cheapest rate possible. This means it wants low interest rates and good repayment terms. The length of time over which the money should be repaid is important and that decision may depend upon current interest

Chapter 5   Functional areas within business

rates and predictions as to whether these will rise or fall.

Sources of finance generally include:

- high street banks, known as commercial banks
- investment banks, which deal with larger companies and can lend greater sums of money
- specialist venture capital companies, which lend money often in exchange for shares in the company or for a seat on the board of directors
- organisations which issue grants and loans, such as the Prince's Trust, which lends money to young people, and regional development agencies (RDAs) which give advice on grants and loans to businesses in their area (see page 32).

A listed public limited company may decide to borrow money by issuing additional shares in the company.

Deciding the best option is a skilled job. It is the task of the financial manager to assess the options and to advise the board of directors which is most appropriate for the company at that time.

An alternative, if the company wants the money to buy new equipment, is to rent or lease the items instead of buying them. Many company cars are leased. They are paid for monthly and at the end of the lease the cars are replaced with new vehicles and a new lease is negotiated. The leasing company also pays for all repairs and servicing. This means the company pays for vehicles out of current profits, rather than having to 'save up' to pay out a large amount at once.

Snapshot

No longer in the top financial league

Borrowing too much money can prove to be a disaster, either for individuals or businesses. All it needs is for something to go wrong and for the organisation to have problems meeting the repayments.

One company which learned its lesson the hard way was football club Nottingham Forest, which became a public limited company in 1997. In 2001, the company's shares were suspended on the London Stock Exchange after it failed to publish its accounts in time. Losses of about £30 million for the last two completed financial years meant that crisis talks were being held with its financial backers. The company's bankers agreed to provide borrowing facilities to keep the club afloat until June 2002.

One of Forest's problems was relegation to the First Division, which meant it no longer had access to the riches to be made in the Premiership. The second was saddling itself with huge debts to buy expensive players.

Spot check

Write down your answers to the following questions:

1. Identify three main functions of a large finance department.
2. Briefly explain why obtaining accurate and prompt financial information is so important.
3. What is meant by statutory accounts?
4. Why does the Inland Revenue require business accounts to be completed?
5. Most businesses provide goods and services for other businesses on credit. Explain the meaning of this term.
6. a How are most employees paid today?
   b Identify three items of information required by finance before wages can be paid.
7. Why do companies often require additional capital even though they are making a profit?
8. a Identify two possible sources of finance for a company which needs additional capital.
   b What is the role of the financial manager in this process?

It makes you think!

1. A small family grocer wants to expand his shop by buying the vacant property next door which is on sale at £80,000. He has the following choices:
   a. Buy the property with a mortgage – pay 5 per cent deposit and then repay the remainder over ten years at a fixed interest rate of 10 per cent.
   b. Borrow the money from the bank on a variable interest rate loan over five years.

   Within your group, discuss the advantages and disadvantages of each option.

2. A florist bought a second-hand van for £5,000 two years ago. This year she decides to sell it and is offered £3,100. The difference between these two figures is the amount the van has depreciated (fallen) in value. Within your group, answer the following questions:
   a. How much has the van depreciated by?
   b. What is this amount as a percentage of the purchase price?
   c. If the van costs £700 in tax and insurance a year, and she has paid £250 each year in repairs and servicing, how much does the van cost to run per year?
   d. If the florist is offered the opportunity to lease a new van at a cost of £2,000 a year, do you think this would be more economical? Give a reason for your answer.

3. You are the owner of a First Division football club. Last year, your team made £2 million profit but you owe £6 million to the bank. You have one star player and have been offered £10 million for him. This would clear your debts but could reduce your performance. There are also two other good players currently on offer from another club for £12 million – and the three good players combined could significantly improve your promotion prospects this year. You could then argue to the bank that the extra money you borrow could be set against increased gate receipts and TV revenues in the future.

   Within your group, decide the advantages and risks attached to these decisions. Then take a vote as to what you should do!

The administration and ICT support function

The purpose of administration and ICT

If you think of a business as a large machine, which constantly produces goods or services, then consider administration and ICT as the 'oil' which keeps it working smoothly. Without them, the machine would grind to a halt because administration and ICT provide the vital support services which are essential for the business to operate effectively.

Traditionally, administration was often **centralised** in a large separate section. Today, it is usually **decentralised** with administrators working in every department. This provides additional flexibility and is largely due to the introduction of networked computer systems which have improved the flow of communications and information between departments.

Administrative and ICT staff are usually responsible for the following key areas:

- **Clerical work** – includes the collection and distribution of mail, record keeping, organising meetings and responding to enquiries.
- **Cleaning and maintenance** – undertaken by specialist staff who may be supervised by an administration or estates manager.
- **Health and safety** – involves all employees but which may be the responsibility of administration in areas such as the use of IT equipment and the maintenance of electrical equipment.
- **Security** – may include day-to-day support for special security staff on the premises.
- **Support for software applications, electronic communications and electronic transactions** – system glitches, crashes and problems can cause havoc and need to be

fixed as quickly as possible. Users also regularly need support and guidance, and rapid assistance with hardware problems.

The role of administration and ICT function

An efficient administration function is essential for the smooth running of a business

Clerical or administrative work

Many different tasks are carried out by administrative and clerical staff during an average day. Some are routine, such as opening the mail, ordering stationery, preparing and filing documents; other tasks also need doing, such as answering the phone, assisting callers, responding to urgent emails or faxes, and so on. This can make administrative jobs very busy, varied and interesting.

The crucial point is the order in which these tasks are done and *how* they are done. Urgent jobs must be done immediately, but routine jobs cannot be neglected. Poor or sloppy administration causes endless problems and can lose customers. A lost order, an abrupt response to an enquiry or a badly typed document give a poor impression of the business and may lose customers. Good administration means enquiries are dealt with promptly and courteously, documents can be retrieved from the files in seconds and the quality of documents is consistently good. In this case, administration as a function is invaluable to both staff and customers. Key duties undertaken by administrative staff include the following.

Collecting and distributing mail

Opening, sorting and correctly distributing the mail promptly around a large company each morning is essential. The administrative staff are responsible for ensuring that all incoming mail is processed and passed to the correct person as soon as possible.

Outgoing mail items must be collected and processed towards the end of the day. This includes routine documents and parcels, some of which may be urgent or need sending abroad. Very urgent items may also be sent by courier.

Keeping records

Records are kept both on paper and on computer. Administrative staff will be responsible for maintaining both types of system:

- **Paper-based records** consist of letters, memos, faxes, reports and print-outs of emails that need to be retained for future reference. All records need to be kept neatly, clearly labelled and stored carefully so that they remain in good condition.
- **Computer records** consist of customer, staff or product files kept on computer, usually in a database. However, there will

also be computer files containing word-processed documents and spreadsheets. Administration staff will responsible for labelling their directories, keeping back-up copies and updating records regularly. Organisations which have **electronic filing** scan incoming documents into the computer system and store them using special software. This reduces the amount of paper stored on the premises.

The test of any record keeping system – and any administrator – is the speed at which an item can be retrieved. If a document or computer file is required urgently, this can be vital.

Organising meetings

Meetings are often held between members of staff or between staff and visitors. Administrative staff are responsible for making the necessary arrangements, including booking a room, organising refreshments, preparing any paperwork, notifying everybody when and where the meeting will be held, taking notes at the meeting and sending copies of these notes to everyone who was invited to attend.

Responding to enquiries

Enquiries will be received internally, from members of staff in other departments, and externally, from customers, prospective customers and other business contacts such as the organisation's bank or accountant. Enquiries can be received over the telephone, by email or in person.

All enquiries must be answered promptly with the correct information, regardless of other priorities. Administrative staff may answer enquiries themselves or pass it on to the relevant person. They also need to know the type of enquiry they are allowed to deal with (such as a routine request for the price of a product) and those which they are not (such as a request for a member of staff's home address).

Other administrative duties

- Preparing documents using word processing, spreadsheet, database and presentation packages.
- Sending and receiving messages by telephone, fax and email.

> I need the information straightaway. Can you get it to me?
>
> Certainly Mrs. Green. I've got everything you need and I'll fax it over immediately.
>
> I need the information straightaway. Can you get it to me?
>
> I'm afraid I don't have access to that information, Mrs Green. I'll transfer you to our finance manager who'll be able to help you.

Enquiries must be dealt with promptly and helpfully in every situation

- Making arrangements for visitors to the organisation.
- Making travel arrangements for members of staff who travel on business.
- Purchasing routine resources required by clerical staff, such as stationery supplies.

Cleaning and maintenance

Cleaners may be employed directly by the company or subcontracted from a specialist cleaning company. Many organisations find it more cost-effective to use specialist companies than to employ their own cleaning staff. Some cleaners undertake light cleaning duties such as vacuuming offices and cleaning toilet areas. Other staff will be employed to do heavy cleaning duties such as cleaning windows. These staff may be part of the maintenance section in some organisations.

Maintenance staff are employed to do general repair work such as mending broken windows or fixing a leaking roof. They may also look after any gardens attached to the premises. Specialist work, such as plumbing, is usually contracted out, although many organisations employ their own electricians.

> **Over to you!**
>
> How often should you change a light bulb? At home, you probably replace it when it fails. Now imagine you are in charge of maintenance in a very large hospital. Would you have a member of staff continually checking the lighting? Or would you do this, say, once a month (which means that some lights might have failed 30 days ago)? Are some lights more important than others, which may affect your decision?
>
> Before you think about this, find out what maintenance staff are employed by your school or college. Find out what jobs they do and which jobs are contracted out to specialists. See if you can find a reason for the difference and whether your maintenance staff agree with it! Then decide what you would do if you ran the hospital. A very large hospital needs many maintenance staff, far more than a school or college. Why do you think this is? Try to identify some of the jobs they do.

Health and safety

While the human resources department might keep all accident records in one organisation, in another only summary records may be kept by human resources, and administrative staff may issue and store accident forms for their area. Administrative staff may be expected to respond to any emergency in their section and many teams include a trained first aider.

In particular, administrative staff are involved in the following areas of health and safety:

- All employees have a duty to work safely. In an office, hazards such as boxes left in a passageway or files piled high on a rickety shelf can lead to accidents. Staff are expected to keep their work areas tidy and are responsible for ensuring that hazards are dealt with promptly.
- Photocopiers and fax machines must be used according to instructions and regularly maintained.
- Hazardous substances such as cleaning materials must be clearly labelled and stored safely according to the manufacturer's instructions.
- Computer and telephone users must have the correct equipment and be trained to use it properly since a badly positioned computer or a flickering screen can cause back or vision problems; overuse of a keyboard can lead to repetitive strain injury (RSI); the constant wedging of a telephone in the crook of your neck may also lead to injury.
- Staff should lift heavy loads such as boxes of photocopier paper correctly. Lifting these without care may cause serious back problems.

More information on the above can be found in Unit 2.

Administrative staff will not only be involved in health and safety record keeping for their own area, but also in any **risk assessments** undertaken. This means identifying possible areas where accidents could occur and minimising the risk as much as possible. One method of doing this is to ensure all administrative staff are trained to do their jobs safely.

Security

Security is another area which is often contracted out to specialist security companies.

Some high-security establishments, such as British Aerospace, employ their own security guards who are responsible for patrolling the premises, reporting security risks, logging any 'incidents' and liaising with the local police when necessary. In many cases, security guards also monitor and report health and safety risks and some may be trained first aiders. The organisation's head of security will advise on security precautions, such as the installation of closed-circuit television.

In many establishments, security guards are located at the main entrance to the site. They check and record the details of all visitors, issue visitor passes and make sure that all passes have been returned.

No matter where you work, you will be expected to cooperate with security staff over security measures, from wearing an identity badge to closing windows at the end of the day.

Support for software applications, electronic communications and electronic transactions

Support for all the IT functions in a business is very important. In any organisation, computer failure causes serious problems. In a company which uses a networked computer system for the creation, storage and transmission of electronic information, computer failure can be catastrophic. Every moment when the computers are 'down' loses business and therefore loses money.

In most businesses there is a specialist IT manager in charge of this function. Even in a small organisation there is likely to be an IT 'guru' who solves basic problems and is responsible for obtaining more specialist help when required.

The basic functions carried out by IT support staff may include the following:

- Purchasing computer equipment and consumable items such as floppy disks and printer cartridges.
- Regularly reviewing IT systems and recommending upgrades to hardware and software as required.
- Advising users on security procedures in relation to computer use, including the issuing of passwords and computer IDs to new users, monitoring of IT usage (especially emails and Internet use) and virus checking.
- Installing security devices such as a **firewall**, which prevents external users from accessing company data (see page 96) and automated protection systems which check email attachments to reduce the risk of viruses being downloaded.
- Providing assistance and guidance on new equipment or software which may include running training sessions.
- Providing ongoing support to users who experience technical problems. This is often done through a **computer help desk** which users can phone if they experience a problem.
- Setting up network services and liaising with users to develop new services that would be useful. This is likely to include maintenance of a company intranet which provides information internally to staff (see pages 94–95).
- Carrying out routine repairs and maintenance.

If the company operates a website or a web store, then specialist staff may be employed to keep this updated. Some websites also include a web store where you can buy goods online such as Amazon, Tesco, Hamleys and Heinemann (see www.heinemann.co.uk/hotlinks). You take your virtual shopping basket around the virtual store, choose what you want to buy and pay for it online.

A computer help desk provides support to users experiencing technical problems

A small organisation may design its own simple website, but businesses with more complex requirements often contract out the creation and design of a website to specialists who will structure it so that updating the site can be done by trained internal staff. A company which has a comprehensive site will employ its own specialist staff to maintain and upgrade the site. These may include programmers and designers. Further information on the IT function and the use of IT in business is given on pages 94–98.

Snapshot

The importance of staying online!

Any company which operates a website needs an internet service provider (ISP) which acts as its web 'host'. A large or specialist company may be its own 'host' and have its own Internet server and employ specialist technical staff to look after it.

This means that small companies, which rely on commercial ISPs, can be more vulnerable if their ISP has technical problems or makes sudden changes without giving advance warning. In some cases, businesses have found that their website simply disappears, or is totally inaccessible to customers.

One way to protect against this is to keep a back-up copy of the site. If an outside agency has designed the site, then it should provide one at the same time as the site 'goes live'. This means that the back-up can be uploaded on the server as an immediate replacement for the original if necessary.

Commercial firms often buy their own domain name so that they have a unique Internet address. The major benefit is that even if the company changes its ISP, its web and email addresses will remain the same. Finally, again as a security back-up, some companies have two telecommunications lines installed, such as a high-speed digital line and a cable line. In this case, if one fails, customers can still communicate with them.

Spot check

Write down your answers to the following questions:

1. Identify three clerical tasks regularly undertaken by administrative staff.
2. Why is it important to respond to all enquiries promptly?
3. Explain two ways in which records may be kept in business.
4. What is the difference between employing cleaning staff and contracting this out to a specialist organisation?
5. Identify three types of maintenance duties that may be required in an organisation.
6. Identify three areas of health and safety which are important to administrative staff.
7. Describe two duties of security staff in an organisation.
8. Why do many organisations operate a computer help desk?
9. Describe four tasks carried out by computer support staff.
10. Briefly explain the main differences you would find between computer support in a large organisation and in a small firm.

Over to you!

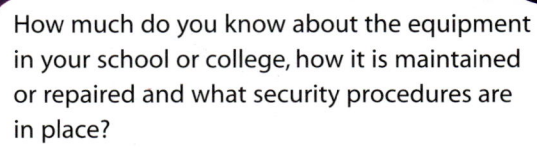

How much do you know about the equipment in your school or college, how it is maintained or repaired and what security procedures are in place?

Start by discussing with your business or ICT teacher the type of system you have in your school or college. Check you know how a networked system operates and the type of facilities found on this. Then find out how the system is protected and what basic steps IT users must take to maintain security. Finally, learn how faults are repaired and who advises users with a technical problem.

Keep your notes safely, so that you can compare this system with those in any organisations you investigate.

The operations function

The purpose of operations

On page 55 you learned that all businesses need resources – buildings, land, equipment, people and materials. The operations function is responsible for:

- obtaining the resources required to produce the goods or provide the service offered by the organisation
- organising these resources so that they are used in the best way to achieve the aims and objectives of the organisation.

What does this mean in reality? Think about the main purpose – or operation – of any business. Honda, for example, makes cars; without cars Honda would cease to exist. Take away all the students from a college and it would have no reason to exist either. In both these cases, the business exists to produce a product or provide a service to a group of people, either customers or students.

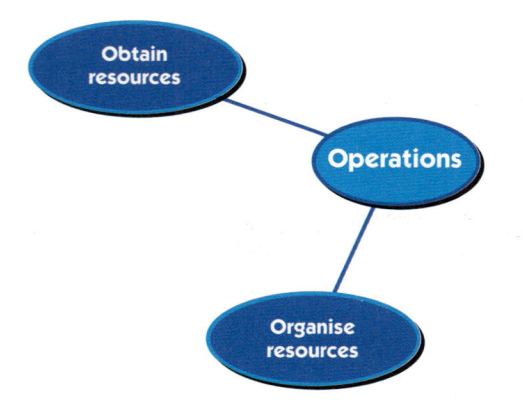

need to buy raw materials and convert them into the finished product. A company making jeans, for instance, requires denim, thread, zips and other fastenings. The list is short. For a car or aeroplane manufacturer, the list would be much longer! All these items need to be available as and when they are needed – and this requires skill. The jeans manufacturer doesn't want thousands of metres of denim fabric lying around – this costs money and takes up valuable space. Neither would it want to run out, because production would stop and the company's profits would be affected.

One type of operation – the production of goods

The role of the operations function

The jeans need to be made with as little wastage as possible. They need to be of good quality, otherwise people wouldn't buy them. They also need to be made within the budget allowed, otherwise the company won't make a profit. Finally, the manufacturer has to make sure the jeans are ready when the customers want them, otherwise it will lose orders.

Making sure that this process goes smoothly is critical to the business and most companies employ an **operations manager** – sometimes called a **production manager**, **manufacturing manager** or **works manager** – to control it.

Producing goods

In many companies, the key operation is making goods, for example cars, computers, clothing, food products. These organisations

Providing a service

Identify three services provided by a travel agent

Many organisations in Britain provide a service, for example banks, travel agents, schools and colleges, and so on. How does operations work in this context?

First, consider what each organisation provides. A bank provides financial services to its customers, travel agents provide travel services, a school or college provides educational services.

Then, consider who is responsible for deciding what will be provided and who is responsible for delivering the service. This way you can identify the key people involved in the organisation's operations:

- In a bank, senior managers will decide on the financial services to be offered and these will be provided through staff in local branches (and on the website).
- In a travel agency, the manager will decide on the travel services to be offered and staff will advise customers.
- In a school or college, the head or principal will decide on the subjects to offer and at what level, and staff will deliver the service to pupils.

In all these cases, both managers *and* the staff are responsible for the operations. In a service organisation, a large number of staff may be involved in delivering the key operation to customers, for example solicitors advising clients.

Types of resources

All organisations need resources, whether they produce a product and/or provide a service. For example, a sandwich bar needs premises, equipment such as a refrigerator, knives and bowls, the basic materials for sandwiches, and labour to produce and sell them. You can apply this type of thinking to all kinds of organisations, no matter what scale of operation is carried out.

The type and quantity of resources required will depend upon:

- the operation being carried out
- the way it is being carried out (e.g. either manually or by automated process)
- the scale of the enterprise. A large organisation obviously requires a greater number of resources than a small firm.

Land and buildings

All businesses – producers of goods and service providers – need buildings and land to operate.

For example, a farmer requires farmland and buildings such as a barn or dairy. A manufacturer needs a factory building. Service providers such as distributors need warehouses, retailers need shops, solicitors and accountants operate from offices, estate agents and travel agents usually need offices but some have shops too.

Equipment

A farmer requires specialist equipment depending upon the type of farm, for example milking equipment, combine harvesters. A manufacturer needs complex equipment related to the goods being produced; a distributor needs vehicles; retailers need cash registers and all offices use a range of equipment including computers, fax machines and photocopiers.

The amount of specialist equipment required will vary, depending upon the extent to which any process is automated.

Automation means that machines do the work instead of human beings. Examples of automation include the following:

- **Robots** – perform dangerous, dirty, monotonous or intricate jobs. Some industrial robots are just 'arms', programmed to do jobs such as welding, paint spraying, machine loading and basic assembly work. Multi-arm robots have been developed to do different jobs simultaneously. Because they can be very expensive, these are more likely to be found in large organisations. Robots are also used in other areas. In medicine, they can be used to help move patients who are immobilised or paralysed. They are also being developed to carry out delicate operations, such as brain surgery, because their movements can be precisely programmed and repeated as required.
- **Digitised telephone systems** – a 'computer voice' answers the telephone and directs customers to select different options depending upon their individual need. This helps to 'screen' calls and directs them to the right person.
- **Automated mailroom equipment** – deals with computer-produced bulk mail-shots. The equipment automatically folds and inserts the documents, seals the envelope, weighs it and franks it with the correct postage.

People

Staff are required at different levels and with different skills. As you will see in Unit 2, **managers** take responsibility for a particular type of function. Supervisors may be employed to oversee the work of people involved in the actual operation such as production workers. They will need **support staff** such as administrators. **Specialists** are also required by many organisations, for example a research firm may employ scientists, a car producer will employ engineers, an accountant will need tax experts.

Materials

All types of businesses require materials. A manufacturing organisation needs raw materials to produce the finished goods. A retail store needs stock to sell, in this case the materials will depend upon the type of goods sold – from shoes to mobile phones. Both organisations also need packaging materials.

Service organisations need specialist types of materials. A travel agency needs holiday brochures, a hotel needs towels and bed linen, hospitals need bandages and medicines.

Snapshot

Design by computer

Automated processes and computers have changed many of the functions of production workers. Today, many products – from wallpaper to cruise liners – are designed using a computer. A <u>computer-aided design (CAD)</u> package enables a designer to sketch a basic shape and then vary the dimensions, angles and sizes of certain parts. The product can even undergo stress testing by computer.

In some industries, CAD packages are linked to <u>computer-aided manufacturing (CAM)</u>. In the carpet industry, a new design can be planned on computer and the tufting machine which makes the carpet (and looks like a giant knitting machine) can be pre-set and controlled to produce the design by computer. Computers also help to monitor the production process. Instead of walking around a large factory to inspect individual machines, production operators can check progress constantly by watching a computer screen or reading a computer print-out. Computers are also used to check quality, as you will see on page 78.

Obtaining resources

You already know that the job of obtaining human resources is the task of the human resources function (see page 56). The task of obtaining land or buildings is usually undertaken when the business is started. Decisions relating to improvements or extensions are usually taken by senior managers, with advice given by the financial manager.

Obtaining specialist equipment such as new computers is often the task of the IT manager, and obtaining routine office equipment, such as photocopiers, is the job of the administration manager.

However, the biggest task relating to obtaining resources is the regular purchase of the materials and general items which are used every day. This is usually the job of specialist buyers in an organisation. They may work in part of production or in a separate purchasing department. In this case, they will buy all the materials required by the organisation. This is usually cheaper because they can buy in bulk and obtain better discounts.

Purchasing staff are responsible for negotiating contracts with suppliers and checking that the terms of these are met. All items are inspected on delivery and any problems are reported back to the purchasing staff who will take up the matter with the supplier. The quality of the materials is extremely important, particularly the raw materials which comprise the finished product. If these are substandard, then the final product will also be substandard. In some industries, quality is critical (think of aircraft components or medicines). In this case, suppliers will have to conform strictly to the requirements of the buyers (see also page 79).

Purchasing is a skilled job because supplies of the correct materials of the right quality must be available when needed. The

It makes you think!

Within your group, carry out the following activities.
1   Copy out the chart below and then try to complete the gaps. Compare your suggestions with other groups.
2   Running the operations of a large, complex service organisation can be as difficult as being production manager of a large factory. Imagine you were to meet the operations manager of an airport. What range of services do you think would be that person's responsibility? Write down all the ideas you can, and then compare your suggestions with those made by other groups.

Business	Type of building or land	Equipment	Specialist staff	Materials
Dentist	Dental surgery		Dental surgeon Hygienist	
Police				Uniforms Petrol Stationery
Cinema		Projectors Catering equipment		
Airline		Aeroplanes Catering equipment Safety equipment Check-in desks		Uniforms Food Drinks Toilet items Cleaning materials
Carpet manufacturer		Computers Tufting machines Cutting machines	Designers Foremen Tufting machine operators	
Garage	Showroom Workshops			

materials must also be purchased at a competitive price (not necessarily the lowest price). Buyers must bear in mind the reliability of different suppliers, the essential quality, storage space available, possible shortages and proposed delivery dates.

Many large organisations ensure that their supplies are delivered 'just in time' for production needs – this is sometimes referred to as JIT. This system reduces the quantity of raw materials held in stock and the storage space required. It also reduces the amount of money which has to be spent on raw materials. However, with this system, the reliability of the supplier is critical, and the organisation may nominate a preferred supplier who will guarantee to deliver goods at a moment's notice. This system is a common feature of the motor trade. Large motor manufacturers rely on nearby suppliers of components who will deliver daily.

Computers have also revolutionised purchasing. Goods can be ordered using electronic data interchange (EDI) (see page 97) where goods are purchased and paid for electronically. However, this system is being replaced by business-to-business (b2b) e-commerce transactions where businesses trade with each other over the Internet. Again, this helps to speed up the process and means fewer items need to be held in stock.

Purchasing staff in many organisations not only obtain resources from within the UK but also from abroad. In this case they need to be familiar with import restrictions and regulations and to know how currency rates may change and affect the cost of supplies.

Good communications are required between purchasing and operations staff. Any changes to a product, or to the production schedule, is likely to mean that changes are required to the type or quantity of materials required or the date when they are needed.

hand. It is exactly the same in business. The organisation functions far better if all the resources are grouped methodically, so that people can use them easily. For this reason, you will find:

- a large site organised with buildings for different operational functions – even a small firm is likely to locate separate functions in different offices
- equipment close to the people who will operate it, e.g. photocopiers close to office areas
- staff grouped together in similar specialisms, e.g. IT staff work in one area, packers in another
- materials sited so that a constant supply is kept on hand with store rooms nearby for the remaining stock.

You can see how this operates when you visit any organisation:

- In a factory, stocks of raw materials are kept near the production area. Items regularly required by production staff are placed where they can be reached easily. The aim is to have the factory so well organised that production flow is always maximised.
- In a retail store, similar products such as household items are grouped together. In a supermarket, fresh produce is in one area, frozen food in another, and so on.
- In a service organisation, both materials *and* different services are grouped together. For example, in a travel agent all the brochures will be arranged in specific sections, such as UK, Europe and long-haul trips. In a hotel, there will be separate areas for checking in (reception), preparing food (kitchens), eating (restaurants). Table linen will be kept close to the restaurant and bed linen near to the bedrooms.

Organising resources

You use resources every day – paper, pens, books and so on – and you probably find that you work more efficiently if you can find everything you need quickly and if it is close at

Using resources

Using resources properly is important for business efficiency. Most organisations have a number of controls, or checks, in place to make sure this is done properly.

- Buildings are expensive as rents and rates have to be paid. The aim is to organise the premises so that as much space as possible is used for operations which will improve profit or the quality of the service. For instance:
    - superstores are planned so that the most profitable lines have the most selling space
    - in hospitals, ward space and bed allocation is critical for the standard of health care provided
    - in a restaurant, tables are grouped so that the maximum number of people can be seated at one time.
- Equipment must be serviced and maintained so that it works efficiently. This is essential in a factory, for example, where a machine breakdown can halt production (known as **downtime**). Manufacturing companies control the use of machines to make sure none are overloaded, over-used or under-used. Some operate a maintenance plan to allow machines to be regularly inspected and serviced. In an office, the breakdown of a photocopier or fax can cause problems, while an IT system crash can seriously disrupt the business's operations. Other examples where equipment failure can damage a business include a restaurant unable to serve meals because of faulty ovens; an evening football match cancelled because the floodlights have failed.
- People should be used wisely! Well-motivated staff are essential to the success of a business's operations and it is more cost-effective for an organisation. Staff should be encouraged to develop their skills so they can do their jobs to the best of their ability (see Unit 2). In many companies, **job enrichment** gives staff greater responsibility over their own work. For example, in manufacturing organisations, staff often work in teams and have responsibility for the quality of the output produced by their own team. This has proved to be more effective than having 'inspectors' to check quality (see opposite).
- Wastage of stock and materials must be kept to a minimum. Stock and raw materials should be stored in a secure area (to prevent pilfering) and issued only to authorised staff. Usage is normally monitored, as a double check. A stock control system allows staff to check stock levels and ensure that stock is replaced when required. This is critical for essential raw materials or items related to the key operation such as clean towels or bed linen in a hotel, bandages or medicines in a hospital and food in a restaurant.

While much information can be obtained from reports and computer print-outs, staff may also use observation to make sure that everything related to the key operation is running smoothly. For example, in a supermarket, staff regularly check and restock shelves; in a factory, checks will be made that operators are working efficiently, that sufficient materials are available and that the machinery is functioning properly.

The importance of quality

Quality is important in all businesses, and vital where the safety of a product is concerned, for example in car engine manufacture.

At one time, manufacturers employed quality controllers to check the quality of a finished product. This is rather like making pizzas and then sampling them to check they are of good quality. While this is still useful, organisations prefer to 'build in' quality at every stage. So the pizza manufacturer would focus on the quality of the food products used, the type of dough, the length of cooking time, even the type of packaging used and the cooking instructions. This is far more effective since some problems and faults might not be evident at the final checking stage.

This system is called **total quality management** (**TQM**), sometimes referred to as **right first time**. Standards are set for each stage of the operation and each operator or team is responsible for checking the quality of its own work. In many cases, the system is extended to supplies, which must conform to certain quality standards. This ensures that any raw materials or components used are also up to the standard set by the buyer.

All businesses must regularly check their products for quality. This applies to businesses providing services, too

The number and type of checks carried out will depend upon the margin for error that is allowable. If a company produces filing cabinets or wrapping paper, then the checking process can be rather less rigorous, because it would not be cost-effective to spend hours on this process. Visual checks may be quite sufficient.

When quality must be more precise computers will be used and part of the quality process will be automated. A machine can test that all items have been manufactured within specified tolerances and automatically reject all those outside the set limit. CAD packages can check that designed components will fit into a total structure. For example, imagine 25 designers working on different parts of an aircraft. A master program coordinates their work to ensure that, when the aircraft is assembled, all the separate sections will fit together and work properly.

Organisations providing a service need to check quality, too. This is often done through customer questionnaires and monitoring complaints. You will read more about this on the following pages.

Spot check

Write down your answers to the following questions:

1. Apart from capital, state the four types of resources required by all businesses.
2. Identify the main operation in each of the following types of organisation and state the type of staff who will carry it out:
   a. a petrol station
   b. a bakery
   c. a football club.
3. Identify at least six important resources that would be required by a health and fitness centre.
4. a. What is meant by the term 'automation'?
   b. Identify two operations which would be automated in a large restaurant but which are probably not automated in your own home.
5. Explain briefly how most large organisations obtain the items they need and use regularly.
6. The organisation of resources is important. How would you see this organisation in action if you visited a large supermarket?
7. Identify two ways in which the use of resources is controlled in business.
8. Explain two ways in which computers are used in business to assist operations.
9. In a local fast-food restaurant, the new manager is keen to monitor operations. What could she do to ensure that operations are always running smoothly?
10. a. Why is quality important?
    b. State two ways in which the quality of manufactured goods can be checked.
    c. Explain briefly how you would 'build in' quality to every stage of the process if you owned a sandwich bar.

Chapter 5   Functional areas within business

Case study

Seabrook potato crisps

Seabrook's distinctive packaging

You may never have heard of Seabrook crisps, let alone tasted them, unless you live in Yorkshire or the North Midlands. This is because – in comparison with major crisp manufacturers – the Seabrook operation is relatively small. But their crisps have an outstanding reputation for taste.

The Seabrook Potato Crisp factory is in Bradford, and has been run by the same family since it started in business 60 years ago. Seabrook is so keen to keep its reputation for high quality that every aspect of production is closely controlled. The crisps are made only from Saturna potatoes which have the ideal sugar content for crisps. They are stored in wooden crates under dim lighting to ensure they do not sprout. Pure sunflower oil – too expensive for many manufacturers – is used, which means the products have less saturated fat than their competitors, and so are healthier to eat. The oil is constantly pumped through a tank so that the same oil is never used twice. Finally, flavourings (from Worcester sauce to Indian tandoori) or sea salt are added.

Every day, 70 tonnes of potatoes are converted into 576,000 packets of crisps. Forklift truck drivers transport the potatoes to a large tank where they are scrubbed, peeled and sliced, and made into crinkly pieces. After being blanched in a vat of hot water at exactly 90°C to remove the sugar and starch, they are fried. The crisps are transported on an inspection conveyor which allows experienced staff to sort, inspect and reject any crisps before they enter the flavouring system. The amount of flavouring is automatically adjusted in relation to the weight and flow of the crisps to make sure that the right amount is added. This is done in a machine like a giant cement mixer to ensure even distribution.

Finally, the crisps are packed (exactly 32 grams per packet), sealed and boxed and then transported to retailers by Seabrook drivers. Customers love them so much that orders are received from British addicts living abroad, and now quality food shops all over the country are interested in stocking them as a result of customer requests.

▶ 1 What is the major operation at Seabrook?
2 Identify two types of equipment and two types of raw materials required by Seabrook.
3 What type of building do you think is required by Seabrook?
4 Identify two types of staff employed by Seabrook.
5 Identify one aspect of production that is automated at Seabrook.
6 Explain how the main raw materials are stored at Seabrook.
7 Seabrook is well known for producing quality crisps. Explain two ways in which it ensures that its crisps are of high quality.
8 Describe one way in which producing high-quality crisps has benefited the company.

▶ 1 Explain the main operation carried out at Seabrook Crisps.
2 Under each of the following headings identify two resources required by

- Seabrook: buildings, equipment, people and materials.
3. Explain how you think the operations at Seabrook will be organised to ensure that the crisp making 'flows' in a logical manner. If you prefer, you could sketch this with a simple diagram.
4. Identify two ways in which crisp production is automated at Seabrook.
5. Most producers think using sunflower oil is too expensive for crisp production. Why do you think Seabrook is prepared to use such an expensive resource?
6. Quality is 'in-built' at Seabrook. Identify three examples of how this is done.
7. The crisp market is highly competitive, yet Seabrook focuses on quality rather than price. Evaluate the benefits and drawbacks of this approach for the company.

The marketing and sales function

The purpose of marketing and sales

Marketing guru Peter Drucker once described marketing as 'Looking at the business through the customer's eyes'. There is no better way of explaining marketing. It is concerned with identifying what the customer needs, and providing it.

Many businesses do not think of marketing as a separate function. Instead, they consider it as fundamental to the way the business operates. This means that *every part* of the business thinks about the customer first. Operations is concerned with quality and providing goods or services on time. Finance is concerned with following up queries about accounts promptly. Human resources is concerned with recruiting staff who are 'customer focused'.

Marketing staff aim to be one step ahead of the customer. They try to identify *future* customer needs – and then the research or design departments try to fulfil these (see page 93). A good example of a marketer is James Dyson, who came to the conclusion that vacuum cleaners would be more efficient if they didn't gather dirt into bags. He therefore invented a bag-less cleaner. The supermarket chains have responded to customer needs by providing wider car parking spaces for families, baby changing rooms and help with packing shopping.

Businesses undertake a range of activities to help meet customer needs including:

- market research – identifies customer opinions on proposed and existing products or services
- promotional activities – to tell customers about the products and services available
- sales – usually undertaken by trained sales staff who advise customers on the best product or service for their needs and keep records to check the type of goods or services which are sold and to which customers.

The contribution of marketing and sales to a business is vital for there is no point in producing goods or offering services that nobody wants to buy. The number of sales directly affects the profitability of a company (see Unit 3).

The role of marketing and sales

Market research

Market research aims to find out customers' needs and views on:

- potential new products and services
- existing products and services.

The information obtained may then be used by a business to design or improve a product or service.

Market research can be carried out by using primary research methods, secondary research, or both.

Primary research

Primary research involves collecting and analysing information at first hand. The advantage of primary research is that the information obtained is original and up to date. The following are the most widely used primary research methods:

- **Postal surveys** – involve sending consumers a questionnaire through the post, which the consumer completes and then returns using the Freepost envelope provided. This is a common method because you can reach a large number of people in a short space of time, but the number of replies received may be small.
- **Personal surveys** – involve face-to-face interviews, often using a questionnaire, with an individual or group of people. Where a researcher carries out an interview in the street, not everyone will be prepared to stop.
- **Telephone questionnaires** – involve asking people questions over the phone. This is the cheapest method, but is time consuming.
- **Observation** – direct observation allows the researcher to see how something is done at first hand; participant observation means that the researcher becomes part of the group being observed (see Unit 2, Chapter 16).

Businesses also use other methods to obtain information:

- They may test a new product or service in a particular area of the country and obtain feedback from users to see if any adjustments should be made before launching it nationwide.
- They can ask employees to test new products, such as food and clothing. One hosiery manufacturer gives new brands of tights and stockings to its female employees to try before putting them on general sale.

Businesses also ask existing customers their opinions (see Unit 2).

Fact file

Choosing who to ask is very important if the research is to be **valid**. This means that the opinions expressed really do represent the 'average' customer.

The first task is to identify **key customers**. They may be identified by gender, by age, by how much people earn (their **socio-economic** grouping) or by ethnicity. It depends on the product. For example, there is no point asking pensioners about mini-scooters or men about nail varnish. Businesses usually have a **profile** of their key customer from their sales records (see page 83).

It is also important to ask sufficient numbers of people to gain a **representative** opinion, or **sample**. If you ask only a few people, some may have unusual views, which could 'skew' the research results.

Designing a questionnaire

This is not an easy task. Businesses will often pay a market research agency to design the questionnaire for them, carry out the research and analyse the results. It is essential to phrase the questions so that you obtain the information you want. The questions also need to be structured, usually with a choice of options, so that analysing the replies is relatively easy.

Questions usually focus on:

- similar products or services used by the customer
- the type of products or services the customer would prefer
- the price paid
- the price the customer would be prepared to pay for additional features
- the newspapers and magazines the customer reads and the television programmes he or she watches regularly
- the places the customer usually shops
- the customer's views on the company's current products and/or services.

The answers to all these questions go towards devising the **marketing mix** for that product or service (see below).

Secondary research

Secondary research involves looking at information that already exists, rather than creating your own. You can look up facts and figures in newspaper and magazine articles, books, published company accounts, and so on. This type of data is usually free and is easily available, for example on the Internet, or in the local library.

Businesses store a vast amount of information on their database systems about existing customers and their buying habits. This is especially true of businesses which operate loyalty schemes, such as Tesco and Sainsbury. E-commerce and Internet transactions also provide companies with information, as customer preferences and behaviour when they access the site can be tracked and this can then be used to automatically offer the customer particular products when he or she logs on again.

Businesses can also buy information from other company databases and obtain government statistics about consumer expenditure and details of their competitors.

(For information on data protection legislation, see Unit 2, Chapter 11.)

Using market research information

The main reason for obtaining market research information is to increase sales. The first step is to decide the **marketing mix** for the product or service. This is made up of four factors – **product**, **price**, **promotion** and **place**, usually known as the 4Ps:

- Product – the type or variety of product or service the customer wants, the preferred design, whether packaging is important, whether a guarantee or after-sales service is required.
- Price – how much the customer is prepared to pay, whether discounts or credit terms would help sales, the price of competitors' products, whether other price-related features would be tempting (such as optional 'add-ons' or being able to trade in an old model).
- Promotion – where it would be best to advertise the product, the type of personal selling that would be the most effective, the sales promotions and publicity to be used, how the product should be displayed in shops (called **merchandising**).
- Place – the type of shops used by potential customers, the magazines and newspapers they read, the television programmes they watch, how the product should be sold (e.g. direct to the customer or in a shop), what regions of the country to cover, what type of transport to use, where to locate shops and depots.

Businesses need to take the 4Ps into account when meeting the needs of their customers because a successful marketing mix boosts sales. The marketing mix is likely to be slightly different for every product or service, even those that seem similar. This is particularly true if the main customer is another business – an industrial customer – rather than a private individual. For example, industrial packs of cleaning products are packed, priced, promoted and sold in a different way from those your family buys in a supermarket or shop.

Snapshot

Beanz means microwaves!

Carrying out market research on an established product can change the marketing mix. Heinz has made baked beans for over 100 years. Today, more than 1.5 million cans are opened in Britain every day. They are sold in 60 countries, including China and Russia. So you may think Heinz knows all about baked beans and the people who eat them.

Not so! Market research showed, unsurprisingly perhaps, that a large number of baked bean buyers were students, living in a bedsit, who didn't know much about cooking. Most could only just use a microwave. Other customers told Heinz that they would like to eat baked beans at work but there was a microwave, no cooker. The answer? Single-portion microwave pots of baked beans which are ready in two minutes. This saves having to open a can, tip the beans into a bowl, and wash it up afterwards. And no cooker is needed!

Market research showed Heinz that there was a market for single-portion pots of baked beans which could be heated in a microwave

Heinz says that people with busy lives can't be bothered with washing up bowls or pans. It had already made life easier for customers by introducing ring-pull cans in 1999 but has now gone one stage further – all to stay 'in touch' with its key customers.

This is because these are different types of customer and so must be treated in a different way.

Promotion

All businesses need to promote their products and services, otherwise customers would be unaware that they exist. The method used will depend on the type of product or service and whether it is being sold regionally, nationally or internationally. Your local takeaway would not use the same promotional methods as Coca-Cola, for example!

The range of available methods includes:

- advertising
- sales promotions
- publicity campaigns
- personal selling.

All promotional campaigns stress the benefits of owning a product or using a service. Their aim is first to draw **Attention** to the product or service; then to create **Interest**; thirdly, to develop **Desire** for ownership; finally, to invite **Action** by telling people how to buy it. This is often known as the AIDA principle. Watch some television adverts and see how they use AIDA!

Advertising

We are bombarded by adverts every day – in newspapers and magazines, on television and radio, in cinemas, on hoardings, in railway stations and on buses. Householders receive direct mailshots through their letterboxes, either as leaflets or as personalised letters. The task of advertisers is to make their particular advert stand out from the rest. This is a skilled job and most large organisations employ an advertising agency.

Adverts are intended to be **persuasive**. They sell an 'image' to the customer (think of car advertisements!). Some are **informational**. These are mainly used for business customers who don't want hype but the facts. For that reason, these are usually longer advertisements.

Businesses use several tactics to encourage people to buy their product or service. The main one is **branding**. This means making a product distinctive through its packaging, its name and the advertising slogans used such as 'Because you're worth it' or 'The real thing'. The aim is to produce **brand loyalty** so that customers will buy a particular brand of coffee or washing powder not because these products really are different from their competitors, but because customers *think* they are.

After deciding the content of the advertisement, the next decision is which **media** to use. The term media is used to describe all the different communication methods available – newspapers, television, and so on. The choice will depend upon:

- the type of product or service
- where the product or service is being sold
- the cost of alternative media
- the habits of the key customer which were discovered during market research.

You are therefore likely to find a leaflet through your door advertising a new pizza takeaway (or an advertisement in the local paper), a television advert for a family car, and specialist computer software and games advertised in a computer magazine. National television advertising is very expensive, so is suitable only for items of interest to large numbers of people. Regional advertising is used for local products and services and specialist advertising sources – such as trade magazines – are used for items of special interest.

Businesses want to check the success of advertising campaigns. The reference code on a form you need to complete to obtain further information will help them to do this. Customer service staff, too, often ask new customers where they heard about the company or product. This is also a standard question on most questionnaires.

Sales promotions

These are campaigns which tempt people to try a product. They include point-of-sale demonstrations (in stores), offering free samples, giving discounts, running competitions and special offers (such as three for the price of two). A company may initiate a sales promotion to boost sales of a particular product if demand has fallen.

> **Fact file**
>
> **Global marketing** means selling worldwide. Today, the Internet is making this possible for small businesses, but care has to be taken because different languages and different cultures can affect how names of products and adverts are understood.
>
> Some years ago, the car manufacture Vauxhall had to change the name of its Nova model to Corsa because 'nova' means 'doesn't go' in Spanish! More recently, Jif cleaning products were rebranded Cif because in some languages 'J' is not pronounced.

Some companies offer dealers incentives to sell their products, such as bonus payments and prizes and provide dealers with special display materials. Manufacturers want supermarkets to display their products in a prime position, often offering them greater discounts to do this. Next time you visit a supermarket, check which items are stocked at eye level (prime position) and which are at the top and bottom of the shelves.

Publicity campaigns

All organisations want as much free publicity as possible as this keeps them and their brand names in the public eye without costing anything! They therefore issue press releases to the media when there is a new development.

Another way of getting publicity is through sponsorship. Many firms pay football teams to wear shirts advertising their name; Barclaycard sponsors the Premiership; Kingfisher sponsored the yacht sailed around the world by Ellen MacArthur. Other companies sponsor particular charities (for example Mothercare supports Great Ormond Street Children's Hospital).

A publicity campaign is when a range of promotional methods are used simultaneously to focus customer attention on a product or service. Television and press advertising may be linked with direct mailshots, publicity in stores and point-of-sale promotions, all over a relatively short space of time.

Sales

Sales staff are employed by organisations which cannot rely only on advertising and promotion methods. They may have different titles and do different types of jobs, depending upon the product or service they are selling. The aim is to make direct contact with the buyer to convert possible interest into a sale.

- **Merchandisers** are employed by companies making household products to visit supermarkets to persuade them to stock their brands, display them prominently and become involved in in-store promotions.
- **Telesales** staff are employed by companies that sell their products or services over the telephone. These include banks and insurance companies which employ telesales staff to follow up enquiries made by customers and newspapers who sell advertising space to local businesses. A few companies are involved in cold calling and telephone people at random. Householders can prevent this by registering their number with the Telephone Preference Service.
- **Sales representatives** are employed by organisations which sell complex or specialist products to industrial and business customers. They travel around the country (or even the world) meeting customers and discussing their needs.
- **Sales staff** are employed by retailers that sell expensive products on which customers will require technical advice and information, such as cars and computers.

Employing a skilled sales force is expensive, particularly if they are paid bonuses or offered incentives to make additional sales. However, there are many benefits:

Sales staff provide technical advice and information

- An effective sales person can make a considerable difference to the number of sales made. Knowledge, experience and good communication skills can persuade a hesitant customer to make a purchase.
- Sales people can build strong links with customers which help to keep them loyal to a particular brand. Many customers like having an individual to look after them.
- Sales staff can obtain information from customers which helps to inform the marketing mix and future sales. Most sales representatives prepare visit reports to summarise their discussions. They may find out that a customer is planning to expand in the future, which will provide sales opportunities.

However, many organisations expect *all* staff to recognise sales opportunities! Travel agency staff 'sell' holidays. Bank staff will 'sell' you a bank service or new account if they think you would be interested.

Finally, email, the Internet and mobile phones have increased the number and type of opportunities for marketing and sales activities (see page 96).

Case study

Uniwho?

You might not have heard of Unilever, but you will certainly know and use some of its products. Unilever is one of the world's top makers of packaged consumer goods. It sells in over 150 countries, has annual sales of over £30 billion and employs about 300,000 people.

Instead of promoting its own name, however, Unilever promotes its brands such as Signal toothpaste, Stork margarine, Walls ice-cream, Knorr soups and stock cubes, Omo washing powder and Comfort fabric softener, so that many consumers actually think they are made by different firms. The company is considered to be the world's number one advertiser, spending about £2.5 billion a year.

Although, traditionally, most advertising is on television and in the press, Unilever is increasing its use of the Internet for marketing and to increase online selling now that more of its customers have a home computer. In 2000, Unilever committed £130 million to e-business initiatives to create 'a shopping mall that never closes'.

In 2001, Unilever moved into the luxury ice-cream market, when it spotted that demand for this product was growing. It bought Ben & Jerry's, a US firm, which promoted its ice-cream with some spectacular marketing campaigns, including Free Cone Days and a competition to find a new chief executive (give your reasons in 100 words!). The first prize was the job, the second was a lifetime's supply of ice-cream! Ben & Jerry's was known in the USA for its caring attitude – handing over 7.5 per cent of its profits each year to fund social and environmental projects and using only hormone-free milk from local dairies.

Unilever is more used to traditional marketing than Ben & Jerry's wacky ideas. There is also talk of changing the name of some flavours such as Chocolate Chip Cookie Dough, Chubby Hubby, Chunky Monkey and Phish Food because these are seen as too hippy and American for a global market.

▶ 1 Identify three products made by Unilever.
2 Explain why you may never have heard of Unilever but have heard about its products.
3 Why do you think television has been the main way in which Unilever has advertised its products?
4 What new method of marketing is Unilever interested in developing?
5 Unilever decided to buy Ben & Jerry's because demand for luxury ice-cream is growing. How do you think Unilever discovered this?
6 Identify one promotional strategy used by Ben & Jerry's to sell its ice-cream.
7 Why might Unilever decide to change the name of some of the flavours made by Ben & Jerry's?

▶ 1 Why did Unilever choose to market its brands, rather than its own name?
2 Unilever is involved in global marketing. What does this mean?
3 State three ways in which Unilever markets its products and explain why the company is keen to develop Internet marketing.
4 Explain two ways in which market research has identified new opportunities for Unilever.
5 Why were Ben & Jerry's marketing tactics described as 'spectacular'?
6 The style of an organisation is often known as its culture. Can you identify the main differences in culture between Unilever and Ben & Jerry's?
7 Identify the extent to which the culture of each organisation determines its promotional campaigns, and assess the benefits and drawbacks of each style.

Spot check

Write down your answers to the following questions:

1. What does the term 'marketing' mean?
2. State one reason why businesses undertake market research.
3. Identify three ways in which market research can be carried out.
4. It is important to select people to answer a market research questionnaire very carefully. Why is this?
5. Identify three types of questions customers would be asked in a market research survey.
6. Explain briefly how the results of a market research survey can affect the marketing mix for a product.
7. Identify one way in which products and service can be promoted to customers, other than advertising.
8. Why do businesses undertake promotional activities?
9. A national company may promote its products through advertising on television while a local business will advertise in the press. How do you explain this difference?
10. Give three reasons why some companies employ specialist sales staff.

Over to you!

Find out more by accessing the Unilever website and Ben & Jerry's at www.heinemann.co.uk/hotlinks. In particular, explore the websites to discover:

- the range of brands produced by Unilever
- how the company uses communications to market its products, particularly in relation to global advertising
- how and why Unilever is keen to increase Internet advertising and what it has done so far
- how it researches what customers want (you'll find this under 'technology and innovation')
- how it differs in its attitude and culture from Ben & Jerry's – comparing the websites should tell you all about this!

The customer service function

The purpose of customer services

Customers are essential to every business because their payments are the income, or **revenue**, of the business. Without customers, a business would not make a profit and would eventually close down.

When customers buy goods or services they expect them to be good quality. The more they pay, the better the quality they expect. Added to this, consumers have specific legal rights when they buy a product or service (see Unit 2, page 282).

Customers also expect staff to:

- give prompt attention and service
- know about the products or services they are selling
- be polite and helpful
- concentrate on their specific needs
- offer extra services that will help them.

Today, many businesses sell the same types of goods or offer the same types of services, so customers have a choice where to go. If they have a positive experience when they visit one business, this will influence them not just to buy, but to return – again and again. Customer service is all about providing this positive experience – all the extras that people need. These include:

- providing information
- giving advice
- providing credit facilities
- delivering goods
- providing after-sales service.

The purpose of customer services is to fulfil their expectations, make them feel important, and provide a range of services which will meet their needs both now and in the future.

> ### It makes you think!
>
> Within your group, compare your own experiences as a customer. Start by thinking of the best experience you have ever had, and the worst. These may have been on holiday, when you were shopping, visiting the cinema or out for a meal.
>
> Now think about the things which make you feel good when you are a customer, and those which irritate and upset you. Then imagine you had your own shop. What qualities would you expect your staff to have?

Providing information

The type of information required by customers can vary. It is doubtful if any customer service assistant could answer *every* possible query immediately – and most customers realise this. The main point is *how* the query is dealt with. A friendly smile, a promise to find out quickly (and doing so) is far more important than being a walking encyclopaedia!

Customers might ask:

- a technical query about a product or service
- a general query about the organisation
- about the range of products or services supplied
- about the location of another store
- about the location of another supplier in the area
- about general facilities available (e.g. 'Is there a coffee shop nearby?').

Customer service staff should have information on products and services and know the range on offer. In a store, they should know where these are located. They should be able to check which items are in stock, which items are not and how long they take to order. In most large organisations this information is stored on a computer database and can be accessed by assistants quickly and easily. A customer database will record the names and addresses of existing customers as well as details of recent purchases and amounts paid. This enables staff to quickly answer queries from a customer who has recently purchased from them. A stock database will give details of prices, delivery times and availability.

Giving advice

Advice is more precise than information. It is tailored to the individual needs of the person making the request and requires greater specialist knowledge. I could give you information about a range of computers, but I would need to know quite a lot about each one – and know what you wanted to use it for – before I could advise you which would be the best for you to buy.

Some types of advice are more critical than others because the consequences of giving the *wrong* advice can be so serious. In particular, advice about medical, financial, legal or safety matters *must* be correct. For that reason, unless staff are specially trained, they should refer queries on such topics to an expert. This is why receptionists in a health centre would refer a request for medical advice to a doctor or nurse rather than answer it themselves.

In many organisations a separate function exists called **technical services**. This area consists of specialists who can answer complex technical queries, normally related to machinery or equipment. If you used an online banking service and had a problem accessing options on their site, and rang the help desk, you would be connected to technical services staff. The same applies if you have a problem as a subscriber to an email service.

In many organisations, specialists are available to give advice on specific topics. Banks and building societies employ financial advisers; colleges and universities have staff who can advise on finance, loans and accommodation; schools and colleges have careers advisers. These are all customer service staff, in that they can give knowledgeable advice to enquirers. The key point to note, when you work in an organisation, is to *always* refer requests for advice to someone trained to help, and *never* guess the answer!

Which person is giving information and which one is giving advice?

Providing credit facilities

Customers often require credit when they buy an expensive item, such as a car. Credit means that they receive the item immediately, but pay for it over several months or years. Many businesses advertise their credit terms as this can tempt people to buy now, rather than keep saving for something.

Private individuals can buy on credit in one of three ways:

- They can pay by credit card, and then choose whether to pay off the account in full the next month, or to pay over several months. This method is not normally used for very expensive items, such as cars, because the price may exceed the customer's credit limit and because the interest to pay each month is usually greater than with other credit methods.
- They can pay in instalments. This is usually done by direct debit whereby a monthly payment is made direct from the purchaser's bank account. Some companies charge *more* if the buyer uses direct debit (such as car insurers) whereas others charge *less* (such as electricity suppliers).
- They can take out a loan from a bank or hire purchase company. Companies which regularly sell expensive items, such as car dealers, are usually agents for a loan company which provides the finance. The buyer then pays the loan company and not the dealer. Again interest is usually added for each year of the loan and there is also an administration charge.

Normally, the greater the range of payment methods available, the more likely it is that the seller will be able to meet each customer's individual needs. Customer services staff need to know all the options available and to be able to give help and advice as to the one most appropriate for each customer. They should also be aware that some customers may be rejected for loans because they have a poor credit record. They may have to explain why there is a problem, tactfully, and in private, to the customer.

Delivering goods

Offering a reasonably priced (or even free!) and flexible delivery service can often make all the difference to a sale. No one wants to buy a heavy or bulky item and then find that they cannot get it home or that delivery is very expensive. In that case, the customer may decide the whole thing is too much trouble and go somewhere else.

Ideally, a business will offer a range of services related to the packing, transportation and delivery of goods. For example:

- a free gift wrapping service for items bought as a present
- physical assistance with packing and loading if the customer wants to take the purchase home by car
- an optional delivery service which is free or low cost, is over a wide geographical area, at times to suit the customer
- a postal or delivery service for goods which have to be ordered, to save the customer having to call back.

In addition, delivery staff should be friendly and courteous and should handle the goods carefully.

After-sales service

If you buy a magazine, you are unlikely to need any service after you have made the purchase. The situation may be very different if you have bought a computer. You would want some assurance that the seller would help you if you experienced any problems.

After-sales service relates to many reasons why a customer may contact the firm after making the purchase. These include:

- goods which are being returned
- goods which need repairing
- goods which need regular maintenance
- general complaints
- technical queries.

Returned goods

Goods may be returned because the buyer has simply changed his or her mind, or because they are faulty. Organisations vary in their policies on returned goods and customer service staff need to know exactly what the policy is.

Some organisations allow purchasers who change their mind later to return any goods, providing each item is in perfect condition, the customer has kept the receipt, and the goods are returned promptly. Some stores allow the buyer to exchange the goods *or* ask for a refund. Others will only allow an exchange to be made.

All organisations *must* allow purchasers to return goods which were faulty when purchased (see Unit 2). They must also be prepared to refund the money paid.

Offering a repair service

Many types of goods can break down after a period of use – from watches to washing machines. Sellers of such items usually operate a service facility. Small items (such as watches) will be taken to the shop where they were purchased. Large items, such as domestic appliances, are repaired in the buyer's own home. The customer calls the service centre, customer service staff check the details on the database, find out details of the fault and arrange for a technician to call. Spare parts which are regularly needed are carried in the technician's van to minimise delays.

Business organisations take out a service contract when they buy expensive equipment, such as photocopiers or computers. Large computer suppliers such as IBM have specialist staff available round the clock to deal with serious computer problems, as the cost and consequences of these can be so high.

Offering a maintenance service

In your home, your family may have an agreement with a heating company to have your central heating system regularly serviced.

Many business organisations also need complex systems serviced regularly. These include burglar alarm systems, lifts and security equipment such as CCTV cameras. Fire extinguishers are also checked and inspected regularly, and must be marked with the date of the last inspection.

Dealing with complaints

Most businesses have an official procedure for dealing with customer complaints. These may be received face to face, when a customer visits the store, over the telephone, or in writing.

Complaints must be dealt with promptly and any serious issues must be investigated properly. If necessary, steps must be taken to ensure that the problem doesn't occur again.

Normally, senior staff monitor complaints as this provides useful information on the standard of the goods sold, the service offered and the helpfulness of staff (see Unit 2).

Dealing with technical queries

You already know that many businesses have a technical support function to assist customers with specific queries. This facility is available to new customers and to those who need help after making a purchase. For example, many people evaluate Internet service providers not just by their connection cost and transmission speed, but also by the speed at which they respond to customers with problems. A reputation for providing excellent technical support attracts more customers to use that particular ISP.

Snapshot

Online support

Suppliers of computer equipment and software now offer technical support online for their products. Most users find this the easiest and quickest way of obtaining help and technical advice.

Buyers of Microsoft products, for instance, have various ways in which they can try to solve a problem. They can access their help screen in their software. If they still have no success, they can log on to the Microsoft site which provides specific help. Users simply click on the type of software they are using and then search for suggestions. The only criticism is that some of the assistance can be too technical for casual users or learners. Microsoft users can also download upgrades or 'fixes' to solve common problems and glitches in software.

Other companies offering similar assistance include Real.com. RealNetworks produces software which enables you to hear sound clips when you access Internet sites and is essential if you are downloading music. Help and guidance to new 'streamers' is available on site. However, you also need the correct hardware (speakers are essential!). Other types of hardware suppliers also have online help, including printer suppliers who also supply printer driver programs online for rapid downloading.

You can find out more at www.heinemann.co.uk/hotlinks.

Spot check

Write down your answers to the following questions:

1. What is the main purpose of customer service?
2. Give two examples of the type of assistance a customer may reasonably expect before he or she makes a purchase.
3. Why is providing good customer service so important?
4. a A customer wants to buy a digital camera. What type of information is she likely to need?
   b The camera costs £500. What other customer services might be offered to tempt her to buy now?
5. a You are thinking of working in IT when you leave school but are not sure. You decide to ask for advice. Why is it called 'advice', rather than 'information'?
   b Why is it important that only trained staff give advice to customers?
6. Identify two types of credit facilities which may be made available to customers and two products for which they may require credit.
7. A hotel buys a 4-metre-high Christmas tree. What additional service will it want the supplier to provide, and why?
8. Identify three types of after-sales service which are often available to customers.

The research and development function

The purpose of research and development

In business, you will normally hear this function called R & D. In many organisations it also includes product design. R & D is concerned with:

- new product developments
- improvements to existing products and additions to existing lines.

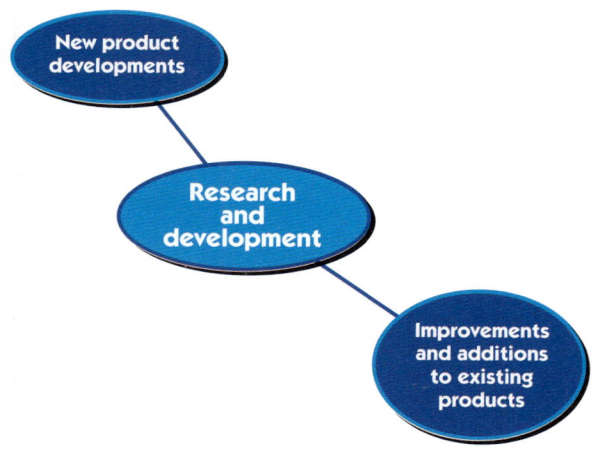

The role of research and development

New products may be developed because of technological or scientific advances, changes in customer buying behaviour or because someone has a good idea – like Trevor Bayliss and his wind-up radio!

Improvements to existing products are often the result of market research findings when customers suggest additional features or differences that they would prefer. Some alterations may be simple – many cans are 'ring-pull' because customers say they can't be bothered finding and using a can-opener. Some are far more complex, such as changes to car exhaust or braking systems.

The aim of R & D is to work with designers to develop a usable product that can be manufactured at a reasonable cost and sold at a competitive price. The type of R & D activities which are undertaken vary from one industry to another. For example:

- Pharmaceuticals and biotechnology companies spend millions of pounds on R & D to develop new medicines and new scientific processes.
- Food manufacturers employ technologists to develop new products such as ready meals.
- Electronic companies develop new technology products, e.g. flat screen televisions, WAP phones.
- Some R & D specialists concentrate on new processes to apply technological advances to production. An example is the way newspapers are printed – with articles input on computer, stored digitally and transmitted to giant printers. Originally, newspapers were typeset by hand, a long and laborious process. The aim of such specialists is to produce high-quality products more quickly and at less cost.
- Most organisations aim to continually improve product design and performance. **Industrial design** relates to the look of a product – from a computer to a car. The designers of the i-Mac wanted their computer to look different and be instantly recognisable. **Engineering design** relates to product performance. In the case of a computer, this means more memory and greater operating speed.

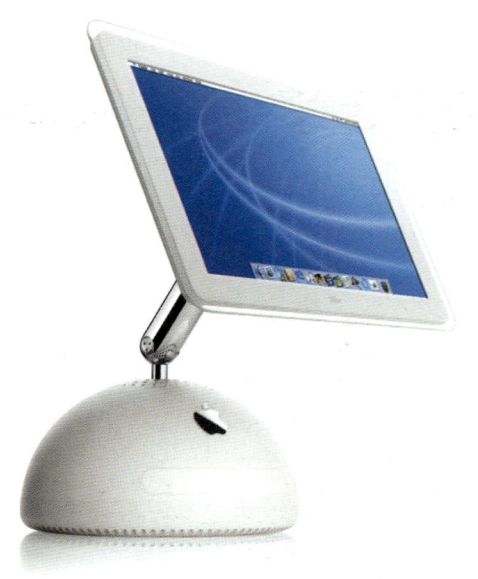

Designers of the i-Mac wanted their product to be instantly recognisable. Do you think they have achieved this?

Organisations are often very secretive about R & D. Car manufacturers are an obvious example. Ford will keep its new car design under wraps in case its competitors find out about it. This means that all the staff involved in the process, including performance tests, will be sworn to secrecy.

The use of ICT in business

Throughout this chapter, you have read about ICT applications in different functional areas. ICT is used today by the vast majority of businesses because it helps to reduce costs and improve goods and services. For example:

- Administrators can produce, check and amend documents quickly using a word processing package, and then send out personalised mailshots at the touch of a few keys.
- Customer data or stock lists can be held on databases and accessed at the touch of a button, which enables up-to-date information to be shared by all staff and customer service staff to be more responsive.
- Computers can be used to check that production processes are operating smoothly and to monitor the quality of finished products.
- Email and the Internet have increased the ways in which businesses communicate with each other, and with their customers.

When you are investigating a particular business, or functional area, it is important to investigate how ICT is being used in that situation. In particular, you should look at:

- electronic communications between departments
- facilities to share common data
- security systems
- external communications
- online support for customers
- electronic transactions.

The information below gives you further guidance on what to look for and explains some of the technical terms you may hear.

Electronic communications between departments

Two methods of communicating information internally and electronically are **email** and an **intranet**.

On a computer network, emails are sent between computer users *without* using the Internet, as you would on a personal computer at home.

The facilities available for staff on email include:

- an 'in box', 'out box' and 'sent messages' box
- the ability to send messages to one person or to a named group or even to everyone in the company
- the ability to attach any type of file (such as spreadsheets) to transmit with an email.

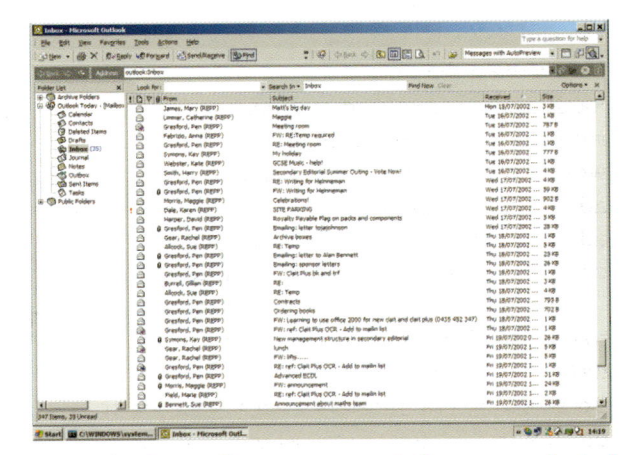

Email facilities allow a message to be communicated simultaneously to a group of people

Security systems will be in place to control the content which is sent or received on a company email system (see page 95).

On an organisation's intranet, information is stored in a secure area of the computer network. It is protected by a **firewall**, which prevents external access. The information can be accessed only internally by staff and may include such items as:

- the staff handbook, describing company facilities, rules and procedures which must be followed
- staff newsletters, giving up-to-date information about staff events
- training information and help notes (e.g. on using equipment or software).

Some schools and colleges operate two intranets – one for staff and one for students. The student intranet may contain course notes and test papers for access by those who have been absent or who need more practice, library book lists and other information. It can be accessed only on the school or college's computer system.

Facilities to share common data

Databases are used to store a great deal of information relevant to the business. Think of a database as a very large, electronic filing system. A business may have internal databases for:

- customer records
- product lines
- spare parts
- staff records
- suppliers
- order files.

Each database record will contain information relevant to that topic. For customers, you would find customer reference number, name, address, telephone number, fax number, email address, previous purchasing record and credit limit (their financial spending limit).

However, each database can also be *linked* to others. This is known as a **relational database**. This means that when an entry is updated in one database, entries in linked databases are automatically updated. For example, if a customer placed an order for a product, this would be entered on the customer record – the product record and the order record would be updated automatically.

Databases allow staff to access up-to-date information quickly and easily. Sharing this data helps everyone as a wide range of queries can be answered rapidly and accurately from information instantly available on screen.

Another type of shared information is financial data. On page 63, you read about management information systems – these contain financial data relating to purchases, sales, salaries, and so on.

When sharing and exchanging electronic data, it's important to be aware of what you are allowed to do and what you can't do. You can read more about Data Protection legislation on page 217.

Security systems

The security of computer systems is paramount. A network will be overseen by a **systems administrator,** but security also requires the cooperation of all staff.

Virus protection

A computer virus is a program deliberately written to cause a malfunction within a computer system or allow unauthorised access to it. Virus protection software is designed to prevent viruses being downloaded on to the system and to repair any files that may have become infected. Some anti-virus software manufacturers provide 24-hour, 365-day online support to their customers, constantly monitoring all servers and workstations on a network and providing an immediate alert if a virus is identified.

Viruses can be downloaded from the Internet, particularly through email attachments. For that reason, certain types of files may be blocked on a network system. However, downloading and installing unauthorised software using an unauthorised floppy disk from outside the organisation can cause the same problem. This, therefore, is normally banned and only authorised software products and disks can be used.

Backup against loss

Backup against possible data loss on a computer system takes place in three ways:

- When developments to the system are being undertaken, a backup of the current version is made before an update is installed. This enables the original to be reinstalled if a 'glitch' or 'bug' is detected in the update.
- Important data and systems should also be stored on backup disks located off site so that these are easily available in the event of a system failure or emergency, such as a fire. Specialist **data recovery** companies advise businesses on these issues and will store backup data in specially secure units. However, this does not protect individual computer users from losing their own data! Backups of important files can be made on floppy

disks, on CD-ROMs, Zip disks or data cartridges. All computer users should know the importance of backing up their own data regularly and storing backup disks safely.
- To protect the confidentiality of data, all networks have an access protection system. Users are 'enabled' by the system administrator who issues each person with a log-in ID (identification). The user must then enter his or her password for the system to operate. The password must be changed regularly (the system will prompt this) and must *never* be written down or disclosed to anyone.

Special access may be given only to managers to read higher-level, confidential data, such as financial data, and this will be controlled by the network administrator. Access to personnel data may also be restricted.

External communications

External communications are sent or received over the Internet. Large organisations are normally connected to the Internet by broadband and are constantly online. In a smaller organisation you may have to dial up the ISP and enter a password before you access the Internet or send an email to someone outside the company. In this case, it is normal to prepare emails offline to save money. Messages are then stored in the 'out box' until the connection is made and then transmitted in one batch.

The Internet can be used for many reasons within a business:

- Market research – specialist market research agencies provide online reports and analyses for a fee. Many businesses subscribe to these services. Professional organisations such as solicitors can access online databases of specialist information, such as legal reports. Again, there is a fee for this type of service.
- Other research – researchers and administrators can access a range of sites to find out relevant information, from train times to information on health and safety. In addition, businesses can arrange to be sent email updates on news features or other topics which concern them
- **Email questionnaires** can be sent to customers asking them for their views (see Unit 2, page 277).
- Companies with a website can use the Internet for marketing and sales promotions. Other online marketing methods include creating a microsite for a specific promotion, online games, site sponsorship and email campaigns. Companies normally use a variety of techniques to promote their company or product.
- Another method which is growing in popularity is **SMS marketing**. Companies send text messages to mobile phones promoting their products, especially to young buyers. For example, *J-17 magazine* and many fan clubs run text clubs. Readers join by texting their age and postcode and receive information, special offers and competition opportunities in return. Text marketing is now being used by organisations, such as Rimmel cosmetics and Costa Coffee shop and also for football score updates.

Online support for customers

Online technical support to customers was described in the Snapshot on page 92. In addition, many businesses provide online support to their customers to keep them informed about progress with a transaction. In this way, when you log on, you automatically find out:

- the status of any orders in progress
- information on new products which may interest you
- details of sales made to you recently.

On some sites, a log-in ID and password or a customer reference number is needed to access your own information. The benefit is that a customer has secure instant access to information and the identity of customers submitting orders is authenticated.

Most sites also have a 'contact us' option so that customer queries can be sent by email at the same time. Other sites may have a PhoneMe button, which the user clicks to make free telephone contact (see www.heinemann.co.uk/hotlinks). An alternative method is to send an email to customers. Many organisations automatically follow up electronic orders with an email confirmation.

Large organisations may also operate an opt-in email system. Customers and website visitors are encouraged to sign up to receive emails from the organisation about products and topics of interest.

Electronic transactions

Electronic transactions refer to any occasion on which the data relating to a purchase or sale, or payment, is processed by computer. Below are some examples:

- Transactions processed by a bar code reader, which automatically 'recognises' the product from the bar code strip. The benefits are less risk of inaccurate keying in of data and no need to price up every product on sale. Price changes can be implemented quickly and easily.
- **Electronic point of sale (EPOS)** systems, usually linked to a bar code reader. These systems enable:
  - information on the quantity of stock sold to be recorded electronically
  - stock sold to be matched against existing stock levels, for later analysis by managers
  - automatic stock re-order lists to be produced
  - prices to be stored automatically through a price look up (PLU) facility
  - till receipts to be printed containing product descriptions and prices, as well as personalised or promotional messages.
- Superstores which use EPOS also link it to any type of loyalty system in operation so that the customer record is also updated automatically (see also Unit 2, page 274).
- Purchasing stock through **electronic data interchange (EDI)** (see page 77) when the order is sent from the buyer to the seller by computer and payment is *also* made by computer. Access is available only by using a special 'smart card' and a personal security code. The payment computer communicates with the banks so that money is transferred immediately from the purchaser's bank to the supplier's bank. A computerised acknowledgement is also sent automatically to the supplier's computer.
- Sales data recorded on special accounting software which then updates the company's accounts and enables invoices and other accounts documents to be produced automatically.
- **Electronic funds transfer (EFT)** systems which are used in the following situations:
  - When a customer pays using a debit card, such as Switch or Delta. The card is swiped through a terminal at a checkout and the funds are transferred electronically from the customer's bank account to the seller's. The customer signs a voucher to validate the sale and may also take advantage of a cash back facility rather than have to go to a cash point.
  - When an online banking customer instructs his or her bank to transfer money to someone else and enters details of the bank account, bank sort code and account name of the person (or organisation) to receive the money.
  - When goods are bought online, using a credit or debit card, from a web store. Companies which operate web stores usually have additional security protection installed on their website. This is to prevent hackers from obtaining card details stored on their site. 'Safe' sections of sites are shown by the appearance of a small padlock at the bottom of a screen. This is to reassure customers that any information they input is secure.

EPOS enables businesses to control the quantity of the stock and may be linked to loyalty cards to find out customers' buying habits

Snapshot

Jargon busting

E-marketing is the term often used for marketing over the Internet – and a host of jargon is used in this business! If you are discussing the topic with a website manager (or 'webmaster') don't be surprised if you hear about:

- <u>search engine optimisation</u> – to make sure the site comes out at the top of search engine lists
- <u>affiliate marketing</u> – when two sites have an agreement that one will feature content or an advertisement designed to tempt readers to the other in return for payment
- <u>viral marketing</u> – a campaign that spreads itself from customer to customer such as when you forward an email advert or SMS to a friend
- <u>microsites</u> – special 'mini' websites created for a special campaign.

Spot check

Write down your answers to the following questions:

1. a What is an intranet?
   b Give one example of information which may be stored on a company intranet.
2. Identify two types of records which may be kept on a computer database.
3. Give two advantages of sharing data electronically among a number of staff.
4. a Describe the type of 'log-in' system normally required for access to a company computer network.
   b Explain briefly why these precautions are necessary.
5. a Why is virus protection necessary in business?
   b Briefly describe one type of virus protection system.
6. Give three reasons why business employees may need to access the Internet.
7. Identify two ways in which the Internet can be used to promote marketing and sales.
8. Explain briefly the type of online support which may be provided to a customer who has just placed an order.
9. Give two examples of electronic transactions.
10. Security is very important for computer installations and for users of web stores. Describe three security precautions you can expect to find in place in a business which operates a computer network and a web store.

Chapter review and practice questions

▶

1. Style Stuff is a sportswear manufacturer. It has seven departments: human resources, finance, administration, operations, marketing and sales, customer service and R & D. Identify the department in which the following tasks would be carried out:
   a. preparing and paying wages and salaries to employees
   b. producing sportswear
   c. preparing sportswear adverts for magazines
   d. preparing adverts for job vacancies
   e. designing new styles of sportswear for next year
   f. keeping records of documents sent and received
   g. responding to customer enquiries and complaints.

2. Your friend is about to start work in the administration function of a large firm, but is unsure about the type of work she will do. Describe three tasks she may be asked to carry out.

3. Most businesses use a computer to help them to work more efficiently and communicate with customers.
   a. Explain two reasons why an administrator might use a computer.
   b. Describe how computers have helped the work of customer service staff.
   c. Identify two jobs which would be undertaken by IT support staff.

4. Identify the businesses below where you would expect to find:
   - sales staff employed specifically to advise customers (rather than just to serve them)
   - a delivery service provided
   - an after-sales service provided.

   a. Computer store
   b. Newsagent
   c. Fitted kitchen centre
   d. Mobile phone shop
   e. Grocery store
   f. Chemist
   g. Insurance company
   h. Retailer of musical instruments
   i. Greetings card shop
   j. Garden centre

   Remember, each business may provide more than one of these services.

▶

1. Tindel Glassware produces a wide range of drinking glasses which are sold in household stores and supermarkets. It is planning to expand next year. Identify the department, or functional area, which will be responsible for:
   a. monitoring the quality of the glasses produced
   b. organising induction training for new staff
   c. obtaining capital to finance the expansion
   d. promoting the glassware to new stores in Britain
   e. organising cleaning and maintenance of the premises
   f. developing a new range of glass tankards
   g. answering queries about deliveries.

2. You visit a company which has a large IT function responsible for IT security, IT support and website development.
   a. Identify three ways in which IT will help the company to be more efficient.
   b. Explain why IT security is important and give two examples of precautions you will find in place.
   c. Describe two ways in which the company website may help to improve customer service.
   d. Describe three functions undertaken by IT support staff.

3. a. What type of resources are required by all businesses?
   b. Identify three ways in which these resources would vary between a large factory making furniture and a furniture retailer.

c   If an employee dispute about the resources available occurred at a factory, which function would be responsible for negotiating with union representatives?

4   Describe four ways in which you could assess the effectiveness of customer service in an organisation.

Chapter 6 Business communications

What you will learn
- Communicating with other people in business
- Methods of communication
- Selecting the best method of communication

Overview: business communications

Types of communications in business

Every day, people working in organisations communicate with other people. They hold meetings, talk over the telephone, send emails and write letters. Some of these communications will be **informal**, such as a chat in the corridor. Others will be **formal**, such as a business letter or a team meeting.

Some communications will be **internal** – they are sent to a person working within the organisation. Others will be **external** and sent to people working for a different organisation.

The need for communication in business

A constant flow of communication is essential for any business to operate effectively because up-to-date and accurate information is needed for decisions to be made. This is normally a four-stage process:

1. Obtaining the information.
2. Sharing information with relevant colleagues.
3. Deciding what action should be taken (often in a group).
4. Communicating the decision or plans for action.

The flow chart on page 102 shows how the process works in practice.

Summary of communications methods

There are four main methods of communication:

- **oral** – such as telephones, meetings, telephone conferencing
- **video** – such as video conferencing, Internet video link
- **written** – such as memos, letters, financial documents, advertisements and email attachments
- **graphical** – such as production drawings, graphics on screen or graphics sent over the Internet.

The best method to use will depend upon the type of message or the particular situation. In this section, you will learn the factors to consider when choosing the best method to suit a particular business need.

The range of communications in business

Internal contacts include the following:

- People **within their functional area**, e.g. one member of the sales team talking to another member.
- People **outside their functional area**, that is those who work in other departments or sections. These contacts are essential as each functional area needs co-operation from the others to be able to operate efficiently. For example:
  - sales staff need to know about production schedules so that they don't promise goods which cannot be made in time
  - operations staff need to know what delivery dates have been agreed with customers so that goods can be produced on time

Example 1

- The marketing manager's assistant tells her boss she is leaving and hands in her notice
- Her boss tells human resources that there is a vacancy. Human resources advertise the job and arrange interviews
- A replacement assistant is chosen
- All candidates are informed of the outcome

Process

- Obtaining up-to-date information
- Sharing/communicating information
- Deciding/agreeing action
- Communicating action to relevant people

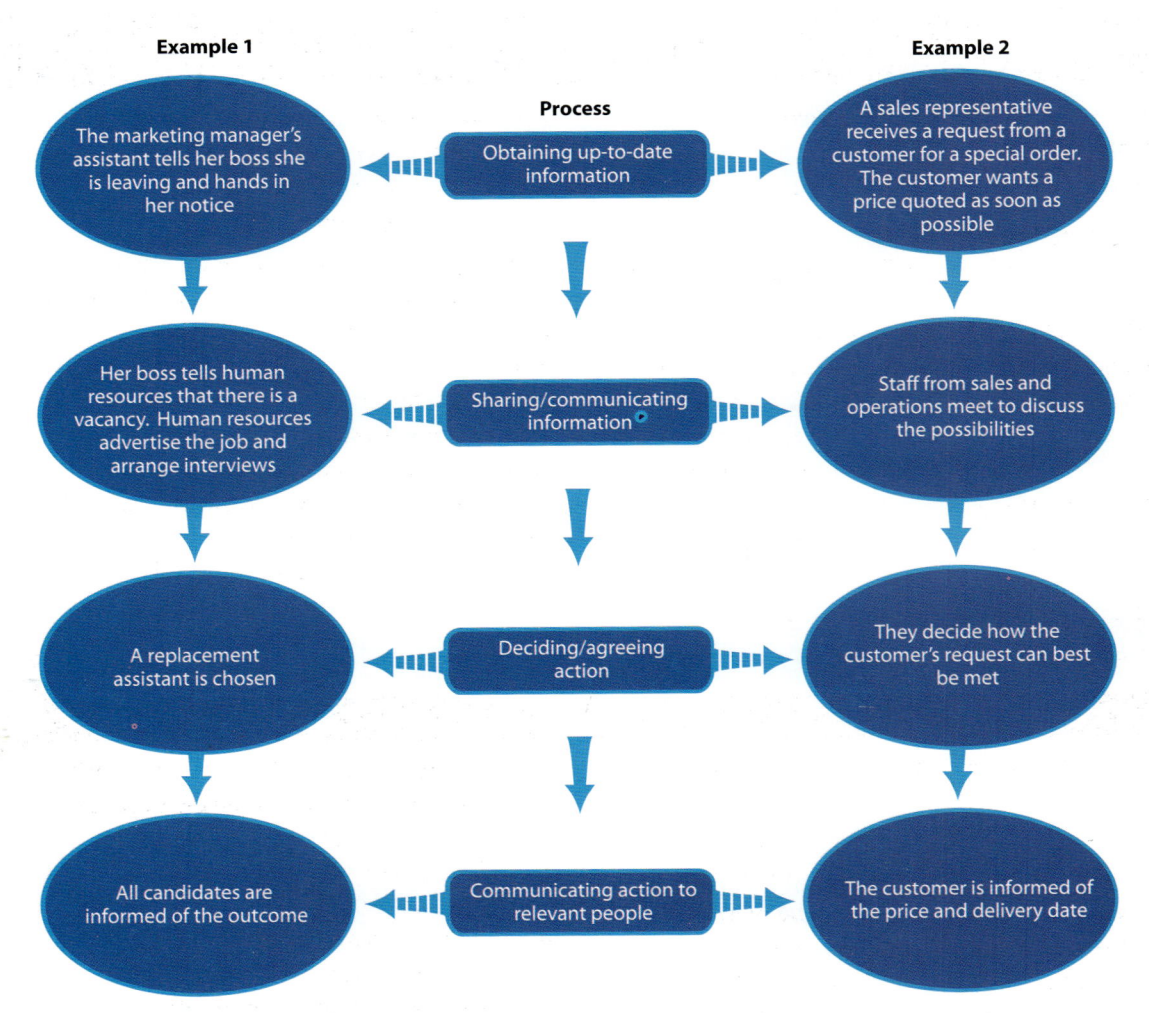

Example 2

- A sales representative receives a request from a customer for a special order. The customer wants a price quoted as soon as possible
- Staff from sales and operations meet to discuss the possibilities
- They decide how the customer's request can best be met
- The customer is informed of the price and delivery date

How communication works in business. Remember that one set of communications can frequently result in another set! For instance, the customer in example 2 may contact the organisation to agree the offer. This information then has to be passed to those who need it, and so on.

- finance staff need to know about sales made and deliveries received so that they can link these to the relevant financial documents
- human resources needs to know about staff training requirements so that appropriate events can be held.

External contacts include other businesses or private individuals. They may be suppliers, customers, prospective customers, shareholders or other people with an interest in the organisation.

Snapshot

The ups and downs of electronic communications

ICT developments are making communication easier, such as text messaging. But there are downsides. It can be difficult to choose the best method in a high-tech organisation which offers a choice of mobile phone, voicemail, email, video conferencing, group chat and an intranet group message board. There is a danger, too, that all these choices mean there is no longer any need to meet or to talk to people personally!

Surveys have shown that email is often over-used, to the extent that some recipients are almost drowned in messages every day. Some organisations have asked staff to stop forwarding 'round robin' or non-business emails to colleagues to reduce the number and the time taken to go through them each day.

Another problem is that online written communications mean that everyone's ability to write a brief, grammatical, well-spelt and properly punctuated message is on view for the whole organisation to see! Even the most junior employees are normally expected to use the company internal email so if their English skills are appalling, this will be obvious. And remember, email spellcheckers do not identify where a 'real' word is used incorrectly!

Spot check

Write down your answers to the following questions:

1 An IT support technician starts his day by ringing a computer supplier to find out when three new laptops will be delivered. He then asks a colleague on the computer help desk for a list of the calls that have been received. The first is from a marketing assistant – her computer is giving problems. The technician checks the machine and replaces a faulty lead. While he is there, she is on the telephone, agreeing the content of an advertisement with the local newspaper.

In each of the cases below, identify whether the communication was:

- internal within a functional area
- internal between functional areas
- external.

   a The IT technician ringing the computer supplier
   b The IT technician checking with the computer help desk
   c The IT technician visiting the marketing assistant
   d The marketing assistant talking to the newspaper

2 Identify two methods of communication which have become available because of technological developments.
3 Identify two methods of oral communication.
4 Identify two methods of written communication.
5 Briefly explain why communication is very important in business.
6 a Your friend is going on work experience, but his spelling and grammar aren't very good. What problems could this cause?
   b He shows you the text of an email he has recently sent to a friend.

> Hi Sam
>
> Grate to here from you again! Hows things in Edinborough? Jason said you started colledge last autum – what coarse are you doing? Our local teem is playing Newcastle next month – could you meat us when we're up their? Let me know quick, if you can, then I can let Jason no.
>
> Mark

   i Spot and correct the 12 mistakes he has made.
   ii Identify the mistakes which would not be picked up by Mark's spellchecker.

Chapter 6   Business communications

Communicating with other people in business

Business communications can be formal or informal depending on:

- the reason for the communication
- the relationship between the people communicating and how well they know each other.

Both of these will influence the type of communication and its **tone**. For example, while you might write a chatty note to a colleague you know well, you wouldn't use the same style in an important message for your boss.

Formal communications are normally used for important or serious matters, when the recipient isn't known very well, or when a paper record must be kept. Examples include:

- information to employees relating to their employment
- complicated instructions or technical schedules which everyone must follow
- financial documents sent to shareholders
- letters sent to customers.

Informal communications are used between people who contact each other frequently, both internally and externally. If you regularly communicate with someone, then it is usual to use an informal method such as an email.

Fact file

The **grapevine** is the network of informal links between staff within an organisation. News and rumour often travel very quickly on the grapevine, usually far more quickly than by formal methods!

Methods of communication

There are four main categories of communications in business: oral (spoken communications), video, written and graphical.

Oral communications

Oral communications may be face to face (when two people or a group meet together) or over the telephone. If you phone someone who is temporarily unavailable, then you can usually leave a message on an answering machine or use voicemail, a type of electronic answering service. Telephone conferencing takes place when several people are linked simultaneously so that they can have a discussion. The type of telephone system in operation will limit the number of links that are possible at any one time.

Many staff carry pagers or bleepers so that they can receive a message at a distance. In a hospital, for example, a bleeper sound prompts the holder to go to the nearest telephone and dial the displayed number. Security guards and engineers may use private radios on which they receive oral messages or instructions and most business people use mobile phones.

Video communications

Video communications have reduced the need to travel to meetings. They enable meetings to be held more easily and more cheaply since staff do not need to travel long distances.

A **video conference** enables two or more people in different locations to hold a meeting. They are connected through telecommunications links to provide both visual and voice links. There are two main options:

- Video conference equipment can be bought or hired. Equipment includes cameras that can zoom in on individual speakers and large-screen VDUs. Participants sit in a virtual conference room and can communicate as if they were sitting together in one room. This system can also be used for presentations and talks, but it is very expensive (especially to buy) and the transmission/communications links also have to be paid for.
- **Internet video link** is a cheaper and increasingly popular option. Staff require

a computer linked to the Internet and the company computer network, a video camera (webcam), microphone, speakers and appropriate software. Two participants can then contact each other. Their voices are transmitted over the network to each other's speakers and the image in front of the video camera appears in a window on their monitor. During a web conference, those involved can send files, share and comment on graphics, show a brief presentation or work on a report together. The drawbacks are the poor quality of the video image in some cases and that only two computers can be linked together at any one time.

A video link enables employees in different locations to hold a face-to-face meeting

Written communications

Written communications refer to text-based documents, such as letters, memos and faxes, which are sent by mail or electronically.

Also included in this category are financial documents which are prepared and distributed by all organisations – from invoices requesting payment to formal accounts for the Inland Revenue (see Unit 3).

Brochures and catalogues advertising products are another form of written communication, as are advertisements whether for products or the recruitment of staff.

Emails may contain attachments – computer files sent with (attached to) the email message such as word-processed documents, spreadsheets or graphics (see below).

Other examples of written communications include telephone messages, notices on staff notice boards, staff newsletters and documents on the staff intranet.

Graphical communications

Graphical communications refer to any type of pictures or graphics which are created on computer, or input by means of a graphics device such as a graphics tablet or scanner – and then transmitted to someone else. Graphics can range from a simple pie chart to a complex engineering drawing. Architects, designers and engineers are examples of professional workers who regularly send production drawings or designs to their colleagues or to a customer. These may be prepared on paper and scanned into a computer, or created on computer using a CAD or graphics package.

Any type of graphic stored on computer can be viewed on screen or attached to an email. However, graphics normally need a computer with a large amount of memory and graphics files are usually zipped (compressed) before transmission over the Internet, to reduce the time needed for the file to download.

Selecting the best method of communication

In business, the method of communication chosen will depend upon the factors outlined below.

The reason

A communication regarding an important or serious matter is usually sent in writing. This makes the communication more formal and provides a written record which can be referred to in the future. Examples include school reports, bank statements and GCSE results.

Over to you!

1. Your friend is getting married and would like to transmit the ceremony, live by video, to her grandad in Australia. Can she do this? If so, how? Visit the following websites to help you answer these questions:
   - BT's video conferencing services at www.hienemann.co.uk/hotlinks
   - Microsoft's NetMeeting at www.hienemann.co.uk/hotlinks

2. Find out more about graphical communications and make a list of all the different types of graphics you identify. Then compare your list with those made by other members of your group.
   a. Start by finding out about graphics packages, such as Paint, on your school or college computers.
   b. Then identify the type of graphics you could create or include on standard text-based packages, such as spreadsheets or word processing software.
   c. Investigate other types of software on which graphics are created. For instance, your tutor may use the presentation package Microsoft PowerPoint, or on work experience you may find a desktop publishing package being used, or special graphics packages such as CAD or Adobe Photoshop. Or you can investigate these on the web. The search engine Yahoo! has a directory of computer and Internet graphics and www.hienemann.co.uk/hotlinks should give you some ideas.

- **Internal communications** include staff meetings, memos, emails and telephone calls.
- **External communications** include business letters, telephone messages, fax messages and advertisements.

Some methods can be used when there are both internal and external recipients, for example video conferencing can be used internally, for people working in different branches of the organisation, or externally if customers are involved. Emails can be sent internally or externally. Text or graphics may be sent as attachments to discuss with colleagues or with customers.

The technology available

The method of communication must suit the technology available; for example, you can only send an email to someone who has a computer linked to the Internet.

This applies particularly to computer attachments as these are stored as specific types of files. The type you send must be compatible with the recipient's computer system; for example, you can only send a PowerPoint file to a computer that has PowerPoint software installed to read it.

It is also pointless to send a large graphics file to a customer whose computer has limited memory because the system will not be powerful enough to load it, even if the customer's computer has the right software.

On an internal network, there are likely to be few problems with compatibility. Such problems are more likely to occur when files and attachments are being sent externally.

The urgency

Some methods of communication are faster than others. Electronic communications – fax and email – are faster than sending a letter through the post.

Instant two-way communications include face-to-face meetings, the telephone, video conferences and Internet video/audio links. These are ideal for discussions when a

The recipient

The recipient (person who receives the communication) may be internal or external. Different methods of communications may be used in each case:

decision or agreement must be reached quickly (see also Feedback, below). If an urgent item cannot be sent electronically, it is usually delivered by courier.

The complexity

Complex information should always be communicated in written form. Many complex documents must be studied at length to be fully understood and are kept for future reference. Examples include company accounts and legal documents such as your contract of employment (see Unit 2, page 186).

Feedback

One-way communications consist of information which is available to those who need it, such as an advertisement for a cinema saying what films are on and the times they are showing. The cinema would not expect customers to contact it except for further information or to make a booking.

Other types of communication are **two-way**. In this case, the communicator needs a response. If you wish to make a doctor's appointment, you need to speak to the receptionist so that you can agree a date and time.

Obtaining a response is often known as **feedback** – you receive comments on your original request or item of information. If you write a letter, leave a message or send an email, you will receive feedback, but there will be a delay. Sometimes this is acceptable – it gives the other person time to think before he or she responds. If feedback is required immediately, a different method has to be used – a telephone call or telephone conferencing.

A face-to-face meeting (includes video conferencing and Internet visual links) is often preferred to a telephone call if a person's *reaction* needs to be assessed. You can usually gain a more accurate idea of what someone thinks of a suggestion when you can see his or her facial expressions and gestures. This is why applicants for a job are interviewed in person – interaction is usually greater when there is visual contact.

Snapshot

It's not what you say, it's the way that you say it . . .

Today, ICT equipment is often used for presentations. An expert on a topic can address an audience around the world, through telecommunications links. Presentations can be prepared on computer using Microsoft PowerPoint and projected on a large screen. Some sales reps use sophisticated PowerPoint presentations saved on their laptops to enhance a sales presentation. On other occasions, speakers can make notes on an interactive white board and take instant copies for the audience.

However, the best equipment in the world won't help if a speaker is ill-prepared, boring or jumbles up the facts so that no one can understand what is being said! One of the hardest tasks is giving a presentation if you are not used to this. Golden rules include:

- checking the length and timing yourself accordingly
- preparing well and making clear, logical notes
- having a good introduction
- illustrating each <u>main</u> point with a clear, simple visual aid
- giving a good summary at the end
- <u>never</u> reading from notes (learn the notes and then use headings as a prompt instead)
- speaking at the right pace and the right volume
- using simple, straightforward sentences.

Experts also say that we like speakers who make eye contact with the audience, who smile and appear enthusiastic. This is because they are not just reciting facts but communicating with us as individuals. Remember this if you have to give a presentation!

Case study

Changing with the times

Jim Woods is a sales representative at Meredith Office Supplies but he has never bothered keeping up with IT developments.

Today, he is giving a presentation about office storage systems to the managers of a large company.

JIM: Right, well, I want to talk to you this morning about our range of storage equipment – well, I suppose I mean the latest type really, because this one is the best. We've sold over 1000 since last year, I think . . . *long pause* Er, let me see . . . *mutters something* . . . I've got the main features here somewhere . . .

MANAGER: I'm sorry, I can't hear you – can you speak up please?

JIM: *Scratches his head* The point is – well, er, I mean – this equipment is really worth buying.

MANAGER: Why?

JIM: *Mutters something at his feet* Well, er, as you can see from the brochures . . .

MANAGER: What brochures? Have you brought some with you?

JIM: *Roots around in his briefcase* Ah, I've one here. Er, no – but I've a description of the units. *Takes out some photocopied pages*

MANAGER: Is this all you've got? *Flicks quickly through the pages.* We can't even see what it looks like. Have you a price list for the units?

JIM: Er, no – but if you let me use your phone I can telephone the office to find out the prices.

MANAGER: *In disbelief* I don't think that will be necessary. If you like, you could email the prices and details of the discounts to my assistant, Martin, this afternoon.

JIM: Er, I'd rather phone if that's OK. *Takes out a pen* Could you give me the number, please?

MANAGER: *Impatiently* His direct line is 283971. Quick question – how long would it take to deliver and install any unit we *may* want?

JIM: I'm not sure. I can check and send you the information later. And a brochure . . .

▶ 1 Jim is communicating externally to a customer. List two methods of oral communication and two methods of written communication which can be used in this situation.

2 Jim should know about prices and delivery and would find out this information internally. List three ways in which he could communicate with his colleagues when he is in the office.

3 The manager wanted the prices and discount details emailed to his assistant. Suggest two reasons why he wanted this information in writing.

4 Why did the manager want to see a brochure, rather than a written description of the furniture?

5 Suggest one reason why the manager was surprised when Jim asked if he could use their phone.

6 Identify four mistakes Jim made during his presentation.

7 Identify two ways in which Jim could have used IT either before, during or after the presentation.

8 Do you think Jim made a sale? Give a reason for your opinion.

▶ 1 Identify the different methods Jim used to communicate with the customer (or suggested he would do so).

2 Jim needs to check the price and delivery of the units. Identify the methods he could use to find out this information both while he is away from the office and when he returns to the office.

3 Jim offered to telephone with the prices and discounts, rather than emailing as suggested. Explain why he did this and why this surprised the manager.

4 Identify two benefits of providing a brochure rather than a typed list of information, and suggest two ways in which Jim could send this quickly to the customer.

5 Identify all the mistakes you think Jim made and then suggest four ways in which IT could have improved his communications with the customer.
6 If you were responsible for suggesting communication improvements for representatives at Meredith Office Supplies, what would you recommend, and why?
7 Evaluate the extent to which communications are important to businesses such as Meredith Office Supplies.

It makes you think!

1 The chart below shows the advantages and disadvantages of the different categories of communication – oral, video, written and graphical. Use it to identify which of the four categories would be most appropriate in each of the following situations:
   a To arrange a time and date for a car to be serviced by a garage
   b To describe six products made by an organisation
   c To show exactly what the same six products look like
   d To show what a house will look like with an extension
   e To discuss a proposed new product with colleagues in the New York office
   f To give information on business travel arrangements
   g To check the layout of a document with a colleague in the next office

	Oral	Video	Written	Graphical
Advantages	Rapid Relatively cheap Voice can be used for emphasis or to show feelings Immediate feedback	Instant feedback obtained Saves time/expense of travelling to meeting Voice and body language emphasises reactions and attitude	Has formal authority Provides permanent record Can be studied at leisure Can be copied for others	Can summarise ideas or main points effectively Helps understanding Often more appropriate than lengthy text
Disadvantages	Clear speech essential Complex/long messages may be forgotten or not understood Other factors may distract listener or speaker	Large group conferences may be difficult to organise or to manage and may be costly Must be pre-arranged Internet video may be jerky unless high speed connection used	Takes time to produce Needs good written and presentation skills Delivery may take time Permanency may be a disadvantage if sent in a rush	Appropriate software needed to create or scanner to input on computer Some graphics need computer with powerful processor/large memory Often need specialist skills to create

2 The chart below provides a list of the different methods of communication you are likely to find in business. Use this to decide exactly which type of communication would be best in each of the following situations, assuming equipment is not a problem. Note that there may be more than one right answer!

   a You need to contact the firm's travel agent urgently to change an airline booking.
   b You have been asked to inform all staff that the canteen will be closed next Monday.
   c You want to ask your boss for a day's holiday at the end of the month to attend a family wedding.
   d Your boss has been asked to provide a reference for a former member of staff.
   e A group of staff in your office want to discuss how to plan a presentation.
   f You have been asked to send a copy of a questionnaire, created on computer, to the London office as quickly as possible.
   g You need to provide a customer with information on the products you sell and their prices.
   h You must contact a travelling sales representative urgently to tell him today's 3 pm meeting is cancelled.
   i You have to help prepare a presentation and show how sales income varies during the year.

Oral	Video	Written	Graphical
Telephone	Video conference	Memo	Hand drawings
Voicemail	Internet video link	Letter	Computer drawings
Answering machine		Email	Clip art
Telephone conference		Email attachments	Pie charts
Pager or bleeper		Fax	Bar charts
Private radio		Telephone message	Graphs
Face-to-face conversation		Report	Organisation charts
Meeting		Summary	Engineering drawings
Interview		Staff newsletter or magazine	Architectural drawings
Presentation		Catalogue	Sketches
		Price list	Product designs
		Advertisement	Illustrations
		Invitation	Cartoons
		Notice	3D graphics
		Meetings document	Animations
		Financial documents	Video clips

Chapter review and practice questions

▶

1. Describe three types of oral communication methods and three types of written methods. Explain an appropriate use for each one.

2. You need to send a document. You can fax it, send it as an email attachment, post it or send it by courier. What factors would you take into account when deciding which method to use?

3. Give two advantages of holding a video conference.

4. Explain the difference between an internal and an external communication and give an example when *each* might be used.

▶

1.
   a. Give two examples of formal communication methods and two of communications that are informal.
   b. What factors would influence your decision in choosing whether to send a formal or informal communication?

2. You are on work experience in the human resources department of a large company. Give two examples when it might be necessary to communicate with:
   a. someone within your functional area
   b. someone working in another functional area
   c. someone external to your organisation.

3. Feedback is an important aspect of many communications.
   a. Identify three methods of communication you could use if you needed immediate feedback.
   b. Give two examples of a situation when immediate feedback would be essential.

4. Identify three occasions when it may be necessary to send a graphical communication.

Chapter 7: External influences on business

What you will learn
- Business competitors
- Economic conditions
- Environmental constraints

Overview: external influences

Types of external influences

In Chapter 1 you learned that businesses may fail to meet their aims and objectives through no fault of their own. If a serious, but unpredictable external event occurs, there may be repercussions for many businesses. In the UK in 2001, the closure of many footpaths due to the foot-and-mouth epidemic in sheep and cattle severely affected rural businesses. The terrorist attacks in the USA on 11 September 2001 affected thousands of businesses. Some businesses, such as airlines, were directly affected because demand for transatlantic travel fell. But business activities are inter-related so other associated businesses such as travel agents and aircraft manufacturers also saw demand for their services or products fall.

Fortunately, not all external events which affect business are so random or uncertain. This chapter looks at three types of external influences which usually affect business in more predictable ways:

- **Business competitors** may bring out a more advanced or cheaper product or offer a better service. Today, most businesses operate in a competitive market. This means that there are many suppliers offering a similar service or product. This gives consumers more choice and helps to keep prices low. You can decide which shops you go to and which products you buy. Each manufacturer and each retailer will compete for your business – and use various strategies to tempt you to buy from them.

- **Economic conditions** can affect the price of goods and the ability of customers to buy goods and services. Customers are tempted to buy more goods when they have money to spend or when borrowing is cheap because interest rates are low. Equally, businesses are more likely to increase production and to expand their operations when sales are high and when they think this situation is likely to continue. This is known as a buoyant economy. If people are worried about jobs or about their future prospects, they may stop spending. Goods remain on the shelves, businesses receive less money so produce fewer goods and may lay off some workers. This means people have less to spend. In this situation, there may be an economic downturn. All governments are keen to avoid an economic downturn and try to take action to manage the economy to keep it buoyant.

- **Environmental constraints** affect the way in which the business is allowed to carry out its operations and dispose of waste materials. In recent years, many laws have been passed to help to protect the environment, including the control and regulation of pollution, the use of resources and the disposal of waste. Such laws and regulations affect business operations. However, many businesses are keen to prove that they are socially and environmentally responsible and often take action beyond those required by the law. They may set environmental targets for themselves or produce environmental reports.

The main point about external influences is not that they exist, but the extent to which they may affect a particular business and how that business responds to them.

Fact file

The **environment** refers to the physical conditions on Earth. These may be damaged by business activities. In 1997, the dangers of global warming led many nations, including the UK but not the USA, to sign the Kyoto Protocol which set targets for reducing carbon emissions.

Pollution relates to the contamination of the environment through the release of any harmful or dangerous substances or gases, whether into the air, into water or on land.

Fact file

A **monopoly** is the term used when one large supplier dominates a market. The monopoly is likely to be very powerful and can therefore stop new businesses from entering the market.

A **cartel** is the term used when several suppliers join together to fix prices. This is illegal in the UK.

Over to you!

The OFT is currently investigating consumer IT services including Internet service provision. It is concerned that consumers are finding difficulty in obtaining information to help them compare the different deals available. Find out about the work of the OFT in encouraging open competition between businesses and helping the consumer by visiting its website at www.heinemann.co.uk/hotlinks

Check the latest press releases on the site to find out what other issues the OFT is investigating.

Snapshot

When big isn't beautiful

Competition is usually good for consumers. If many suppliers offer a similar product, then prices will be lower than if one supplier controls the market. This is because a very powerful supplier can try to restrict other firms from entering the market. This is one reason why Microsoft, which sells 85 per cent of computer operating systems, was being investigated by the US government and the European Commission. It dominates the industry to such an extent that there were allegations that it was abusing its position by deliberately designing its Windows software to be incompatible with its competitors' products.

In Britain, no one company is allowed to control 85 per cent of the market. The Competition Act 1998 allows the Office of Fair Trading (OFT) to investigate a company which has a dominant position in the market (usually more than 40 per cent of the total) to check that it is not imposing an unfair price, is not deliberately limiting production to keep the price high, and is dealing with all its customers fairly.

The Act also prevents suppliers deliberately limiting production or taking other actions to prevent open competition, such as agreeing between them to control prices. In 2002, the OFT ruled that a manufacturer and several retailers were guilty of price-fixing replica soccer kits. The OFT has the power to fine businesses involved in price-fixing 10 per cent of their sales turnover, even if the price-fixing agreement is an informal one.

Spot check

Write down your answers to the following questions:

1. Identify two types of external influences on business.
2. Give two reasons why a business is interested in the actions of its competitors.
3. Why is competition normally good for consumers?
4. What is meant by a buoyant economy?
5. a Suggest two reasons why you, as a consumer, might want to spend less.
   b How would your actions affect businesses?
6. a What is meant by the environment?
   b State one way in which business activities can affect the environment.

Business competitors

Businesses need to sell their products or services in order to survive. Most businesses also operate in a market in which they compete with other suppliers of the same, or similar, goods. The 'market' consists of all the individual consumers who want to buy those particular goods, for example mobile phones or sportswear. Companies compare their success in the market by identifying their **market share**. This is always given as a percentage of the whole market.

When a new product, such as mobile phones, is launched, demand may be high and the market is growing. Eventually, the market reaches saturation point – when everyone who wants the product has one. At this point, the size of the market is virtually static and suppliers have to use other methods to keep sales high. At the same time organisations are competing against each other for the same customers to increase their own share of the market.

The main tactic used by businesses is to make their own product or service slightly different in some way. How they do this depends on:

- the type of goods or services they offer
- the aims and objectives of the organisation
- the type of customers they have (e.g. individual consumers or industrial buyers)
- the type of competitors they have and the actions of their competitors.

Competitive features

Various features make a product or service competitive. The main ones include:

- the **price** buyers are asked to pay
- the **quality** of the goods or service and/or the reputation or image of the business
- the **availability** of the item(s).

Other competitive features can be introduced, as you will see.

The importance of price

All organisations have a pricing policy for their goods or services. They may choose to sell at:

- a low, highly competitive price
- a middle-range price
- a high price

or they may produce or sell goods at all three prices, for example Tesco has a Value (low price) range, a Finest (high price) range and sells other goods in the middle range. In this way, Tesco tries to satisfy the needs of a variety of customers (see page 117).

Supermarkets, which sell the same or similar products, need to find a way of differentiating themselves and they usually do this by competing on price.

Many clothing stores also compete on price, although again they may be grouped into low-price stores (e.g. Matalan), mid-range stores (e.g. Next) and high-price stores (e.g. Jaeger). In this case, each store's main competitors are those which sell goods in the same price band, so Next competes with Debenhams and River Island but not with low-price stores.

The wide difference in pricing is because organisations take into account several factors when deciding what price to charge:

Competition usually benefits customers

Matalan's selling point is its low prices

The chart shows the main internal and external factors affecting price.

Factors affecting price

Internal factors	External factors
Cost of making product	Prices of competitor's products
Cost of research and development activities	Discounts allowed to retailers
Cost of marketing and advertising	Demand for the product
Organisation's aims and objectives	What customers expect to pay
Product image	What customers are prepared to pay

- Organisations usually sell goods at a price which covers the costs of production and distribution – plus a profit (see Unit 3). Sometimes a business may sell below cost, perhaps to win business from a competitor. However, low prices cannot be sustained as the business is making a loss on each item.
- Some organisations, such as Gucci and Ferrari, trade on the exclusive nature of their products and charge higher prices accordingly. Lowering prices would actually damage their exclusive image and they would lose their key customers.

Price competition includes special offers, payment terms and discounts. Discounts and special payment terms are often used in industry to gain a large contract when the total amount and the length of time over which payment can be made may be the subject of lengthy negotiations. Payment terms are frequently used in the car industry to boost sales, such as 0 per cent finance deals, which means money can be borrowed at no charge.

Chapter 7   External influences on business

> **Fact file**
>
> Some items are more **price sensitive** than others – if the price increases, fewer people will buy the product. This happens if there are substitute products available. For example, if the price of oranges suddenly tripled, many people would choose apples instead.
>
> Goods which are less price sensitive include petrol, alcohol and those with no obvious substitute such as salt. In this case, people may try to use less but will still buy.

The importance of quality

Quality can relate to the raw materials used, the type of service offered and to the reputation of the business. Generally, the best quality costs money, so high-quality goods or services will be more expensive. If you stay at a luxury hotel you would expect superb service and facilities, but you would also have to pay for these. However, even if consumers are buying a cheap product they expect it to be of satisfactory quality – indeed, this is a legal requirement. So even the cheapest pair of trainers mustn't fall apart within weeks!

Some manufacturers try to gain a **competitive edge** by offering better quality than their competitors at a *slightly* higher price – and try to convince customers it is worth paying the difference. L'Oréal's advertising slogan 'Because you're worth it' aims to help customers justify spending slightly more on themselves!

Businesses which sell to industrial customers are keen to stress their quality of service and their reputation as this may be more important than price. This is because industrial customers placing large contracts will insist on minimum standards of quality and after-sales service. In some cases, safety is also an issue. A company which builds bridges or hospitals will have to give assurances that the materials used will be of a certain standard and that they will abide by health and safety and environmental regulations.

The importance of availability

Availability is part of providing an excellent service. It may include availability of the product or service, of related items (such as spare parts), of staff and of the business itself. Strategies used by businesses include:

- extended opening hours so that customers who work unsocial hours can still buy goods without any problems – many supermarkets and filling stations now open 24 hours, 6 or 7 days a week
- a large range of stock and regularly replenished shelves and racks so that customers have a wide choice available
- an in-store or telephone ordering service for special items or items which are out of stock with the offer to deliver the item to the customer's home (or work) address
- a catalogue or Internet mail order service so that customers can buy from their own homes.

Organisations which provide a service must also consider availability. A business which provides a maintenance or repair service can gain a competitive edge if it employs enough staff to be able to guarantee prompt service at a previously agreed time.

Additional competitive features

Although a business can differentiate itself from its competitors through price, quality and availability, there are other ways. For instance:

- a clothing shop offering a free alterations service to customers
- loyalty or discount schemes enabling regular customers to make savings on their purchases
- meeting other related needs of its customers, e.g. travel agents offering a currency exchange service
- regularly reviewing existing ranges, adding new features and bringing out new models to tempt customers to make further purchases.

Knowing the customer

A business which understands its customers, knows what they need and does its best to provide this will always have an advantage. You have already learned that businesses try to find out about their key customers (see Chapter 5). They do this by obtaining a **customer profile** which includes details on:

- the **age range** of their customers
- their **gender** – whether they are mainly male, mainly female or both
- their average annual **income**
- their **lifestyle**, e.g. whether they have children, how they spend their leisure time, where they go on holiday.

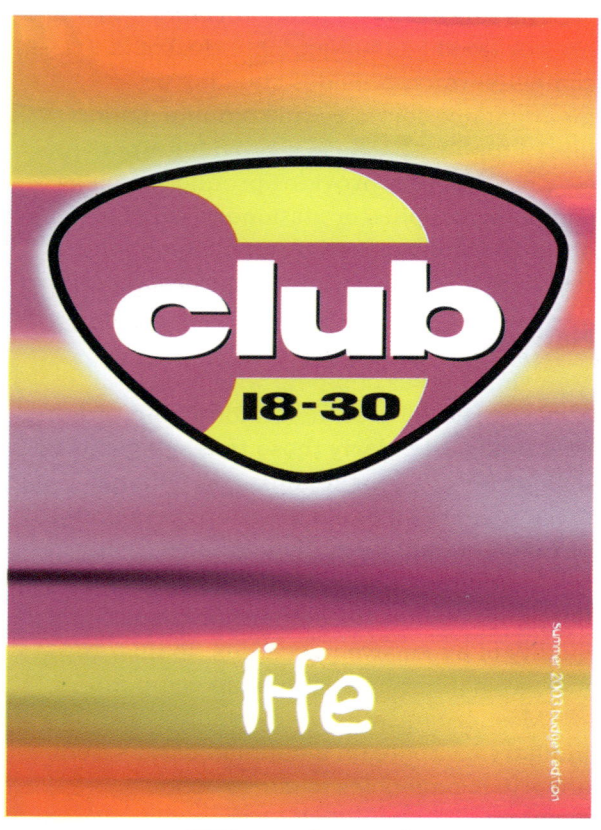

Club 18–30 knows what its customers want – and provides it

This information helps them to develop additional products linked to their customers' needs and promote them to the right people. For example, Club 18–30 offers holidays geared to people between these ages. By surveying this age group, the company can decide which type of activities will be most appealing, and the most appropriate prices to charge for their holidays. By contrast, Saga specialises in holidays for the over 50s – mainly outside the peak holiday season because its customers are often retired and want to take a break in the winter months.

Some businesses have different types of key customers and will develop specific products and services to appeal to each group. For example, Ford produces a range of vehicles such as sports cars, people carriers and hatchbacks – its models are provided for different key customers, with different needs. Another example is the cosmetics industry, for example Boots' 17 range is produced for young customers and its No 7 range for older customers. Dividing up a market into different types of customers with different needs is known as **market segmentation**.

In some cases, identifying the needs of different customers enables a business to benefit from **price differentiation**. This is when different prices are charged for the same service to different groups of customers. One example is train travel which is cheaper during quieter periods. The highest prices are charged to business passengers and commuters who travel during peak times.

Fact file

Direct competition refers to competition from suppliers or sellers of the same product or service such as the Next and River Island clothing stores.

Indirect competition relates to competition from different goods or services which all compete for a share of a consumer's income. There is only one National Lottery but competition here includes other types of gambling such as the football pools.

> ## Snapshot
>
> ### Who knows about your buying habits – and how?
>
> Computer databases store customer data, but a new technique called data mining is now used to extract more detailed information on individual customers. This is often part of an overall strategy of <u>customer relationship management (CRM)</u> used by businesses to find out more about their customers.
>
> All companies want to persuade existing customers to spend more money with them, so they need to know more about individual customers' buying habits, tastes and spending levels. They want to make better use of existing information on customers and to analyse it thoroughly to help them attract new business.
>
> To do this, a variety of CRM IT systems are used by call centres, marketing departments and website teams. Although customer information obtained is by phone, personal visit or Internet, it is the last which can provide the greatest insight into customer behaviour. This is because a company can record the buttons a customer clicks, the pages viewed and responses to different aspects of the site.
>
> Web monitoring may lead to a business making changes. For example, Victoria's Secret, a lingerie retailer, believed most of its customers to be women in their 20s and 30s. Website monitoring showed that most visitors were men aged 40–55 – and this resulted in a change of website design.

The location of competitors

Telesales and the Internet have increased selling opportunities for many businesses. Some traditionally local businesses, including butchers and fishmongers, have their own websites and now supply to customers all over the UK and even abroad. While options and choices available for customers have grown, there has also been an increase in the number of potential competitors in certain business activities.

When you are investigating the type of competitors a business has, the first step is to identify whether the business is selling locally, nationally or internationally. In most cases, its competitors will be doing the same thing.

Local competitors

A business will have local competitors if it provides convenience goods to a local community or a personal service. You are unlikely to travel far to buy a sandwich, hire a video or have your hair cut. However, your local florist *may* be under competition from businesses which provide a national delivery service and customers may stop visiting a local newsagent if they find buying a magazine is cheaper if they take out a subscription.

The same applies to organisations which provide goods or services to industry. A company which provides cleaning or maintenance services will compete against local suppliers because it provides a personal service. One that provides products such as computer supplies or stationery, which can be ordered locally or nationally by telephone or Internet, will have a wider range of competitors.

National competitors

Many businesses compete with other organisations all over the UK for their customers' business, particularly those that sell goods by mail order or over the Internet. Although these types of sales are currently less than 10 per cent of total sales, they are increasing.

In addition, consumers are likely to travel or search further to compare prices and quality of expensive purchases, so this increases the range of possible competitors.

Most organisations which supply to industry compete on a national basis – from advertising agencies to construction companies. Some may be less used to competing internationally, but this, too, is becoming increasingly common.

International competitors

Many organisations operate internationally, particularly those that sell to industry or to governments across the world, such as pharmaceutical companies and civil engineering companies, which build roads and bridges.

Although many overseas websites offer products direct to British consumers, such purchases are not always practical. This is because other factors such as import duties, delivery charges and customs regulations need to be taken into account. There may also be difficulties if the product later develops a fault. Generally, most individuals buy from abroad only when they visit a country. However, this has meant that some shops and stores on the south coast of England now compete with French superstores for their customers – who may prefer to cross the Channel to save money.

Fact file

A **multinational** company is one which produces and sells goods all over the world, for example oil companies (such as BP and Texaco), car producers (such as Ford and General Motors) and computer giants (such as IBM). Multinationals often customise their products to suit different markets.

What can go wrong?

Sometimes competition can be *too* intense and some companies will go out of business. These are likely to be the ones that cannot afford to promote and market their goods to the same extent as more powerful suppliers. Many experts have argued that Microsoft's dominance in the computer industry has restricted the choice available to consumers.

In many industries, it is difficult for new or smaller companies to compete on price because their expenses are higher in relation to the number of products they make or sell. This is why your local shop cannot compete with a superstore on price and why small car producers operate only in specialist markets as they simply cannot compete with large, multinational car producers.

Elsewhere, despite legislation, large suppliers sometimes act together to try to put new entrants out of business. Large organisations have the ability to cut prices to the extent that new businesses cannot compete. When the new business leaves the market, the others simply raise their prices again.

Besides pricing, businesses can use other methods to limit competition. The high street banks, for example, have been criticised for making it difficult for small businesses who want to bank elsewhere. Changing over all their banking arrangements can be such a nightmare that many people can't be bothered. The Competition Commission recently called this a 'complex' monopoly because the big four banks – Royal Bank of Scotland (includes NatWest), HSBC, Barclays and Lloyds TSB – have 90 per cent market share between them.

Spot check

Write down your answers to the following questions:

1. Identify two types of business which often compete with each other on price.
2. Why might businesses such as Gucci and Ferrari actually lose customers if they dropped their prices?
3. Explain why a business may try to improve quality without increasing the price of a product.
4. a What is meant by the term 'availability'?
   b Give two examples of the way in which a business could try to improve the availability of its products.
5. a Why do companies try to find out detailed information about their customers?
   b Identify two types of information in which they would be interested.
6. Explain briefly how computers and the use of the Internet can help businesses to understand customer behaviour.

It makes you think!

Within your group, answer the following.

1. Draw up a consumer profile (see page 117) for each of the following items:
   a Barbie dolls
   b washing machines
   c power drills.

   For each profile, decide one way in which the manufacturers could use this information to their advantage.

2. Identify whether each of the following businesses would have local, national or international competitors. In each case, give a reason for your choice.
   a A manufacturer of DVD players
   b A company which specialises in demolition work
   c An optician
   d A textiles manufacturer which makes towels and bathrobes
   e A chiropodist
   f A theme park

3. Select one local organisation of your choice. (Use Yellow Pages or the Thomson Local directory if you need ideas). Then summarise:
   a the aspects and features on which you think it will compete (e.g. price, quality, availability, etc.)
   b the type of business which will be its main competitor.

4. The market share of the major supermarkets in 1995, 1998 and 2000 is shown in the chart below. Briefly comment on the performance of each of them during this period.

UK supermarkets – comparative market shares

Supermarket	1995	1998	2000
Tesco	13.9 per cent	17.2 per cent	18.3 per cent
Sainsbury	12.4 per cent	12.2 per cent	12.8 per cent
Asda	7.1 per cent	8.7 per cent	9.6 per cent
Safeway	7.4 per cent	8.0 per cent	8.2 per cent

Case study

Competing for a market share

The computer games industry is worth £14 billion a year which is why 2002 saw three mighty players competing for the prize. The contestants are the Sony PlayStation 2, the Nintendo GameCube and the Microsoft Xbox. British consumers are likely to see several benefits from this match. When the GameCube was launched in Japan, Sony promptly responded by cutting the price of its PlayStation 2 by £60 though at the time it claimed this was due to production savings.

The limited number of GameCube games available at the Nintendo launch was disappointing. However, at a starter price of £150, some consider the GameCube will be very attractive to buyers. In its first two months of sales in the USA, 2.7 million were sold.

The Xbox, at a starter price of £299, is Microsoft's bid. Microsoft promised that 60 Xbox games would be available by summer 2002. They also argued that the Xbox is technologically more advanced than its rivals. 1.5 million were sold in the US between November and January 2002.

You can find out more at www.heinemann.co.uk/hotlinks.

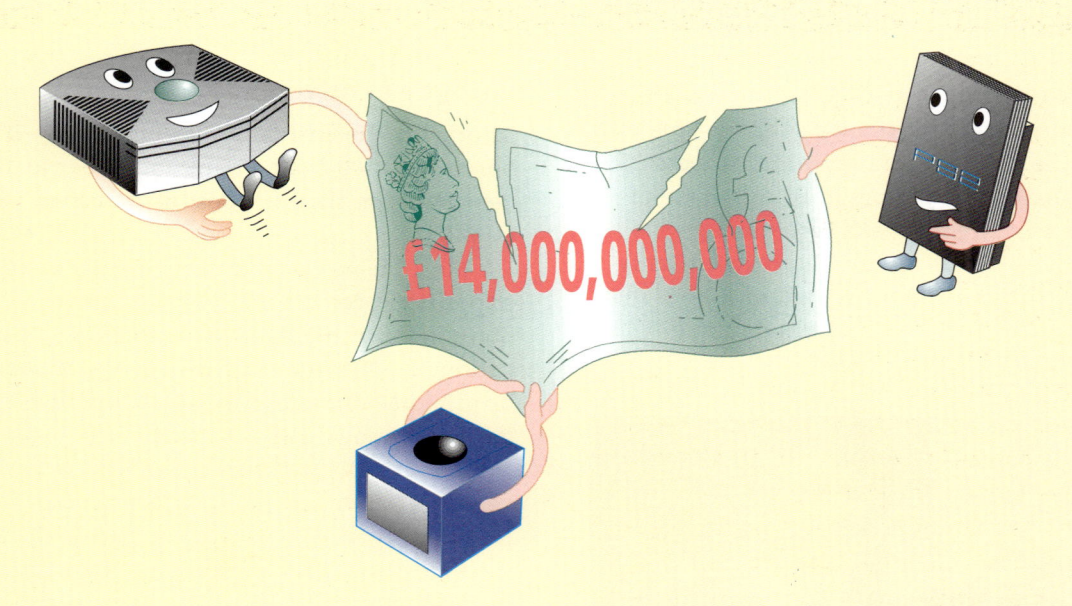

Three major companies compete for market share of the computer games industry

▶ 1 How many competitors are there for the computer games' console market?
2 How much is the overall market worth?
3 Do the companies compete on a local, national or international basis? Give a reason for your answer.
4 Why is it better for consumers that there are three suppliers of games consoles, rather than one?
5 As a group, decide what you consider to be the customer profile of a computer games player in terms of:
   a age   b gender
   c income   d lifestyle.
6 State two ways in which manufacturers could use these customer profiles to help to sell more consoles.
7 Do you think Microsoft, Nintendo and Sony are competing mainly on price, quality or availability? Give a reason for your answer.

▶ 1 Nintendo and Microsoft are new entrants to the games market. Suggest why they have chosen to enter this market and identify two benefits to consumers.
2 Sony claimed it cut its price because of production savings. Suggest one other reason why it took this action.

3 If a new manufacturer entered the market, would it need to compete on a local, national or international basis? Give a reason for your answer.
4 a Draw up a customer profile of a computer games player in terms of:
      i   age   ii gender
      iii income   iv lifestyle.
   b Do you think the profile will be identical for each manufacturer, or do you think there could be any differences? Give your reasons.
5 How could the manufacturers use the information they obtain from visitors to their website to fine-tune their customer profiles?
6 Assess the main needs of computer games players in terms of price, quality (e.g. reliability and technological advances) of the console and availability (of both the console and games). Then suggest the key areas on which manufacturers should concentrate their future developments. (*Note:* there isn't one 'right answer' to this question as games players may vary. The most important point is that you can give a reason for your opinion.)

Chapter 7   External influences on business

Economic conditions

The term 'economy' refers to all the wealth and resources in a particular country. This unit looks at the British economy which affects all the businesses and people in Britain. One of the UK government's tasks is to manage the economy and this is mainly the responsibility of the Chancellor of the Exchequer, who is advised by the Treasury and the Bank of England.

The Chancellor of the Exchequer is responsible for managing the economy

The economy is affected by the behaviour of people and businesses, all of whom act independently. So forecasting what might happen in the future can be difficult. If people or businesses act in a way that might create economic problems, the Chancellor will try to change this behaviour. For example, if people are spending too much, the Chancellor can increase the taxes people pay. This deprives them of money and, theoretically, should reduce spending. If people are spending too little, the Chancellor could reduce taxes so that they have more money in their pocket.

Changes in the economy

There are three main changes in the economy that you need to understand:

- changes in **interest rates**
- changes in **prices**
- changes in **exchange rates**.

Each of these has a direct affect on business *and* on the behaviour of consumers.

Changes in interest rates

Interest is the cost of borrowing money. If you borrowed £100 from a bank for a year at 10 per cent interest, then the cost of your loan would be £10.

Most businesses borrow money to pay for expansion projects, to upgrade their equipment or machinery or to develop new products. They may borrow several thousands or millions of pounds. Let's assume that a large garage borrows £500,000 for an expansion project. It aims to repay the money over five years at 10 per cent interest and knows that if its sales are on target it can afford to do this.

If, during that five years, interest rates increase, then the cost of the loan is greater. At the end of year 1, if interest rates are 12 per cent, then interest for that year is now £60,000, not the £50,000 which was calculated originally. If at the end of year 2, interest rates have increased again, then the cost will be even higher. The business either has to repay more money than it forecast each year *or* arrange to repay the loan over a longer period.

The problem for many businesses is that increases in interest rates will also affect the behaviour of other businesses *and* consumers. Many people have mortgages which become more expensive if interest rates rise. This leaves people with less money to spend. People are also less keen to borrow money to make expensive purchases when interest rates are high. So our garage may suffer twice. First, because it is having to pay more for its loan. Secondly, because it will sell fewer cars than originally anticipated.

Businesses are also affected if interest rates fall. In this case, the original loan will cost less and sales may increase at the same time. For this reason, most businesses prefer interest rates to be low.

Mortgages are cheaper when interest rates are low, and this encourages people to buy and sell housing

Fact file

The official interest rate in Britain – called the **base rate** – is decided by a Bank of England committee. This is not the same rate that you are charged by a bank or credit card company for borrowing money. These rates vary, depending upon how much profit the lender wishes to make on the loan. You can compare rates by looking for the Annual Percentage Rate (APR) which, by law, must be advertised. So whereas the official interest rate may be 4 per cent, a credit card company may still charge 19 per cent and some store cards may charge you 30 per cent in interest!

Changes in prices

Prices of goods and services can increase or fall. If the general level of prices is rising, this is known as **inflation** and causes problems for both businesses and individuals. People on fixed incomes (such as pensioners) cannot keep pace with the increasing cost of living because the goods they need are more expensive. People who work often expect employers to give them pay rises each year to cope with the increase. Trade unions often bid for pay rises to match any rises in the cost of living.

Snapshot

Winners and losers when interest rates change

In January 2001, the base rate in Britain was 6 per cent. By November, interest rates were at a 37-year low – at 4 per cent. The interest rate cuts were made for two reasons:

- *Manufacturers in Britain were having problems selling their products abroad because the pound was very strong (see page 125). The global economy was also deteriorating and this was affecting sales. Things became even worse after 11 September. Lowering interest rates reduced the cost of loans taken out by manufacturers so their overall costs were less.*

- *At the same time, the government wanted to encourage consumers to spend more money. This would help to boost the sales of goods. The reduction in interest rates reduced mortgage payments, leaving consumers with more income to spend. Lowering interest rates also encourages consumers to borrow money. These actions would help to keep the economy buoyant.*

However, not everyone gained. Savers lost income as the interest rates paid on savings were also reduced. This particularly affected older people who had paid off their mortgage and needed interest from savings to supplement their basic income.

Businesses are likely to find that raw material prices have increased. In addition, their workers are demanding pay increases. To meet these extra costs, the business may be forced to increase its selling prices. This has three effects:

- The increases may cause inflation to get worse.
- If the business exports goods, it may sell fewer of them because they have become more expensive and therefore less competitive.

- Consumers may prefer to buy cheaper imports rather than more expensive home-produced goods. If sales fall because of the price rise, the business may have to reduce production and lay off staff.

From this, you can see that it is important for a country to have a stable and predictable economy and the government will act to try to achieve this. In Britain, the government's policy is to keep inflation low. In 1997, it set a target of 2.5 per cent inflation. By the end of 2001, prices were rising by less than 2 per cent. To control inflation the government has to take action over the factors that cause it. These include the following:

- **Excessive consumer spending**. If demand for goods rises more quickly than the goods can be supplied, then prices are likely to rise. As an example, think about parents at Christmas, all desperate to buy the latest toy for their children. Because there is a limited supply of the item they want, the producer or retailer can increase the price and, in effect, sell the last one to the highest bidder! This can happen in the economy as a whole, when there is a shortage of goods and consumer spending is high.
- **Lack of competition**. You have already seen that when one large organisation, or a few of them, control a market they can charge higher prices. In Britain, this used to be the case with gas, electricity and telephones, but now that there is greater competition, prices have fallen.
- **Higher costs to businesses**, such as high wage settlements or increases in interest charges. Businesses try to cover these costs by raising their prices.
- **Higher taxation**. When the government increases tax on alcohol or tobacco products or increases VAT rates this directly affects the final price of goods.

The government can try to restrain consumer spending by increasing interest rates, but this, as you have seen, can cause problems for business. It therefore has to do a juggling act, depending on which area of the economy it most wants to change! If inflation is low, and stable, there is no need to risk causing problems for business by increasing interest rates, even if consumer spending is rising. If, however, there is a danger that inflation will start to increase significantly, then action must be taken, even if this causes unfavourable effects in other parts of the economy.

Snapshot

What does it cost you to live?

Inflation – or the cost of living – is measured by the retail prices index (RPI). *This is a basket of 650 goods covering 147 areas across the UK. How much the basket costs for one period is then compared with how much it cost for the last period. The latest RPI figures can be obtained from the Office for National Statistics at their website –* www.heinemann.co.uk/hotlinks.

In 2001, international competition was one reason why prices of many goods actually fell. Audio-visual equipment today costs less than 40 per cent of its price in 1987, household electrical appliances are 10 per cent cheaper, and the price of women's clothing has also fallen. Government action to increase competition in the gas, electricity and telephone industries has also resulted in lower prices.

However, the cost of services has increased by more *than the overall level of inflation and, at the end of 2001, was about 4 per cent. Dental examinations, eye tests and hairdressing services had increased the most, the cost of entertainment had increased sharply, and so had the cost of taxing and insuring a car. Rail fares increased by 112 per cent between 1987 and 2001!*

While inflation must be kept low, it is important that it does not fall so low that deflation *occurs. This is the opposite of inflation and means that overall prices are falling. While this may sound good, it brings its own problems. Think of your home, your possessions and your savings being worth* less *each year and then think about this happening all over Britain!*

Changes in exchange rates

As a private individual, the only time you are likely to be interested in the exchange rate is when you are going abroad on holiday. Then you will need to swap your British currency and the exchange rate will affect how much foreign currency you receive.

In January 2002, 12 out of the 15 European Union (EU) member states (excluding the UK) replaced their notes and coins with a common currency, the euro. At that time, a euro was worth about 62 pence. If you had £620 to spend on holiday in Spain, you would have received 1000 euros (620 ÷ 0.62).

But what happens if the pound/euro exchange rate changes. If the pound gets stronger against the euro, then you will receive *more* euros; if it gets weaker, you will receive *fewer* euros. Assume you are going on holiday in June, and you are told that the exchange rate is 1.7 euros to the pound. In this case, the pound is stronger – it is buying more euros. In exchange for your £620 you would now receive 1054 euros (620 × 1.7). In September you are told the exchange rate is 1.5 euros to the pound. The pound is weaker and is buying fewer euros. In exchange for your £620 you now have only 930 euros to spend (620 × 1.5).

You obviously want the pound to be strong so that you have more money to spend when you go on holiday. But French friends coming to visit you in Britain would want the *opposite* to happen – they would want the pound to be weak against the euro so their holiday would cost less.

The same applies to British goods. When British goods are sold abroad, foreign buyers pay in their own currency. If the pound is strong, then British goods cost more for foreign buyers. If the pound is weak, then British goods are cheaper. More tourists come to Britain, too, because holidays here cost less.

In general, therefore, businesses prefer exchange rates that keep their prices competitive abroad. They are worried if the pound is very strong as this increases the prices of the goods they export.

However, some businesses prefer the pound to be strong. This is because they buy raw materials from abroad but mainly sell to UK customers. In this case, a strong pound keeps their prices low! British consumers also prefer a strong pound because goods from abroad and foreign holidays are both cheaper.

The biggest problem for businesses is that exchange rates fluctuate. This makes it difficult for businesses to predict their profits on international transactions. The government can try to keep exchange rates stable through its interest rate policy. If interest rates increase, foreign investors want to invest their money in Britain and buy pounds to do this. This increases the value of the pound. If interest rates fall, then investors sell their pounds to invest elsewhere. However, as you have already seen, changing interest rates affects other factors as well, so the government is limited in the extent to which it can affect exchange rates.

This is the main reason why many manufacturing businesses which deal with European businesses would prefer Britain to join the euro. This would remove the uncertainties of fluctuating exchange rates and also reduce the costs incurred when changing money into foreign currency.

Fact file

The value of the pound fluctuates because of **demand** and **supply**. When many people 'demand' pounds, then the value increases – so the pound is strong if many people buy pounds to invest in Britain or to buy British goods. On the other hand, if more people are selling pounds than are buying them, the value falls.

The law of demand and supply applies to most goods. This is why inflation can occur if consumer demand is high, yet there is a shortage of goods. Think of an ice-cream seller. On a hot day, with a limited supply, he can raise the price because many people want to buy ice-creams. He is still likely to run out before he closes. On a wet Saturday, he will lower the price to get rid of his surplus stock before he closes.

Managing the national economy

The management of the UK economy is shared between the government and the Bank of England. Their aim is **stability** which means that:

- businesses can confidently plan their future activities
- customers can plan their spending and saving activities.

Stability is mainly achieved in three ways:

- The government and the Bank of England decide on specific targets they wish to achieve, for example 2.5 per cent inflation. They publish these so that businesses and consumers know the aims of the government.
- They constantly monitor the state of the economy against these targets and take action – such as increasing or lowering interest rates – to 'fine-tune' the economy and to try to keep it on target.
- They avoid drastic action wherever possible; for example, interest rates tend to rise or fall by only small percentages at a time, usually 0.25 or 0.5 per cent. This is to prevent undesirable side effects occurring too quickly.

What can go wrong?

It is difficult to make totally accurate economic predictions because no one knows exactly how individuals will behave. In addition, the world economy and particularly the US economy affects Britain.

Governments are limited in the actions they can take. They mainly try to control the economy through interest rates and taxation, but this does not guarantee success. If there is a delay between government action and consumer response, the government may try to do too much. This happened in the 1980s. The government wanted to slow down consumer spending but it took months before anything happened – then everyone stopped spending at once. This caused an **economic recession** (a contraction in the economy). The government then had to try to 'kick start' the economy.

Some business people are worried that if Britain joins the euro, the government will have less ability to act because the UK will no longer be able to control interest rates.

Spot check

Write down your answers to the following questions:

1. Explain what is meant by the term 'interest rate'.
2. Give one reason why many businesses prefer interest rates to be low.
3. Give two reasons why a rise in prices may adversely affect a business.
4. Explain the action that a business is likely to take if its costs suddenly increase.
5. a What is meant by the term 'inflation'?
   b How is inflation measured in Britain?
6. a If the exchange rate for US dollars is 1.4 to the pound, how many dollars would you receive if you had saved £500 towards an American holiday?
   b Would you be better or worse off if the exchange rate changed to 1.2 dollars to the pound?
7. What happens to the price of UK exports if the pound suddenly falls in value? Explain whether this is good for British business or bad.
8. Explain briefly why business people prefer stable economic conditions.
9. Give one example of an action the government can take to manage the national economy.
10. Some manufacturers would prefer Britain to belong to the euro. Give one reason for this.

It makes you think!

Within your group, imagine that you are part of the Bank of England's monetary policy committee. You have to decide whether to cut interest rates, increase them or leave them alone. The date is July 2002 and the official interest rate is 4 per cent. Your facts and concerns are as follows:

- Manufacturers want lower interest rates and, preferably, a weaker pound to help them sell abroad. If you reduce interest rates, you will help manufacturers.
- Consumers have been borrowing at record levels because interest rates are low, so debt is cheap. At present, too many people are borrowing more than they can afford to repay. This situation will be made worse if many manufacturing businesses fail and unemployment increases.
- The government is worried that excessive consumer spending could trigger price rises. Although inflation is low, prices in the service sector have not fallen and increased demand for services could make this worse.

Decide what you will do. Then find out what has happened to interest rates between July 2002 and now, why these changes occurred, and how they affected businesses.

Environmental constraints

Industrial skyline showing factories in Halifax, West Yorkshire in the 1950s

If you turned back the clock 50 years and studied the way in which the activities of business *and* ordinary people affected the environment, you might be surprised. In 1950, you would have struggled to get to and from school on some days because of blanket smog caused by smoke pollution from factory chimneys. In some areas, you might have lived next to a large, noisy factory which operated all night long, making sleep nearly impossible. Local rivers and streams were badly polluted and a swim in the sea might have left you with a severe stomach upset. Businesses and individuals didn't think much about the items they used and how they disposed of them.

Since then, attitudes have changed, initially through the work of pressure groups such as Friends of the Earth, Greenpeace and the Worldwide Fund for Nature. Their campaigns, together with warnings from scientists, have resulted in greater public awareness of environmental issues such as global warming, acid rain and pollution. Governments and individuals are starting to realise that unless we change the way we live, work and use natural resources, we are in danger of permanently damaging our planet.

Business activities and the environment

The actions of both individuals and businesses are important in protecting the environment. Laws control business activities that would have a damaging effect on the environment. The UK government has set specific targets to be met; for example, by 2010 electricity supply companies in Britain will have to obtain 10 per cent of their energy from renewable sources.

The UK government department responsible for many environmental initiatives and laws, such as those relating to air quality and transport, is the Department for the Environment, Transport and the Regions (DETR). The major body responsible for environmental issues in the UK is the Environment Agency. The agency promotes public and business awareness of environmental issues and also has the power to enforce environmental legislation and prosecute businesses which flout the regulations. The agency is supported by local authorities which are responsible for the local environment and have the power to take action against offenders.

Business activities can cause a variety of environmental problems. These are described below.

Air pollution

Air pollution occurs when substances which are harmful or dangerous to humans or to the environment are released into the atmosphere. For example, processes in industries such as power stations and cement works create harmful emissions which are released into the air. Another major cause of air pollution is traffic. Cars and lorries emit a variety of pollutants which can significantly affect air quality in an area.

Laws control the type of emissions allowed by industry and vehicles. Every time a vehicle undergoes an MOT test, emissions equipment analyses the exhaust gases. To pass the test, dangerous emissions such as carbon monoxide must be within a certain limit.

The Environmental Protection Act 1990 regulates air pollution by industry. This Act states that manufacturing processes should be:

- operated using the best available techniques without leading to excessive costs
- operated in a way which minimises the environmental impact on air, water and land.

The Act divides manufacturing processes into:

- significant emissions from major processes – these relate to about 3,000 manufacturing plants in Britain and are monitored and authorised by the Environment Agency
- less significant emissions – these are monitored and enforced by local authorities and cover approximately 20,000 industrial processes.

The Pollution Prevention and Control Act 1999 covers businesses not regulated under the Environmental Protection Act. It also covers several new areas, such as energy, water and raw material efficiency, waste minimisation and recovery, in addition to minimising pollution.

Snapshot

Good air day?

In summer, TV weather forecasters regularly talk about 'air quality'. The air quality reading tells you how clean the air is in your region. Air pollution may be described as low, moderate, high or very high. If you are asthmatic, for example, you would be concerned if the reading was high.

The problem is that air quality can be poor even in rural areas. This is because pollution doesn't stop at national or regional boundaries – even emissions from Europe can carry over to the UK (and vice versa) if the weather conditions are right.

Businesses need to be aware of how the weather and other geographical factors can affect them. Castle Cement, in Lancashire, encountered problems because the processing plant is in a valley. The surrounding hills, together with the prevailing winds, led to chimney gases being pulled back down to ground level. Local residents protested because of the smell and the effect on air quality in the area. To reduce the problem the company installed a special gas cleaning system at a cost of £5 million to reduce sulphur dioxide emissions. This system also costs £750,000 a year to run – for some industries, improving environmental performance and taking account of local concerns can be expensive.

Following the adoption of National Air Quality Standards by the government in January 2000, local authorities are responsible for monitoring and controlling air quality in their area. They are responsible for ensuring that central government targets on pollutants will be met by 2005.

Noise pollution

Noise pollution describes noise which may affect your sleep, your health or that generally annoys you. You can create noise pollution yourself – simply by playing a ghetto-blaster at full volume where other people can hear it, whether they like it or not! This is an offence – and a neighbour could report the problem to the local authority's environmental health department.

Noise is measured in decibels. The World Health Organisation recommends a maximum daytime level of 55 decibels. Unfortunately, many people regularly suffer higher levels, mainly from traffic or trains. People living near airports may also be affected by the noise of low-flying aircraft, although night-time flights are restricted.

Various Acts of Parliament, primarily the Environmental Protection Act 1990, help to regulate noise and give residents the right to complain if they are annoyed by noise from any source such as factories or burglar alarms. Most people are prepared to tolerate noise for a short time, for example from road or building works. Persistent unwanted noise is more serious and inspectors can use equipment to measure the noise level.

A European Directive restricting noise emissions from equipment used outdoors such as construction machines and lawnmowers came into effect in July 2001.

In December 2001, the Environment Minister launched a three-month consultation exercise to develop a noise strategy. It involves gathering information about noise and identifying actions to be taken. It will help to prepare the UK for a European Directive on the assessment and management of environmental noise expected in 2002.

Water pollution

Since 1999, the Environment Agency has recorded and classified all water pollution incidents. Water pollution occurs when undesirable or hazardous substances are discharged into rivers, lakes or the sea. Each year in the UK there are about 18,000 incidents. In 1999, the main source of pollution was industry, mainly from construction businesses.

Agriculture can also cause pollution. Cattle slurry and other organic waste may pollute water sources, particularly during high rainfall or in flood conditions. Other pollutants found in water include chemicals, dyes, diesel and other fuels.

Generally, however, water quality in Britain is improving. Fish, such as salmon, and seals have been sighted in several rivers in England and several beaches now conform to European safety standards. Legislation strictly controls the substances which can be discharged in Britain. Under the Control of Pollution Act 1974 it is an offence, without consent, to allow the discharge of any pollutant in controlled waters. Businesses must also check the location and routes of drains used to take away storm and surface water and ensure no pollutants enter them. The Groundwater Regulations 1998 also restrict activities such as the storage of chemicals which could result in the pollution of groundwater.

Flying the clean beach flag

Wasteful use of resources

All businesses use resources such as water, energy, paper, glass and other materials. The aim of resource management and waste minimisation is to reduce and reuse waste.

This can be done by:

- operating more efficiently to minimise waste
- recycling waste materials
- disposing of dangerous or special waste responsibly and according to the law.

Waste minimisation

Britain is running out of space for landfill sites

According to the Environment Agency, each person in the UK consumes 60–80 tonnes of material each year. In addition, 11 tonnes of raw materials are used to produce just one tonne of product.

Businesses may undertake an environmental audit to monitor how they are using resources, the results of which show them where improvements need to be made. An audit can involve:

- checking the resources used in production processes to reduce waste (e.g. by reusing resources where possible) and to avoid the use of potentially environmentally harmful materials

- reviewing the production process to use clean and eco-efficient techniques
- assessing the design of products to make the best use of raw and recycled materials
- assessing the use of energy to ensure efficiency, e.g. checking insulation and heating levels, turning off equipment when not in use
- assessing usage of water to ensure efficiency, e.g. reusing water in the production process
- reviewing the amount and type of packaging used to reduce the quantity and to ensure the use of recyclable materials
- checking the ordering and storage of materials to minimise waste and deterioration
- monitoring the disposal of waste materials (see below) to ensure these are dealt with appropriately.

The Packaging (Essential Requirements) Regulations affect companies which pack or fill products with packaging and aims to minimise the amount of packaging used and to increase the amount that is recycled. The EC Directive on Packaging and Packing Waste requires that at least 50 per cent of the UK's packaging waste must be reused through recycling or similar recovery methods.

Fact file

Recycling involves reprocessing waste into new products. Many waste materials can be recycled, including paper, glass, cardboard, plastic and metal. Some hazardous wastes can also be recycled.

Dealing with waste

Even the most efficient business will produce some waste materials. Some of these will be hazardous substances known as **special waste**.

Traditionally, much waste was dumped in landfill sites. The 1999 European Union Landfill Directive restricts the type of waste which can be put in landfill sites (such as biodegradable waste) and requires other types of waste to be pre-treated. The aim is to reduce the amount of waste being disposed of in this way through increased recycling and the proper disposal of hazardous materials, which normally involves incineration. A landfill tax is imposed on all waste disposed of at licensed landfill sites to encourage industry to change to more environmentally friendly methods of disposal. Otherwise, we will simply run out of space for rubbish!

Various laws control the disposal of waste. The Special Waste Regulations 1996 control the disposal of toxic or hazardous materials such as chemicals. In addition, the Environment Agency regulates waste management through a licensing system. Under the Environmental Protection Act 1990, all businesses must ensure that their waste is stored safely and disposed of by someone who is authorised to take it and deal with it.

Snapshot

On the scrap heap?

The motor industry is concerned about a new EU Directive which will make car manufacturers legally responsible for taking back, scrapping and recycling the 1.8 million used vehicles each year which are no longer roadworthy. After 2007, manufacturers will be responsible for every car they have made. The Directive sets a target of recycling 85 per cent of cars by 2006 and 95 per cent by 2015.

The Society of Motor Manufacturers and Traders (SMMT) estimates this could add up to £300 to the cost of a new car, as manufacturers try to recoup the cost of recycling. The DTI (Department of Trade and Industry) has estimated it could cost businesses £161 million to £346 million a year between 2006 and 2015 and up to £438 million a year after that.

The SMMT believes that the costs of recycling should be shared between the manufacturers, owners, insurance companies, finance houses who lend money to buy cars, and the government.

What can go wrong?

Despite many laws and regulations to protect the environment, many people think that too little is being done. In a report to the United Nations, the Intergovernmental Panel on Climate Change forecast that the average surface temperature on Earth would rise by 2100 and sea levels would also rise. It believed the only way to protect the environment is to change the current system of mass production, mass consumption and mass waste to one which focuses on efficient production, efficient consumption and full recycling. Industry should aim at zero emissions of global warming gases and zero discharge of wastes.

This needs every government's involvement. There are particular worries that the US refused to sign the Kyoto Protocol as it is the world's worst polluter. Industry and consumers around the world will need to agree on a rejection of the 'use and throw away' society and put the environment ahead of individual needs and wants.

Over to you!

Investigate the environment in your own area and the support given to businesses by your local authority, and by other agencies, such as the Groundwork Trust.

Start by visiting the website of the Environment Agency at www.heinemann.co.uk.hotlinks. Follow the links to 'What's in your own backyard?' and type in your postcode. Then you can investigate the businesses in your own locality and obtain a pollution inventory.

Next, visit the website of your local authority (you can find this through a search engine). Click on its environmental links to see how it monitors and controls the environment in your area. Find out which areas have been set aside for industrial use as industrial sites or business parks. In these areas, businesses are allowed to undertake activities which would not be permissible near to residential areas.

Ideally, ask your tutor to arrange a visit from someone who works for your local authority's environmental health office, Groundwork or Business Link to tell you about the type of activities which are restricted to businesses, particularly in residential areas. Ask what happens when businesses submit plans to change their business activities in a way which may affect the environment and what happens to existing businesses if new regulations are introduced which affect their activities.

It makes you think!

If you undertook an environmental audit of your school/college or home, how do you think it would score? You can think of both of these as 'production' centres, if you consider that schools and colleges produce successful students (or aim to!) and homes 'produce' food, clean clothes and other essentials needed by those who live there. How efficient are the buying systems, the production systems and the waste systems? Do you recycle waste paper, do you have a shower rather than a bath to save water, do you take old bottles to the bottle bank? Do you walk or ride a bicycle to school or college, or use public transport, or are you taken by car?

Within your group, decide on 12 actions which would save energy, water or materials *either* at home *or* at school or college. You can gain ideas for this by accessing the Environment Agency's website at www.heinemann.co.uk.hotlinks and finding tips on waste minimisation. Then try to ensure that at least two are put into operation.

Spot check

Write down your answers to the following questions:

1. a What is meant by air quality?
    b Identify two factors which can contribute to poor air quality.
2. Which government body or authority monitors businesses which:
    a produce significant emissions as part of their industrial process
    b produce less significant emissions as part of their industrial process?
3. Noise is measured in decibels. What is the maximum daytime level recommended by the World Health Organisation?
4. a In your own words, define noise pollution.
    b Identify two locations where residents may suffer from noise pollution.
5. If new neighbours moved next door and continually played loud music all night long, ignoring your pleas for quiet, what could you do?
6. Identify two ways in which water may become polluted.
7. Identify three ways in which waste can be minimised.
8. a What is a landfill site?
    b Why are additional regulations being introduced to restrict the use of these sites?
9. A company produces toxic waste as part of its industrial process. How can it legally dispose of this?
10. a What is recycling?
    b How does recycling help the environment?

Chapter review and practice questions

1. Identify one major retailer in your area and identify:
    a three major competitors
    b how the businesses *mainly* compete, e.g. on price, quality, availability or other features.
2. You have been asked to draw up a customer profile for a local video rental store.
    a What information would you need to find out?
    b Give two reasons why the video store would find this information useful.
3. The Bank of England has just announced a cut in interest rates. The pound has also fallen in value against the euro. How is this situation likely to affect:
    a retailers who sell to British consumers
    b British holidaymakers travelling to mainland Europe
    c British manufacturers who sell their goods in mainland Europe
    d British manufacturers who import their raw materials?
4. A firm producing computer monitors needs to package these carefully to avoid damage in transit.
    a Which regulations relate to packaging materials?
    b What action must the firm take to ensure it complies with these?

7 Give two reasons why there was a record number of car sales in 2001.
8 How are car manufacturers trying to help drivers to check that their vehicle will not fail an emissions test?
9 Why is research continuing into new types of engines?
10 Do environmentalists think that further research will help to protect the environment completely? Give a reason for your answer.

▶ 1 Give three reasons why environmentalists dislike the petrol engine.
2 Identify three ways in which research has helped to make car engines more environmentally friendly.
3 MIRA and other European organisations advise the European Union before laws relating to cars and the environment are passed. Suggest one reason why the EU needs the views of expert researchers on this subject.
4 a What is a pollution camera and what does it do?
 b How are car manufacturers reacting to this development?
5 In 2002, UK interest rates were low. How did this affect car sales, and why?
6 In 2002, what strategies were used by the car manufacturers to increase sales?
7 Experts consider that competition between car manufacturers is 'a trade off between price and quality'. As an example, they say that Ford sales fell in the USA because of a record number of faults reported.
 a What do you think is meant by 'a trade off between price and quality'?
 b Identify two car manufacturers which you think compete mainly on price.
 c Identify two car manufacturers which you think compete mainly on quality.
 d How would you explain the difference in these policies?
8 a Identify two actions taken by the government to try to lessen the effect of cars on the environment.
 b Suggest one way in which the government could try to reduce consumer spending on new vehicles.
9 a Identify two types of research which are currently being undertaken to further improve cars.
 b Why is this research considered necessary?
10 Environmentalists are still unhappy about the situation.
 a Why is this?
 b What is meant by 'radical' action?
 c What further action do you think the government could take to try to reduce vehicle usage by private individuals and businesses?

Portfolio evidence for Unit 1

Overview: portfolio evidence

What is a portfolio?

Unit 1 is assessed through a portfolio of evidence. Your portfolio is a file that you create which contains specific information. The file must be structured and organised so that the information is grouped together logically.

What type of information do I need?

OCR has stated the information you must obtain as you investigate *two* contrasting businesses (see pages 138–140). The different ways in which you can obtain it are listed below.

You must use the information to write about each business. However, it is *how* you use the information that determines the grade you will receive. This is explained on page 138.

Investigating two businesses

You need to investigate *two different* businesses to obtain your information. *Both* must be medium-sized or large organisations because you are unlikely to be able to find everything you need in a small business. Because you have to *compare* the businesses in some ways, it is advisable to investigate businesses that are as different from each other as possible.

Primarily, they should:

- operate in different **sectors** – primary, secondary or tertiary (see page 38 if you need reminding about sectors!)
- undertake different **activities**. This is very important if, for instance, you have no choice but to investigate two businesses in the same sector.

You may also find it easier if the businesses:

- have different types of ownership – for instance, you could choose one which is privately owned and one in the public sector, or a private limited company and a public limited company
- have different types of location, or different reasons for choosing their location
- are different in size
- operate in different types of markets, with different types of **competitors**.

Where to find your information

You should discuss the best options with your tutor, but you might like to think about your opportunities before you do this. You could choose:

- an organisation you know, e.g.
  - where you go on work experience (see Appendix 1 on work experience, page 408)
  - where you work part time
- an organisation which is familiar to someone you know, e.g.
  - where a member of your family works
  - where a friend of your family works
  - where your tutor has a contact.
- another organisation which can provide you with the information you need. For example, many public limited companies have a comprehensive website and publish company reports and brochures. You will find additional information in newspaper reports and articles. However, to obtain the detail you require, you will also need to arrange to visit someone in the business to ask specific questions.

If obtaining information direct from an organisation proves to be difficult, your tutor may arrange:

- for you to obtain your information from *one* business and then give you a case study for the second
- for your class, as a whole, to obtain different types of information from different businesses or even the same business and then share this. However, you must remember that your portfolio evidence must be *all your own work*!

Over to you!

The chart below shows details of the information you need to obtain and the accounts you need to write to obtain different marks. These marks are then converted into your grade for the Unit. The range of grades you can achieve is from A*A* to GG.

Study this information now, and talk to your tutor about anything you do not understand.

Unit 1 assessment evidence. Maximum marks = 50. Remember, each outcome builds on the last to achieve the maximum marks

Section	What you must find out	What you must then do	Points to consider
A	<ul><li>What each business does (i.e. its main activity)</li><li>Its aims and objectives</li><li>Its type of ownership</li><li>Its location</li></ul>	Write an account of *both* businesses. • If you *describe* the activity, aims and objectives, ownership and location properly, you will achieve up to **4 marks**. • If you also *identify the main differences* between the two businesses in relation to the activity, aims and objectives, ownership and location, you can achieve a further **3 marks**. • If you also *suggest and justify changes* that *each business* could make to be more effective, you can obtain a further **3 marks**. **Total possible marks = 10**	Activity – what the business does and what sector it operates in. Is this area growing or declining, how is this business affected, how does it respond? Location – where it is situated and why. Why is it there, are there any plans to relocate? Ownership – who owns it, how many owners are there, what is its legal status, is this right for the size/type of business? Aims and objectives – what it aims to do and how it will achieve these aims. Are these realistic/appropriate for the business? You may be able to suggest a change in only *one* area, e.g. location, or you may find difficulty suggesting any improvements. This does not mean you cannot obtain a high grade. However, you would have to say *why* you think *both* businesses are operating as well as they possibly could. For instance, you may say that although a private limited company *could* change its ownership to a plc, there could be disadvantages (say what these are) and given its current levels of activity it has the most appropriate type of ownership.

B	The purposes and activities of *three* functional areas for *one* business	Write an account of these areas for *one* business. • If you *describe* the type of work carried out by each functional area you have chosen, you can obtain up to **6 marks**. • If you then state how these areas *work together* to support the overall business activity, and use examples to illustrate your answer, you can obtain up to a further **4 marks**. • If you *evaluate* how effectively these areas work together to achieve the aims and objectives of the business, you can obtain a further **3 marks**. **Total possible marks = 13**	You can choose which functional areas to investigate from those discussed in Chapter 5. It is advisable to choose areas which you understand and find interesting and about which you can find the most information. For instance, you may find a business is prepared to give you more information about its sales function than finance or if you worked in a finance office on work experience, you may wish to include this area. You then need to identify why these areas contact each other and how they work together. Use specific examples. You may find it useful to re-read the section about interactions between departments in Chapter 6 on pages 101–2. If you are *evaluating*, you are looking at the way the areas work together more critically and identifying the good points and any problems. You need to assess – for *each* area – whether it always effectively contributes to the overall purpose of the organisation or if there are occasional difficulties. Try to be specific and give an example of a problem and how it was solved, or the difficulties that occurred because it was not.
C	The different ways in which different functional areas communicate in *one* business	Write an account of the methods of communication used in *one* business. • If you describe the different oral and written methods of communication *and* describe, with examples, how the business uses ICT to communicate and operate, you can obtain up to **7 marks**. • If you then *analyse* how effective different communications methods are: 　– inside a functional area 　– between functional areas 　– with people and organisations outside the business	Your investigation should cover oral and written methods (both internal and external) *and* how the business uses ICT to communicate and operate. Note that the last part follows on quite naturally from the second. If you say that email is used between functional areas, you may comment that it is an effective and speedy method of communicating internally between departments, but occasionally there may be a problem if someone is absent. In this case, you could suggest an alternative. For instance, many email systems have the facility for the mailbox holder to set up an automated reply if he or she is absent and state who is

Section	What you must find out	What you must then do	Points to consider
		you can obtain a further **5 marks**. • If you suggest alternative or improved methods of communications: – inside a functional area – between functional areas – with people and organisations outside the business and *justify* (i.e. give good reasons) for your choices, you can obtain up to a further **3 marks**. **Total possible marks = 15**	answering urgent messages. If this system was introduced, it would help to solve the problem. If you are studying an organisation which appears to have *excellent* communications, you can still obtain a higher grade by saying *why* you think it is so good and suggesting any problems you think could occur (e.g. if the company grew in size or was very busy) and how these could be solved.
D	The external influences which affect *both* businesses. These must include competitors, location and environmental constraints	Write an account of their effect on *both* businesses. • If you identify all the main external influences on *both* businesses and refer to competitors, location *and* environmental constraints, you can obtain up to **5 marks**. • If you explain how *both* businesses are affected by *changes* in external influences, you can gain up to a further **4 marks**. However, you must look at changes with reference to competitors *and* location *and* environmental constraints. • If you then suggest ways in which *both* businesses could respond to these changes and justify your suggestions (i.e. give good reasons for them), you can gain up to a further **3 marks**. **Total possible marks = 12**	All businesses are affected by changes, but the impact of change will vary depending upon the type of business and the type of change. Competitors – these may enter or leave the market, offer cheaper or better-quality goods, spend more on advertising. Location – refer back to your information from Section A, but compare location here with the location of competitors. Environmental constraints include new laws and regulations which affect the business. If one of your businesses has experienced relatively little change recently, find out what type of changes in each area *would* affect it and suggest what action it should take if these occurred.

Contacting an organisation

Your tutor may do this on your behalf. If you choose to investigate a business you know yourself, then you need to go about it in a responsible and professional way.

You will need to arrange to visit the business and meet someone who can answer your questions. You may have to make a few visits to find out everything you require. If you are working at the organisation, don't be surprised if you are told the meeting must take place outside your normal 'working hours' – when you have other work to do. Also, remember that any meetings must take place at the convenience of the business person, not to suit you! If a meeting takes place in class time, make sure your tutor knows.

Other points to remember include the following:

- It is always easier to make arrangements with someone you know, or if someone has mentioned your name in advance, than with a complete stranger in an unknown organisation. In this situation, be prepared to introduce yourself properly.
- You will need to explain clearly why you are contacting the business and/or would like to meet someone. Say that you are investigating a business for your GCSE Applied Business award.
- You should give a positive reason for choosing the business (not because it's the only one you know!). You could say you think it would be very interesting to study.
- Although you may need to find out general information about finance and human resources, you should stress that you do not need to find out anything that is confidential.
- Ideally, you need to talk to someone who has a good, overall view of the business.
- If you arrange to visit, it will impress the person concerned if you write a letter to confirm the arrangements, providing your letter is well written and set out.
- Before your visit, do some research. Find out as much as you can about the business and what it does. This will convince the person you are seeing that you are serious about what you are doing and genuinely interested in his or her business (see also page 144).

Attending a meeting

A checklist for the meeting is shown on page 142. Read through this now and make sure you understand all the points.

You will need to ask various questions to obtain your information. To help you, a list of questions which covers all the main areas for each section is also shown below. Read this through and add any questions you want to ask, based on your research and what you already know about the business (see page 144).

Meeting checklist

1. Write down:
   - the name of the person
   - his or her full job title
   - the name and address of the company
   - the time and date of the meeting.
2. Check that you know where the company is located and can get there easily. Work out how long it will take you to arrive and then add on another 20 minutes!
3. Dress appropriately. If you are at school, your tutor will probably expect you to attend in school uniform, if you wear one. If you are at college, or don't wear uniform (or if the interview is at weekend), dress smartly – this means no jeans and no trainers!
4. Remember to take your question checklist and a note of any other questions you want to ask, a clean notepad and a pen. (If you would prefer to take a tape recorder, ask permission first!)
5. Aim to arrive five minutes early. Give your name to the receptionist and state the name of the person you are seeing.
6. When you enter the room try to smile, no matter how nervous you are!
7. Expect some questions about your course and your portfolio work. If someone has been kind enough to offer to help you, and is showing an interest in what you are doing, then the more you tell them, the better he or she will understand what you are trying to find out and why.
8. Ask the questions, but don't gabble or ask quick-fire questions! Be prepared to go 'off script' if something important is mentioned.
9. Tick each question as you ask it and make a clear note of each answer.
10. If you are offered a tour of the business, accept gratefully. This will give you a better understanding of how the company operates and what it does.
11. At the end, ask if you can contact the person again if you find there is anything you need to check. Then write down his or her phone number or email address. You may prefer to arrange a follow-up discussion, especially if you are finding out information for every section – one visit is unlikely to be enough for this.
12. Remember to say 'thank you' at the end of the meeting.
13. After the meeting, label your notes clearly with the date, the name of the organisation and the name of the person.
14. Don't be surprised if the person you are meeting asks to see a copy of your final work. You could even offer to send a copy to them voluntarily!

Business investigation questions checklist

The checklist is subdivided into information required for both businesses and information needed for just one business. However, your tutor *may* prefer you to obtain *both* sets of information for *both* businesses, and then decide which to use for sections B and D later.

For both businesses (Sections A and D):

- What is the name of the business?
- What is the size and scale of the business (e.g. number of employees/number of customers/whether customers are local, national or international)?
- Who owns it (e.g. is it in the public or private sector, is it a private or public limited company)?
- How does the ownership link to the size and scale of the business?
- In which industrial sector does the business operate?
- Is this sector increasing or decreasing?
- What types of activities are carried out by the business?
- Has the business changed in size or changed its activities over the last few years? If so, why?
- Does the business expect to change in size in the near future?
- What is the main aim of the business?
- What are the main objectives of the business to meet these aims?
- Where is the business situated?
- How long has it been located there?
- What was the reason for the original location, and has this changed at any time?
- Has the business ever relocated, and if so, why?
- What factors could cause the business to relocate in the future?
- Who are the main competitors?
- How does the business ensure it competes successfully?
- What actions could competitors take which would seriously affect the business?
- If this happened, what would the business do, and why?
- Does the business have any aims or objectives related to the environment?
- What environmental policies are there?
- How does the business make sure it operates within environmental laws?
- Who in the business is responsible for keeping up to date with environmental laws?
- Are there any new environmental laws which the business will have to consider? If so, what changes might it make?
- Are there any other environmental considerations the business will have to take into account in future? If so, what will it do?

For one business (Sections B and C):

- What functional areas are there?
- What type of work does each one carry out?
- How do the functional areas work together to support the main activity?
- Which functional area(s) are responsible for achieving the different aims and objectives of the business?
- Are there any improvements you would like to see in the way the functional areas work together?
- What oral methods of communication are used in the business?
- What written methods of communication are used in the business?
- How is ICT used to enhance the choice of communications?
- In what other ways is ICT used in the business?
- Which communication methods are mainly used within functional areas?
- Which communication methods are mainly used between functional areas?
- Which communication methods are mainly used for external people and organisations?
- How effective do you think communications are in all these areas?
- How do you think communications could be improved, both internally and externally?

Help and guidance

Your tutor will give you help and guidance when you are collecting your evidence and writing about the business. In particular, make sure that:

- your tutor fully approves of your choice of business(es)
- your tutor knows how you intend to obtain your information
- you see your tutor regularly to discuss the information you have obtained and how you intend to use it
- you keep to any deadlines for the submission of work. You may find you are given different deadlines for completing different sections of your portfolio work.

The last point is very important. Your tutor will want to see your work and make suggestions on how you can improve your evidence. You then need time to amend your work to take account of these comments.

Remember, there will be a fixed deadline for the completion of all your evidence for this Unit, so your tutor will have scheduled specific dates to allow time for all this. If you miss your deadlines and end up in a rush, there is less time to improve your evidence and obtain the best mark you can.

Action plan

1. Check you understand *exactly* what information you need (see pages 138–140).
2. Check the deadlines for obtaining each type of information and writing about it.
3. Agree with your tutor which businesses you are going to investigate and how you will contact them.
4. Start to collect the information.
5. Organise the information neatly, into clearly labelled folders:
   - so that you can always find what you need
   - so that any information you include in your portfolio is in perfect condition!
6. Based on the information, start to produce the evidence required. Make sure that any copied information you refer to is acknowledged properly (see below).
7. Submit your evidence to your tutor for comments. Make sure this is in the requested format, e.g. if you have been asked to word process it, make sure this is how you do it!
8. Revise your work after receiving comments. If there are any you do not understand, talk to your tutor about them.
9. You are likely to find it much easier if you complete each section of your portfolio before starting the next. However, you may wish to refer to the same information in more than one section.
10. You may also have to keep a record which 'tracks' the work you have completed against the scheme, or your tutor may do this on your behalf. If this is your responsibility, your tutor will give you guidance on how to do it.
11. When you have completed all the sections to the best of your ability, file them neatly into a folder, in the correct order.
12. If you are including printed company information in the folder, put this at the back, as an appendix. It is sensible to give each piece of information its own number, e.g. appendix 1, 2, and so on. You can then refer to these throughout your evidence.

Referring to sources

You may find information in a company brochure, in a newspaper, on a web page or in a book, such as this one, which you find useful. If you decide to *copy* this information, you must quote your source.

If your source is a newspaper or magazine, state the title and date. If you have used a book, give the title and author. If you visited a business, state the name of the organisation, the date you got the information and the name and position of the person you spoke to.

The simplest way is to list this information *at the end* of your portfolio on a sheet headed 'References'. However, you will find this much easier if you are neat and methodical and make out the list as you go! Trying to find and complete all your references at the end is much, much harder!

Hints and tips

Creating a portfolio can be a daunting task, but very satisfying. It depends how you approach it!

- It is easy to be overwhelmed at first. Take each section a step at a time and this will help to give you confidence.
- Be organised! Decide what you need to find out, then do it! Use the business investigation questions checklist on page 143 to help you.
- Collect all your information on one section, sort through it and decide what is relevant *before* you start to write anything.
- Don't get distracted with irrelevant information. Stay focused. It is harder to sort through 30 pages than ten! If you access the Internet, try to print out only the information which is useful. If you have a problem deciding what is relevant and what is not, discuss this with your tutor.
- *Think* about what you are going to write. Remember that you must cover the areas on pages 138–140. If you write two paragraphs about how helpful the security staff were when you arrived, while this might be interesting you won't get any marks for it!
- When writing about two businesses and describing different features, you may find it easier to describe one business first, and then the second. Then you can start to expand your answer to cover any comparisons you need to make.
- Use headings and bullet points (as in this book) so your comments are easy to read.
- Include graphics where you can, such as tables, charts and diagrams, if these will help you to explain something more easily.

- Don't confuse quantity with quality. Writing two or three pages which state the key points clearly is better than writing six pages which miss the point, repeat information or contain irrelevant details.

Over to you!

You can make a start on your evidence collecting as soon as you have decided on *one* business you are investigating.

Go through the business investigation questions checklist above and talk to your tutor about any questions you don't understand. Think about any questions you could add and discuss these with your tutor.

Now mark each item **A** or **B**. Items marked **A** are those you have to find out from someone at the business. Items marked **B** are those you can start researching now.

Make a list of ways in which you could find out this information, such as in your school or college library or on the Internet. Remember, the better the 'picture' in your head about the business you are investigating and the current trends which are affecting that business, the more you will impress the person you will be talking to – and the more you will understand what you are being told!

Special note

Readers of this book have the unique opportunity to use Richer Sounds, a national retailer of audio separates and related equipment, for one of their business investigations. Information about Richer Sounds is given on the StudentZone on the Richer Sounds website at www.richersounds.com – you will need the following password to access this zone: RICHERLEARNING. The StudentZone has been designed especially to help you.

Unit 2: People and business

Introduction to Unit 2

No business can operate without people. Two important groups are employees and customers, and while the smallest businesses may have only one or two employees, they will normally want to attract as many customers as possible.

This unit looks at how businesses try to attract and keep customers through good customer service. It deals with the main laws which protect consumers.

However, offering excellent customer service does not simply mean operating within the law. It means understanding the customer, asking the customer's opinion and responding to the answers. You will learn how businesses do this and how they can use IT to help them.

Businesses also want to attract and retain good staff for the various types of jobs which must be undertaken in the organisation. You will learn about the different types of jobs people do and the various working arrangements which exist. Again, the law protects both employees and employers and the unit looks at your legal rights and responsibilities as an employee. You will also find out about the rights and responsibilities of your employer. Good employers don't just want to fulfil their legal responsibilities, they also want to encourage staff to develop their skills and abilities. This has benefits for everyone. This unit will give you information on all aspects of recruitment and training – from applying for a job and attending an interview to understanding the different types of training you may be able to undertake.

Other people have interests in business organisations, besides employees and customers. Collectively, this group is known as stakeholders. This unit starts by introducing you to the different types of stakeholders and the type of influence they may have on business activities. You will also learn that you are a stakeholder yourself, in many organisations, although you may not think you have much personal influence over their operations!

This unit is all about the people who are essential to the operation and success of business organisations. As a customer, an employee and a stakeholder, therefore, this unit is all about you, too!

What you will learn

- **8** Stakeholders
- **9** Investigating job roles
- **10** Working arrangements
- **11** Rights of employers and employees
- **12** Resolving disagreements
- **13** Recruitment and training
- **14** Personal job applications
- **15** Staff development and training
- **16** Customer service

Chapter 8: Stakeholders

What you will learn
Understanding stakeholder groups

Overview: stakeholders

What is a stakeholder?

A stakeholder is any person or organisation which has an interest in a business. You are a stakeholder in many businesses. As a student, you are a stakeholder in your school or college. As a customer, you are a stakeholder in all the shops and cinemas you visit, or anywhere else where you spend your money as a consumer. If you are a football fan or member of a leisure centre, then you are a stakeholder in the club or centre, too. You are a stakeholder because if any of these businesses closed down or changed in some way, this would affect you.

Students are stakeholders in their school or college

Stakeholders and influence

All stakeholders have some influence on the business, but this can vary hugely. In your school or college, you and your friends may have influence over some decisions which affect you. You may be able to give your views through a student panel or committee. In many colleges and universities there are student union representatives who will put forward the views of students to staff. This is because students are key stakeholders of these organisation and so their collective views are very important.

Whether you are a key stakeholder to other types of organisations will vary. If you and your friends buy sandwiches each day from a local shop – and then suddenly stop – the owner may be concerned at the loss of trade. If you return, you might be asked why you had stopped going there and the owner would be keen to hear your response. You are unlikely to get the same reaction if you suddenly stop buying Coke or changed your mobile phone. This is because you are one out of millions of customers, so your individual action wouldn't be noticed. Only when many customers do the same thing will there be a reaction. For example, some years ago, Coca-Cola changed its formula. People didn't like the new taste and stopped buying the drink. Powerful though Coca-Cola may be, this affected sales so much that the organisation returned to the old formula.

The types of issues which interest stakeholders and the amount of influence they have varies between different groups of stakeholders and different types of businesses. In some cases, stakeholders may hold conflicting views, which can create further problems, as you will see in this chapter.

Fact file

Stakeholders include:

- **customers** – who buy the product or service
- **employees** – including the managers of the business
- **owners and shareholders** – both of whom have invested money in the business
- the **local community** – who are directly affected by the actions and operations of the business
- the **government** – which wants all business to thrive and also act within the law
- **pressure groups** – who represent specific interest groups
- **suppliers** – who rely on the business for orders
- **financiers** – who have provided money to the business.

Some have more power and influence over the business than others.

It makes you think!

You are a stakeholder in your local pharmacy if you go there to buy over-the-counter medicines. In 2001, the Office of Fair Trading ended the practice of pharmaceuticals manufacturers setting the prices of over-the-counter medicines. This allowed supermarkets to sell them at lower prices than those charged by independent pharmacists because the latter cannot buy stocks in bulk at the same low prices and may have higher business overheads per customer.

The National Pharmaceutical Association is worried that many small pharmacies will lose business as a result, leading to their eventual closure. It believes as many as 25 per cent may close in the next few years and people will no longer be able to get the friendly and expert local advice they are used to receiving.

Within your group, decide your answers to the following:

1. Are the type of customers who buy medicine from their local pharmacist different in any way from the customers who buy medicine in supermarkets? To help, identify the occasions when you would prefer to shop locally and other types of people who like to do this.
2. Do you think pharmaceuticals manufacturers prefer to supply their products to a small local shop or a supermarket, or does it not matter to them? Give a reason for your opinion.
3. Look back at the different types of stakeholder and decide which groups are most likely to be:
   a stakeholders in a local pharmacy
   b stakeholders in a supermarket.
4. Of all the stakeholder groups you have identified, which do you think might be the most powerful in each case?
5. Overall, do you think the Office of Fair Trading did the right thing? Give a reason for your opinion.

Compare your ideas with other members of your class and keep your answers safely. Then see if you would reach the same conclusions when you have completed this chapter.

Understanding stakeholder groups

Customers as stakeholders

As you use this book, both you and your tutor are stakeholders in it! So is the publisher. If you and your tutor find it useful, and recommend it, then sales should rise. For that reason, authors and publishers like to produce books which meet the needs of their readers – or stakeholders.

Customers, however, can go by different names and have different interests. Both you and your parents are stakeholders in your school or college. But some of the changes which may worry you, such as a favourite tutor leaving, might not bother them. Parents will be concerned about the facilities and the record of examination success, so all stakeholders are apt to view the business from a personal point of view.

Other examples of customers who are stakeholders include:

- patients at a local hospital, health centre or dental practice
- fans of a local football team
- visitors and tourists in a holiday resort
- members of a group or association – from the Venture Scouts to the local library.

Unless a customer knows the owner personally or the business is very small, it is the collective views of customers which influence business activities. For that reason many organisations try to find out the views of their customers (see pages 276–277). Interactions between customers and business can vary, depending upon the business, activity, the size of the business, and its attitude to individual customers.

Issues which usually concern customers include:

- the opening hours and availability of staff
- the range of goods or services offered, the price of these and the quality, and the range of additional facilities and services such as free home delivery
- the attitude of staff
- the overall efficiency of the organisation, e.g. speed of service, staff expertise
- the overall performance of the organisation.

Employees as stakeholders

As an employee, your interest in a business will be different from that of the customer. You are most likely to be concerned about the following:

- The way staff are treated, e.g. you will want to be treated fairly and to do interesting work. You will also want to work in a safe environment with an appropriate range of facilities.
- Rates of pay – and how often pay rises are awarded. You will want to be paid a fair rate in relation to other people of your own age, with the same qualifications and experience, who are doing the same type of job as you, and to receive sick pay and holiday pay.
- Job security. If the business is doing well, there are likely to be promotion opportunities. Where a business is performing poorly, there may be the threat of redundancy.

Managers' interests in the business are much the same as employees'. In addition, they like the opportunity to make decisions, to prove that they can do the job well and to be given responsibility – just like other good employees!

The influence employees have varies from one business to another. If there is a recognised trade union, then there is likely to be more formal discussion between trade union officials, representing the employees, and management. The business will take into account the views of employees where appropriate. Some organisations are non-unionised; instead, there may be a staff committee or association which raises employee concerns with management. The most important point is that the business is aware of the importance of employees as stakeholders and listens to their views. This makes employees feel more valued even if individual suggestions and ideas cannot be implemented.

Over to you!

Suggestion schemes are one way of obtaining both customer and employee views. Within your group, decide on answers to the following:

1. As a student at your school or college, how do you make your views known? Is there a formal way to do this, or is it mainly informal, through your tutor? (Note that neither way is wrong, providing it works!)
   If you had to make *one* suggestion to your tutor, what would it be? How representative is your view among your group or class? How do you react if you are told that, while your idea is quite good, there are problems implementing it? Would you feel happier if you knew what these are?
2. Find out how your tutor can influence your school or college as an employee. This may be through staff meetings, informally in discussion with managers or as a member of a trade union. Find out the type of issues which would be raised at each type of event and how these differ.

Owners and shareholders as stakeholders

If you have already studied Unit 1, you will know that some businesses are very small, such as your local newsagent, and may be run by one person. Other businesses are very large, such as Virgin and Tesco. They have several hundred thousand shareholders. A smaller, private company will have far fewer shareholders. Shareholders are the owners of the business.

Owners and shareholders have a common interest. They have each invested money in the business. If it is successful, they will make more money. If it is not, they will lose money.

Shareholders hope to make money in two ways. If the business does well, then the value of their shares increases. They could then sell their shares, and take a profit, or keep them and hope they would increase further. The danger is that the shares could fall in value, in which case the shareholders would lose money.

Shareholders also expect the company to pay a dividend (usually a few pence per share) twice a year. This is their reward for investing in the company (owning shares), rather like interest on a savings account. The amount of dividend paid per share will vary each time depending upon the company's profits and its financial commitments. A company's directors may decide to pay no dividend or only a very small dividend, for example if they wished to use the money to expand the business. In this example, the interests of shareholders and the company's directors are likely to conflict.

Individual shareholders' power to influence a company's decision depends upon two things:

- How much money the shareholder has invested. All shareholders have one vote for each share. Small investors may own only a few shares in a company, so their influence on the company is small. Large institutional shareholders such as a pension fund or insurance company may hold several hundred thousand shares, and they can use their votes to influence the way a company is run (see below).
- The number and views of other shareholders. A private company may have only family members and a few employees as shareholders. At a shareholders' meeting, all the views are likely to be heard and discussed. The voting may be more evenly balanced and all the shareholders may agree with a decision. However, if they don't, those with the most shares can still outvote the others!

All shareholders are invited to attend the annual general meeting (AGM) of the company. Sometimes these meetings run very smoothly, at other times there can be arguments or disputes. The directors and managers are aware, however, that if many shareholders are dissatisfied with the company's performance or the management's decisions, they can decide to sell their shares. If many shareholders sell at the same time, the value of the shares will fall. (This is another version of the consequences of demand and supply that was discussed in Unit 1, page 125.)

When the value of shares falls, the overall value of the company is less. Another organisation may try to buy the company and the remaining shareholders might agree with this and the current directors could even lose their jobs. Shareholders can also vote some, or even all, the current executives off the board of the company. This makes large shareholders very powerful and extremely influential as stakeholders!

Snapshot

Double the interest!

Many employees are also shareholders in their organisations. This makes them stakeholders twice over! However, the interests of employee shareholders may be different from those of other investors. In Germany, employees of the electronics company Siemens own 10 per cent of the company's shares. In January 2002, the shareholders' association said that no employees would take part in a vote of confidence in the company's management at the next AGM because of 16,000 job cuts made in 2001. The employees felt that the management could have responded more quickly to company problems and that the cuts could have been avoided.

The local community as a stakeholder

The local community has an interest in many of the business activities taking place in an area. For example, residents of a large housing estate might welcome a supermarket opening on the edge of their estate but be concerned about the number of lorries making late deliveries to the store.

Local people may also be concerned about business activities and operations that could result in damage to the local environment such as the building of housing on green-field sites. Some residents might worry that some business activities will reduce the value of their property.

Some issues that concern communities and which they might object to include:

- the building of ring roads and motorways which would damage the environment and might result in increased traffic in residential areas
- air-borne pollution from factories, chemical sites and nuclear processing plants – and fears about long-term health and safety
- the building of prisons or remand centres in semi-residential areas – because of the fear of escapes.

Some people feel strongly enough about these issues to take direct action. Some chain themselves to trees and form barricades to stop developers building new motorways, ring roads or airport extensions which would destroy countryside and turn it into concrete. Most people don't act in such a radical way, but they can object in other ways. If a local community disagrees with a decision made by the government, the council or a local business it has several options:

- If the business depends on local trade, then the community, as customers, can boycott the company.

Campaigners protest against night flights and plans to build a new runway at Heathrow Airport

- The community can make its views known to local and national media and hope that the publicity will make the company back down.
- The community can get in touch with other groups of stakeholders who would be sympathetic to their cause.
- The community can lobby their local councillors and MP.
- The community can lodge a formal appeal against the decision. This is the most likely course of action if a community objects to a proposed business plan. If the appeal is complex, a special hearing or inquiry may take place. At the end of the investigation, the inspector in charge makes a decision and submits this to the Secretary of State for the Environment. Normally, the inspector's decision is accepted, although the Secretary of State does have the power to overrule it.

Snapshot

For better or for worse?

Greenham Common, Berkshire, came to fame in the 1980s when a group of women, concerned about the stationing of cruise missiles at the US airbase there, set up a protest camp. Since 1992, when the Ministry of Defence declared the airbase redundant, the hangars and main buildings have been developed into a business park and the runways have been demolished.

However, a new group of protesters is set to blockade Greenham Common after finding out that Sainsbury's want to build a 79-foot high warehouse there. They argue that this will ruin the view from the surrounding countryside as well as increasing traffic on local roads with hundreds of articulated lorries thundering past.

Sainsbury's plans to operate day and night have also annoyed residents because the area would be illuminated with artificial lights all night.

Some radical protesters are talking about blocking the site with cars and agricultural machinery. Others have written to West Berkshire council. They are arguing that use of the site as a business park for light industry does not mean that the council should agree to the building of a huge warehouse.

Sainsbury's, however, argues that the warehouse will create 750 jobs in the area, it will not generate huge amounts of traffic and night lights will be shielded. It has also promised to landscape the site to enhance the area.

Spot check

Write down your answers to the following questions:

1. Who, or what, is a 'stakeholder' in business?
2. Explain why, as a customer, you might have more influence on some businesses than others.
3. Stakeholder groups often have different interests. Identify two types of interests you would have as:
   a   a customer
   b   an employee
   c   a member of your local community.
4. What is the main interest of owners and shareholders as stakeholders?
5. Give an example of an occasion on which the interests of shareholders and the company's directors might conflict.
6. Re-read the snapshot about Sainsbury's proposed development at Greenham Common. Do you think that any local people might welcome the plans? If so, state why they might be in favour.

The government as a stakeholder

In Unit 1, you learned that the government's policy is to have a strong UK economy. This is possible only if British business does well. The government is therefore a stakeholder in every type of business – from the very largest, exporting goods all over the world, to the smallest which provides employment for local people.

Governments are also interested in business for political reasons. All governments want to retain power and aim to be re-elected. So how can businesses help governments to stay in power?

Quite simply, if the economy is healthy, then the government receives more money. Businesses pay tax on their profits so the higher their profits, the more money the government receives. People pay tax on their earnings so the more people who are employed, the more taxes that are paid, and the government will be able to spend less on benefits to those out of work.

A government which is receiving a large amount in revenues has the scope to do more. It can spend money on new hospitals, schools and transport, which will please voters. It may even be able to lower taxes, which may please them even more. But if business is doing badly, many people are unemployed and taxes are going up, then the electorate may vote another party into power at the next general election in the hope that it will do better.

However, the government is aware that without any laws or regulations some undesirable business activities may take place. Smaller businesses would be at the mercy of large, powerful enterprises. Consumers' rights may be ignored. Dangerous products may be offered for sale. People may be cheated on price. Some executives may embezzle money or defraud the company. Employees may be treated badly. This is why legislation is needed to control the way businesses are run. The government therefore has a significant influence on businesses as it can make an activity unlawful (illegal) and therefore effectively control business operations. The government also monitors operations through watchdog bodies such as Ofcom and Ofgas, and sets standards, for example trading standards, safety standards and environmental standards, which all businesses should follow.

Building new hospitals pleases voters

Governments also want to encourage businesses as well as regulate some of their activities. They therefore introduce supportive measures, such as regional aid programmes, and protective measures. Competition legislation, for instance, protects smaller businesses as well as consumers by making it an offence for large businesses to join together to set prices (see page 113). Health and safety legislation protects employees and also gives employers legal protection against unsafe actions by workers. Employment legislation protects employees and employers by giving both parties specific rights and responsibilities.

The government also promotes business abroad – at trade fairs and British weeks – to help exporters. It tries to encourage overseas businesses and governments to deal with Britain and invest their money here. It offers incentives to multinational companies to open manufacturing plants and branches in the UK and publishes a large amount of information and statistics which are useful to businesses.

Over to you!

Explore some of the information provided by the government. Agree with your tutor whether you should undertake each of these activities yourself, or share them out as a group and then compare your findings. Links to the websites mentioned are provided at www.heinemann.co.uk/hotlinks.

1. Visit the DTI website and use the site map to see a summary of all the different types of information provided by the DTI. Find out about Business Support, that is the help the government gives to small and new businesses, to businesses which want to expand and to businesses which are concerned about their environmental responsibilities.

2. Look at the Trade Partners website and assume you are a UK carpet manufacturer who wants to sell your carpets abroad. Find out about the help Trade Partners can give you and the contacts on the site.

3. Access Invest UK and assume you are a Japanese motor manufacturer thinking of opening a European factory. Find out more about Britain (particularly your own region) and whether you should invest here. (You can also click on student information to obtain more guidance.)

4. Visit the Online for Business website and find out what the government is doing to encourage British businesses to develop e-commerce opportunities. Additional information is also available at the DTI website.

Many of these websites provide information on specific industrial sectors. On the DTI site these are listed under 'Help for particular industries'; at the Trade Partners site you can find out about companies which are already UK exporters and at Invest UK there is a summary of different industrial sectors in the UK. All the sites provide valuable information when you are researching an industry as part of your portfolio work for Unit 1.

Pressure groups as stakeholders

A pressure group is an organised group of people which aims to influence more powerful bodies such as the government, local authorities or large businesses. Some of these groups are very large, and operate internationally on a permanent basis, have millions of supporters and champion a particular cause. Others are much smaller and may be formed for a particular purpose and then be disbanded.

There are thousands of pressure groups in Britain including:

- trade unions and the TUC which lobby the government about the causes of workers, e.g. the National Union of Students (NUS) campaigns on student rights and issues
- most charities, e.g. Amnesty International, Shelter and the NSPCC
- many famous environmental groups, e.g. Greenpeace, Friends of the Earth and the World Fund for Nature
- business, trade and professional associations – the largest is the Confederation of British Industry (CBI) which represents 200,000 businesses; others represent specific trades or professions, such as the Society of Motor Manufacturers and Traders and the British Medical Association
- local groups, such as Residents Associations, which campaign about issues in their own neighbourhood.

The aim of a pressure group is to influence powerful decision makers. Many are very successful, for example environmental issues taken up by the European Union and the British government were originally highlighted by environmental pressure groups. Pressure groups enable groups with a common interest to make their views known. On many occasions, this has prevented powerful organisations making decisions which would be against the interests of many individuals.

How do pressure groups become stakeholders in business? The interests of a specific pressure group will depend upon who it represents.

- Pressure groups such as the CBI and trade associations represent the views of business to the government and will argue in the interests of business organisations.
- The TUC and trade unions represent the views of employees and campaign on issues such as health and safety, employment rights and working hours.
- Some charities actively campaign about business issues such as Parents at Work (see below). Other charities depend upon business sponsorship and support to help them to promote their causes. For example, international telecommunications giant – Cable & Wireless – combined with children's Internet charity Childnet International to run the C&W Childnet Awards, an international awards programme which rewards children and those working with them who are developing outstanding Internet projects that benefit other children. See www.heinemann.co.uk/hotlinks
- Environmental groups may campaign against the plans or actions of big businesses. Many oil companies, such as Shell and BP, have had to improve their environmental and human rights records following bad publicity when pressure groups highlighted their activities.

Identify each of these pressure groups. Check their websites to find out about their campaigns

Snapshot

Rights for parents!

Parents at Work is a charity group which lobbies to improve working life for parents. It also gives awards to Britain's best employers and bosses nominated by parents. Its chief executive, Sue Monk, was a member of the Work and Parents Taskforce, set up by the government to see if parents' needs for more flexible working patterns could be achieved without losing business efficiency.

Other members of this taskforce included representatives from the TUC, CBI, business organisations and the Equal Opportunities Commission (EOC). One result was legislation to be introduced in 2003 which gives employees the right to make a written request for flexible working. The request could be refused but the employer then has to give 'clear business reasons' in writing. The employee could appeal against the refusal.

This legislation could benefit the 3.8 million working parents with children under the age of 6. In addition, parents with disabled children under 18 can also apply.

The CBI was concerned that small businesses with only a few staff may struggle to agree flexible working without losing their efficiency or adding to their costs. They argued for businesses to be able to refuse a request on business grounds and won this concession.

You can find out more at www.heinemann.co.uk/hotlinks

Suppliers as stakeholders

You already know that without customers a business cannot survive. Imagine you produced ready meals which you sold to Tesco or Asda. These stores would then be *your* customers – and you would be one of their suppliers. You would obviously have a key interest in these businesses. You would want them to do well and to keep buying from you, preferably in greater quantities every year.

This is why suppliers are stakeholders in all the businesses to whom they sell their goods and services. To be successful themselves, they need to keep receiving orders from buyers.

But what if a major customer said it wasn't buying from you any more? Could you influence its decision? Or what if it suddenly said you must reduce your prices to get further orders? Could it insist or could you argue and still keep the business? This would all depend upon whether you were a powerful supplier.

When are suppliers likely to have more power?

- If there are few other companies supplying the same item or no substitutes for it. Many companies have argued that Microsoft's plans to levy additional charges for upgrading software across networks will affect them badly. However, they have little alternative but to accept, given that Microsoft is the major supplier of computer operating systems and software.
- If it has many customers and the company threatening to change its supplier or demanding lower prices places only small orders.

When are suppliers likely to have far less power?

- If there are only a few buyers for their product or service, e.g. suppliers of specialist equipment with only a small market.
- If there are many suppliers of the same product or service and the market is highly competitive. In this case, the buyer can 'shop around' and change supplier easily.
- If the buyer is very large and powerful and the customer is heavily dependent on its orders to continue in business. Suppliers can have serious problems if they are too dependent upon a few large buyers, for the loss of any one of these can have disastrous consequences. For this reason, suppliers will try to have a range of buyers so that the loss of one is less important.

Some suppliers dislike being dependent on business buyers so they extend their operations to sell direct to the final consumer; for example, many breweries own their own pubs and restaurants and petrol companies have their own petrol stations.

Equally, some business buyers don't like being dependent on suppliers. In this case, they may decide to produce their own supplies, for example a cider producer with its own apple orchards.

Financiers as stakeholders

In Unit 3, you will learn about the different ways in which businesses obtain finance. They may need money to start up or to expand at a later date. Finance can consist of:

- grants – which do not have to be repaid
- loans – which must be repaid.

A person or organisation which puts money into a business is called a financier. If a grant has been provided, there will be checks to ensure the money is used as agreed. If the financier has provided a loan, the business must honour its repayment commitments. In addition, some organisations will provide finance only in return for shares in the company or for some other influence on how the company is run. In all these cases, the investment gives the financier a key interest – or stakeholding – in the business.

Financiers can include the following:

- The government – which finances public sector organisations, including schools, hospitals and local authorities. All these organisations have to produce accounts and have these audited (checked

Case study

The cost of a pint

In 2002, members of the Farmers for Action (FFA) group threatened to blockade Tesco's distribution depots. The FFA claimed that Tesco was forcing down milk prices to unacceptable levels and that the supermarket chain was refusing to listen to the farmers. It argued that a litre of milk cost 22.5p to produce but Tesco, which was buying it for 20p, wanted the price to be 18p.

In reply, Tesco said that it bought its milk from the processors, not from the farmers, so the price had nothing to do with them. Others disagreed with this, commenting that Tesco is such a powerful buyer that it can dictate prices to its suppliers and virtually hold them to ransom. They also claimed that cheap milk sold by supermarkets is threatening the livelihoods of many in the industry, including farmers, dairies and milk delivery people. In reality, many people realise the supermarket chains could be putting local butchers, fishmongers and milk delivery people out of business, but still want the convenience of supermarket shopping and low prices.

One of the leading voices of the FFA, David Handley, was one of the organisers of the fuel protests in autumn 2000, when petrol supplies were blocked at refineries. This was in protest at government tax increases which raised fuel costs and, at the time, virtually brought Britain's roads to a standstill. David Handley is quite willing to blockade the milk processors as well as Tesco, though he knows this type of action is illegal.

The government is talking about creating a 'prices watchdog' to monitor prices and relations between farmers and supermarkets (not just on milk, but on meat and vegetables, too). Supermarket chiefs are furious about the proposal. They argue that their price-competitive policies have produced major benefits for customers, who will be the ones to be inconvenienced if supplies are blocked. After all, it was ordinary individuals who were mainly affected by fuel shortages in 2000, though people like David Handley would say this was necessary to achieve their aims.

▶ 1 Both Tesco's customers and employees are stakeholders in the company. For each of these groups, identify one major interest they have in the company.
2 What type of group is the FFA?
3 Who does the FFA represent?
4 Why does the FFA have an interest in Tesco?
5 Why do Tesco's suppliers have an interest in Tesco?
6 Are Tesco's suppliers powerful or not? Give a reason for your answer.
7 If you were a Tesco shareholder, how would you want the company to perform? Give a reason for your answer.
8 Identify one conflict of interest between different stakeholder groups in the Tesco dispute.

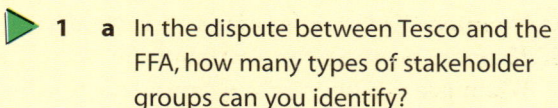

▶ 1 a In the dispute between Tesco and the FFA, how many types of stakeholder groups can you identify?
   b For each of the stakeholder groups you identified above, state a major area of interest.
2 Give two reasons why Tesco is considered to be a powerful buyer.
3 Explain who the FFA represents, and why it is in dispute with Tesco.
4 If Tesco distribution depots are blockaded, which stakeholders would be inconvenienced?
5 Tesco's directors and the government are also in conflict. Explain why the government is interested in Tesco and why Tesco's directors disagree with the government.
6 How do you think Tesco's shareholders might feel about the dispute? Give a reason for your answer.
7 Evaluate the extent to which the interests of the different stakeholder groups influence their individual views and contribute to the conflict.

thoroughly) to make sure they are correct. This is to prevent misuse of any finance provided by the government.
- Local authorities and the European Union – which offer a wide range of grant and loan schemes (see Unit 1, page 32). Again, strict checks are kept on any business which receives money from these sources. The Prince's Trust and Shell LiveWIRE provide grants and loans to young people wanting to set up in business. Applications are scrutinised and the businesses which receive money monitored.
- Financial institutions – such as commercial banks and investment banks. Banks will want to study the business plan before they agree to lend any money and will also want copies of recent accounts. They will expect to receive regular repayments for loans and will take an active interest if there are any business problems which could affect this.
- Venture capital companies – which offer finance in return for shares in the business, e.g. 3i. Venture capitalists aim to invest in growing companies with good prospects. They may offer additional support and often expect to have a seat on the company's board of directors.
- A **business angel** – a private individual who wants to invest in a growth business. The business angel may also provide help and advice, will obviously want a return on the money invested and is likely to want a percentage of the ownership of the business.

All public limited companies have a credit or investment rating. The better this rating, the easier it is for them to borrow money. The rating is based on their past history and current financial performance. If business is poor, their rating may be changed and this can affect their ability to borrow money.

Financiers can be very powerful stakeholders. Banks can 'foreclose' on a company which is defaulting on loan repayments and make it sell everything to repay the money. This means it has to go into liquidation and close down. Very large organisations can also be put under pressure by financiers. The threat of calling in a large loan or refusing to extend a loan can cause the share price to fall dramatically. In some cases, powerful financiers, such as venture capitalists, have insisted on major changes at the company, such as a complete change of management, if there are problems.

Shell LiveWIRE help young people to set up in business by providing grants and loans

What can go wrong?

Businesses can have problems with stakeholders who hold strong views and attract media attention. This results in bad publicity for the organisation. In some cases, businesses may be tempted to give in to the demands of the most powerful groups and ignore those who hold conflicting views, simply because this is easiest. On other occasions it is just impossible to please everyone.

Stakeholders can have problems if they are dealing with an organisation which ignores their demands or requests, or if their views are in a minority.

Snapshot

The dot.com fiasco

Many financiers had their fingers badly burned when the dot.com bubble burst. They invested in new dot.com start-ups, hoping to make money quickly. Unfortunately, many of the dot.com entrepreneurs, such as boo.com, had very shaky business plans and the young managers had no experience of running a company. Equally, many financiers had little knowledge of the Internet and invested without enough guarantees. The consequence was too many dot.coms forming too quickly, and many went out of business, with the financiers losing their money. Today, financiers are much more cautious about investing in Internet-based companies and insist on more careful checks on future prospects and profitability.

Shareholders are, of course, another type of financier (see page 152–3) with a stakeholding in business. Even when the relatively successful dot.com company Lastminute.com floated on the London Stock Exchange, many shareholders lost money when the price of the shares fell from its original launch price of £3.80 each to less than £2 in the first month of trading.

Chapter review and practice questions

1. Your friend's parents have recently bought a Chinese takeaway business. It is situated in a row of shops on a small estate. They used their savings so did not need to borrow any money. They employ one person to help them at weekends.
   a. Identify **four** stakeholder groups in their business.
   b. Out of the groups you have identified, which do you think is the most important – and why?

2. a. What is a pressure group?
   b. Give two examples of pressure groups.
   c. Give one reason why a pressure group may be a stakeholder in a business organisation.

3. Your brother works for a software company which is based 40 miles from his home. He doesn't drive and has a rail season ticket from his local train company, Connex. Sometimes he stays overnight near the business in a small hotel. Because he is a regular customer, he is good friends with the owners.
   a. State three business organisations in which your brother is a stakeholder.
   b. Identify your brother's main interests in all these organisations.
   c. In which organisation will your brother have the most influence? Give a reason for your choice.
   d. Connex supplies your brother's travel. Would you say it is a powerful supplier? Give a reason for your opinion.
   e. If Connex was losing money, which stakeholder groups would be most concerned?
   f. If Connex responded to the problem by raising its prices, which stakeholder group would now be affected?

1. Some stakeholders are more powerful than others.
   a. Why does this difference occur?
   b. Give an example of a stakeholder with a great deal of influence in business, and give a reason for your choice.
   c. Give an example of a stakeholder with little influence, and explain your choice.

2. a. Give an example of two situations where stakeholders may have competing interests.
   b. Suggest how a business may respond to one of the situations you have identified.

3. In 2002, the Transport and General Workers Union (TGWU) was campaigning to save jobs at the Goodyear tyre factory in Wolverhampton. The union was worried about possible major job cuts at the factory and was concerned that

its US owners might decide to close it completely. The TGWU argued that Goodyear jobs were not the only ones at stake, but also jobs at smaller firms which rely on the plant. The football club Wolverhampton Wanderers might also be affected as Goodyear is one of its main sponsors.

a What type of group is the TGWU besides being a union?

b Why are smaller businesses stakeholders in Goodyear?

c Who else are stakeholders in Goodyear? Name as many as you can.

d Explain why the aims of the US owners (and financiers) differ from those of the trade unions.

Chapter 9: Investigating job roles

What you will learn

Understanding organisation charts
Understanding job descriptions
Key job roles and their differences

Overview: job roles

Job roles in business

Everyone who works in business has a particular job to do. Each job is likely to differ in several ways:

- the tasks or activities carried out by the job holder
- the level of responsibility and the types of action the job holder can take without specific permission
- the security of the job, that is whether the job holder could lose his or her job at any time or looks forward to being in the same job (or organisation) for several years
- the type of decisions which have to be made and the range of problems which have to be solved
- the skills, qualifications and personal qualities needed by the job holder
- the amount the job holder is paid and any other benefits.

As you probably know, some people are paid more than others. If you have very scarce skills and talents and are very valuable to your organisation, then you might be paid very highly.

In most businesses, people are usually paid in relation to their level in the organisation. The more senior a person, the higher the pay. This is because senior staff have to take difficult decisions which could cost the business dearly if they make a mistake. In effect, they are paid to get it right!

Job levels in business

Jobs can often be categorised in three levels. These are often shown in the shape of a pyramid simply because there are fewer people in the higher roles and more in the lower roles.

Pyramid diagram showing from top to bottom: Owner/Directors, Managers, Supervisors, Operatives or support staff

Job levels in business

However, even within this structure there can be differences. In many organisations, for instance, support staff have their own career structure – from junior to senior administrators – and their job roles and pay may be quite different.

Investigating jobs in business

Jobs are usually clearly defined, so that the tasks undertaken by everyone together cover all the duties and activities which need to be undertaken for the organisation to run smoothly and efficiently.

Fact file

- You can see how jobs fit together and how each job relates to the others by looking at an **organisation chart**. This is a diagram which shows the structure of an organisation.
- In addition, each person's activities and duties will be set out in a **job description**.

Over to you!

Make a list of the staff who work at your school (see below for a college) and their job titles. Keep this safely. You will need this information later to convert it into an organisation chart.

If you are studying at a large college, then find out about the staff who work in the section or department where you are a student. You don't need the names of every person, but you do need to know the different levels, the numbers of staff and their job titles.

Understanding organisation charts

An organisation chart is a diagram which shows the job titles of all the employees and their relationship with each other. Some charts do not include people's names, as these can go out of date very quickly. At the top of the chart are the more senior staff. They have more responsibility than those lower down.

- **Horizontal lines** on the chart show staff who work at the same level as each other.
- **Vertical lines** show the staff for whom a particular manager or supervisor is responsible.

Some organisations have a **flat structure** – there are only two or three levels. This type of organisation usually operates informally as the managers or supervisors will be in constant contact with the other staff. The structure is suitable for small businesses and those which have to react quickly to change; for example, small manufacturing companies, new media and IT businesses, and those businesses where there is a group of skilled operators and a manager such as a high street travel agency.

Other organisations have a **hierarchical structure** – with many levels. If you asked for an organisation chart for your local authority or hospital, you might see six or even seven levels. The same applies in some large manufacturing companies or large service organisations. In this type of structure, you are likely to find more specialists and greater opportunities for promotion. The organisation is likely to operate on a more formal basis. Employees will have to follow specific rules about hours of work, holidays and methods of working to ensure that everyone is treated the same. Staff are likely to be on specific salary scales linked to their job. Some may rarely see a very senior manager as they deal only with the supervisor or manager in their own section or department.

It makes you think!

Below is an organisation chart for Hanley and Barker, a small garage. Look at the chart carefully and answer the questions below.

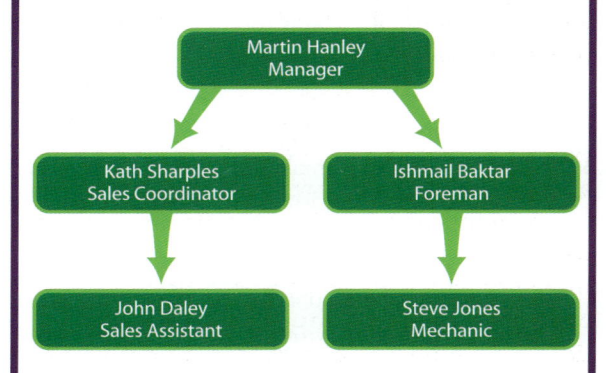

```
         Martin Hanley
            Manager
          /          \
  Kath Sharples    Ishmail Baktar
  Sales Coordinator   Foreman
       |                  |
   John Daley         Steve Jones
  Sales Assistant      Mechanic
```

Hanley and Barker's organisation chart

1. How many people work at Hanley and Barker?
2. Who is in charge?
3. How many levels are there?
4. How many people report directly to Martin Hanley?
5. Sometimes, supervisors have other job titles. Find two people who work at this level and state their job titles.
6. a Operatives can have other job titles. Find two people who work at this level and state their job titles.
   b For each person state the name of his or her line manager.

Check all your answers with your tutor.

Fact file

The term **line manager** is used to describe the person immediately above you and to whom you are responsible. The reason for the term is easy to understand when you see an organisation chart – this person is linked to you by a vertical line.

The number of staff under the supervision of a manager (or supervisor) is called the **span of control**.

Changes and additions to organisation charts

If a company grows or expands, then more staff are employed. This obviously changes the organisation chart.

Each new person, apart from the most senior person, must report to someone. Each person also needs placing at the correct level and linking to other members of staff.

At Hanley and Barker, Martin Hanley decides to recruit two new people: a deputy manager who will report to him and an administrative assistant to do the accounts, deal with enquiries and general paperwork. The administrative assistant will also report to Martin Hanley.

- A deputy manager is shown immediately below the manager on the chart and linked to the higher job by a solid vertical line. This indicates that the deputy could be eligible for promotion to that position if a vacancy occurs.
- Support staff are often shown in a different way on an organisation chart and are linked to their line manager by a dotted line. This is because they 'assist' the manager but are not eligible for his or her job if there is a vacancy.

At Hanley and Barker, the organisation chart now looks like this:

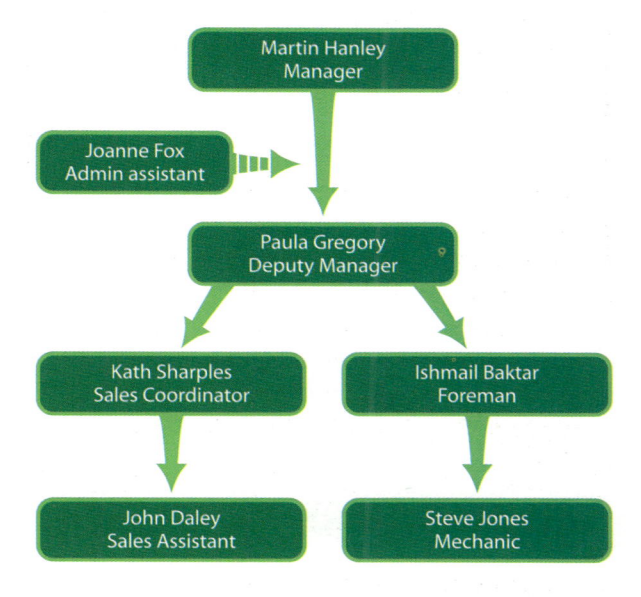

```
                    Martin Hanley
                       Manager
                          │
Joanne Fox ···→           │
Admin assistant           │
                          │
                    Paula Gregory
                    Deputy Manager
                     ┌────┴────┐
                     │         │
              Kath Sharples  Ishmail Baktar
              Sales Coordinator  Foreman
                     │         │
               John Daley   Steve Jones
              Sales Assistant  Mechanic
```

Organisation charts and large companies

Organisation charts may be very complicated. To make things easier, many produce one chart which shows the senior managers and individual charts for sections or departments.

Another way is to show the title of staff employed in a department at a certain level, and putting the number of staff in brackets. If Hanley and Barker was a larger organisation, the number of sales assistants or mechanics could be shown thus:

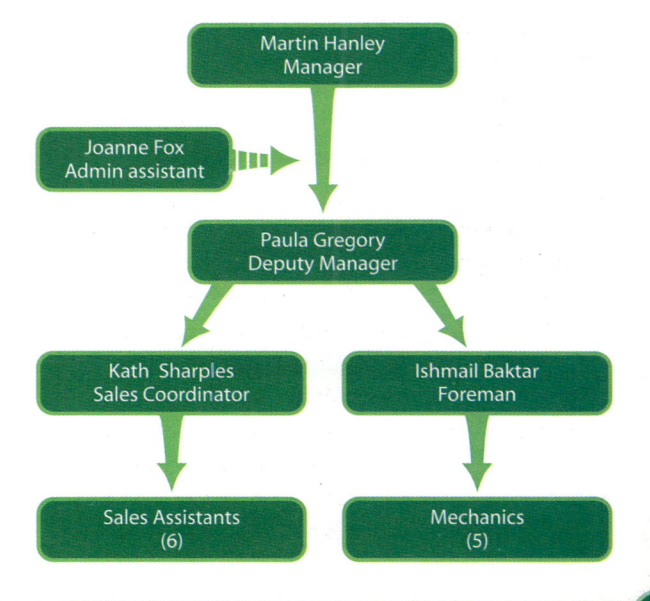

```
                    Martin Hanley
                       Manager
                          │
Joanne Fox ···→           │
Admin assistant           │
                          │
                    Paula Gregory
                    Deputy Manager
                     ┌────┴────┐
                     │         │
              Kath Sharples  Ishmail Baktar
              Sales Coordinator  Foreman
                     │         │
              Sales Assistants  Mechanics
                    (6)          (5)
```

Shapes and styles of organisation charts

The organisation charts shown above are fairly typical, but you need to be aware that charts can be drawn in different ways, particularly in larger businesses, for example:

- 'side on' – where the most senior staff are placed on the left-hand side
- 'staggered' – simply to fit more people on one piece of paper, but this can make it harder to work out different levels.

Hanley and Brown's organisation chart has been redrawn so that it is both side on and staggered. See if you can still follow it!

The value of organisation charts

Advantages – what you can see at a glance

- How the business is organised and the functional areas into which it is divided.
- The job titles within each area – these should suggest the activities which take place and the type of work which is done.
- Levels of staff – the most senior staff, staff at the same level as each other, managers of other staff, subordinates to other staff.
- The size of each function, and how many staff each manager has to supervise.
- The number of levels in the organisation. Although you can draw some conclusions from this (look back to page 164), check how these apply in the organisation you are studying. All businesses are different!

Disadvantages

- The chart may not be up to date.
- It's not possible to tell if there are any informal links between staff, either within or between departments.
- You cannot see how departments or sections communicate with each other. The importance of this was discussed in Unit 1, Chapter 6, but these **lateral links** are never shown on organisation charts.
- It does not reveal whether the company style is formal or informal, whether staff morale is good or if the business is doing well or not. Neither can you tell which member of staff works hardest, who is likely to be promoted next, nor who takes on the most, or the least, responsibility.
- The chart doesn't show which members of staff hold 'power' in specific circumstances. Generally, this type of power is held by specialists and will cover the whole organisation. For instance, the chief executive or managing director would take advice from:
  - health and safety staff on risks, hazards and accident prevention
  - security staff on security alerts and emergencies
  - IT staff on computer security and virus alerts.

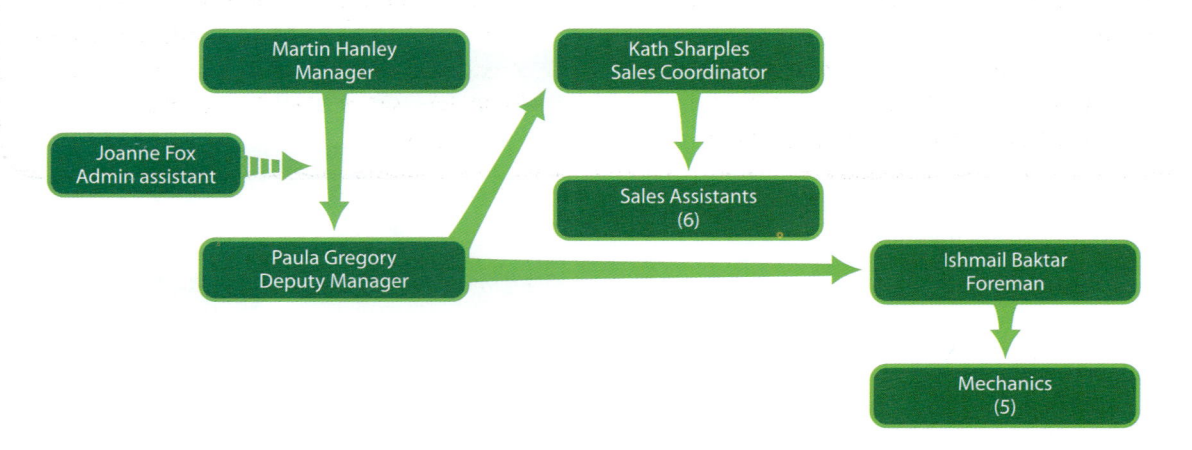

Hanley and Barker's organisation chart from side on and staggered

Snapshot

Titles at the top

A director may not be the highest-ranking person in an organisation. In a company, it may be the managing director or chief executive. Some government departments use the title director general and the head person in the government is, of course, the prime minister. Colleges have principals, schools have head teachers, newspapers have managing editors. It all depends what type of business you are studying. The chairman of an organisation is also important, but less likely to be involved in the day-to-day running of an organisation.

Many industries have specialist job titles for supervisors and staff, too. A publishing company will have publishers and editors, a research firm may have scientific officers, and a new media firm may have project leaders and account managers. These are not 'managers' in the usual sense of the word – they are usually operatives who manage certain client accounts. This term is also frequently used in advertising and marketing companies.

Wherever you work, it is sensible to find out the title and name of the most important person. Also, don't jump to conclusions about people's titles until you understand how the business is structured. Only then can you accurately assess each person's true job role.

Spot check

Write down your answers to the following questions:

1. Identify two differences between job roles.
2. State two different levels of staff you are likely to find in an organisation.
3. What is an organisation chart?
4. Susie Jarvis is the office manager of a small employment agency. There are two employment consultants who report to her. Susie also has an administrative assistant who helps her. Draw a chart to show the structure of this business.
5. Identify two job titles used to describe the most senior person in a business organisation.
6. For each of the following types of organisations briefly explain what the term in bold means:
   a. an organisation with a **flat** structure
   b. an organisation with a **hierarchical** structure.
7. A security supervisor wants the managing director to move her car urgently because of a security problem in the car park. Can he (politely) insist on this? Give a reason for your answer.

It makes you think!

Jennings is a large manufacturing company. The organisation chart is divided into two: one showing the senior managers and the other, the individual departments. You are investigating the human resources department and have been given the two relevant charts. Use these to answer the questions that follow.

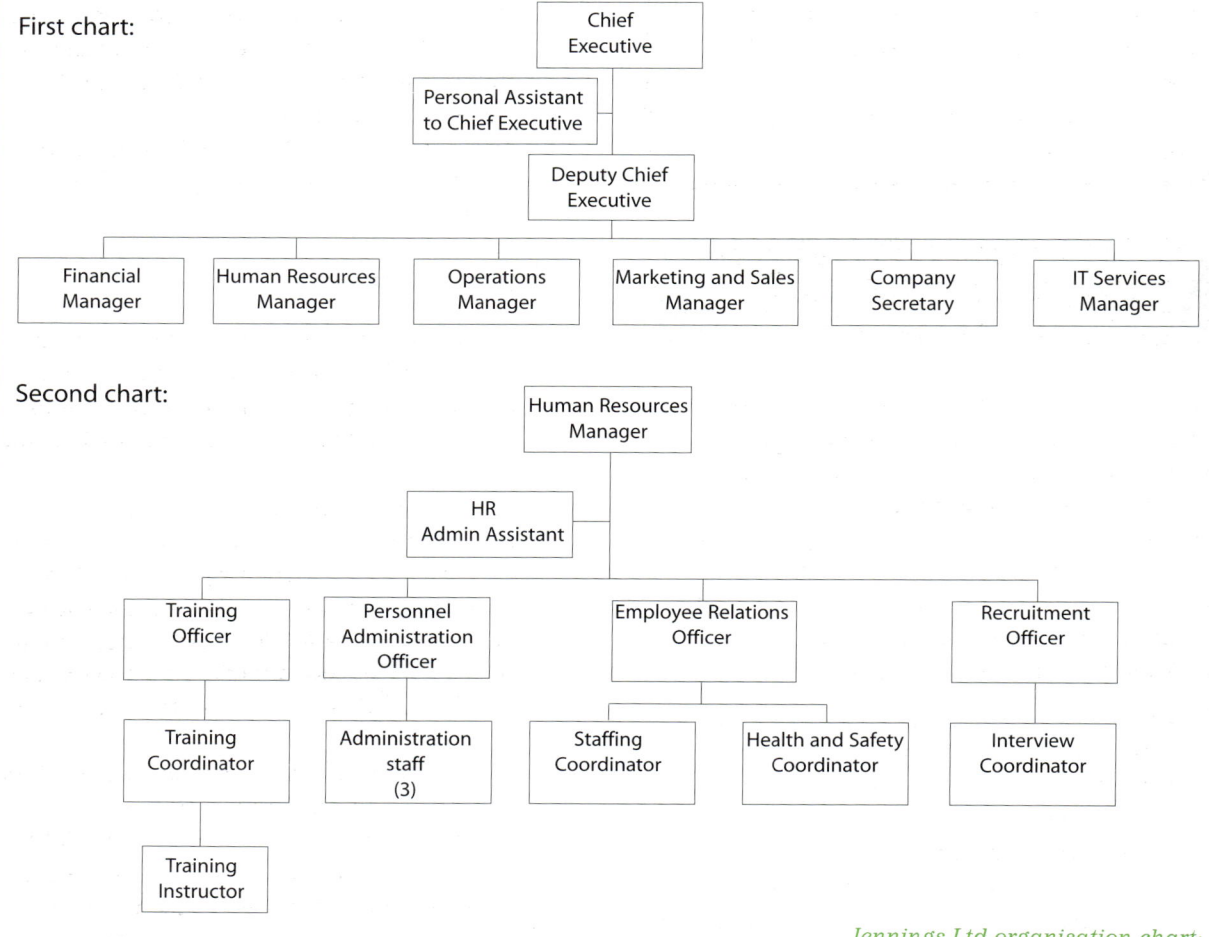

First chart:

- Chief Executive
  - Personal Assistant to Chief Executive
  - Deputy Chief Executive
    - Financial Manager
    - Human Resources Manager
    - Operations Manager
    - Marketing and Sales Manager
    - Company Secretary
    - IT Services Manager

Second chart:

- Human Resources Manager
  - HR Admin Assistant
    - Training Officer
      - Training Coordinator
        - Training Instructor
    - Personnel Administration Officer
      - Administration staff (3)
    - Employee Relations Officer
      - Staffing Coordinator
      - Health and Safety Coordinator
    - Recruitment Officer
      - Interview Coordinator

Jennings Ltd organisation chart: human resources department

1. What is the title of the most senior person in the organisation?
2. Who is in charge when the most senior person is absent?
3. How many people work in the human resources department?
4. a What is the title of the most senior person in the human resources department?
   b Who is this person's line manager?
   c For how many staff is this person directly responsible?
5. How many levels are there:
   a in the human resources department
   b in Jennings as a company?
6. a How many people work at supervisory level in human resources?
   b State one of the titles used.
7. If the training coordinator was absent one day, and the training instructor had a problem, to whom should she go to for advice? Give a reason for your answer.
8. Suggest two aspects about working in the human resources department that the organisation chart cannot tell you.

> **Over to you!**
>
> Start by adding to the information you obtained about your school or college (see page 164) by finding out the level at which each person works and his or her line manager. Then draw an organisation chart to show the structure of your school or college department.
>
> Be prepared to do a draft copy first, and check this with your tutor.

Understanding job descriptions

A job description (sometimes called a **job outline**) summarises all the basic facts about a particular job and/or the role of the job holder. It is often prepared or revised when a vacancy is created and before it is advertised. A copy may be sent to all the applicants. As you will see in Chapter 6, a job description is usually a key part of the recruitment process.

A job description may include:

- the title of the department or section where the job holder will work
- the job title or a summary of the job role
- the normal hours of work
- the salary or salary scale
- the person to whom the job holder is responsible (that is his or her line manager)
- any staff for whom the job holder is responsible, if the job is for a supervisor or manager
- the main duties and responsibilities of the job holder.

The more senior the job role, the more likely it is that the job description will be lengthy and detailed.

The value of job descriptions

Advantages

- Drawing up a job description gives the organisation the opportunity to think carefully about the job role. This helps to ensure the best person is recruited.
- The type of tasks and the level of job can be compared to other jobs in the organisation to ensure that the salary offered is fair.
- If a job description is updated when a job holder leaves, this gives the organisation the opportunity to change duties and responsibilities as necessary.
- Job applicants and job holders can see exactly what they are supposed to be doing.

Disadvantages

- It is almost impossible to list every single type of task or activity a job holder may be asked to carry out. For that reason, most job descriptions include a 'catch all' at the end.
- Unless a job description is written carefully, the list of tasks could be so long it would be overwhelming, so most job descriptions cover only broad tasks and don't go into detail. For this reason, most people undertake a variety of tasks which aren't specifically listed on the job description.
- It is tempting to think that the tasks which take up the most space on a job description will take the longest to do! In fact, the opposite can occur. An employee may spend much of his or her week on one particular type of task, which takes up only two lines of the job description!
- A job description doesn't always accurately indicate the variety of work undertaken by the job holder. Some tasks may be done every day, but others may be done only every week, month or even once a year.
- Some job holders may try to stick grimly to their existing job description even if conditions change. Most contracts of employment prevent this (see page 186) but there can still be a dispute about whether an additional task is a 'reasonable' request or not.

It makes you think!

The human resources manager at Jennings considers that the department needs a receptionist/administrator to cope with all the visitors and telephone calls which are constantly taking up staff time. Below is shown the job description for this person.

1. Work through this job description and check with your tutor any terms or words you do not understand.
2. How varied do you think this job would be? Give a reason for your answer.
3. Your friend's father owns a small grocery store. He wants to employ a new sales assistant to work there three days a week – Wednesday, Friday and Saturday. When you mention what you know about job descriptions, he asks you to write one for him. Within your group, decide the main tasks and activities the sales assistant would carry out. Then draw up the job description. Although he would normally write the hours of work and salary himself, try to guess what these might be. Then check your ideas with your tutor.

JENNINGS LTD – Job Description
Department: Human Resources
Job title: Receptionist/Administrator
Hours of work: 9 am–5.30 pm, Monday to Friday
Salary scale: £9,000–£12,000
Responsible to: Personnel Administration Officer
Responsible for: Not applicable
Job purpose: To provide support for the Human Resources team in dealing with visitors, telephone calls and general enquiries

Duties and responsibilities

1. Receiving and directing callers to the Human Resources Department.
2. Receiving telephone calls, dealing with general enquiries and referring these to the correct person. Taking telephone messages for staff as necessary.
3. Keeping reception area neat and tidy and checking heating and ventilation.
4. Making appointments for staff and visitors.
5. Receiving and recording all requests for application forms, training forms, accident forms, etc.
6. Receiving and recording all self-certification forms from staff and all departmental staff absence notifications.
7. Ensuring an adequate supply of stationery and HR forms are available in the reception area and in relevant offices.
8. Attending any training course that may be considered appropriate by the Personnel Administration Officer.
9. Maintaining staff confidentiality at all times and being aware that breach of this could lead to instant dismissal.
10. Undertake any other relevant duties which may be identified.

This job description is not intended to be fully prescriptive and will be the subject of regular review and possible amendment. The post holder may be required to undertake related tasks which are not specifically mentioned above.

Job description

Key job roles and their differences

You have already seen that there are different levels of staff. Before you start investigating jobs at different levels, you need to understand the type of responsibilities and activities carried out by managers, supervisors, operatives or members of the support team. You also need to understand the other ways in which these jobs are likely to vary, including job security, the decisions or problems that must be faced, the skills and qualifications required and the type of pay and benefits the job holders will receive.

Before reading on, you need to be aware of the following:

- If you are comparing levels of jobs and differences *within* one organisation, then you can expect to make useful comparisons. There should be a clear difference between, say, the responsibilities, activities, skills and experience required or undertaken by staff at different levels. But *do not* try to make comparisons across two different organisations. You cannot, for example, accurately compare the job of a senior manager in a large, multinational company with that of a junior manager in a much smaller business. Their management roles may be very different, as the first has a far more responsible and complex role than the second.
- Whatever investigations you carry out into job roles, *never* ask anyone how much they are paid or what other benefits they receive. There are two ways in which you can investigate comparative pay and benefits:
  - Look in a local or national newspaper to find advertisements for the jobs you are investigating. Be aware that pay rates differ in each locality and for different types of organisations. Your tutor will give you guidance on this for your own area.
  - If you are on work experience, ask a member of the human resources team if you can have a copy of one or two job descriptions. Ask, too, if they would let you have details of typical pay scales. These give the bottom and top rates for a job. A member of the human resources staff should also be able to tell you about typical benefits available to staff, if there are any.

Fact file

If you are investigating the activities of the head or main office of a company, you will find that it has directors. A director may have a seat on the **board of directors** and make policy decisions on behalf of the organisation as a whole. In this situation, directors are senior to managers.

Some organisations have only **managers**. In this case, this is the most senior title. This happens if the head office is elsewhere, if the company is owned by a much larger organisation or if, in a private company, the owners prefer this title.

The job role of managers

As you have seen, managers can vary in several ways:

- There may be different levels of managers within an organisation, such as senior and middle managers. The term 'middle' is used because these managers are in between the senior staff and the supervisors.
- Whereas some managers are in overall charge of the business, others have a line manager themselves. Your local supermarket or bank manager will report to, and receive instructions from, head office. A departmental manager in a large company will report to and receive instructions from his or her own line manager, who may be one of the directors. In contrast, the most senior manager in a small company may be in overall control of the whole business and free to make decisions as he or she chooses.

Key responsibilities and tasks or activities of managers

Most managers are responsible for other people *and* for ensuring that certain tasks are carried out. The 'balance' between people and tasks can vary, depending upon the job role.

One writer, Peter Drucker, described management as 'getting things done through other people'. This sounds like a manager can just order other people to do all the work! In reality, it is far more difficult. Some people will do the work well, others will not. Others may be overloaded and unable to cope. Occasionally, some tasks may require skills no one has, or need to be completed by tight deadlines. It is the manager's job to resolve all these problems, to deliver high-quality work by the target date and still keep all the staff happy and motivated!

The main responsibilities and activities of managers are shown in the chart below.

A manager's job

Key responsibilities	Main tasks or activities
• Running the business or a major department • Controlling operations by balancing the needs of staff with getting jobs done on time and to the required standard • Planning for the future, bearing in mind the needs of stakeholders and possible changes in the industry • Deciding on and operating within a fixed budget • Deciding on and achieving important targets and objectives, such as future sales or expansion targets. These are usually identified in the strategic plan of an organisation • Co-operating with other managers in the organisation over strategic issues and problems • Ensuring that legal requirements are met	• Carrying out the instructions of the line manager (if there is one) • Scheduling and allocating work for own area or department • Deciding/agreeing future plans and targets that will affect own area • Checking that staff are meeting agreed targets and doing their work effectively • Making decisions which relate to the running of own area • Resolving any disagreements in own area and solving day-to-day problems • Keeping line manager (if there is one) informed of developments, progress or problems • Keeping staff informed of non-confidential organisational developments • Carrying out personnel and administrative duties relating to own area, including checking staff training needs and carrying out staff appraisals • Undertaking professional development to keep up to date in own field and in relation to trends and developments in the industry • Liaising with other managers in the organisation about current issues and developments in which they have a joint responsibility

Job security

This depends upon the success of the organisation and the level of manager. In the 1980s and 1990s many businesses 'cut out' middle managers to save money. They decided the organisation could run just as well without them. Since then, this type of thinking has been challenged, but it does highlight that not all managers are secure in their jobs.

Probably the most risky job is that of a football manager! The main thing to remember is that managers need the business to continue to grow and expand if they are to have job security. Otherwise, if business operations contract, they could lose their jobs.

Fact file

Two business terms you may hear are **strategic** and **operational**.

Strategic relates to the whole organisation. So a **strategic plan** is the plan for the whole business. Senior managers work at a **strategic level** and make decisions and plans for the business as a whole.

Operational relates to the way a job is done. So **operational plans** relate to plans for a specific department and the work it will carry out. Supervisors normally operate at **operational level** and are responsible for how the day-to-day work is undertaken.

Managers need:
- Management skills
- Financial skills
- Leadership and 'people' skills
- Planning and decision-making skills
- Communication skills

Skills required by managers

Decision making and problem solving

Senior managers are involved in making strategic plans and decisions. In addition to thinking about their own area of work, they have to think about the organisation as a whole and how it will be affected by external influences on the business and trends in their particular trade or industry over the next few years. In a school, a head teacher will consider the needs of the whole school over the next few years, bearing in mind government educational plans and initiatives, local authority requirements, the needs of all the different stakeholders and how to manage the budget and obtain the best resources! This is no easy task.

A manager also has to deal with day-to-day problems which cannot be resolved by anyone else. These may relate to issues such as staff absences, disagreements about resources and serious complaints. Usually, a problem is referred to a manager when it affects more than one area of the business or if it could have serious consequences for the business.

Skills, qualifications and personal qualities

All managers need to have the ability to manage their staff. They also need to understand business finance and be able to make critical financial decisions about their business. Most senior managers are guided by a specialist such as a management or financial accountant, but need to be able to understand and apply the information they are given.

Some managers are technical specialists. However, the higher managers climb, the *less* they may need technical skills, as they will usually have a technical adviser to help them.

Some people believe that management skills are so different from technical skills that an excellent manager can almost run anything! Richard Branson, for example, openly admits he knew nothing about the airline industry when he first bought Virgin Atlantic. Instead, he employed people who did and then *applied* the information they gave him to running a business. This is where management skills such as planning, organising and controlling a business enterprise become so important.

Managers require excellent communication skills. They may have to write complex reports and be expected to give presentations to important customers. Leadership skills are also essential to motivate and encourage staff.

The qualifications held by managers vary. Some senior managers in business, such as Richard Branson, never went to university but started their first business instead. However, this is unusual. Today, most organisations want to employ managers with appropriate qualifications, often both technical *and* managerial. For example:

- human resources managers are usually members of the Chartered Institute of Personnel and Development (CIPD) – they achieve this status only after taking high-level qualifications in personnel management

- accounting managers are often members of the Chartered Institute of Management Accountants (CIMA) – another qualification which takes several years of study
- marketing managers may be members of the Institute of Marketing and possess a diploma in this subject.

Other managers may have studied a general management qualification, such as the Diploma in Management Studies or an MBA (Master of Business Administration). These can be taken at many business schools and universities around the country.

To obtain promotion, managers also need a good 'track record' in business. They have to prove that they have consistently met targets and achieved success. In some areas, such as sales, this may be considered more important than high-level qualifications.

If you were deciding upon the personal qualities of a manager, you might want to include patience, sense of humour and kindness. However, these would not be top of the list for most organisations! Managers often have to make difficult decisions which some people won't like. Having the strength of character to do this is an important quality. Others include: vision, enthusiasm, energy, ability to grasp situations quickly, ability to consider and evaluate different points of view, ability to cope with pressure, good judgement, trustworthiness and discretion.

Related pay and benefits

Most management jobs are advertised with salaries of £20,000–£60,000 per year, depending upon the size of organisation and level of responsibility. However, there are exceptions. You may see senior managers', or directors', jobs advertised at far higher rates.

You will also frequently see advertisements which say 'bonus and benefits'. These can include:

- a share option scheme – so that the manager can buy (or be given) shares in the company
- a bonus scheme linked to performance and the achievement of targets
- private health care for the manager and his or her family
- company pension scheme
- company car or car allowance
- assistance with relocation (that is payment of the costs of moving home to take up a new job).

The importance of supervisors

Supervisors *assist* managers who run a large department or section. Sometimes supervisors are called first-line managers because they are at the first level above the operators. They also have day-to-day contact with their staff.

Key responsibilities and tasks or activities of supervisors

Someone once described the difference between managers and supervisors as 'the point at which the talking stops and the action starts'. This means that whereas managers are responsible for planning what must be done, supervisors are responsible for making sure it gets done – to the right standard and by the required deadline.

A supervisor has similar responsibilities to a manager but over fewer staff and, often, in relation to a specific set of tasks. His or her tasks and activities are also similar but over a smaller area. These are shown in the chart on page 175.

Supervisors assist managers in running a business department

Over to you!

Arrange to talk to a manager about his or her job role. An obvious person to ask could be your head teacher or the head of a college department. Or your tutor may know another manager from industry who would be willing to talk to you.

Before the talk, divide into groups and list the questions you want to ask. Then combine your ideas and make a final list of about 12 good questions, covering all the main areas, for example responsibilities, activities, skills. Remember to be tactful! Don't ask about pay and don't ask personal questions! If you want to know about personal qualities, don't say 'What personal qualities do you think you have?' but 'What personal qualities do you think a good manager needs?' It is useful – and courteous – to let the manager have a copy of the questions in advance, so he or she knows what to expect.

You may also find it helpful to find out what the manager thinks are the main differences between his or her current job role and jobs at a lower level such as the supervisory or operative job roles he or she has held in the past. (This will be useful for when you move on to the next part of this section.)

A supervisor's job

Key responsibilities	Main tasks or activities
• Ensuring own section runs smoothly and safely • Controlling day-to-day operations to ensure output targets are met, standards are achieved and deadlines are kept • Allocating resources in own area to meet requirements • Resolving operational issues and problems promptly • Managing and motivating own staff • Keeping line manager informed of problems and developments and advising on future issues	• Carrying out instructions of line manager • Reporting daily or weekly progress to line manager • Scheduling and allocating work between operatives • Checking that staff do the work properly and that specific targets on quality and output are being met • Making operational decisions which relate to the way the tasks are carried out and in what order relating to own section • Solving day-to-day operational difficulties • Carrying out administrative and personnel duties relating to own area of work, such as completing progress reports and identifying staff training needs (including their own!) • Suggesting operational changes and improvements to line manager • Keeping own staff informed of non-confidential developments that will directly affect them • Liaising with other supervisors when there is an operational issue over which they have a joint responsibility

Job security

Job security can be variable, although supervisors may be slightly *less* vulnerable to business changes than managers, mainly because they cost less. Again, job security depends upon the industry. When many dot.com businesses closed, everyone was made redundant, at every level. If all the operatives go, then supervisors aren't required either! Similarly, if the number of operatives required is less, then fewer supervisors are required.

Decision making and problem solving

A supervisor must be good at making rapid decisions relating to operational issues and difficulties and to decide how resources can best be allocated in his or her own area. For example, if work is falling behind, a supervisor may move more operatives on to a job to make sure it is done on time. If there is an equipment problem, a supervisor must decide how to resolve this quickly, preferably without affecting output. If this is impossible, he or she will work out when the job can now be completed and consult his or her manager.

Many of the problems faced by supervisors will be technical ones, related to their own specialist area. An IT supervisor, for example, will be expected to solve technical issues experienced by programmers or IT support staff and give specialist guidance on alternative methods of solving difficulties.

Skills, qualifications and personal qualities

All supervisors must have technical skills relating to their own area. Normally, they will have done the job themselves, at the level of operative, and have been promoted. However, they then have to take a broader view of the job. Often this means gaining greater understanding and knowledge over a wider range of technical skills.

Other important skills are the ability to communicate well in writing and to understand budgets, financial targets and output statistics.

The major new skill required, however, is the ability to manage people. All supervisors need this ability if they are to run their own section effectively. Therefore, they may be encouraged to study for a specialist qualification, such as the NEBSM Certificate in Management or the Edexcel Certificate in Management Studies.

Skills required by supervisors

Many supervisors hope eventually to move on to management level. In certain areas, therefore, such as human resources, accounting and purchasing, they may choose to take higher-level professional qualifications.

The personal qualities required by supervisors include several needed by managers, such as drive, enthusiasm and energy. They need to be good communicators with their staff and be able to keep them motivated. Good supervisors also have an enquiring mind, the ability to see things from different points of view *and* a keen eye for detail, all of which should enable them to solve problems.

Related pay and benefits

Generally, supervisors are paid at a lower rate than managers. You can expect to see job advertisements with pay rates of £18,000–£30,000. However, rates will vary depending upon the size of the company, the locality, and specialist skills required.

Fewer benefits are likely to be offered at this level, although this often depends on the job. Most sales supervisors, for instance, will be offered a company car. Supervisors may also receive more holidays than operatives.

Companies are usually aware that it is unfair to offer benefits only to senior staff and may have a benefits 'package' which is offered to all staff (see below).

It makes you think!

A variety of benefits can be offered by organisations, as shown in the chart below.

1. Go through the list and rank the benefits in the order you would like to receive them. Rank your highest preference as number one. Then compare your answers with those of other members in your group and draw up a final list which takes into account everyone's views.
2. Now check the comments column and decide which you would offer if you were an employer, and which you would not, if you were offering a package of any five benefits. Check any terms you do not understand with your tutor. Then discuss the additional factors you had to bear in mind from an employer's point of view.
3. Now decide the advantages both to staff and employers of offering a flexible package, available to all staff, up to a certain limit. Can you think of any disadvantages?

Staff benefits

Benefit	Comments
Buying shares in the company, usually at less than the market price	Good if shares rise in value, depressing for staff if they fall. May be restrictions to prevent immediate sale. Benefit must conform to Inland Revenue rules. Helps staff think like 'owners'
Profit-sharing or bonus scheme	Bonus is variable, depending on company performance and/or achievement of targets. Staff pay tax on money
Health insurance, either private medical insurance (PMI) or health cash plan	PMI is expensive, especially if it includes the whole family. Health cash plans pay out for specific benefits, e.g. days in hospital or an appointment with a specialist
Extra holidays (e.g. whole day or half day)	Cheap popular benefit – costs money if cover needed for absent staff. Difficult to remove this benefit once in place
Childcare/nursery vouchers	Helps to pay for childcare costs for staff who need it
Gym membership (free or subsidised)	Gyms offer discounts for groups. Organisation can pay whole bill or just pass on saving to staff. Helps keep staff fit!
Company car, car allowance or cash alternative	Popular with staff but expensive for employers because of taxes to pay. Cheaper for employer to offer cash alternative
Dental and/or optical care	Employer pays dental bills and/or optical bills, but may be an upper limit or number of visits may be limited
Vouchers	Vouchers available for large retail firms, short-break holidays, days out, and so on. Makes reward into a treat
Loans	Range of loans can vary. Some firms offer season ticket loans and deduct payments monthly from wages. Others offer cheap loans to staff after minimum time employed
Company goods at discount prices	Only appropriate if company makes goods employees would want to purchase!

The importance of operatives

Operatives are vital to the success of any organisation because they are the people who do all the essential basic jobs such as:

- packing goods in a distribution warehouse
- keying in text in a newspaper office
- cooking fries in a fast-food outlet.

An operator is anyone who is responsible for carrying out a key task and isn't responsible for supervising other staff. Using this definition, you could include many jobs – nurses, teachers, journalists, travel consultants, computer programmers, sales representatives and other skilled professional people. Therefore, don't let the term mislead you into thinking that 'operative' always means unskilled or low-paid staff. Sometimes this may be true, but often it isn't!

Key responsibilities and tasks or activities of operatives

Whereas the main responsibilities of all operatives are similar, their actual tasks or activities will depend upon their specific job role. Those undertaken by a sales representative, for example, are very different from those of an assembly worker! In general, you can expect operatives to have the responsibilities and undertake the tasks and activities outlined in the chart below.

The operative's job

Key responsibilities	Main tasks or activities
• Doing own job in a professional manner • Meeting own targets or deadlines • Producing high-quality work • Informing supervisor of any difficulties or problems which cannot be resolved or which are outside own area of responsibility • Making positive suggestions which could improve the quality of own work or overall workflow • Keeping up to date with job and identifying own training needs	• Carrying out specific duties related to own training, experience and job role • Solving day-to-day problems in own area of work which are not outside the limits of the job role • Keeping supervisor informed of own progress • Assisting other team members when there is an urgent job or deadline to meet

Job security

This can be very variable. In late 2001 and early 2002, many operatives in manufacturing organisations were made redundant. This was because a fall in orders or sales meant fewer staff were required and businesses also wanted to cut costs. Unskilled operatives are always more vulnerable than skilled staff because it is easier to rehire them if times change, but both may lose their jobs if the company cuts back its operations sharply.

Jobs are also likely to be more at risk in new or very small companies, which may not survive very long, than in larger, well-established businesses.

Decision making and problem solving

Operatives are expected to make routine decisions and solve standard problems relating to their own jobs. Some operatives, however, are allowed more flexibility and discretion than others. For instance, someone cooking fries at a fast-food outlet would have to follow precise instructions, while an experienced engineer would be expected to use his or her own judgement about deciding the best way to do a job.

Similarly, the type of problems to be solved would be different. The person cooking fries might be told to refer any problems immediately to the manager while the engineer would only consult his or her supervisor over anything which could be serious or affect the costs of the job.

Skills, qualifications and personal qualities

The skills required by operatives vary hugely and are specific to the job and the industry. Some operatives need no specific skills, others are highly trained. However, all employers look for operatives who have certain general abilities. They expect them to be:

- hard-working and conscientious
- able to get on with other people in their team
- capable of using their common sense and, preferably, their own initiative when doing the job
- reliable.

Operatives who deal with customers need additional personal skills such as good communication skills and a pleasant manner and personality.

Operatives need:
- Team skills
- Technical skills
- Routine problem-solving skills
- Communication skills

Skills required by operatives

Specific qualifications exist in a wide variety of trades and industries for staff who start at the level of operative. Many are National Vocational Qualifications (NVQs). These can be taken over a wide range of occupational areas and at different levels. They are designed to be taken by people at work and are also studied by young people who go on a Foundation Modern Apprenticeship (FMA) or Advanced Modern Apprenticeship (AMA) scheme (see Snapshot on the following page).

Personal qualities required by operatives can vary, but the most important will include: honesty, loyalty, discretion, attention to detail, sense of humour and the ability to cope with pressure.

Related pay and benefits

Pay rates vary enormously between routine operative jobs and highly skilled operatives. All workers must, by law, be paid at least the national minimum wage (see below).

The lowest rates of pay are usually made to unskilled workers. Operatives who have a trade or specific skill are paid more – on average, £14,000–£22,000. Salaries for IT staff are often good because there is a shortage of skilled workers in this area.

Operatives who work in the public sector, such as in hospitals, local authorities and schools, will be on specific salary scales. Those who work in the private sector will have more variable salaries because individual companies decide their own pay rates. At the top of the scale, an operative in a City financial firm may be earning as much as £50,000 a year, or even more with a bonus.

The benefits offered to operatives will vary, depending upon the organisation (see page 177). One of the best benefits at this level, however, can be ongoing training to help improve skills and abilities (see Chapter 8).

Fact file

The **national minimum wage** is set by the government.

In November 2002 it was £4.20 an hour for most workers over 21 years old. Between 18 and 21, the rate was £3.60 per hour and also for workers aged 22 or over when receiving training in the first six months in a new job. Under 18, the minimum wage rate doesn't apply, but for those over 18, it is illegal to pay wages below the minimum level.

Rates usually change annually, so if you read this after autumn 2003, it is worth checking whether the rates above still apply.

Snapshot

National Vocational Qualifications

Nearly 3.5 million people obtained NVQ awards in 2001 over a wide range of occupational areas. NVQs are divided into 11 different 'frameworks' which cover groups of occupations, including construction, engineering, manufacturing and transportation, as well as the provision of goods and services, the provision of health, social and protective services and communications. They cover a wide variety of jobs from cleaning to dog grooming, retailing to library services, journalism to fashion design, hairdressing to telesales.

Many managers, supervisors and support staff undertake NVQs in the framework area Providing Business Services. These include accounting, administration, customer service, IT, purchasing and management.

NVQs are offered at five levels. Most people start at level 2, which is the level usually appropriate for school leavers with GCSEs. Levels 4 and 5 are high level and are available only in certain areas.

NVQs are taken by young people who join Modern Apprenticeship schemes. There are two levels, Foundation and Advanced. All Modern Apprentices work and study at the same time. In addition to doing an NVQ in their chosen occupational area, they also study for a Technical Certificate and for certain Key Skills awards.

Find out more at www.heinemann.co.uk/hotlinks

It makes you think!

1. Decide whether each of the people below is most likely to work at management level, supervisory level or operative level. In each case, give a reason for your decision.

   a police sergeant
   b guard on a train
   c ward sister
   d postal delivery worker
   e head buyer
   f warehouse worker
   g firefighter
   h trainee finance officer
   i chief accountant
   j despatch clerk
   k veterinary nurse
   l production controller
   m graphics designer
   n customer services assistant

2. Select any one of the above jobs and suggest the specific responsibilities and duties this person would have.

The importance of support staff

Look back at Unit 1, pages 67–72, to remind yourself of the type of support staff required by an organisation.

Support staff assist the operatives, supervisors and managers to do their own jobs by undertaking all the other key tasks that need to be done in an organisation. These include:

- administrative duties – which may involve clerical staff, word processing operators, administrators and secretaries
- IT support – which usually requires computer programmers, maintenance engineers and general IT support staff (such as the person who works on the help desk)
- security checks – security staff are responsible for ensuring the safety and security of both staff and property
- maintenance, cleaning and catering.

Levels of support staff

Support staff can operate at different levels. Administrators, for instance, may work at operative or supervisory levels. Junior administrators or administrative assistants will be operatives whereas departmental or senior administrators may operate at supervisory level and be responsible for more junior staff.

The same can apply to IT support staff, particularly in a large department where highly qualified staff work in IT services and maintain a website. In this case, they will have their own supervisor and manager who may also be classed as a (senior) member of the support staff.

Key responsibilities and tasks or activities of support staff

These vary, depending upon the particular area in which the person works and the level. If the job involves supervisory or management duties, then it will have the same responsibilities you read about on pages 172 and 175.

The general responsibilities and duties of support staff are shown in the chart below.

Job security

It is rare for an organisation to operate without any support staff, and this helps to provide some job security. Also, because members of a support team often have skills which are required by a wide range of organisations, if one employer is reducing staff, it is likely they can obtain a job somewhere else. IT staff, for instance, are usually in constant demand, as are administrators.

Some support staff may not be employed by the organisation for whom they work. Security staff and cleaners, for example, may be employed by specialist companies which provide these services. If one organisation cuts back, then the worker will be redeployed elsewhere.

Some support staff use this to their own advantage. Administrators and IT staff may prefer temporary contracts through an agency. In this case, they are actually employed by the agency who 'hires out' their services. Some highly skilled workers prefer to operate on a freelance basis. This means they are self-employed and hire out their own services to different organisations.

Decision making and problem solving

All support staff will be expected to make decisions which relate to their specific job, but the degree to which they can implement these without someone else's approval will depend upon the level at which they are working. Similarly, a junior administrator, for example, may have to solve only basic problems (such as how to remedy a simple fault on the photocopier) whereas a senior administrator may have to schedule all the administrative work of the section, allowing for deadlines and staff absences.

The job of support staff

Key responsibilities	Main tasks or activities
• Doing own job in a professional manner • Meeting deadlines • Producing high-quality work and/or providing a high-quality service • Communicating clearly, promptly and appropriately with customers and colleagues • Informing supervisor of any difficulties or problems which cannot be resolved or which are outside own area of responsibility • Making positive suggestions which could improve the quality of own work or overall workflow • Keeping up to date with job and identifying own training needs	• Carrying out specific duties related to own training, experience and job role • Responding to requests to provide support from members of staff for whom responsible • Solving day-to-day problems in own area of work and referring serious difficulties to own supervisor or line manager responsible for the area • Keeping supervisor informed of progress and any problems which could affect deadlines • Assisting other team members when there is an urgent job or deadline to meet

Skills, qualifications and personal qualities

Important skills for most support staff include IT literacy, good communication skills and the ability to deal with a wide range of people. Most support staff have to deal with customers. Support staff also need job-related skills. Administrative staff will need to know about office procedures and how to use different software packages, IT staff will be expected to have IT skills relating to computer networks and hardware as well as computer software.

Instead of NVQ qualifications, support staff may choose to take a skill qualification, such as word processing, or continue studying through a part-time degree course. Alternatively, they may decide to take a professional qualification. An administrator who deals with budgets may, for instance, take an accounts qualification.

Support staff are expected to provide high-quality work and a good service so need personal qualities which will help them do this, including enthusiasm, commitment, loyalty, discretion, a positive attitude, an eye for detail, reliability, and being able to cope with pressure and act calmly in a crisis.

Support staff need:
- Job related skills eg. IT/Customer services etc
- Team skills
- Routine problem–solving skills
- Communication skills

Related pay and benefits

Unskilled support staff such as cleaners may be paid at the minimum wage rate (see page 179). Skilled support staff will be paid according to their specific skills and level. It is relatively easy to research the pay of administrative and IT staff in your own area. Administrative salaries can range from £8,500 for a junior in some regions to around £30,000 for a senior position in London. Starting salaries for IT staff tend to be higher.

Benefits will be the same as for other staff employed by the organisation, although staff who are sub-contracted to work for the organisation or who work freelance will not be eligible for these.

Over to you!

Agree with your tutor whether you should undertake these tasks on your own, or within a small group.

1. Decide on an business-related occupation or profession you would like to investigate further.
2. Visit your local careers or Connexions service and find out how people can enter this type of work.
3. Obtain at least one copy of your local newspaper and/or visit your local JobCentre and try to find at least two examples of job advertisements or vacancy notices for this job. Then make a note of the job requirements and salaries offered.
4. Find out what qualifications can be taken by people doing this job. You can find out about NVQs by accessing the QCA website, which lists all the NVQs available. You could also contact your local college for more information.
5. Prepare a brief talk (about five minutes) to summarise the information you have obtained to give to the rest of your class.

Case study

A day in human resources

Jan Whitehouse has just taken over as human resources manager in a large organisation. She is anticipating a difficult day. Human resources lacked importance at Jacobs Electronics until the new managing director was appointed six months ago. He has given her an instruction to 'sort things out'.

Jan starts the day with a meeting of her key staff. Martine, the recruitment/training officer, is also a new appointment, but Jack, the staffing officer, has been there for some time and expected to get the job of human resources manager. Since Jan started, Jack has been uncooperative and unhelpful. Jan is trying to think of new responsibilities she can give to Jack to help him cope better with the change. The problem will be money. The managing director has made it clear that salaries are frozen this year, given the company's poor sales. It is either that or cut more jobs. Already the number of assembly workers has been reduced by 20 per cent, and more could follow.

Jan has four items for discussion at the meeting.

First, she is concerned that job descriptions are out of date or non-existent for most jobs in the organisation.

Secondly, the organisation chart which was produced about five years ago has never been updated. She thinks a new one will highlight several points and problems. In particular, IT staff are scattered all around the company. Several departments have taken on IT staff and another group provides support and runs the company website. They don't seem to report to anyone. Marketing and sales staff say that they should operate the website as this would help sales.

Thirdly, many of the support staff are leaving after only a few months in the job. It is expensive to recruit and train staff and if they leave quickly, all this money is wasted. However, Jan doesn't know how well she can trust the figures she has been given and would like a wider survey across the whole company. She also thinks that leavers should attend a short interview with human resources staff so that their reasons for leaving can be assessed and recorded.

Finally, Jan wants to discuss the costs of recruiting staff. Jack seems to hand all vacancies over to a local agency which costs a fortune in commission. Jan reckons that with the savings she could make from filling vacancies themselves, she could start to draw up some suggested benefits for staff. She decides to give the job of drawing up a possible package to Jack – perhaps it will help to bring him round – and motivate more of the support staff as well!

1. a What level of job does Jan Whitehouse hold?
    b Identify two responsibilities she will have at this level
2. What level of job is held by:
    a Jack, the staffing officer
    b Martine, the recruitment/training officer
    c the assembly workers?
3. Suggest two tasks or activities Martine will have to carry out.
4. Identify two problems Jan wants to resolve and one decision she has made.
5. a What is meant by a 'package of benefits'?
    b Why does Jan think these would a good idea?
6. What is job security like at Jacobs Electronics? Give a reason for your answer.
7. Suggest two advantages to Jacobs of drawing up job descriptions for all the staff.
8. Suggest one advantage to Jacobs of having an up-to-date organisation chart.
9. Identify two personal qualities Jan Whitehouse needs to be able to succeed in her job.

1   a   From the case study, identify one example of:
        i   a manager
        ii a supervisor
        iii an operative
        iv a support worker.
    b   Choose one of these jobs and suggest two key responsibilities the person will have.
2   Explain how the lack of job descriptions and the out-of-date organisation chart are hampering Jan and identify the information she would need to produce these documents.
3   a   Identify two further problems Jan has discovered
    b   Identify two decisions Jan has made since she started the job
4   a   Why is the company experiencing financial difficulties?
    b   How does this situation affect the workers?
5   What skills, qualifications or personal qualities do you think Jan possesses that enabled her to get this job?
6   Assess Jan's strategies for motivating Jack and suggest how she can check how successful these are.
7   Evaluate the potential benefits to the company of
    a   restructuring the IT department,
    b   interviewing leavers and
    c   introducing a package of benefits for staff.

What can go wrong?

All organisations have an organisational structure, and most have an organisation chart. This does not always mean the business is structured in the best way to achieve its aims and objectives. Problems can occur if:

- the organisation structure is inappropriate for the aims of the organisation and doesn't help staff to work or communicate effectively
- the organisation has expanded or contracted but the structure has never been reviewed.

To prevent this, most organisations revise their structure and may **restructure** (make changes to the structure) to bring it up to date. This will affect people's job roles. Some staff may even lose their jobs if the organisation is contracting. Most organisations, however, prefer to lose staff through **natural wastage** – staff who leave are not replaced. Alternatively, staff may have to move to another department.

A restructure or reorganisation is also likely to affect the tasks carried out by staff. Those transferring to a new department may have to learn new skills. If staff numbers are being cut, then the remaining staff may have more work to do – and more responsibility. If the company is not performing well, employees may be expected to do this without additional pay.

Chapter review and practice questions

1   Identify two advantages and two disadvantages of organisation charts.
2   a   State two benefits of preparing a job description.
    b   Suggest two tasks which would be on a job description for a customer service assistant in a large store.
3   Jim Evans works as a sales assistant in a store that sells sportswear and fitness equipment.
    a   Identify the level at which Jim is working.
    b   Suggest one key responsibility he will have.
    c   Identify two tasks or activities he will carry out regularly.

    d Suggest one problem he may encounter as part of his job.
    e If sales fell, how could this affect his job security?
    f Suggest two skills or qualities which would make Jim a good sales assistant.

4 Shahid Patel is a sales representative who has applied to be promoted. If he's successful, Shahid will have the title area supervisor and will report directly to the area sales manager. There are six other sales representatives in the company and one other area supervisor.
    a Draw a simple organisation chart to show the structure of the sales section as it is at present.
    b Identify two tasks likely to be on the job description of area supervisor.
    c Suggest one one new skill Shahid will need and two qualities his boss will be looking for at the interview.
    d Identify one benefit provided to most sales representatives.

▷

1 a Explain the main purpose of organisation charts.
   b Identify two drawbacks and two benefits of organisation charts.
   c Suggest two reasons why it is important that organisation charts are kept up to date.

2 Lameesa Iqbal is an administrator who has just been given the job of departmental administrator. She will now be senior to the three other staff in the office.
    a Suggest two new tasks or activities Lameesa will now have to undertake.
    b Identify four qualities which her boss would have been looking for at the interview.

    c Lameesa now needs to find a replacement for herself. Suggest three skills that will be needed by the new job holder.
    d Explain how Lameesa's key responsibilities will have changed as a result of this promotion.

3 Explain *either* why salaries *or* job security can vary:
    a from one level of job to another
    b between different types of jobs at the same level
    c between organisations.

4 An insurance company employs a customer service team of six. They are overseen by a customer services supervisor who reports to the sales manager. The sales manager has an administrative assistant. She is also responsible for the sales supervisor and the sales team of eight.
    a Draw an organisation chart to show the structure of the sales department.
    b Identify which person should respond to each of the following enquiries or problems:
       i a customer enquiry for insurance
      ii a request by the marketing director for a copy of a report on sales trends
     iii working out a new rota to cover for staff illness in the customer service team
      iv a routine customer complaint
      v a customer enquiry for a complicated insurance quotation
     vi a very serious customer complaint threatening legal action.
    c The sales manager wants to introduce a staff training scheme.
      i With whom should she discuss this?
     ii Suggest an appropriate qualification for one of the teams.

Chapter 10: Working arrangements

What you will learn

- Understanding contracts of employment
- Different types of working arrangements
- The need for flexibility
- Changing working arrangements

Overview: working arrangements

What are working arrangements?

When you start a job, you probably know that you cannot just turn up or leave when you want to. You will be employed to work for a specific number of days and hours. You also have to work in a certain place and take holidays by arrangement.

All these factors relate to your 'working arrangements'. These vary between employees. Some people may work full time and others part time. Some may work shifts or regularly do overtime. Others may work at home rather than in an office. You saw in the last chapter that the pay and benefits can vary between staff.

In this chapter you will learn about the different types of working arrangements which exist and also why working arrangements may be changed. Generally, employers like flexibility. This means they can increase staff hours easily when there is more work to do – and reduce them when there is not. This is better than making staff redundant. Redundancy is when staff are laid off because there is no work for them to do (see Chapter 4).

What is a contract of employment?

A contract of employment is a very important document. It is a formal agreement between an employer and employee.

Every employee and employer *must* abide by the terms of the contract. In other words, when you receive a contract of employment – and sign it – you have to do what you have agreed, otherwise you are breaking the law. Equally, the contract safeguards you because your employer has to abide by it, too. In this chapter you will learn about the different aspects of work and working arrangements that may be included in a contract.

Over to you!

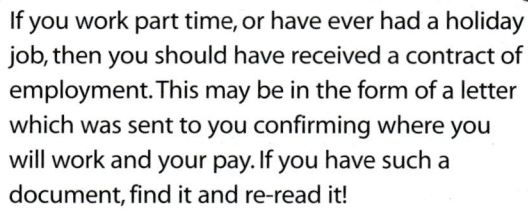

If you work part time, or have ever had a holiday job, then you should have received a contract of employment. This may be in the form of a letter which was sent to you confirming where you will work and your pay. If you have such a document, find it and re-read it!

If you haven't, see if any of your relatives has a contract they will show you. Anyone in your family who works should have one. Do be aware, however, that they may want to cover up the amount they are paid before you see it!

Understanding contracts of employment

After you have been working for an organisation for more than one month your employer must, by law, provide something in writing about your **terms** and **conditions** of employment. You have this right whether you are employed full time or part time. Most employers issue an official document called a contract of employment, but you might instead receive a written statement of the main terms or the details in a letter.

You are also likely to receive two copies of the document. One is for you to keep. You will be asked to sign and return the copy to your employer as proof that you are agreeing to the terms and conditions. For that reason, it is sensible to read it and to think about what you are agreeing to do!

Important points about contracts

A contract is a legal agreement between two parties. In this case, it is an agreement between you, as an individual, and your employer, who may be an individual or a company. Quite simply, you both commit yourselves to keeping to the terms of the contract, unless there is a *mutual* agreement to change it.

If you fail to do what you have agreed (or **breach** the contract in legal terms), then your employer can take disciplinary action. If your employer breaches the contract, then you have legal protection. Both these aspects of employment are covered in Chapter 4.

Key items in a contract

Your letter, contract or statement of main terms must contain the following items:

- your job title
- your hours of work
- the place of work
- the terms and conditions of employment
- your pay and any other benefits including sick pay and holiday pay
- the date on which your employment commenced
- the name of your employer
- your name.

Additional information

Employers must also provide other items of information, but this can be given in a separate document:

- If your job is temporary, the date on which the job will end – or the length of time the employment will last.
- Details of any trade union agreements which affect you.
- Details of your employer's grievance and appeals procedure (see Chapter 4).

You should also be given the following information, or be told where you can obtain it:

- details about sickness benefits and sickness entitlement if you are ill
- pension scheme details
- how much notice you must give if you want to leave the job
- details of your employer's disciplinary rules and procedure.

It makes you think!

Because a contract of employment may be a very lengthy document, many organisations issue a statement of the main terms and refer to other documentation in this statement. Look at the example on page 188. Then answer the questions.

1. Try to identify all the items listed in the statement.
2. a Decide what the term 'notice' means in this situation.
   b Suggest two reasons why an employee may want to 'give notice'?
   c How much notice must Andrew give after he has worked one month in the job?
   d How much notice would Jacobs Electronics give to Andrew after he had worked there for eight years?
3. When Andrew starts work he discovers that a colleague, who has worked there for ten years, has four more days' holiday each year than he does.
   a Why do you think some companies give extra holidays to employees who have worked there longer?
   b Andrew doesn't think this is fair and wants to complain. Do you think he has the right to do this? Give a reason for your answer.
4. What must Andrew do if he wakes up one morning with flu?
5. Why do you think Andrew isn't paid sickness benefit from the first day he starts working for the company?
6. Do you think it is fair that all employees can be searched if items go missing? Give a reason for your opinion.

Snapshot

Fair shares for all

Britain has about six million part-timers and this number is growing every year. Many people like the flexibility of working part time and may even prefer two part-time jobs to one full-time job!

At one time, part-time workers used to have fewer legal rights than full-time workers. However, this changed in July 2000 when the Part-Time Workers (Prevention of Less Favourable Treatment) Regulations came into force.

These regulations mean that there must be no difference between the terms and conditions of part-time and full-time employees. They must be paid the same rate of pay and their sick pay, maternity pay, pension entitlement, training and holidays must be calculated on a pro rata basis. Part-timers also have the same basic legal rights in relation to parental leave, time off work, unfair dismissal and redundancy pay.

The term 'pro rata' means 'at the same rate' or 'proportionally'. Therefore, if a full-time employee works 35 hours over 5 days, is paid £175 a week and has 20 days' annual paid leave; a part-time employee who works 21 hours a week over 3 days must be paid £105 and receive 12 days' annual paid leave.

Flexitime

Flexitime is a flexible working pattern agreed between employer and employee. Everyone must be at work during **core time** – usually between 10 am and 4 pm – to ensure that the busiest periods of the day are covered. Outside core time employees can choose to work either between, say, 8 am and 4 pm or between 10 am and 6 pm.

This enables people who feel at their best in the morning to start work early and finish earlier. Those who don't can start later, and finish later. However, staff are not normally free to pick and choose on a daily basis! They usually have to nominate which flexitime hours they will work for a week or more in advance.

Some organisations allow flexitime workers to build up credit hours by working more hours than are required for their contracted hours that week. Staff can then take a day off in lieu. Most staff like working flexitime as they feel they have more control over their own working hours. Employers benefit because the organisation can open longer hours with the same number of staff.

Overtime

Overtime is the hours worked in addition to the weekly contracted hours. In many jobs overtime is paid, but not in all. It is at the employer's discretion to offer overtime and, when it is paid, the rate may vary depending upon when the overtime is worked. Traditionally, evening and Saturday work was paid for at a lower rate than Sunday or bank holiday working. However this, too, has changed as more organisations operate seven days a week.

Whereas paid overtime is normal in manual jobs, many office and managerial staff, especially at higher levels, are expected to work overtime without payment if there is urgent work to do. They may be given time off in lieu, but not always.

Fact file

Many shops open all week and staff may be asked to work on a Sunday. However, the law protects workers who refuse. No employee can be disciplined or dismissed for refusing to work on Sunday. There are also similar rights for many staff whose work involves handling betting transactions.

Breaks from work

Breaks from work may be required for a variety of reasons. All employees have a legal right to be absent from work in certain circumstances, such as:

- to attend ante-natal classes
- for maternity/paternity leave
- for emergencies involving a dependent, e.g. a child
- to carry out public duties, e.g. a school governor
- to take part in trade union activities or to train as a safety representative or employee representative (see Chapter 4)
- to find another job or arrange training if they are being made redundant
- for those aged 16 or 17, to study or train for certain qualifications and, at 18, to complete training already begun.

The law sets down minimum requirements, but some employers are more generous and these terms will be stated in the employee's contract of employment. For instance, the law states that all employees have the right to take time off to deal with an emergency involving a dependent but it does not include a legal right to be paid. Some employers, however, will pay staff during this period, particularly if they have worked for the company for some time.

You will see in Chapter 4 that some of the legal rights of employees depend upon them completing a minimum period of **continuous employment**. It is important, therefore, that any breaks from work do not affect this. Absence for any of the reasons listed above would not affect continuity, neither would absence because of sickness or injury, for normal holidays or other absences agreed beforehand with the employer.

It makes you think!

Within your group, decide two advantages and two disadvantages for an employee of:

a having a full-time, permanent job
b having a part-time, permanent job
c working part time
d being able to work flexitime
e having the opportunity to work paid overtime
f having a temporary job
g doing shift work.

Compare your answers with the ideas put forward by other groups.

Places of work

A **fixed place of work** is still the norm for most employees. The contract of employment will state the place of work and the employer's address. It will also state whether the employee is required to work at more than one location.

The most usual locations for people working in business are **offices** and **retail outlets**, although 'offices' may be found in large establishments such as hospitals, government buildings and universities. The main difference between types of retail outlets is that small shops have no legal restriction on Sunday opening hours whereas large shops can open for only six hours between 10 am and 6 pm. This can affect the working hours and days of those who work in retail outlets, although workers do not have to work on Sunday (see Fact file above).

If your contract identifies a specific place to work each day, then you are legally obliged to go there during your contracted hours. You may expect to have your own desk and chair and a place to call your own, but not always (see Hot desking below).

Teleworking

This is when employees use ICT equipment to enable them to work away from the business's main location. All that is needed are a personal computer and modem, to link the employee to the organisation and its software, and a telephone. Many teleworkers are highly qualified, such as computer consultants who design new software programs at home and transmit them electronically. Other examples include administrative staff, data entry clerks, journalists, designers, researchers and training specialists.

Mobile working

This is when work is carried out in different places. Examples include hairdressers who visit clients' homes rather than own premises themselves, sales representatives, merchandisers who visit supermarkets and large stores to arrange stock displays for their companies, plumbers, electricians and service engineers.

Most employees still go to a fixed place of work

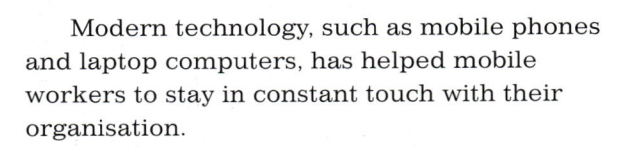

Mobile workers such as hairdressers have no fixed place of work

Modern technology, such as mobile phones and laptop computers, has helped mobile workers to stay in constant touch with their organisation.

Home-based working

This involves a person working from home. There is obviously a link between teleworking and home-based working, but in this case it is less likely that ICT equipment will be used.

Many home workers carry out repetitive manual work, and may be poorly paid. They may be involved in packing, assembling, painting or hand-finishing garments. Or they may be using clerical or selling skills such as Betterware or Avon representatives.

Hot desking

Some organisations allow flexibility for staff to vary their workplace. They may work from home some days and call into the office on others to attend meetings or do work which cannot be done at home. On other days, they may even be mobile, calling on customers. This type of arrangement means fewer people are in the office at one time and reduces the resources required. A system of hot desking may be in operation, whereby each person, instead of having his or her own desk, is expected to use any available desk, when in the office.

It makes you think!

Gemma Scott is a skilled IT worker and can use word processing, spreadsheet and presentation packages with ease. She has worked for a local company for the past two years, enjoys her job very much and is friends with several of her colleagues. To reduce its costs, the company is moving to a new site 20 miles away. Gemma now has three choices:

- She can travel every day by train (she has no car and lives two miles from the nearest train station).
- She can resign and look for another job near her home.
- She can become a teleworker. (The company is prepared to provide her with the equipment to work from home if she wishes.)

Gemma has two weeks to make a decision. At the moment, she is quite tempted by the idea of teleworking. Her best friend, however, thinks that Gemma would soon get fed up working on her own.

Within your group, discuss the advantages and disadvantages of each option and decide which action Gemma should take.

Pay, benefits and holidays

Pay

The rate of pay will be clearly stated in the contract of employment, as will the frequency of pay (weekly, monthly, and so on).

Some organisations start new staff at a fixed point on a salary scale. This is usually the case in the public sector. The salary scale gives the lowest and highest rate for the job. Between these two rates are other amounts, called **increments**. A new employee will normally move up the scale by one increment a year until he or she reaches the top. At this point, he or she may be hoping for promotion to move on to a different salary scale which starts at a higher level. In the private sector you are less likely to find salary scales, especially among small firms.

A benefit of a salary scale is that you know you will receive more money – in the form of increments – for the next few years. Otherwise, you are reliant on the employer giving you a pay rise. In many organisations, the trade union or staff association will try to negotiate annual pay rises to at least cover the cost of living (see Unit 1, page 124). However, pay rises are at the discretion of the employer and there may be none if the business has had a bad year.

In some jobs you may be entitled to additional payments or benefits (see Chapter 9, page 179). If you are entitled to regular bonuses or commission, then this will be stated in the contract of employment. However, *discretionary* payments will not. For instance, your boss may give you an extra payment as a reward for working very hard or helping to meet a special target. This is unlikely to be in your contract because it would commit your employer to giving you the reward according to the terms stated in the contract.

Every employee has the legal right to receive an itemised pay statement which states:

- gross pay (pay before deductions)
- fixed deductions (such as pension payments or trade union subscriptions)
- variable deductions (such as income tax and National Insurance)
- net pay (amount after deductions).

However, remember that you have no legal right to insist you are paid in cash. Most organisations today pay their staff by credit transfer, direct into their bank account (see Unit 3).

Holidays

Holidays are a legal right for all employees, both part and full time, from their first day of employment. All full-time workers have a right to a minimum of four weeks' paid annual leave and this must be calculated on a pro rata basis for part-time employees (see page 190). All workers also have the right to pay in lieu of any leave owing to them when they leave their employment, or the employer may ask them to take any remaining leave during their notice period.

This is the minimum an employee can receive. However, many organisations are more generous and the total number of holidays will be clearly stated in the contract of employment. In addition, as you saw in the example on page 188, many reward long-serving employees with additional holidays for their service and loyalty.

Holidays may be divided into statutory days and personal leave. Statutory days are official public or bank holidays when many (but not all!) businesses are closed, such as Christmas Day, Good Friday and May Day. Some employers today also allow Muslim staff to take Eid as a holiday. Personal leave relates to your individual entitlement which can be taken on other days. However, you have no legal right to be given public or bank holidays, whether you work full or part time. This is another reason why it is important to read your contract of employment!

Finally, most organisations have an official system for booking holidays. Businesses need to make sure they cover all their key operations, especially during busy times. Your employer, therefore, has the right to negotiate with you when you take time off to fit in with business commitments and the needs of other staff.

Fact file

Sick leave is the term used when a person is absent through illness or an injury. Sick leave is *not* a legal entitlement. Unless you are genuinely ill, you are supposed to be at work! If you are ill, you will normally have to notify your employer promptly, as part of your contract (see example on page 188).

Sick pay describes the money paid to you when you are ill. You do *not* have a legal right to sick pay. Most employees have the right to receive Statutory Sick Pay (SSP) which is paid at a lower rate than their main salary, after they have been ill for a qualifying period (currently more than four days). However, an employer may be more generous, and agree to pay the full salary for a specified number of days. After this time, the employee would receive only SSP. The length of time for which an employee will be paid sick pay is stated in the contract of employment.

Spot check

Write down your answers to the following questions:

1 State three items of information you would find in your contract of employment.
2 State the main difference between full-time and part-time working.
3 Give two reasons why an employee may need a break from work. At least one of your examples should relate to a legal right of the employee to take a break from work.
4 Give one benefit of working flexitime to the employee and one benefit to the employer.
5 What is the difference between teleworking and home-based working?
6 Give three examples of mobile workers.
7 Decide whether each of the following statements is true or false:

   a Employees have a legal right to bank holidays.
   b Part-timers must be given the same terms and conditions of employment as full-time workers.
   c Flexitime means employees can choose their own hours.
   d All employees have a legal right to an itemised pay statement.
   e All employees have a legal right to be paid overtime.
   f A temporary worker is employed only for a fixed period.
   g Shift work patterns vary between organisations.
   h All employees receive sick pay when they are ill.
   i All employees have a legal right to receive details of their employment in writing.
   j Teleworkers use ICT equipment.

The need for flexibility

Imagine the following scenario. A business employs 20 permanent, full-time staff. They work Monday to Friday, 9 am to 5 pm, and have one hour for lunch. They are on fixed pay scales which give them an increment every year for the first few years of their employment. What does this mean in reality?

- The company can answer customers' enquiries during weekdays, but not in the evenings or at weekends.
- If the company wants staff to work additional hours, it has to negotiate this and pay overtime.
- Some staff have skills in high demand and some less so. Yet everyone is there all the time, and the company needs to find work for everyone to do.
- The company's salary bill is increasing every year and there is little it can do about this if times are hard, apart from making people redundant. The company may not want to do this if it believes business will quickly recover.

From this, you can see that businesses require flexibility, while staff would like some job security. It is possible to match these two requirements by recruiting a variety of staff, on different types of contracts, to meet both needs.

Varying the working arrangements of staff allows employers to open longer hours, pay for the skills they want when needed and take on additional staff at busy times. The needs of different employees are also met, providing full-time and part-time jobs, permanent and temporary work.

Changing working arrangements

Employers may need to become more flexible for various reasons. Normally, identifying the need, and doing something about it, has major benefits for the company. However, many employees don't like change and prefer to keep things as they are.

If an employer wants to change the working conditions for existing employees, then the terms of the contract of employment must be changed. Employees must be notified in writing within one month of the change.

The change may be beneficial to most, if not all of the employees, or it may not. If the change is detrimental (for example involves shorter holidays, more travelling or longer/more unsocial hours), then employers often try to negotiate an agreement with the employees, usually through a trade union or staff association.

If no agreement is reached, the employer can still go ahead, but does not have the right to make sweeping changes which would severely worsen a person's terms and conditions of employment. In this case, the employee has legal rights and could refer the matter to an Employment Tribunal (see Chapter 12, page 229).

It is better for both parties if agreement is reached and, as part of any negotiations, the reasons for the changes should be thoroughly discussed. Possible reasons are shown in the diagram below.

Working arrangements may need changing to:
- Increase productivity
- Improve the quality of products
- Introduce new technology
- Be more competitive than other businesses
- Introduce team-working and multi-skill practices

Reasons for employers changing working arrangements

Changes to increase productivity

Productivity relates to the amount of work people can do in a given time. If people work

Fact file

A different type of 'team' is when two people **job share**. This involves two people doing one full-time job between them, each working half the hours.

For a job share to work successfully, there must be good communications between the pair. But there are many advantages, particularly for full-time staff who want to reduce their hours but still work for the same employer. The employer benefits by retaining skilled, experienced staff.

Spot check

Write down your answers to the following questions:

1.
   a. What is meant by 'productivity'?
   b. Why would an organisation wish to increase its productivity?
   c. State two actions an organisation could take to do this.
2. Suggest one way in which working arrangements may be changed to help to improve the quality of the items produced.
3. Identify two ways in which technology has affected the working arrangements of employees.
4. A business is keen to offer a more competitive service.
   a. Suggest one way in which it could do this.
   b. Identify how this would affect working arrangements in the company.
5. An employee is recruited as a member of a customer service team. Briefly explain why the working arrangements of the team must be co-ordinated.

Snapshot

Open all hours

Traditionally, most bank employees worked from 9 am to 5 pm on a full-time, permanent basis. They worked in bank branches, which closed at 3.30 pm to give staff chance to 'cash up' for the day.

Today, the situation is very different. The introduction of cash machines meant fewer staff were required in banks. Telephone and Internet banking has accelerated this trend. Many banks now offer customer advice and telephone banking through call centres which operate 24 hours a day, 7 days a week. These are at various locations in the country, not necessarily near to the traditional bank branches.

As more staff work varying hours and patterns, this increases the demand for other services around the clock. Many large supermarkets operate 24 hours a day, and so do many petrol stations and some cinemas. Television programmes used to end at about 11 pm, now most go on all night. In the USA, there are even more types of outlets and services which claim 'we never close', particularly in large cities. Perhaps it won't be too long before the same happens here!

Case study

Working arrangements

Jez has just got a job with a large mail order company. On his induction course, to familiarise him with the company and how it operates, he met several other staff including:

- Tom, a security guard, who is responsible for patrolling the grounds and checking all visitors entering the premises
- Aziz, a maintenance engineer, who carries out machine maintenance in the packing department
- Jacqui, a merchandiser, who visits the company's retail outlets
- Mark, an accounts clerk, who works in the finance department
- Sue, a computer programmer, who is involved in software developments in the company
- Paula and Louise, marketing assistants who job share.

Jez plans to visit Australia in a few months. At present, he is covering for a member of the human resources staff who is on maternity leave.

The company operates for longer hours from October to cope with the extra demand before Christmas.

- The factory operates for 18 hours a day between 1 January and 30 September, but for 24 hours a day, 7 days a week, from 1 October to Christmas.
- Office staff work from 8.45 am to 5 pm all year but staff in telesales work longer hours from October to Christmas – from 7 am to 10 pm.
- IT staff normally work office hours but from October at least one member of staff is on duty overnight in case there is a computer problem.

The company recruits a large number of temporary staff from early September onwards. Most of these are unskilled packers, but additional, experienced telesales staff are also hired.

1. From the staff Jez met, identify those who would be most likely to:
   a. be employed in a full-time, permanent job and work from 8.45 am to 5 pm most of the year
   b. be employed on a part-time basis
   c. operate on a mobile basis
   d. work shifts.
2. a. How will Jez's contract be different from those of the others? Give a reason for your answer.
   b. Why is Jez happy to have this type of contract?
3. The company has many different types of working arrangements for staff. Give three benefits to an organisation of operating in this way.
4. a. Why does the mail order company have different working hours for three months of the year?
   b. Suggest one reason why local people may appreciate being offered temporary work at this time.
5. Sue confides in Jez that she is hoping that she may be able to work from home on some days.
   a. Suggest one reason why Sue may wish to do this.
   b. Do you think her boss might agree? Give a reason for your answer.
6. All the people Jez met are happy to have different working arrangements. Suggest two reasons why staff like to have this type of choice.

1. Identify five different types of working arrangements which exist at the mail order company.
2. Identify three areas in which shift working operates in the autumn. In each case, state why this is required.

3. One member of staff Jez met says that he could be called out in the middle of the night if there is a machine problem.
   a. Who is this person?
   b. In what document will this condition be stated?
   c. What type of payment will be made in this situation?

4. Jacqui tells Jez that she couldn't bear the idea of sitting in an office all day, which is why she likes being mobile.
   a. What is a 'mobile' worker?
   b. Suggest two ways in which Jacqui will use ICT equipment to stay in touch with the office.
   c. Suggest one way in which the company can control the work carried out by mobile staff like Jacqui.

5. The mail order company is anxious to stay competitive. Identify how working arrangements could change to enable the company to cope with each of the following situations.
   a. There is a backlog with packing because they were particularly busy in late November.
   b. People are complaining that they cannot get through to telesales staff.
   c. The installation of a new computer system in June could improve order processing by 30 per cent.

6. Assess the importance of flexible working arrangements to a company such as Jez's and explain the benefits both to the company and its employees.

What can go wrong?

For employees, the most disastrous effect of changes to working arrangements can be a unilateral (one-sided) change by the employer which adversely affects them. Obviously, the employee can look for another job, but this may not be easy. The employee then has three basic choices. To accept the change, to leave and claim constructive dismissal (see Chapter 12, page 228) or to accept 'under protest' and hope a compromise can be negotiated. If not, and the change was very detrimental, the employee may have grounds to take legal action if no agreement is reached.

For employers, the difficulty can be in trying to negotiate changes if employees are unwilling to adjust their working patterns. Employers must comply with the law but still need to try to improve business prospects and this often requires flexibility and the co-operation of the workforce. Agreement can often be negotiated if additional money is offered to employees, but a struggling firm may not be able to afford this.

Finally, there may be a conflict between an employers' need for flexible working arrangements and the needs of young families. This is one of the reasons why the government has been keen to balance the needs of organisations with the needs of families in the Employment Bill (see Snapshot, page 210).

Chapter review and practice questions

▶

1. Your friend has started work and received a contract of employment, but doesn't understand it.
   a. Explain the purpose of a contract of employment.
   b. Identify six items included in this document.
   c. Give two reasons why your friend should read it carefully.

2. a. Identify three reasons why an employer will want staff to work flexibly.
   b. Identify one way in which each of the following types of working arrangements can improve flexibility:
      i. introducing flexitime
      ii. offering overtime
      iii. employing temporary staff.

3. Jenny has been appointed to work as a member of a team.
   a. Give one benefit of team-working to:
      i. Jenny's employer
      ii. Jenny herself.
   b. Jenny's contract says that she is employed for 36 hours a week, her hours will be between 8 am and 5 pm as arranged with her team leader.
      i. Jenny wants to start at 9 am. Can she insist on this? Give a reason for your answer.
      ii. Suggest one reason why her team leader is responsible for Jenny's hours.
      iii. What would be the difference if Jenny was offered a flexitime job instead?

4. An administrator listed the advantages and disadvantages of different types of working arrangements – see the chart below – but put the wrong ones under each heading. Re-arrange them correctly.

Working arrangement	Advantages	Disadvantages
Temporary employment	Can arrange hours around family commitments	Involves working unsociable hours
Permanent part-time employment	No travel involved	Can be very tiring
Home working	Allows 24-hour operations	No job security
Overtime	Can work when need the money, then leave	Can be lonely
Shift work	Enables extra money to be earned on top of salary	May limit career prospects

▶

1. Josh and Kenny have both obtained jobs for the summer and have received a contract of employment. Josh has a temporary job in a theme park – he will do 40 (variable) hours a week. Kenny will be working at a nearby hotel six evenings a week, and intends to continue working there for extra money in the autumn.
   a. State six items of information which will be on both contracts.
   b. Josh's contract is on a special form, but Kenny has received only a letter. Does this matter? Give a reason for your opinion.
   c. Why have their employers asked them to sign and return one copy in each case?
   d. Identify two main differences between the two contracts.
   e. If Kenny wants to work only three evenings a week after September, what action must be taken *both* by him and his employer?

2 Sunway Travel is always very busy in January and February when people make summer holiday bookings. The offices are normally open from 9 am to 5 pm, six days a week. The owner would like to open longer hours during the busiest period. Suggest two ways this could be achieved without taking on additional staff.

3 Dragon Software has its offices in London where rent is expensive. The firm is growing rapidly and there is an acute shortage of space. Suggest how the owner could cope with this problem without moving and having to pay additional rent.

4 a Identify two situations in which employees have a legal right to have a break from work.
 b Mandy's mother is ill in hospital and Mandy wants to be with her. However, she doesn't know whether she will be paid for this time. How could she check this?
 c Suggest how an employer could cope with a long-term break from work of a skilled employee.
 d Explain how team-working and multi-skilling can help an employer to cope with short-term breaks by employees.

Chapter 11: Rights of employers and employees

What you will learn
- Employer rights
- Employee rights
- Employers, employees and the law

Overview: rights of employers and employees

The expectations of employees and employers

When you start work, you will have certain expectations of your employer. You can reasonably expect, for instance, that the work you are asked to do matches the duties which were discussed at the interview, and which are specified on your job description. You may also expect to work in a safe environment, not to be asked to do anything which is dangerous or against the law and to be treated fairly. These are probably your minimum expectations – you may have several more!

Your employer will also have expectations of you. You will be expected to have the skills you claimed to have at the interview, to turn up for work regularly and on time (unless you are genuinely ill), to be honest, co-operative and obey reasonable requests.

Normally, there are no problems in any of these areas between most employers and employees, but this might not always be the case. What if you thought you weren't being treated fairly, or were asked to do something which was very risky? What could you do? Similarly, what if you started staying at home after every late night out? What could your employer do? To resolve problems like these fairly, both employees and employers have specific legal rights to protect them. These rights are the focus of this chapter.

Employer rights and the law

When you are working, your employer will have certain legal rights. For example, your employer will expect you to sign a contract of employment and abide by it. If you sign it and then ignore it, the law will be on the side of your employer who can take disciplinary action against you.

An employer can expect all employees to:
- meet the terms of their contracts
- co-operate in meeting the objectives of the business
- follow health and safety regulations.

In this chapter, you will see how these rights affect employees in business.

Employee rights and the law

As an employee, you also have certain legal rights. For example, you have the right to be paid at the rate specified in the contract of employment. If you are not, then your employer has broken the agreement and the law is on your side.

All employees can expect to be:
- paid according to their contract
- provided with a safe working environment
- appropriately trained
- permitted to join trade unions or staff associations
- allowed access to any confidential computer records kept on them as employees.

This chapter looks at how businesses operate to ensure they comply with the law.

The main legal requirements

There are many laws and regulations which relate to the workplace. You need to know the main principles of the laws most likely to affect you. These include the law on:

- equal pay
- discrimination linked to disability, gender and race
- employment rights and working hours
- health and safety
- access to information such as your personal records.

Fact file

Statutory rights refer to the employment rights laid down by Acts of Parliament and regulations, for example the Working Time Regulations (see page 209). These rights apply to everyone and are the *minimum* legal entitlement.

Your **contractual rights** refer to the specific terms and conditions listed in your contract of employment. These may be better than the legal minimum and can never be worse.

Employer rights

Employer rights and the contract of employment

When you sign a contract of employment you agree to:

- work the hours stated
- turn up for work, unless you are ill (in which case you must comply with your employer's requirements by informing your supervisor, or the appropriate person, of your absence and providing sick notes)
- do the work you are asked to do as part of your job
- comply with any other conditions stated in the contract.

Employer rights and business objectives

Your employer also has several rights beyond the terms listed in the contract – see the box below. The reason they aren't included is because they are considered to be so obvious that they are taken for granted!

It makes you think!

You learned in the last chapter that all employees over the age of 18 years have the right to be paid at or above the minimum wage. Start by checking if the rates quoted on page 179 are still the same, or have increased.

Now calculate how much you would earn if you were paid at the standard minimum wage rate and worked 40 hours a week. Bear in mind this would be your gross pay. You would still have to pay tax and National Insurance. Deduct about 20 per cent for these.

Now decide whether:

- you could live on the minimum wage if you lived at home
- you could live on the minimum wage if you lived on your own
- it would make any difference whereabouts in the country you lived and worked.

Compare your answers and ideas with other members of your group.

These additional employer rights mean that employees must work in a way which enables their employers to meet their business objectives. This would be impossible if the employee was incapable of doing the work, would not carry out instructions, gave confidential information to competitors, and so on.

Additional rights of all employers (the implied terms)

All employees must:
- be reasonably competent and have the skills they claimed to possess at the interview
- be 'ready and willing' to do the work and do what a 'reasonable' employee would do in any situation
- work towards the objectives of the organisation
- take reasonable care of the employer's property (including equipment and furniture)
- be prepared to carry out reasonable instructions and requests, which might include complying with a company 'dress code' especially if the employee comes into contact with the general public or does work which is regulated by hygiene and food handling laws
- be honest
- not give away confidential information
- behave responsibly towards other people at work
- be prepared to change when the job changes, e.g. when new technology is introduced into the workplace.

Fact file

Specific conditions which are stated in a contract are called **express terms**. Look back at the contract shown on page 188. All the items listed are express terms.

Implied terms refers to all the conditions which are considered to be so obvious they do not need to be stated – see box above.

An employee also has two types of contractual rights. Your express rights are stated in your contract. Your implied rights are that your employer will:
- treat you reasonably
- give you the opportunity (not the right) to participate in and be consulted on company matters which would directly affect you.

Employer rights and health and safety

Employers have a legal responsibility to comply with health and safety legislation. Employees have the same responsibility and must co-operate with their employers over health and safety issues. These are statutory requirements of all employers and employees (see Health and Safety at Work Act on pages 212–213).

An employee who ignores health and safety might endanger other people. He or she could be prosecuted for committing a criminal offence and be dismissed from his or her job. Employers who disregard health and safety can also be prosecuted (see page 212).

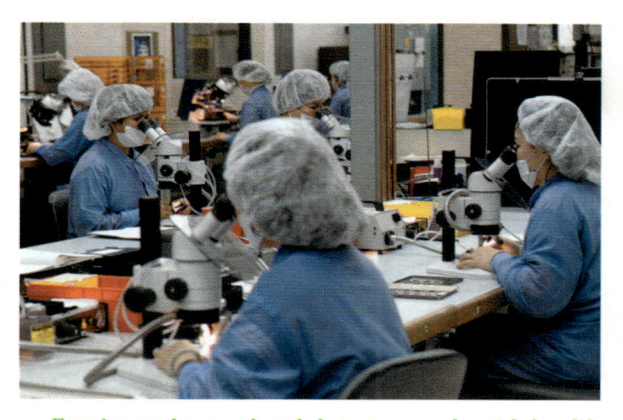

Employers have a legal duty to comply with health and safety legislation. As an employee, you will be expected to follow health and safety rules

Employee rights

You have a statutory right to receive details of your employment terms within two months of starting work. Normally, this is in a contract of employment. You also have a right to be consulted over changes which will significantly alter your terms and conditions and to be notified about these, in writing, within one month of their implementation.

Employees' other main rights are discussed under the headings below.

Employee rights and pay

All employees have the right to:

- be paid a wage or salary which is at, or above, the national minimum wage
- be paid in accordance with the details stated in their contract of employment
- receive an itemised payslip showing gross and net pay and any deductions
- a minimum of four weeks' paid holidays (or the pro rata equivalent if they work part time)
- be paid for up to 26 weeks if they are suspended from work on medical grounds
- receive redundancy pay if they are dismissed because of redundancy and they have worked for that employer for more than two years.

Employee rights and a safe working environment

You have seen that compliance with health and safety legislation is a statutory requirement for both employers and employees. Your employer therefore has a legal responsibility to provide a safe working environment for all employees (see pages 212–216).

Employee rights and training

- *All* employees have the right to receive essential health and safety training to enable them to work safely.
- Trade union officials have the right to undertake relevant training related to their duties.
- Safety representatives and employee representatives must also be allowed time to undergo specific training for their role (see page 263).
- All employees aged 16 or 17 years have the right to study or train for a qualification (usually up to NVQ 2) which will help them to do their job more effectively.
- Employees aged 18 years, who change employer, have the right to complete training they have already begun. Reasonable time off must be given, with pay, regardless of whether the employee studies at work, at college or with a specialist training provider.

Where training is given, it must be available to everyone who is entitled to it. **Discrimination** – the unfair treatment of a person or group of people – in employment is illegal (see pages 208–209). For example, training cannot be restricted to male employees.

Employee rights and trade unions/staff associations

All employees have the legal right to join a trade union. (An employee also has the right *not* to join.) It is illegal for employers to discriminate against employees or victimise them if they belong to a union. Neither can an employer refuse to employ someone because he or she is a union member.

An employee who also serves as a trade union official has the right to paid time off to carry out specific duties, as well as time off (without pay) for training.

There is no automatic statutory protection for members of staff associations or works committees, although this *may* be a specific contractual term if the association or committee is formally recognised by the employer.

The situation is different for formally elected **employee representatives**. This employee represents the interests of other workers to management about important issues such as health and safety. The employee representative has a right to time off for relevant duties and is protected against discrimination because of his or her responsibilities.

Employee rights and confidential computer records

The Data Protection Act 1998 is intended to prevent data (information) held in an organisation's computer records or in paper files being misused. This includes confidential employee data as well as data on customers, potential customers and suppliers.

Under the Act, anyone who has data held on them has the right to access. You could therefore formally request to see a file or computer records held about you by most organisations such as your bank or your employer. You can then check that the information is accurate and up to date.

There are some types of records you cannot access because the data in these files is exempt. Usually, these include police records, tax records, educational and health records.

Fact file

All employees can reasonably expect their employer not to **breach** (break) the contract of employment. Examples of a breach include:

- harassment at work (see page 210)
- unfair accusations of misconduct
- failure to pay your wage or salary
- a significant change in your terms of employment or your job without consultation
- a major change to your work location without notice.

If any of the above occur, an employee can accept the situation or resign claiming constructive dismissal (see Chapter 5, page 227). An employee who remains in his or her job can still try to claim compensation for breach of contract.

Spot check

Write down your answers to the following questions:

1. a   Identify three examples of specific information (express terms) you will find in your contract of employment.
    b   Give three additional items (implied terms) which are not included because they are considered to be obvious.
2. Why is it important that all employers *and* employees follow health and safety regulations?
3. Maria has heard about the Data Protection Act and decides she wants to find out what information the Inland Revenue holds on her. Can she do this? Give a reason for your answer.
4. Martin, aged 17, has a job and is also studying for an NVQ 2 in Administration one day a week at college. He is offered a better job at another company but the owner says he will not be able to continue his studies. Is this true? Give a reason for your answer.
5. Amelia and Sanjay have both started new jobs. Amelia has just joined the trade union which operates at her organisation. Sanjay tells her that there is no trade union where he works, but he found at the interview that all employees are encouraged to join the staff association which operates.
    a   Could Amelia have refused to join the trade union?
    b   Are Amelia's rights in relation to trade union membership statutory rights *or* contractual rights? Explain your answer.
    c   How can Sanjay quickly check if he has a legal right to join the staff association?
6. a   What is an elected employee representative?
    b   What additional rights does such a person have?

Employers, employees and the law

In Chapter 3 you learned about the Part-Time Workers (Prevention of Less Favourable Treatment) Regulations, which state that all part-timers must be treated in the same way as full-timers and offered the same terms and conditions. You may also have remembered reading about the Employment Bill and 'family-friendly policies' on pages 157 and 200. In Chapter 2 you also learned there is a national minimum wage. All these are examples of employment rights which are protected by law.

There are many other laws in Britain which provide protection both for employers and employees. There is legislation which covers employment law, health and safety, and data protection to ensure that organisations follow certain minimum standards. In this section you will learn about important laws which regulate the relationship between employers and employees.

Employment law and equal pay

For many years, it has been a government aim to ensure that men and women who do the same or equivalent work are paid the same wage. The Equal Pay Act 1970 was introduced to make it unlawful to offer different pay and conditions simply because one person is male and another is female. However, it is necessary to ensure that the jobs are 'equal', especially when the duties of each person may be different:

- A woman is doing 'like work' to a man if she is employed to do the same type of job. For example, if a woman and a man are both packers, and the women packs carrots and the man packs apples, they must both receive the same rate of pay.
- A woman must be paid the same as a man if the jobs have been rated as the same under a job grading study.
- If there has been no job grading study, a woman can claim her job is of 'equal value' to a man's. In this case, an independent specialist may be appointed to decide on the value of each job. In one case, a women who worked as a cook in a shipyard canteen was able to prove her job was of equal value to a male shipyard worker.

An employer can put forward two defences for differences in pay:

- The employer may claim that the difference between a man's and a woman's contract is because of an important difference between the two people, which has nothing to do with their gender. For example, the man may have worked for the company much longer or be better qualified.
- The employer may claim that there is an important difference between the two jobs. For example, a man is expected to do heavy cleaning jobs and cannot be compared to a woman who does light cleaning duties.

Men and women who do the same job must receive equal pay

Employment law and equal opportunities

Many organisations today have equal opportunities policies. They may include a statement in their job advertisements which says that they do not discriminate against anyone 'on grounds of colour, race, nationality, ethnic or national origin, sex, being married or disability'.

The following laws protect against discrimination:

- **Sex Discrimination Act 1975** (as amended) makes discrimination illegal on the

Sex Discrimination Act 1975 (as amended)

This Act makes it illegal for anyone to be discriminated against on grounds of gender (or gender reassignment), either directly or indirectly. In employment, this applies to recruitment and selection for jobs and promotion, training, the way you are treated in a job, dismissal and redundancy. Discrimination can occur in two ways:

- **Direct discrimination** is where one gender is obviously excluded, e.g. 'only men need apply'.
- **Indirect discrimination** is where a *condition* would make it more difficult for one sex to comply, e.g. 'only those over 1.98 m need apply'.

There are some exceptions, such as acting and live-in jobs, if the employer can show that a genuine occupational qualification (GOC) applies to that job.

Race Relations Act 1976 (as amended by the Race Relations Act 2000)

This Act makes it unlawful for anyone to be discriminated against on grounds of colour, race, nationality or ethnic origin. Both direct and indirect discrimination applies. An employer advertising 'only white people need apply' would be guilty of direct discrimination. One advertising 'only those who can speak English as their first language need apply' would be guilty of indirect discrimination.

There are certain special circumstances under which discrimination may be justified, such as Chinese waiters in Chinese restaurants for authenticity, but these are relatively rare.

Disability Discrimination Act 1995

This currently applies to businesses with over 15 employees. From 2004, it will apply to all businesses.

The Act is concerned with discrimination against people with disabilities in employment, when obtaining goods and services or buying/renting land or property. The disability may be physical, sensory or mental but must be relatively long term (that is, last more than 12 months). Employers must not treat a disabled person less favourably than able-bodied persons whether in recruitment, training, promotion or dismissal unless it can be justified. Employers must also be prepared to make reasonable adjustments to the workplace to enable a disabled person to do the job. In this case, discrimination is not divided into 'direct' or 'indirect' but is 'less favourable treatment that cannot be justified'.

Anyone who suffers discrimination, whether on grounds of sex, race or disability, can appeal to an employment tribunal (see Chapter 5).

---

grounds of sex, marriage or gender reassignment (a sex change).
- **Race Relations Act 1976** (as amended) makes discrimination unlawful on the grounds of race, colour, nationality or ethnic origin.
- **Disability Discrimination Act 1995** (as amended) makes it illegal to treat someone less favourably because they are not able-bodied.

Discrimination is not just unlawful when people apply for jobs. It is unlawful at any stage of the employment process, including training, promotion and dismissal.

The main points of each of the three Acts are shown in the box.

Employment law and working hours

The Working Time Regulations 1998 restrict how many hours most people can legally work in the UK. This law applies to full-time, part-time and casual workers. Under the regulations, employees need not work more than 48 hours a week, averaged over a 17-week period, and are entitled to a minimum of four weeks' paid holiday each year. Employees can sign a separate agreement to work more hours but, if they change their minds about this later, they have the right to cancel the agreement. There are a few exceptions: the regulations do not apply to many transport workers, nor to trainee doctors, the police, the armed forces and the self-employed.

For all other workers, the regulations also allow for rest breaks of at least 20 minutes for working days of over 6 hours and a minimum 11-hour break between working days, unless shifts are worked. In addition, there must be at least one 24-hour rest period in every seven days. Night workers have slightly different entitlements, as do workers aged 16–18, who are entitled to longer breaks and rest periods of 30 minutes after four and a half hours.

Snapshot

Keeping up to date with employee rights

Employment rights change quite frequently and it is important that all employers and employees learn about the changes. A major law was passed in 1996 – the Employment Rights Act. This covered maternity leave, the right to 'opt out' of Sunday working, the right to a minimum period of notice depending upon length of employment and the right to redundancy pay after two years' continuous employment. Many of the employee rights to time off that you read about in Chapter 3 were introduced through this Act and these have since been extended through the Maternity and Parental Leave Regulations and amendments.

In 1999, the Employment Relations Act improved maternity leave, introduced parental leave and gave workers the right to take time off in a family emergency. Further changes are expected in April 2003. Since 1999, the government has also introduced the Employment Bill 2001, which covers work and parents – and the issue of requesting more flexible hours – and also aims to end discrimination against temporary workers who are treated less favourably than permanent workers. It is also concerned with how disputes should be resolved at work and how the employment tribunal system can be improved (see Chapter 12).

Another proposed development is legislation to provide protection against unfair discrimination and harassment across Europe. This is likely to mean a new law which also forbids discrimination on the grounds of age, sexual orientation and religion. In addition, further changes to the Disability Discrimination Act and Race Relations Acts are planned.

Finally, the Young Workers' Directive, which is likely to become law in late 2002, will limit 16–18-year-olds to working a maximum number of hours a week (probably 40), and restrict night work.

Fact file

Harassment describes 'unwelcome behaviour' which upsets, offends or frightens someone. It is sexual harassment if the behaviour is linked to gender and racial harassment if it is linked to ethnic origin or culture. The law protects employees against harassment by the Protection of Harassment Act 1997. All organisations should make sure that employees know how to report any instances of harassment or discrimination.

Victimisation is when one person is singled out for unfair treatment by another person.

It makes you think!

Laws don't always provide a magic solution to problems. In 1970, when the Equal Pay Act was introduced, there was a difference of 31 per cent between women's and men's wages. In 1990, the gap had fallen to 23 per cent, but since then progress has been slow. In 2001, the figure had fallen only to 19 per cent. The government wants to halve this gap by 2006.

The chart below identifies some of the reasons which have been given for the continuing pay gap. It also includes some of the suggestions that have been made to improve matters. As a group, decide which you agree with, and which you don't. Then propose *your* solutions for equality in the future and decide whether women could do anything to help the situation themselves.

Reasons	Possible solutions
Women are paid less because:	The problem could be solved if:
1 they are more likely to work in low-paid, low-status jobs, such as sales assistants and check-out operators, in child care and clerical work	1 employers had to publish any gender pay gap in an annual report each year and the media 'named and shamed' those with a poor record
2 they are less competitive and ambitious and less interested than men in being promoted to high level, responsible jobs – there are fewer than ten female executive directors in large companies in Britain	2 employers received a government subsidy (payment) for women to undertake high-level qualifications
3 most businesses in Britain are run by men who prefer to promote their male colleagues to high-level jobs	3 employers had to pay higher rates for part-time workers – which would directly affect many women
4 employers see a woman's main role as wife and mother – many take career breaks or work part time because of child care responsibilities	4 all employers had to undertake an annual pay audit and identify discrepancies between pay rates
5 women often do lighter or less demanding work than men	5 women themselves were more ambitious in terms of the careers they choose and their promotion prospects
6 fewer women have high-level qualifications	6 men took on an equal share of parental responsibilities to support women who wanted a career
7 the starting salary people are offered in a new job is based on their existing salary, not upon the job itself; as women are often on lower rates to start with, this perpetuates the system	7 more women worked in male-orientated sectors, such as IT and computing, where skills shortages have increased wages
8 women are still seen as 'cheap labour' by many employers	8 women were given the legal right to find out easily what their male colleagues with similar experience earn

To investigate this issue further, visit the Equal Opportunities Commission website at www.heinemann.co.uk/hotlinks.

The law and health and safety

Most employees expect to work in a safe environment. The law requires both employers and employees to conform with health and safety legislation.

Many organisations have a health and safety officer who is responsible for advising management about health and safety policies and training. He or she will also ensure employees are kept informed. This is because health and safety laws place a responsibility on *both* employers and employees, so if you do not co-operate with your employer in this, you are guilty of an offence.

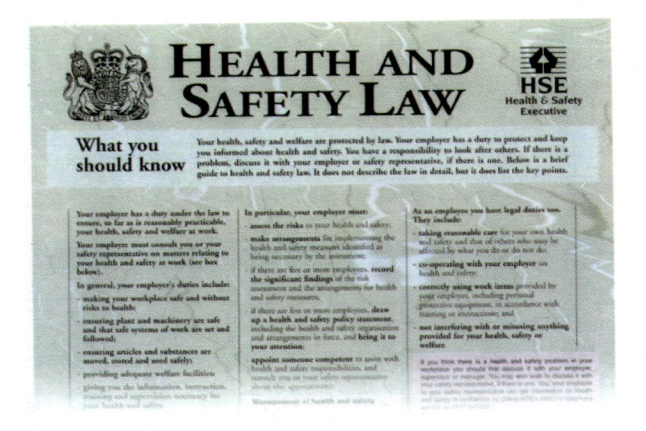

Look out for this legal notice – it must be displayed clearly in all workplaces

Health and Safety at Work Act 1974

This is the most important Act of Parliament relating to health and safety, and is often referred to as HASWA. The Act sets out the general duties and responsibilities that employers have to their employees and to members of the public, and those that employees have to themselves and each other. HASWA is an 'umbrella' Act which includes various regulations that can be revised to ensure the law is kept up to date. The Workplace (Health, Safety and Welfare) Regulations 1992, for instance, give more specific details of the responsibilities of employers under HASWA.

All organisations must display details of the Act in a prominent place, and this includes your school or college. A person who is negligent under the Act can face criminal prosecution for breaching a health and safety requirement.

The agency which enforces the Act is the Health & Safety Executive (HSE). An HSE inspector can visit any industrial premises without warning to investigate an accident or complaint or to inspect the premises. Offices and shops are visited by an environmental health officer employed by the local authority. If the inspection shows that there are unsatisfactory working practices, then the employer is issued with an Improvement Notice, which gives a specific time by which any problems must be sorted. If working practices are so poor that the safety of the workers or the public is at risk, then a Prohibition Notice can be issued. In this case, the employer must stop operations immediately. An employer can appeal if the decision is considered unfair. However, if the employer loses the appeal and still fails to put matters right, the company can be fined or the owner imprisoned.

Since 2001, an organisation's safety representative (see page 215) who believes that his or her warnings are being ignored can also issue a 'final warning' to employers who endanger the safety of employees. If the employer ignores the notice, it will be passed on to the HSE inspectors.

The main requirements of the Health and Safety at Work Act and the Workplace (Health, Safety and Welfare) Regulations are shown in the box on page 213.

Health and Safety at Work Act 1974

1. Applies to all work premises. Anyone on the premises is covered by and has responsibilities under the Act, whether employees, supervisors, directors or visitors.
2. Requires all employers to:

- 'as far as is reasonably practicable' ensure the health, safety and welfare at work of their employees, particularly regarding:
  - safe entry and exit routes
  - safe working environment
  - well-maintained, safe equipment
  - safe storage of articles and substances
  - provision of protective clothing
  - information on safety
  - appropriate training and supervision
- prepare and continually update a written statement on the health and safety policy of the company and circulate this to all employees (where there are five or more)
- allow for the appointment of safety representatives selected by a recognised trade union. Safety representatives must be allowed to investigate accidents or potential hazards, follow up employee complaints and have paid time off to carry out their duties.

3. Requires all employees to:

- take reasonable care of their own health and safety and that of others who may be affected by their activities
- co-operate with their employer and anyone acting on his or her behalf to meet health and safety requirements.

Workplace (Health, Safety and Welfare) Regulations 1992

Most of the regulations cover specific areas of health, safety and welfare to supplement general duties on employers.

1. **Work environment:**
   - effective ventilation
   - reasonable temperature
   - adequate and emergency lighting
   - sufficient space
   - suitable workstations
   - protection from adverse weather for workstations outside a building.
2. **Safety:**
   - traffic routes for pedestrians and vehicles to circulate in a safe manner
   - properly constructed and maintained floors
   - safe windows and skylights
   - safely constructed doors, gates and escalators
   - safeguards to prevent people or objects falling from a height.
3. **Facilities**:
   - sufficient toilets and washing facilities
   - adequate supply of water
   - adequate seating
   - suitable storage for clothing
   - rest areas
   - provision for non-smokers in rest areas
   - adequate facilities for people who eat at work.
4. **Housekeeping:**
   - proper maintenance of all workplaces, equipment and facilities
   - cleanliness of workplaces.

Health and Safety Regulations

Since HASWA, several other regulations have been introduced. You will need to know and abide by the ones that apply to your job:

- The **Reporting of Injuries, Diseases and Dangerous Occurrences Regulations (RIDDOR)** require organisations to notify the HSE of any serious or fatal injuries and keep records of certain specific injuries, dangerous occurrences and diseases.
- The **Control of Substances Hazardous to Health Regulations (COSHH)** state that hazardous substances must be stored in a special, safe environment and users provided with protective clothing.
- The **Electricity at Work Regulations** relate to the design, construction, use and maintenance of electrical systems.
- The **Noise at Work Regulations** relate to noise hazards. Employers must check and reduce these where possible and provide ear protectors to employees where necessary.

- The **Management of Health and Safety at Work Regulations** require employers to carry out risk assessments, to eliminate any unnecessary risks, control significant risks and provide information on risks to all employees.
- The **Display Screen Equipment Regulations** require employers to assess the risks of staff using VDUs and workstations, pay for eye tests and spectacles or lenses if these are prescribed for VDU work and plan work activities to incorporate rest breaks.
- The **Provision and Use of Work Equipment Regulations (PUWER)** are concerned with the maintenance and safety of all work equipment. Employers must make regular checks and inspections and provide appropriate training and instructions for users.
- The **Manual Handling Operations Regulations** relate to lifting and handling items. Where possible an automated or mechanised process must be used, but employees who have to move items manually should be trained properly in order to minimise injury.
- The **Fire Precautions Regulations** require all designated premises to have a fire certificate showing a plan of the building with the position of fire-resistant doors, fire extinguishers and break-glass alarms. There must be a fire alarm system and a protected means of escape. Businesses which do not comply can be issued with Prohibition and Improvement Notices or prosecuted by the fire authority.
- The **Health and Safety (First Aid) Regulations** require businesses to provide and train sufficient first-aiders, depending upon the risk level of the working environment. A low-risk environment should have one first-aider for every 50 employees. High-risk environments (such as oil rigs) have a higher ratio.
- The **Health and Safety (Safety Signs and Signals) Regulations** require safety signs to be displayed to identify risks and hazards. There must be written instructions on the use of fire-fighting equipment. All signs must be to a specified design and in the correct colours – red for a prohibited action, blue for a mandatory (must do) action, yellow for warning and green for a safe condition.
- The **Employers' Liability (Compulsory Insurance) Regulations** require all employers to take out insurance against accidents to and ill health of their employees. This means that employees injured in the course of their work can claim compensation and this would be paid by the employer's insurers.

Snapshot

Playing games could seriously damage your health

Many people think that accidents and industrial injuries only happen in factories, on farms, on construction sites and in other hazardous places such as oil rigs. This is dangerous thinking! Computer users, for instance, should be alert to risks. Keyboarding too much can increase the risk of repetitive strain injury (RSI). Staring at a screen for long periods can cause eye problems and headaches. Even sitting at a computer can cause back and neck problems! To alert computer users to these risks, the Display Screen Equipment Regulations were introduced.

However, recent research has shown that playing computer games for long periods can also cause problems. In 2002, a 15-year-old was diagnosed as suffering from hand-arm vibration syndrome after playing a driving game in vibration mode for up to 7 hours a day on his Sony PlayStation 2. This is normally a condition associated with miners and other users of heavy equipment. Other problems reported by computer gamers include joystick digit, mouse elbow and central palmar blister. If you play games regularly, read the guidance issued by Sony and take 15-minute breaks every hour as a first step.

Health and safety in practice

Organisations cannot 'trust to luck' that they meet the health and safety laws and regulations. They need to have policies and ways of operating to ensure they stay within the law.

Firstly, a business should draw up a **safety policy** which is a legal requirement for organisations that employ five or more people. The policy should state the aims of the company regarding the health and safety of employees. It should also include key members of staff and arrangements for carrying out the policy. This is likely to include training and instruction, company rules, emergency arrangements, the system for reporting accidents and the identification of risk areas. The policy must be revised regularly to make sure it stays up to date.

The business will decide its own **codes of practice** which state the procedures employees must follow in the event of an emergency, such as a fire or an accident occurring. This will include how to contact a first-aider, where the medical room is, how to contact a doctor or send for an ambulance and when an accident report must be completed. All organisations must record accidents and those with over ten workers must keep an accident book and accident records for over ten years. In addition, organisations usually record 'near misses' as these indicate where improvements should be made.

In many organisations a **safety committee**, made up of representatives from management and employees, operates. The committee checks that legal requirements are being met and reports to management on any working conditions which breach safety regulations or company policy. If there is no safety committee, these duties may be undertaken by a **safety officer**. The committee, or officer, will also check local accident trends and recommend preventative action. They will consider reports of particular accidents and suggest actions which would prevent any recurrence. They regularly report on safety matters and make recommendations to managers.

Many businesses also have **safety representatives** who attend meetings of the safety committee. These representatives are appointed by recognised trade unions and elected by union members and not by the employer. They follow up complaints made by employees relating to health and safety, carry out inspections every three months and are involved with any consultations involving HSE inspectors. They must also be consulted by the employer about any changes in the workplace that might affect the health and safety of the employees or any information or training the employer plans to provide for staff.

Safety representatives and safety officers are also involved in investigating accidents. The safety representative or officer can recommend improvements, where required, and then check that recommended action has been taken. They can also check completed accident report forms and accident records and monitor accident rates to ensure these are not above the national average and that there is a regular improvement in standards.

Snapshot

Young, free – and at high risk!

Injuries and ill health cost industry between £14 billion and £18 billion each year. About 25 million working days are lost each year because of employee absence. The government wants to reduce this number by 30 per cent by the year 2010.

Young people are particularly vulnerable. In 2000, six employees under 19 years lost their lives at work, 1,551 suffered serious injury and a further 5,310 needed to take more than three days off work because of a work-related illness or injury.

Employers must carry out a risk assessment to take into account a young person's lack of awareness of existing or potential risk and their inexperience. They are then responsible for providing proper training to ensure no unnecessary risks are taken. Young people are also encouraged to (politely) question what they are being asked to do, particularly if they have any worries or concerns. Anyone going on work experience should receive similar training, as the law considers students on these programmes to be 'employees' for the duration of their stay at the company.

Over to you!

If you have a part-time job or go on work experience, collect any information you are given on health and safety or which you receive as part of your training. You might find it useful as a basis for your portfolio investigations. It is likely to include information on fire drills, how to report and record accidents, the name of safety officials, and so on.

In addition, you should be able to add to it from information given to you at school or college. Look for the Health and Safety at Work Act poster which should be prominently displayed – and read it!

Then find out more about the work of the HSE by accessing its website at www.heinemann.co.uk/hotlinks.

It makes you think!

1. Look back at the box describing the main parts of the Health and Safety at Work Act (see page 213). Read it carefully and then decide which part of the Act the following actions would contravene:
    a   An office worker overloads a high shelf above a desk with some heavy files.
    b   A caretaker leaves a stack of boxes behind the office door.
    c   A science technician leaves a bottle of acid on top of a desk.
    d   An employee insists on using the lift when the fire bell sounds. She says it's only a practice so it doesn't matter.
    e   An office worker accidentally breaks a glass and throws it, unwrapped, into the waste-paper bin.
    f   A hairdressing trainee finds the box containing gloves is empty just as he is about to start colouring a client's hair.
    g   An office trainee is told to mend a paper jam in the photocopier, even though she has never used it before.
    h   Two students in a college set off a fire extinguisher as a joke.
    i   On a hot summer's day, the officer supervisor finds an old fan in a cupboard. Although the plug is loose and the wires are frayed, he switches it on.

2. Check through the Workplace (Health, Safety and Welfare) Regulations shown on page 213. Identify one example, in your own school or college buildings, where each requirement has been fulfilled.

3. The Health and Safety at Work Act requires all employers 'as far as is reasonably practicable' to ensure the health, safety and welfare of their employees.
    a   What do you think is meant by the phrase 'as far as is reasonably practicable'?
    b   You are the employee representative and have been approached by employees to improve safety in the corridors. They say the tiles are slippery, especially when they are wet, because people have walked on them with wet shoes. Some are demanding mats at the front and back doors, others want the area to be carpeted.
        i   Which solution would be the cheapest and which the most expensive?
        ii Are either, or both, 'reasonably practicable'? Give a reason for your answer.
        iii If you wanted to support your recommendation to your manager, what part of the Health and Safety at Work Act could you quote?

The law and data protection

Data protection is concerned with protecting the collection, storage, processing and distribution of personal information. The first Data Protection Act regulated the use of information processed on computer. This was introduced because there was concern about the type of information which was held about individuals on computers, such as whether the data was correct, whether personal and sensitive details were held against people's wishes and whether the information could be given or sold to someone else without the person's consent. The Act gave people rights about the information which could be held about them, who could hold it and how it could be used.

The Data Protection Act 1998 extended the original Act to cover data held in manual (paper) filing systems.

Businesses which hold data on individuals are called **data controllers**. All data controllers must be registered and included in a national register held by the Information Commissioner's Office. This office is responsible for enforcing the Act and ensuring freedom of information. If an organisation fails to comply or contravenes the Act, then the Information Commissioner has the power to issue an enforcement notice or an information notice against that data controller. An enforcement notice instructs the data controller what action to take (or what activities it must stop). An information notice is a request for details. The Information Commissioner also has the power to search premises if there is evidence of contravention. Failure to comply with a notice or to obstruct a search are criminal offences.

An employee who wishes to obtain access to his or her personal files can be charged for this. The maximum in January 2002 was £10. The employer then has to provide information to which the employee is entitled. The employer must also:

- acknowledge that he or she is processing personal data
- give details of the personal data which is held
- state why this data is being processed
- state any other organisations or individuals who might receive this information.

The Information Commissioner is currently looking at the uses of personal data by employers and is currently drawing up codes of practice to tighten control on:

- employee surveillance, such as the use of CCTV, the interception of email and the monitoring of Internet use and telephone calls
- automated processing of employee data, such as the scanning of CVs or recording of aptitude tests
- the collection of any particularly sensitive information, such as the result of alcohol or drug tests.

Snapshot

I know what you're surfing!

Organisations can check which Internet sites their staff visit

The Regulation of Investigatory Powers Act 2000 has given the managers of a business organisation the right to read any electronic communications. As a result, many businesses now routinely monitor all incoming and outgoing emails and attachments as well as Internet use by staff. Staff who send emails with unsuitable content, spend their day emailing friends or colleagues about social arrangements and surf the Internet for cheap holidays during working hours can be disciplined.

The introduction of the Act resulted in several newspaper reports of staff being sacked for abusing their email or Internet facilities. However, recommended good practice is for the company to draw up a computer use policy which defines the rights and obligations of employees when using computers at work. This policy would be referred to in the contract of employment and the consequences for breaching the policy would then be clear.

In any organisation, you should check if there is a computer or IT policy that you must follow. This includes your school or college.

It makes you think!

Details of the Data Protection Act are given in the box opposite. Read this carefully and then answer the questions:

1. Three of the following types of data are included in the Act. Which are they?
   - a Employee records held by the employer
   - b Customer records held by a supplier
   - c A database of your friends on your home computer
   - d Police records
   - e Files on individuals held by a credit reference agency.

2. Three of the following are an offence under the Act. Identify them.
   - a A business sells its personnel database to an insurance company so that it can sell its products to the business's employees by direct mail.
   - b Your employer provides information about your income to the tax office without your consent.
   - c You write to your bank asking for details of the information they hold on you, but they refuse, saying this is confidential.
   - d Your local college asks if you will voluntarily identify your ethnic origin when you enrol on a new course.
   - e Your brother, who runs a small business, refuses to register as a data controller. He argues that the Act doesn't apply to small businesses.

Data Protection Act 1998

The Act requires all organisations and businesses which process personal data on individuals (a **data subject**) to be listed in the register of **data controllers**, unless they have already registered under the 1984 Act. They must give:

- their name and address and the name of their representative, if any
- a description of the personal data being processed and the types of data subject which it covers (e.g. customers, employees)
- a description about why the data is being processed
- a description about any recipients to whom it may be disclosed
- a description of any countries outside the European Union (EU) to which it may be sent.

The term 'data' which is covered by the Act relates to:

- information recorded or processed by computer
- information which is part of a relevant filing system or forms part of an accessible record, e.g. health records, social services records, and so on.

All data controllers must comply with the eight Principles of the Act when handling personal data:

1. Data must be obtained and processed fairly and lawfully. Normally this means the individual has given his or her consent. Explicit consent is required for 'sensitive' data relating to religious or political beliefs, racial origin, trade union membership, physical or mental health or sexual life, criminal convictions.
2. Personal data must be held only for one or more specified and lawful purposes and should not be processed for another reason.
3. The data should be adequate, relevant and not excessive.
4. Personal data must be accurate and kept up to date.
5. Personal data must be kept no longer than is necessary.
6. It must be processed in accordance with the rights of data subjects (see below).
7. It must be stored to prevent unauthorised or unlawful access, loss, destruction or damage.
8. It must not be transferred outside the EU unless the country to which it is being sent also protects the rights of data subjects.

The rights of individuals (data subjects) include:

- the right to access data held about them
- the right to prevent processing which would cause damage or distress
- the right to prevent processing for direct marketing purposes
- rights in relation to automated decision taking (e.g. evaluating job performance or creditworthiness on the basis of personal information)
- the right to take action to correct, block, erase or destroy inaccurate data
- the right to compensation if damage is suffered through contravention of the Act.

The Act allows for certain **exemptions**:

- purposes of national security
- crime detection and taxation purposes
- health, education and social work
- research, history and statistics
- domestic use only.

Case study

Read the following email Emma has sent to her friend, Kate.

Hi Kate

Remember I said I would be working this summer? Well, forget it! I've had a terrible week and never want to see a sandwich shop again in my life.

I started last Monday at Lite Bites in the High Street. They said it was for six weeks. Although they told me I would have to wear a uniform at the interview I never realised I was expected to look like a clown. What with hair net, hat and special overalls – and hardly any make-up and no jewellery!

This guy Dominic spent the whole of the first day telling me about health and safety, about clean hands (as if I'd never washed my hands before) and clean work surfaces, about reporting any cuts or tummy upsets and wearing special gloves and a blue plaster if I cut myself. He's only a sad little college student and has worked there for a couple of years in the holidays – and on Saturdays – but the way he went on he sounded like my father! He also cleans the equipment each evening with another man, called John. How exciting!!

Anyway, on Wednesday, I was serving at the counter and looked up to see this gorgeous lad, called Mark. On Thursday, I tried to fix it so I could serve him and chat to him! He was really sweet but I could hardly impress him in that beautiful outfit they make me wear, could I?

On Friday, the manageress had to go out around lunchtime – just before Mark was due. So I took off all the clown clothes, put on some make-up and rushed out to serve him when he came in. It didn't help I'd just cut my finger but I hadn't time to find the plaster box or I would have missed him. Just as I was serving him the manageress walked back in and went mad. In front of everyone she ordered me away from the food counter and told me to get my stuff and leave! It was awful. How dare she? I told her that I didn't need her stupid job anyway. Apparently, that Dominic is paid 50p an hour more than me, which I know is discrimination.

Anyway, that's it and I've left. My only problem now is lack of money. Are there are any jobs going at your place?

Emma

▶ 1 Identify one express term of Emma's employment, which was explained to her at the interview.
2 Do you think Lite Bites complies with health and safety regulations? Give a reason for your answer.
3 Why do you think Lite Bites is keen to stress hygiene regulations to staff?
4 Could Lite Bites insist that Emma wears a hat and hairnet? Give a reason for your answer.
5 Identify two reasons why Dominic's wage can legally be higher than Emma's.
6 The manageress sacked Emma because she 'deliberately endangered the health of other employees and customers.' Emma obviously doesn't agree. Who do you think is right? Give a reason for your opinion.

▶ 1 Identify two express terms that would be included in Emma's contract of employment.
2 Explain what is meant by an implied term and suggest two implied terms which applied to Emma.
3 a Which law requires all employers to give staff training on relevant aspects of health and safety?
   b What other type of training did Emma receive before she started work?
   c Why do you consider that Lite Bites includes all these aspects in its training programme?
4 Identify two ways in which Emma breached her contract of employment.
5 Emma was paid less than Dominic. Do you think this is fair or unfair? Give a reason for your answer.
6 Do you think the manageress was within her rights to ask Emma to leave when she did? Give a reason for your answer.

What can go wrong?

Despite laws to protect employees and employers, problems can still occur. Some small firms may not know about all the laws they have to follow, even though ignorance is never an excuse. An unscrupulous employer may treat staff badly and ignore the law, and take the chance that employees won't complain or take legal action.

Employees, too, can create problems for employers. Not everyone is hard-working, loyal and honest! In these situations, the employer needs to take action to protect the business.

In addition, employees may have disagreements with each other or with their boss. These need to be settled rapidly, and fairly, so that everyone can concentrate on their job again.

To solve the problem of disagreements, employers have grievance policies to help employees to resolve problems. They also have disciplinary policies and procedures which can be used if employees are at fault. You will learn about these in the next chapter. You will also learn what happens when problems cannot be sorted out within the company and must be resolved elsewhere.

Chapter review and practice questions

▶

1 a What is meant by the term 'discrimination'?
   b Identify which law protects employees in each of the following situations:
      i   A man and a women do exactly the same job but he is paid more than she is.
      ii A young Asian woman is ignored for promotion even though she is highly qualified.
      iii An employee in a wheelchair cannot attend a training course because it is held on the second floor and there is no lift.

2 a Suggest the type of personal records which would be held by the following organisations:
      i   a doctor
      ii a clothes shop
      iii a football club
      iv a school or college
      v   the police.
   b Which law protects individuals about the type of personal information held about them by organisations?
   c Shahida wants to obtain information held about her by her employer.
      i   Can her employer refuse her request? Give a reason for your answer.
      ii Can her employer charge her for finding this information?
   d Customers, too, can request information, but not in every situation. From the list of organisations given in (a) above, identify those which would have to comply with a request for information, and those which would not.

3 a What is the major law relating to health and safety in Britain?
   b Identify two other regulations which would apply to someone working in an office in a business organisation.
   c At Jack Martin's factory there is an accident when a young worker traps his hand in a door.
      i   What records would need to be completed to record that the event had occurred?
      ii Who would be contacted to help the worker?
      iii Who would investigate whether the accident could have been avoided?
      iv What difference would it make if the accident had occurred because the young worker had been chasing his friend at the time?

▶

1 a Explain the difference between discrimination and harassment.
   b What is an equal opportunities policy?
   c Why do many firms have equal opportunities policies?
   d Three separate laws protect different groups of people from discrimination. Identify each of these laws and, in each case, state which group of people are covered by the law.

2 Max has recently read that he has a right to obtain details of personal information held about him by organisations. He decides to find out as much as she can.
   a Which law has Max read about?
   b As Max's friend, suggest three types of organisations he could contact, and three he could not.
   c Max is intrigued when his employer provides a report attached to his personal details. State two items of information this report will contain.
   d Max is annoyed when another organisation has obviously recorded his age incorrectly and he wants it changed. Can he insist on this? Give a reason for your answer.

3 a State two requirements of employers and two requirements of employees in the Health and Safety at Work Act.

b Louise works with computers every day.
  i Which regulations specifically apply to this type of work?
  ii Under these regulations, what action could Louise take if she started suffering from regular headaches?
c Explain the role of a safety representative and identify three duties carried out by this person.
d Your friend has started work in the office of a small business and states that health and safety is unimportant in this situation. What arguments could you put forward to prove he was wrong?

Sometimes an arbitrator such as ACAS is able to offer a solution to a dispute

The European Court of Justice

If a person does not agree with the decision of the employment tribunal then, under certain circumstances, the case may be referred to a higher level such as one of the UK's appeal courts or even the European Court of Justice.

This European Court consists of 13 judges appointed to represent the European Union (EU). It is responsible for making judgments in relation to the following:

- **EU regulations** – which must be obeyed by all member states from the moment they are introduced
- **EU directives** – which must be obeyed by all member states, but individual countries can decide when and how to introduce them
- **EU decisions** – which are binding on the state to which they directly apply (not necessarily to all member countries).

The European Court of Justice represents the European Union

A UK court has to follow the European Court's rulings on:

- equal pay directives
- employee rights
- human rights
- freedom of movement of workers from country to country
- health and safety.

Snapshot

For better or for worse?

Sometimes action by one person can lead to a change which other people don't like! A case which reached the European Court of Justice involved a woman who worked for South West Hampshire Area Health Authority. She was told she had to retire at 60 but objected, complaining this was discriminatory as her male colleagues could work until they were 65.

She won her case and the British government was told to review the difference between male and female retirement ages. The government concluded that it could not afford to pay the state pension to men at 60. It therefore changed the retirement age for women. From 2020, women will have to work until they are 65 before they can claim the state pension.

Case study

In 1993, Belinda Coote lost her job at Granada Hospitality. She took the case to an employment tribunal claiming sex discrimination, as she had been dismissed because she was pregnant. She won the case and received £11,000.

Belinda Coote took her case to the European Court of Justice, and won

When she tried to get a job in 1995, she was unsuccessful because Granada Hospitality refused to supply her with a reference. She took the case back to a tribunal claiming victimisation. The tribunal dismissed her claim because she was no longer an employee of Granada.

Mrs Coote then appealed to the employment appeal tribunal which asked the European Court of Justice to rule on the case. The European Court ruled in her favour and this decision has changed UK law. It is now illegal for employers to victimise former employees who have won a discrimination case by denying them a reference. In January 2000, Mrs Coote was awarded £195,000 for loss of earnings during the five years she spent fighting the case. She was supported in her claim by her union, the GMB, and also by the Equal Opportunities Commission.

It is not, however, illegal for employers to refuse to give a reference in other circumstances, but the law requires all references to be 'accurate' and 'fair'. This means that all statements must be true and not misleading. To prevent problems, or claims of inaccurate judgements, some firms refuse to give any references. Others simply stick to the facts, for example starting and leaving dates, position held and reason for leaving. Even though employers may be nervous about writing a reference, virtually all firms request one – to confirm the claims made by the job applicant in their CV and at interview.

▶ 1   Why did Belinda Coote go to an employment tribunal?
　 2   Did she win her case? Give a reason for your answer.
　 3   Explain the difference between racial discrimination and sex discrimination.
　 4   When she returned to the tribunal she claimed victimisation. What does this mean?
　 5   What was the eventual outcome in the European Court?
　 6   Why do people wanting to work in another organisation need to ask their past employer for a reference?
　 7   Why would it affect an employee's future prospects to be refused a reference?
　 8   Under normal circumstances, can an employer refuse to give a reference? Give a reason for your answer.

▶ 1   Explain clearly the grounds on which Belinda Coote first went to an employment tribunal.
　 2   What was the result of this case? Give a reason for your answer.
　 3   Identify the stages Belinda Coote went through before the case was referred to the European Court of Justice.
　 4   Did Belinda Coote win her case in Europe? Give a reason for your answer.
　 5   What does the decision mean for other employers in Britain?
　 6   State the main role of the Equal Opportunities Commission and say why it would be involved in this case.
　 7   What is a reference?
　 8   What is the law in relation to references in normal circumstances?

Over to you!

Belinda Coote was supported in her claim by her union, the GMB, and also by the Equal Opportunities Commission (EOC). In Chapter 11, you were asked to find out more about the EOC by accessing its website on www.heinemann.co.uk/hotlinks. Now, investigate how the Commission for Racial Equality and the Disability Rights Commission support people with claims by visiting their websites at www.heinemann.co.uk/hotlinks.

What can go wrong?

It is usually better for everyone if a disagreement is settled quickly and within the workplace. Although the law protects employees who are treated unfairly or unjustly, it is often very stressful to take legal action. Even if a complaint is upheld, it is often unrealistic to expect the employee to want to return to work for that employer, and any monetary award can rapidly disappear if the employee finds it difficult to obtain work again. The danger is that, because all tribunal cases are made public, the person is then branded as a 'trouble maker' by future employers.

Employers, too, can have problems. It takes time and money to prepare a defence and release people to attend a tribunal hearing. If the case against the employer is upheld, then this is damaging to the employer's reputation and of concern for existing employees. In some cases, although ignorance of the law is no excuse, smaller firms have struggled to keep up with all the additions to employment law. They can find it hard to cope with difficult situations such as continuous absence by an employee because of illness and stay within the law. In larger organisations, it can be difficult to control the actions of individual managers and supervisors who may not have had specialist training and may not be clear about their legal 'limits'. Generally, this is why it is better if there is a human resources expert who can advise both managers and employees, and union representatives who can advise employees properly.

Chapter review and practice questions

1. Decide whether each of the following incidents relates to *either*:
   - an employee grievance against the employer, *or*
   - an employer having a valid reason to take disciplinary action against the employee.
      a. Ishmail is told he could be sacked for joining a trade union.
      b. Kevin spends half his time at work surfing the Internet looking for cheap holiday offers.
      c. Paula won't use the telephone to talk to customers and refuses to go on a training course.
      d. Fatima asks for time off to look after her young son who is ill, and is refused by her boss.

2. Tom has changed jobs and works alongside an older woman, Jill. The two of them don't get on. Tom thinks Jill is 'picky' and hates it when she is critical of him in front of other people. Jill thinks Tom is lazy and sloppy. Tom's manager is involved when Jill reports Tom for repeatedly taking home floppy disks from the stationery cupboard. Tom retaliates by claiming Jill victimises him.
    a. Who is initially responsible for sorting out the problem?
    b. Do you think Tom has a valid complaint? Give a reason for your answer.
    c. Do you think Jill has a valid complaint? Give a reason for your answer.
    d. If Jill is correct about Tom taking disks from the cupboard, what action is the manager likely to take?

3. Eleanor thinks she has a justified complaint against her employer. She has read about each of the following but doesn't know who to go to first. Put them into the correct order for her.
   - the European Court of Justice
   - her trade union representative
   - an employment tribunal
   - employment appeal tribunal

1   a   Explain clearly the basic difference between grievance procedures and disciplinary procedures.
    b   Give one example of behaviour by an employee which would most likely result in:
        i   a verbal warning
        ii   a final warning
        iii instant dismissal.
    c   Give two examples of a situation in which an employee would have a valid reason to complain about the actions of his or her employer.

2   Tania is on maternity leave when she receives a letter saying she has been dismissed. Caroline leaves the same firm because she is fed up with her boss. He is constantly pestering her and she feels she can't put up with it any longer. Suhail is upset when he is dismissed for constant bad time-keeping. Joanne says she is seeing a solicitor when she is sacked for refusing to work in a shop on Sunday and John is furious when he is given only two weeks' notice after working for a firm for five years.
    Identify which employees:
    a   have been sacked fairly
    b   can bring a case for unfair dismissal
    c   can bring a case for constructive dismissal
    d   can bring a case for wrongful dismissal.

3   a   What is the role of ACAS in relation to disagreements?
    b   Under what circumstances would a disagreement be taken to an employment tribunal?
    c   If the European Court of Justice makes a judgment on a case, can the British government ignore this? Give a reason for your answer.

Answers to **It makes you think!** on page 225

1   The employee has to comply with reasonable requests and using new equipment is likely to be a term of her contract of employment. She has no legitimate grievance.
2   All employees have the right to time off work for dependants, even though this can be unpaid. She has a legitimate grievance as her employer is acting unlawfully.
3   Employee records must be available under the terms of the Data Protection Act. The employer can charge a maximum of £10 for this service. The employer cannot legally refuse this request.
4   The young man misled the employer at interview and doesn't have the qualifications he claimed to possess. He is incapable of doing the job and this is a legitimate reason for dismissal.
5   The representative knew that being able to drive was an essential requirement of the job. His employer has the legal right to dismiss him.
6   No woman can be sacked for being pregnant or taking maternity leave. This is unfair dismissal and the woman can take this to an employment tribunal.

Answers to It makes you think! on page 228

1. All *could* result in instant dismissal and this is likely to be the result in cases **a**, **b**, **c**, **g**. In cases **h**, **i** and **j** it would depend upon the seriousness of the offence and/or whether the employee had been warned previously. In cases **d**, **e** and **f** the employee would normally be warned but could be dismissed if the behaviour continued.

2. Any of the following: taking bribes, divulging confidential information, clocking in for someone else, repeatedly being incompetent/careless despite having been trained, harassing another employee.

3. The employer must always check the previous conduct of the employee and check that the allegations are accurate. If theft is alleged, the employer does not have to provide proof in the same way the police would have to. If there is strong evidence of dishonesty, this is sufficient.

4. Behaviour out of hours which could have an effect on what that person does at work is a valid reason for dismissal.

5. The dismissals are fair because the manager has strong evidence of dishonesty and has treated them all equally.

Chapter 13 Recruitment

What you will learn
Understanding recruitment
Steps in the process

Overview: recruitment

The recruitment process

All organisations need staff to fill new posts and to replace staff who leave. Sometimes people are promoted to a higher-level job within their own organisation. The advantage for the company is that the abilities of these staff are known to them. Also, because existing staff know how the company operates, they need less training at the start. Promotion helps to motivate existing staff to work hard because they know they can progress.

On other occasions, new staff are brought in from outside. This is because existing staff may not have the specialist skills that are required. In addition, new staff bring in new experiences and knowledge to the company. For this reason, most companies try to recruit using both methods.

Recruitment, however, isn't easy. There may be many applicants for a job, so selecting the best one can be difficult. In addition, employment legislation means each applicant must be treated fairly and equally. Staff involved in recruitment must be aware of this and know what they can do and what they must not do.

Knowing about the recruitment process helps you to understand what happens when you apply for a job yourself. It means you can write your application in a way that will help you to have a better chance of obtaining an interview. If you know what employers are looking for during an interview, this also helps your own performance (see Chapter 14).

1 Identify the vacancy
Agree that a particular job is available

2 Draw up a job description
Summarise the roles and responsibilities of the job

3 Draw up a person specification
Identify the skills and experience that will be required

4 Advertise the vacancy
Select from a range of methods

5 Shortlist applicants
Reduce the number of applicants to those most suitable to be interviewed

6 Interview applicants
Involves one or more people

7 Select and appoint the most appropriate candidate
The main focus of the interview

Steps in the recruitment process

Understanding recruitment

The right person for the job

Recruitment is the process of finding the right person to do a particular job in an organisation. This is usually the responsibility of the human resources department, if the organisation has one. For skilled or higher-level jobs, the manager of the relevant section will also be involved. In a small business, the owner or manager is likely to be in charge of recruitment.

Managers take a keen interest in recruitment because they want the best person possible to be offered the job. Identifying who should be interviewed, and then who should be

It makes you think!

Below is a job advertisement for a job in a Human Resources Department. Study it carefully and then, within your group, answer the following questions:

1. Why has the job become available?
2. What are the main skills and qualifications that the company says are essential for this job?
3. What other skills or qualities does the company think are desirable?
4. Tom has 3 GCSEs but has never had a part-time job. Karen has 2 GCSEs and worked at McDonald's over Christmas. Who do you think is in the better position to be offered an interview and why?
5. What type of work do you think the successful candidate will be doing? (You may wish to look back to Unit 1, Chapter 5 and Unit 2, Chapter 9 before you answer this!)

CALIBRE SOFTWARE LIMITED
Human Resources Trainee

Following the promotion of one of our members of staff, an excellent opportunity exists for a young person with a keen interest in working in a busy Human Resources team.

The successful applicant must have a minimum of 3 GCSEs at grade C or above. Preferably these will include English. Good verbal communication skills and neat handwriting are essential, as is some experience of working with computers, preferably using Microsoft Office. A formal ICT qualification is desirable.

School and college leavers will be considered, but experience of dealing with people in a commercial environment, for example in a part-time job, would be an advantage.

The successful candidate will be required to work towards higher-level qualifications and career prospects are excellent.

Hours: 9 am–5.30 pm. Salary negotiable, depending upon age and experience.

For further details, including a job description and application form, contact Amy Watts, Human Resources Assistant, on 03781 404020.

Calibre Software is an Equal Opportunities employer and welcomes applications from all sections of the community

---

appointed, is not easy, but it is important for the following reasons:

- The recruitment process is expensive. Apart from advertising costs, it takes time to look through applications and to interview.
- If unsuitable staff are hired, this can have undesirable consequences, e.g.
  - if they do not have the right skills, they may struggle to do the job properly
  - if they do not have the right attitude, they can annoy or upset existing staff and/or customers
  - if they do not 'settle in' and leave, the recruitment process has to take place all over again.

Recruitment policies

Most organisations have a policy for recruitment which states what must be done when new staff are being recruited. Normally, all staff involved in interviewing and selection are trained so that they act within the law and know how to interview to get the best results. A copy of Calibre Software's recruitment policy is shown opposite.

This type of policy reduces the possibility of an applicant being treated unfairly. It also tries to ensure that the best applicant is offered the job. The policy covers the main steps in the recruitment process and states what staff should do at each stage.

Understanding the law and ethics in recruitment

You learned about employment law in Chapter 4. With regard to recruitment, discrimination is illegal; that is, a candidate for a job must not be treated unfairly or unfavourably because of race, gender or a disability *at any stage* of the process. For example:

CALIBRE SOFTWARE LIMITED
Recruitment policy

1. Each vacancy must be approved by the departmental manager before it is notified to the Human Resources Department.
2. Each job must be detailed on a job description which states the job title, hours to be worked and lists the tasks to be undertaken.
3. For each job, a person specification must be prepared which states the qualifications and previous experience required by the applicant.
4. All jobs must be advertised within the company as well as externally.
5. Jobs can be advertised at the Jobcentre and in the local paper. The Human Resources manager must agree to national adverts or job placements with recruitment agencies or any other method of advertising.
6. All advertisements must clearly state the essential qualifications and experience required by candidates.
7. On application, all candidates must be sent a job description and must apply by completing a company application form. Two referees are required.
8. Shortlisting must take place by at least two people who are also involved in the interview. Only candidates who have the essential qualifications and experience can be shortlisted.
9. Interviewers must complete an interview checklist. It is expected that the highest-scoring candidate will be offered the job, providing the references are satisfactory.
10. No candidate must be appointed until references have been obtained. A candidate can be offered the job 'subject to satisfactory references' if these are to be obtained after the interview

- tests should not be set which require a high level of written English *unless* this is important in the job
- women attending an interview should not be asked questions about family responsibilities unless men are asked the same questions
- if one candidate is in a wheelchair, an interview room should be chosen to which all candidates have easy access.

The word 'ethics' is used to describe behaviour which is good practice. Acting unethically is bad practice. This may happen if one candidate is treated with favouritism. For example, if an interviewer is immediately impressed by the appearance and looks of a candidate, so chats to that candidate for over half an hour. The interviewer then gives the other candidates only ten minutes each and asks them very difficult questions. Such favouritism is not illegal, unless another candidate could prove discrimination.

Ethical organisations train their interviewers and are strict about the procedures they follow. In particular, interviewers are told to:

- ask the same questions of all candidates and act in the same way to all candidates
- guard against being overly impressed by appearance at the outset
- be careful not to favour an interviewee because he or she attended the same school or is 'a friend of a friend'.

For this reason, many organisations prefer interviews to be carried out by more than one person.

Steps in the process

Agreeing the vacancy

New staff cost money. They need to be recruited and then trained. They are therefore hired only when they are necessary and when the company can afford to pay them. Most departments have a budget for staff and a manager will be allowed to recruit a new person only if it has been agreed that more staff are necessary and the additional money is available.

Similarly, even if someone has left, or been promoted, there has to be agreement that the vacancy must be filled. In some cases, this may not be necessary or it may be decided that the job has changed so the replacement person needs different skills. Equally, a company in financial difficulties or experiencing a fall in demand may decide not to replace staff.

For these reasons, it is usual for vacancies to be formally agreed as the first step in the recruitment process.

Drawing up a job description

A job description summarises the key facts relating to the job. These include the title, salary and main duties and responsibilities.

Most large organisations produce job descriptions, although this is not a legal requirement. Many small firms may not. If a job description is produced, applicants may be sent a copy when they ask for an application form. This enables them to check carefully that the job covers the range of tasks they expected and is at the expected salary level before they formally apply. It also enables candidates to focus their application better and to respond more appropriately at the interview.

An example of the job description for the human resource trainee is shown below.

CALIBRE SOFTWARE LIMITED – Job Description

Department: Human Resources
Job title: Human Resources Trainee
Vacancy No: 489
Hours of work: 9 am–5.30 pm, Monday to Friday
Salary scale: £9,500–£12,500
Responsible to: Human Resources Assistant
Duties and responsibilities
1. Receiving and logging requests for application forms.
2. Sending application forms to enquirers.
3. Receiving and logging completed application forms.
4. Maintaining all files related to job applications, shortlists and interviews.
5. Assisting the Human Resources Assistant in arranging interviews and writing to candidates.
6. Recording staff leave requests and maintaining absence records on computer.
7. General correspondence and filing as required by the Human Resources Assistant.
8. Collecting incoming mail and delivering outgoing mail to the mailroom.
9. Other routine office duties which are commensurate with the job.

Drawing up a person specification

The person specification relates to the person who will do the job. It identifies the essential and desirable qualifications, skills and attributes of the person required. A person specification:

- enables the employer to think about the best type of person for the job
- helps the person drafting the advertisement to highlight the essential and desirable qualities clearly
- enables the applications to be compared more fairly and easily
- helps to identify further training needs which the applicant may have.

An example of a person specification for the human resources trainee is shown on page 239.

Advertising the vacancy

The next stage is for potential applicants to find out about the job vacancy. This involves advertising the job or placing it with an agency. The method chosen will depend upon the type of staff required and how much the company is prepared to spend. Usually, the scarcer the skills required, the more costly it is to recruit staff because more expensive methods need to be used. The chart opposite shows different types of jobs and sources of recruitment.

A job advertisement is usually drafted from the information given in the job description and person specification. The essential requirements should be made clear because anyone without these is normally not considered for interview.

The advertisement should also include information on the conditions of employment – for example, salary and hours worked – and applicants must be informed how to apply or find out further information. Applicants may be asked either:

- to telephone the company – usually this is required only if the company wants to check how candidates sound over the telephone, such as when the vacancy is for a telephone sales job

CALIBRE SOFTWARE LIMITED – PERSON SPECIFICATION

Department: Human Resources
Job title: Human Resources Trainee
Vacancy No: 489

Personal attributes	Essential	Desirable
Qualifications	3 GCSEs grade C or above	GCSE English, ICT
Experience	None	Work experience/part-time work involving dealing with people
Skills and abilities	Verbal communication skills Neat handwriting Computer experience	Use of Microsoft Office
Personal attributes	Keen interest in working in Human Resources Willing to undertake further study Neat and tidy appearance	Friendly personality

Sources of recruitment

Type of vacancy	Source	Cost
Junior/Modern Apprenticeship vacancy for school or college leaver	Careers service, Connexions, local schools or college	Nil
Mainly adult semi-skilled or unskilled	Jobcentre	Nil
Qualified staff in a particular area or temporary staff	Recruitment agency (many specialise in certain types of jobs, e.g. accounts, administration)	Relatively high
Experienced managers or senior staff	Employment consultant	High
Jobs which could be filled by local people	Adverts in local press	Relatively high
Specialist skilled staff not available locally	Adverts in national press or trade journals	High
Promotion opportunities for existing staff	Internal adverts – on noticeboards and by email	Nil

- to call in to the human resources department – this is sometimes used for Jobcentre vacancies, where skilled or unskilled manual workers are required or when temporary seasonal staff are needed urgently
- to write a letter and attach their curriculum vitae (CV) (see Chapter 14, pages 248–249).
- to complete an official application form – these range from simple forms for routine jobs to more complex forms for skilled or senior jobs (see pages 247–248).

The advertisement will also include a closing date after which no applications will be considered. Finally, most organisations also include a statement about their **equal opportunities policy**. (Look back to page 236 at the example of the job advertisement for the Human Resources trainee.)

Spot check

Write down your answers to the following questions:

1. Put the following activities in the interview process into their correct sequence:
   a. Advertise the vacancy.
   b. Draw up the job description.
   c. Draw up the person specification.
   d. Agree the vacancy.
2. a. What is a recruitment policy?
   b. Why do many companies have one?
3. What is the difference between a job description and a person specification?
4. Why do businesses try to fill vacancies both from within the company and through external applications?
5. If you are applying for a job, which is the more important – the essential characteristics or the desirable characteristics required – and why?
6. State four main items in a job advertisement.
7. Identify three ways in which applicants may be asked to apply for a job.
8. Two of the following types of behaviour are illegal and one is unethical. Identify them, and give a reason for each answer.
   a. A woman applied for a job on the security staff at a large store but was told only men would be considered.
   b. The daughter of one of the managers has applied for a job at her father's company. All the other candidates are given a difficult test to do, but she is not.
   c. A black applicant for a customer service job is offered a lower starting salary than the other white applicants.

It makes you think!

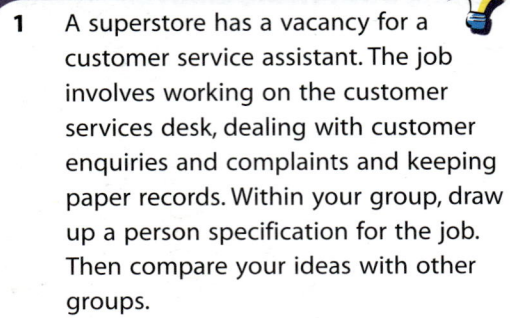

1. A superstore has a vacancy for a customer service assistant. The job involves working on the customer services desk, dealing with customer enquiries and complaints and keeping paper records. Within your group, draw up a person specification for the job. Then compare your ideas with other groups.
2. Along with the job description, some organisations send out information about the company, its location and the working conditions to applicants. Within your group, discuss the following:
   a. Why do you think companies do this?
   b. How helpful do you think this would be if you were applying for a job?
3. Look at the person specification for the human resources trainee on page 239 and compare this with the advertisement on page 236. Discuss the following within your group.
   a. Two characteristics were omitted from the advert. What are they?
   b. Why do you think these were omitted on this occasion?
   c. Do you think all characteristics on the person specification should always be included, or not? Try to think of the advantages and disadvantages in both cases. Then give a reason for your decision.

Shortlisting applicants

A well-written advertisement for a good job is likely to attract far more applicants than a company can interview, so someone has to go through the applications and select the best ones. This can be a difficult task.

It is important that shortlisting is done against the criteria set out on the person specification. It is usually done in stages:

1. Check which applicants have the essential characteristics. Those that haven't are rejected.

Shortlisting means only the best candidates are interviewed

2. Check the desirable characteristics. Those who possess all (or most) of the desirable characteristics would go forward first.
3. Take other aspects into consideration, such as the neatness and style of the application itself. (This stage is required only if there are still too many people for interview.)

The shortlisted applicants – now known as candidates – then receive a letter asking them to attend an interview.

Interviewing applicants

There are different types and styles of interview. These usually depend upon the size of organisation and the type of vacancy:

- One-stage interviews, undertaken by human resources staff, are usual for manual or junior vacancies in medium and large companies.
- One-stage interviews, undertaken by a manager, are common in small companies.
- Two-stage interviews, the first by human resources staff and the second by the manager of the new employee, are usual for higher-level or highly skilled vacancies.

A panel interview, where a group of people interview the candidate, is frequently used for senior jobs.

Interviewers should be trained so that they know *how* to question candidates and the *type* of questions to ask. Good interviewers will ask 'open-ended questions' which can't be answered with a simple 'yes' or 'no'; for example, 'Why do you want this job?' rather than 'Do you really want this job?'. This encourages candidates to talk about themselves, even if they are shy. Interviewers are also trained to 'follow up' very brief or unsatisfactory answers and, where necessary, to query such things as a 'gap' in an employment history without any reason given.

The same questions should be put to all candidates, for fairness, even though the discussion that follows may be different, depending upon the response. As you saw on page 237, certain questions cannot be asked at interview because they are discriminatory.

Some interviews contain a psychometric assessment or skills test to check the abilities of applicants and their suitability for this type of job. For some senior jobs, candidates may have to attend an assessment centre and undergo a variety of tests and activities under observation.

The interview should make the terms and conditions of the job clear to all candidates and cover areas such as holiday entitlement, sick pay, whether overtime is paid and so on.

It is normal to ask each candidate if he or she has any questions. This is often a further 'test' – and questions about career prospects and company plans are always considered more favourably than questions about pay rises and holidays!

At the end, candidates should be thanked for attending and told how, and when, they will be notified of the result.

Selecting and appointing the most appropriate candidate

The process used to make a final decision may vary considerably from one organisation to another. There are two views:

- Some people believe there are fewer errors and misjudgements if candidates are scored numerically at all stages. The candidate with the highest score is offered the job, regardless of the interviewer's personal opinion.
- Others believe that some characteristics can be difficult to score accurately, e.g. 'friendly personality', and yet can make all the difference. Therefore, the interviewer's personal opinion should be the deciding factor.

The best approach is usually a combination of these methods, for the following reasons:

- Scoring candidates is more objective and fairer. Candidates would get points for their application, performance in any tests and performance at the interview.
- If the scoring system is comprehensive and well balanced, it will include all the vital requirements related to the job.
- Scoring is useful if an unsuccessful candidate asks for 'feedback' and the interviewer has to explain why he or she was unsuccessful.

- Scoring can be important if a candidate claims that the interview was unfair and he or she suffered discrimination (see page 237).
- Scoring helps interviewers to remember how all candidates performed.
- The opinions and views of an experienced interviewer are important because he or she will know which applicant would best fit in with the rest of the staff. This is difficult to include on a scoring sheet.
- Two candidates may be equally matched – then it's down to the personal judgement of the interviewer.

The usual process, at the end of the interview, is to check all the scoring sheets. Those candidates who performed less well are rejected. This may leave two or three whose attributes will be discussed. This is the stage at which 'fitting in' with the organisation and its existing staff is considered important. Before a final decision is made, references will be checked if this has not already taken place.

References

Organisations usually ask for two referees. One should come from a 'current' source, such as a recent teacher or tutor, or the person's current manager or supervisor. Quite naturally, though, many people applying for a job do *not* want their employer to be contacted for a reference at this stage because they do not want to risk losing their current job because their boss thinks they are job hunting! For this reason, applicants are within their rights to ask that a current boss is not contacted unless they are offered the job, and organisations must abide by this. However, it is normal for a prospective employer to ask for references and check that these are satisfactory before confirming a job offer.

Making an offer

Once a person has been selected, the organisation makes a formal job offer. The other candidates are not contacted at this stage, in case the first-choice candidate refuses the offer. In that case, an offer may be made to the second choice. Only after the offer has been accepted are other candidates told they have been unsuccessful.

Spot check

Write down your answers to the following questions:

1. What is meant by 'shortlisting'?
2. Why is shortlisting necessary?
3. a What is meant by an 'open-ended question'?
   b Why are open-ended questions used at interviews?
4. Give two advantages of scoring candidates at interview.
5. Why do you think unsuccessful candidates are not notified until one person has officially accepted the job?

What can go wrong?

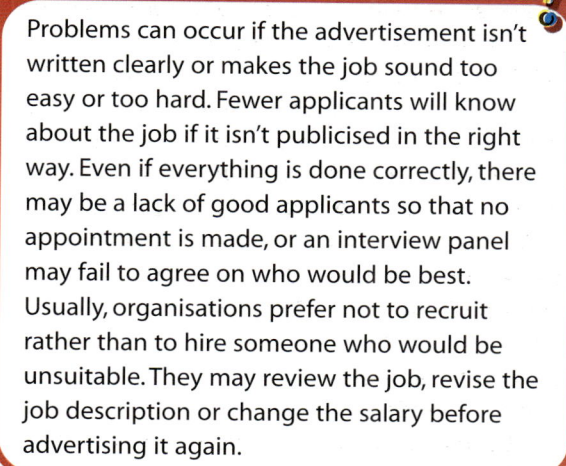

Problems can occur if the advertisement isn't written clearly or makes the job sound too easy or too hard. Fewer applicants will know about the job if it isn't publicised in the right way. Even if everything is done correctly, there may be a lack of good applicants so that no appointment is made, or an interview panel may fail to agree on who would be best. Usually, organisations prefer not to recruit rather than to hire someone who would be unsuitable. They may review the job, revise the job description or change the salary before advertising it again.

Chapter review and practice questions

▶

1. An employer advertises a job and receives 30 applications. Six candidates are chosen for interview.
   a Why would an employer not interview all 30 people?
   b What is the name for the process when the number is reduced for interview?

2. In a small business, all job applications have to be addressed to the manager. In a large business, all job applications have to be sent to the human resources department. Give one reason for this difference.

3. Good interviewers ask 'open-ended' questions.
   a Why do they do this?
   b Give an example of an open-ended question.

4. a Identify two advantages of scoring candidates during an interview.
   b If two candidates have equal scores, what might be the deciding factor?

5. a What is a reference?
   b Why is it useful for interviewers?

▶

1. What is meant by the 'recruitment process'?
2. Why is the recruitment process likely to be different in a very small business and a large business?
3. a Give two reasons why interviewers should be trained.
   b Suggest two topics that would be included in a training course for interviewers.
4. Briefly explain how interviewers will make their selection after the interviews are over.
5. At what point in the process would unsuccessful candidates be informed of the result and why?

Case study

Who should get the placement?

Clearview Veterinary Practice was contacted last month by Deepdale High School. Several of the students had requested a placement with a vet for their work experience, but Karen Phillips, the manager, was determined this wouldn't be the disaster it was last year. A student who fainted at the sight of blood was not the best choice!

Karen started by checking with the senior vet, John Parkes, that they could take on a work experience student. Next she listed the tasks the person would do, working mainly on reception. This would include helping customers and taking payments for pet supplies and pet food. She then decided on the qualities and abilities the right person should possess. The tutor had sent her a list of ten students and from this Karen had chosen four Year 11 students to be interviewed. She then summarised the key information about them:

Mark   Likes science and ICT. No pets. Wants to study science at higher level. Tutor's comment: serious and hardworking.

Kerry Likes English and ICT. Has a rabbit and a dog. Wants to work 'with people'. Tutor's comment: lively but rather easily distracted.

Tahira Likes ICT, business and French. Has a cat. Wants to work training guide dogs. Tutor's comment: bright and always interested.

Simon Likes science and business. Has a cat and a dog. Wants to continue to study business at higher level. Tutor's comment: good worker but occasionally over-confident.

At the interview, Mark is very pleasant but difficult to talk to. Answers have to be dragged out of him. Kerry is outgoing and has a bubbly personality but is a bit giggly. Tahira is very earnest and eager to please and admits to loathing snakes and being frightened of spiders. Simon is very keen, but arrived five minutes late and seemed disappointed that he would have to work on reception most of the time.

1 The veterinary practice had a student on work experience last year.
   a What went wrong?
   b How could this have been avoided?
2 Karen wants the work experience person to help out on reception: dealing with customers and taking payments for pet food and pet supplies. What other tasks do you think the job holder would be expected to do?
3 If you were Karen, what type of person would you be looking for? Karen has already decided that qualifications and experience are not important, though she would prefer someone who is interested in relevant subjects. But she is very keen that the person has the right skills and abilities and personal attributes.
   List the skills and abilities in one column and personal attributes in another. Sub-divide your lists into essential and desirable requirements.
4 Suggest three questions which Karen could ask during the interview which would help her to decide who to choose.
5 Karen has asked for the student's tutor to comment on them. Why do you think she did this?
6 a For each of the following stages in the recruitment process, list the actions that Karen took:
      i   agreeing the vacancy
      ii drawing up the job description
      iii drawing up the person specification
      iv shortlisting applicants
      v   interviewing applicants
      vi selecting and appointing the best candidate.
   b Which stage could Karen miss out, and why?

7 The day before the interview, a veterinary nurse tells Karen that she knows Mark, one of the candidates, because he is a friend of her son. She asks Karen if she wants to know more about him but Karen says 'no'. Why do you think Karen refused her offer?

8 Read through the descriptions of each candidate and list their strengths and weaknesses. Then decide who you think would be the best person to do the job. Compare your answers with other students and be prepared to justify your decision.

Chapter 14: Personal job applications

What you will learn

- Application forms
- CVs
- Job application letters
- Making your application different or special
- The interview

Overview: job applications

Applying for a job

At some stage, you will apply for your first full-time job. You may already have a part-time job and/or have visited at least one organisation on work experience. You may have had to complete official forms or attend a short interview in either of these situations. However, when you apply for a permanent job you are likely to find that the procedure will be more formal. This is because the organisation is making a much greater commitment if it employs you. It needs to be certain that the arrangement will benefit both parties!

What type of job?

The first step is to think about the type of work you want to do. This is important because it is difficult to be enthusiastic about a job which doesn't appeal to you. Before making a decision, you should investigate different types of jobs, talk to your careers adviser and your tutor.

Once you have decided on the type of work you would like to do, try to stay open-minded about the actual job or career you want to follow. Sometimes it is better to make this decision when you have had more experience at a general level and can more accurately assess which areas of work you prefer. Generally, however, you can expect:

- to have a more specialised job role in a large organisation, e.g. if you worked in a finance office, then you would deal with financial documents
- to have a wider job role in a smaller organisation, e.g. you may be expected to do a range of duties relating to several areas of the business.

Investigating jobs is important – try to stay open-minded and don't make any decisions until you've done your research

Finding a vacancy

The next step is to investigate vacancies in the areas in which you are interested. You may obtain information on a vacancy from:

- the careers service Connexions or the Jobcentre
- your careers teacher/tutor or student services at a college
- your local newspaper
- a local recruitment or employment agency.

You may also have the opportunity to join a Modern Apprenticeship scheme. If you become a Foundation Modern Apprentice, then you will study up to NVQ 2; if you become an Advanced Modern Apprentice, you will study up to NVQ 3. (Occupational areas related to business include NVQs in accounting and administration.) In both these cases you will have a permanent job, but the vacancy will be suggested by a training agency or other organisation, who will send you for an interview. You will also be given time to study for your NVQ. If you are interested in this option, talk to your tutor about opportunities in your area.

Applications and interviews

Knowing how to make an application is important because you will be applying for a job in competition with other people. Your careers adviser, tutor or the advertisement will tell you how you should make an application. You may have to:

- send your CV (see below) with a covering letter
- complete and return a job application form
- write a formal letter of application.

Whichever method you are asked to use, it is essential that you prepare your application well to give you the best possible chance of obtaining an interview. This chapter will give you guidance on how to do this.

Your excitement at being offered an interview can soon evaporate if you are wracked with nerves at the very thought! It may help to know that interviews can be an ordeal for even the most experienced employees. Yet a good performance is absolutely essential if you are going to convince an interviewer that you really are the best person for the job (see pages 256–258).

The skills you need

At all stages of the job application and interview process, you need to know:

- how to complete an application form, prepare a job application letter and/or CV, and the 'golden rules' of interviews
- how to 'sell yourself' so that you provide information that will impress the reader or listener. This includes:
  - describing your own skills
  - listing your achievements in and out of school
  - identifying your range of interests
  - demonstrating your enthusiasm for the job
  - saying what you might bring to the job in the future.

Over to you!

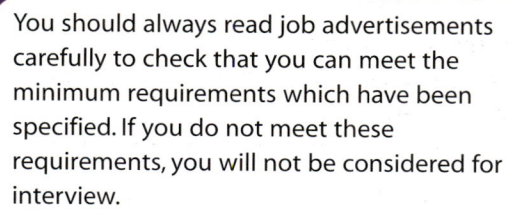

You should always read job advertisements carefully to check that you can meet the minimum requirements which have been specified. If you do not meet these requirements, you will not be considered for interview.

Look through your local newspaper and find two job advertisements which would not be appropriate for you now but would be if you were more skilled or experienced. Think about what skills you would need to develop in order to do them.

Select one advertisement which would be suitable for you and discuss with your tutor why you think this is the case.

Application forms

This section will guide you on the best way to fill in application forms.

Preparations for completing the form

Start by photocopying the form. You can practise on this, have it checked and then complete the original form when you are certain you have done the best you can.

Golden rules

- Read the form through before you do anything.
- Collect all the information you need before you start, e.g. examination results.
- Check if you have to use a particular type of pen (black ink is often required) and that it is 'blotch free'.

- Make sure you understand every question.
- Check where you should use block capitals.
- Check if you need to include the names of any referees – if so, ask for their agreement *before* you include their names.
- Check if there is a section where you have to say why you are applying for the job – this is the most tricky part to complete and is dealt with on page 250.

Common mistakes

- Putting the current year for your date of birth.
- Writing the postcode in the wrong place (check if it should be in the address part or in a separate part).
- Scruffy or illegible handwriting.
- Spelling errors.
- Forgetting to sign and date the form at the end, if this is asked for.
- Completing a section which is clearly headed 'for office use only'.

When you start

- Take your time.
- Make sure you are practising on the photocopy, not the original.
- Think about your answers in relation to the amount of space you have been allowed.
- Make sure you write clearly and legibly.
- Check in a dictionary the spellings of words you are not sure of.

When you have finished your draft

- Read it through and correct any errors.
- Ask someone else, such as your tutor or careers adviser, to read it through. Accept any suggestions or corrections positively, not resentfully!

When you start the original

- Take your time. If there has been a few days' gap between finishing your draft and starting the final version, read through the instructions again to refresh your memory.
- Write *very* neatly.
- Make sure you include any corrections or improvements that have been suggested.
- Check the form through carefully at the end.
- Take a photocopy of the finished version *before* you post it, then you can read it through again before the interview.

Help! What if something goes wrong?

Even with the best care in the world, something can go wrong; for example, your pen runs dry part-way through or you miss out a word or make some other mistake.

Here are some remedies:

- If your pen runs dry, use another pen *in the same colour and texture* as the first. Never start off with a black 'fine' pen and then continue in blue or with a pen which writes in 'medium' strokes.
- Use liquid paper to correct *minor* mistakes. Use a new bottle and put on a tiny amount very carefully – you can always add more if required. Only correct the mistake when the fluid is *completely* dry.

In the last resort, telephone the organisation and ask for another form.

CVs

A CV or **curriculum vitae** is a summary sheet about you and your achievements. It must look professional so you should create it on a word processor and only send an original document, not a photocopy.

Golden rules

- Keep it short – one A4 page is ideal, two is the maximum.
- Set it out clearly – use bold and different type sizes to make the headings stand out.
- Put your personal information first.
- List your achievements in reverse chronological order so that your most recent qualifications and experience are at the beginning.
- Concentrate on what you have done since starting secondary school.

- Include the names of two referees – remember to ask for their agreement *before* you include their names.

Common mistakes

- Attaching a photograph – unless this is asked for.
- Writing too much.
- Exaggerating your qualifications. *Never* claim to have a qualification or a grade you haven't achieved.
- Exaggerating your skills or abilities.

Sections in a CV

A CV is normally divided into sections under specific headings – see below. At the very top, you can either put the heading CURRICULUM VITAE – this is the traditional method – or your name.

Personal details

- Your name (if this is not part of the heading)
- Address
- Telephone number (you could also include a mobile number or email address)
- Date of birth
- Marital status (optional)

Educational details

- Secondary school(s) attended and dates
- GCSE results
- Any examinations taken where you are awaiting the result
- Other awards at school/positions of responsibility held
- Work experience details

If you have left school and are at college, then you must also state the name of the college, date you started there, course attended and current examinations/awards being taken.

Employment details

- Current job held, if you are working, with a brief description of the duties
- Previous jobs held and areas of responsibility (if applicable)
- Details of any part-time or Saturday jobs you have done if you are a full-time student

Other useful information

- Details of any hobbies, interests, sports or voluntary work you have done
- Details of any organisations to which you belong
- Any other useful, relevant information, e.g. driving licence

Referees

It is usual to give two names. One should be a current tutor who knows your work well. It is useful if your other referee knows how you work in business, so this could be your employer if you work part time or someone who supervised you on work experience. Avoid putting the name of a member of your family. Most organisations would think that such a person would naturally be biased towards you!

Job application letters

Types of job application letters

There are three main types.

Brief covering letters

If you are sending your CV, it is usual to attach a brief covering letter that explains why you are sending it. This is different from a formal job application letter as all the main information is given in the CV so there is no need to repeat it. However, this letter must:

- include your home address
- be dated
- be addressed to the correct person
- include any reference numbers specified in the advertisement
- be easy to read – you can prepare the letter on a word processor unless the advertisement says otherwise
- be signed by you.

A letter justifying your application

A harder letter to write is one in which you are asked to say why the job interests you. This type of letter is dealt with below.

A formal job application letter

It is rare, these days, to be asked to apply by letter without a CV. This is because it is easier to assess applications from CVs. If the organisation receives a long letter, every word has to be read to extract the information.

However, just because writing an application letter without a CV is rare doesn't mean it is unknown! It is therefore useful to know the difference if the advertisement simply asks you to apply in writing.

Golden rules

- Keep the letter fairly short – three or four short paragraphs is sufficient.
- Use the standard format for a business letter (see page 255).
- Check if the advertisement says you must apply in *writing* – otherwise, you may word process the letter if you prefer.
- Make sure there are no spelling, punctuation or grammatical errors.

Structure of a job application letter

- The *first paragraph* should say where you saw the advertisement (or found out about the job) and formally state that you would like to apply for the position.
- The *second paragraph* should give general background information about yourself – at school, college or work. At this stage, if you are enclosing a CV, you would refer to it. Otherwise you will need to go into more details about your qualifications and the work you have done.
- The *third paragraph* should state your reasons either for wanting this job or to work for this organisation – or anything else to make your application different or special.
- The *final paragraph* should say you are available for interview at any time or state when you are *not* available.

Making your application different or special

The hardest task is talking positively about yourself! You will have to do this:

- on an application form, if there is a box in which you must say why you want the job
- in a letter, if you are asked to say why you are applying for the job
- in some cases, on the CV itself. If you are asked to send *only* a CV, you can write a brief personal statement about yourself and put this at the top, underneath your name.

Even though it might sound like hard work, every application should be tailored to the particular job and, if possible, the organisation. Don't produce one standard CV and one standard letter and sending it off in response to every advertisement that appeals to you!

You should also emphasise your own personal skills and achievements that, where possible, link with the essential and desirable requirements stated in the advertisement. Before you do this, think carefully about your skills and achievements. The activity on page 254 will help you to do this.

Writing about your strengths

One way to help you do this is to think about your strengths in 'groups', for example:

- **Describing your skills**: 'I enjoy working with ICT equipment and can use a wide range of software. I also enjoy working as a member of a team. I have undertaken several group assignments and have been told I am a productive and positive member of the group.'
- **Listing your achievements in and out of school**: 'I am a keen runner and won in the 400 metres town championships. I am also an active member of the school computer club and this year have been responsible for helping younger students who have recently joined the club.'
- **Identifying your range of interests**: 'I am interested in outdoor activities and am working towards my Duke of Edinburgh

bronze award. As part of this award, I have been working with a local environmental group, helping to clean up an area close to the canal.'

- **Demonstrating your enthusiasm**: This is easier to do if you are a naturally enthusiastic person! Use words and phrases to stress how keen you, e.g. 'I am very interested in . . .', 'I really enjoy . . .', 'I would very much like to work in sales because . . .'.
- **What you might bring to the job in the future**: This is more likely to be important at the interview. At this stage, you should indicate that you would welcome the opportunity to develop your skills and take further qualifications so that you will become more valuable to the company in the future. It also helps if you have some idea of a career plan in your mind!

What are your strengths? Write some headings on a sheet of paper, then jot down your thoughts

Case study

Applying for a job

Adam Bradshaw has seen a job which appeals to him in the *Mellington Gazette*. The advertisement is shown below.

> **AQUA SOFT DRINKS plc**
> **Marketing Trainee**
>
> Enthusiastic, well-organised person required to join our busy marketing team. Duties will include assisting with direct mail, updating the customer database and marketing administration. Excellent opportunity to learn e-marketing and develop sound marketing communications skills.
>
> Good English and basic IT skills are essential. Experience of dealing with customers and working in a team would be an advantage.
>
> This position would be suitable for a school or college leaver who has the required skills and is prepared to study for higher-level qualifications.
>
> Hours: 8.30 am–5.15 pm. Salary negotiable, depending upon age and experience.
>
> Please send your CV, together with a brief letter stating what interests you about the job, to Joanna Marsh, Marketing Assistant, by 16 January 2003.
>
> Aqua Soft Drinks plc, Abbey Road, Mellington MG3 6PT
> *Aqua Soft Drinks is an equal opportunities employer*

Adam prepares a CV and a covering letter, as instructed – see pages 254–255.

▷▷

1   Identify the essential and desirable requirements of the job.
2   Decide whether Adam meets these requirements, or not. Give a reason for your opinion.
3   Identify whether Adam has done each of the following. In each case, find evidence to support your view:
    a   described his own skills
    b   listed his achievements
    c   identified his interests
    d   demonstrated his enthusiasm
    e   said what he might bring to the job in the future.
4   Do you think Adam has prepared a 'general' application or tailored his application to this particular job? Give a reason for your opinion.
5   Using Adam's technique, refer to *either* the job advertisement on page 236 or the one opposite. Alternatively, your tutor may prefer

you to use an advertisement from your local paper. Then write your own CV and letter. Include a short paragraph saying why you are particularly interested in that job. Check your letter and CV with your tutor and make any suggested amendments.

ADAM BRADSHAW

Address: 14 Centenary Way, Mellington, MG6 3ML
Telephone: 03781 683737
Nationality: British
Date of birth: 12 June 1988
Marital status: Single

EDUCATION
2002–present: Mellington College, part-time Internet Technology course
1997–2002: Westward High School, studying for GCSEs

QUALIFICATIONS OBTAINED
June 2002 – GCSEs:
English (B)
Applied Business (Double Award) (BB)
Maths (C)
Applied ICT (Double Award) (CC)
Science (Double Award) (CC)
French (D)

QUALIFICATIONS TAKEN BUT RESULTS NOT YET KNOWN
Jan. 2003 – OCR, Internet Technologies Stage 1

WORK EXPERIENCE
March 2002: Parker and Scholes Accountants – I worked in the marketing office and helped prepare and distribute financial newsletters to customers.

EMPLOYMENT
In my last year at school I worked each weekend at the Latest Releases Video Store in Hightown. When I left school they offered me a full-time job because I was used to helping and serving customers. This has helped me to understand the business better and to see how the customer database is used to improve sales.

ADDITIONAL INFORMATION
I studied an Internet Technology course at college on a part-time course to help my career prospects. I am very interested in ICT and how it is used in business. My hobbies include playing football – I play for a local charity team – and going to the cinema. I am also learning to drive.

REFEREES
Mrs J Brookes, Tutor, Mellington College, Newby Road, Mellington, MG1 3SL, telephone 03781 382798
Mr T Harper, Manager, Latest Releases Video Store, Swan Street, Mellington, MG2 5KS, telephone 03781 603982

14 Centenary Way
MELLINGTON
MG6 3ML

10 January 2003

Ms Joanna Marsh
Marketing Assistant
Aqua Soft Drinks plc
Abbey Road
MELLINGTON
MG3 6PT

Dear Ms Marsh

MARKETING TRAINEE

I would like to be considered for the position of Marketing Trainee which was advertised in the Highgate Gazette yesterday.

I left Westward High School last July and since then have been working at Latest Releases Video Store. I have just completed a part-time course at Mellington College where I studied Internet Technology. I am attaching my CV which gives full details of the qualifications I have taken and my results to date.

I would very much like to be considered for this job for several reasons. I am very interested in both marketing and IT and this is why I tried to develop my customer service and Internet skills after leaving school. I am used to using customer databases and helped with a customer mailshot when I was on work experience. I would really enjoy learning more about e-marketing and would welcome the opportunity to obtain higher-level qualifications. I am very familiar with the range of products made by your company, which are excellent quality and value for money. I also know your organisation has an excellent reputation for training staff.

I am an enthusiastic and conscientious worker. I am also used to working in a team – both at Latest Releases and as a member of a local charity football team.

I can attend for interview at any time.

Yours sincerely

Adam Bradshaw

Enc

It makes you think!

1. Do the skills audit below and write a short paragraph about:
   - the skills you think you have
   - those you think you need to develop
   - those you are not sure about.

   Add a second paragraph in which you list any skills which you think you have but which are not included in the list.

2. Next, complete the quiz on page 255 to analyse your personal strengths and weaknesses. Write a brief summary after completing the quiz which lists these.

3. Finally, make three further lists:
   a. List *all* your achievements, both in and out of school. This is a 'feel good' activity at this stage. So if your first achievement was learning how to swim, write it down! You can refine your list later.
   b. List *all* your interests. Make it specific, rather than general, e.g. playing cricket (rather than 'sports'), reading science fiction books (rather than 'reading').
   c. List any other facts about yourself which other people might find interesting. This can include school or out-of-school activities, voluntary work, membership of any organisation, visiting a foreign country on an exchange visit and so on.

4. Arrange an opportunity to talk to your tutor to review and refine your lists. This should be a positive session, not a critical one! It is also an opportunity to see how other people see you. If you are an optimist, then you can hope your tutor spots strengths you haven't listed. If you are a pessimist, you will probably worry he or she will find more weaknesses! The aim of this exercise is to end up with lists of:
   - your strengths, skills and abilities
   - developmental areas, which you can prioritise with your tutor
   - achievements which your tutor thinks you should highlight in any job application
   - relevant interests and other information which would be helpful to an employer. However, it shouldn't look as if you are so occupied with leisure interests you haven't time to go to work!

Job skills audit

How good are you at job skills?
Give yourself a rating of 1–5 (1 = very good) for each of the following:

- using the telephone
- speaking to people
- answering queries
- writing letters or reports
- writing neatly
- spelling
- working accurately
- finding and correcting my own mistakes
- working with details
- using ICT equipment
- using a range of software
- using the Internet
- finding what I put away
- organising paperwork
- organising my own work
- meeting deadlines
- being punctual
- planning how to do a job
- solving problems
- making decisions
- thinking up new ideas
- handling cash
- dealing with numbers
- business calculations
- listening to other people
- dealing with customers
- helping other people
- working as a member of a team

Personal skills audit

Achievement profile
1. Are you competitive or laid back?
2. Do you accept responsibility for your own actions and mistakes, or expect other people to 'rescue' you when you have a problem?
3. Do you enjoy new challenges or worry about them?
4. Do you set yourself realistic targets and goals?
5. Do you regularly achieve the targets and goals you set?
6. How do you react to failure?
7. Do you keep going if a job is more difficult than you expected, or give up?
8. Do you stay calm under pressure, or panic?
9. Do you ever put the blame on other people when something goes wrong?
10. Would you ever cheat to get what you want?

Emotional profile
1. Do you get upset easily?
2. Are you easily bored? If so, do you show it?
3. Are you easily depressed?
4. Do you enjoy arguing, or do people in authority make you feel nervous (e.g. a boss or your tutor)?
5. Do you lose your temper easily, or rarely?
6. Do you get annoyed if someone suggests you could have done something better?
7. How tactful are you?
8. Do you sulk or bear grudges?
9. Do you think before you speak?
10. Can you 'give in gracefully' when necessary?

Social profile
1. Do you make friends easily?
2. Do you like to have a busy social life?
3. Is it very important to you to be 'in' with the crowd?
4. Do you like being on your own?
5. Are you always friendly?
6. Can you keep a secret?
7. How do you react if you find out someone doesn't like you?
8. Are you easily impressed?
9. Do you respect other people's opinions, even if they differ from your own?
10. Can your friends rely on you for help and support?

Life profile
1. Are you always in a rush?
2. Do you burn the candle at both ends?
3. Do you like to keep fit?
4. Are you a 'self-starter', or do you need someone to give you a push?
5. Do you work quickly?
6. Do you regularly meet deadlines?
7. Are you a worrier, or does nothing bother you?
8. Do you quickly grasp how to do a job, or prefer to have a task spelt out in detail?
9. Do you live for today, or plan for the future?
10. Are you energetic and enthusiastic about new things?

The interview

At interview, people often worry that:

- they won't know what to say
- they won't be able to answer the questions
- they will talk too much, or not enough.

Preparing for an interview will help you to feel more confident. This is likely to mean that you talk more easily and positively and give a better impression of yourself.

Remember also that:

- an interview should be a two-way process – *you* should also be finding out whether the job is suitable for you
- if you aren't successful, you can count the experience as good practice – there are other jobs out there, this one just wasn't for you.

Tests

Your interview may include one or more tests.

You may be asked to take a psychometric test which will help the employer to find out more about your skills and abilities. Psychometric tests usually cover:

- your verbal abilities
- your numerical abilities
- how well you understand abstract concepts
- your mechanical skills
- how well you deal with other people
- how you think
- your coping skills.

In most jobs in business you can expect an interviewer to be interested in areas such as verbal abilities, some numerical abilities, people skills and coping skills.

Some organisations will ask you to do communication and numeracy tests, depending on the job. For an administration job, a keyboarding test may be given if you have no formal qualification in this skill.

Preparing for interview

Before the interview

- Check the date, the day and the time.
- Find out where the organisation is located, how to get there and how much travelling time you will need in order to arrive in good time.
- Think about what you will wear. Make sure your clothes are clean and neatly ironed, and that your shoes are clean. Always be more conservative than normal.
- Check your personal appearance – make sure your hair and nails are clean.
- Find out about the organisation. How big is it? What does it do? Is it local or national? Have you read any of its advertisements?
- Think about the job and what type of skills you must stress you have. To help, re-read your lists about your skills and achievements. Highlight the ones you want to mention during the interview.
- Try to think about the type of questions you may be asked, e.g. 'Why did you decide to apply for this job?', 'What interests you about this job?', 'What subjects did you enjoy most at school/college?', 'Why do you want to work in this area?'
- Be ready with an explanation should you have a gap in your CV or work history – the interviewer is likely to explore this.
- Decide what to take with you to the interview, such as your Progress File or Record of Achievement, a reference from a part-time employer or examples of excellent work you have produced.
- Think about questions *you* can ask at the interview. Most interviewers invite you to ask questions so you should always have one or two ready, e.g. 'Will I be able to continue to study for a qualification?', 'What are the exact hours of work?', 'If I worked hard, could you tell me what my promotion prospects might be?' Avoid questions which focus on holidays or pay rises!

On the day

Some ways to make a good impression:

- Arrive a few minutes early.
- Give your name to the receptionist and say why you are there. Remember to be polite and to smile. Other staff may be asked what they thought about you later!
- Take a deep breath and try to relax when you are asked to meet the interviewer.
- Knock before you enter the room.
- Concentrate when you are told the interviewer's name. Try to use the person's name once or twice to refresh your memory, e.g. 'Hello, Mr Jackson' rather than just 'Hello'.
- If the interviewer holds out his or her hand, shake it firmly.
- Smile when you are first introduced.
- Sit down only when invited to do so.
- If you are holding a bag, put it on the floor.

The sequence of the interview

A trained interviewer will usually follow a set sequence. An untrained interviewer may not! This may happen if you apply to work for a very small business where the owner interviews you.

The structured interview

During *stage one*, the interviewer will try to help you relax and may comment on general events or whether you found the building easily. Make polite replies. You may also be told how the interview will proceed.

Stage two normally relates to your application form, CV or letter. The interviewer may take you through this and ask questions relating to the content.

At *stage three*, the interviewer will tell you more about the job and the tasks you will undertake. You can now expect to be asked more in-depth questions about your own skills and abilities and how these would relate to the job itself.

At *stage four*, you will be asked if you have any questions or any other comments you wish to make. This is the point at which you:

- prove you have done some research about the company and have a keen interest in working there
- highlight any relevant skills or achievements you have which haven't been discussed so far
- make it clear that you really want to work hard and develop your skills and career.

Stage five is the end of the interview when you will be told what will happen next. The standard close is tell you that you will hear from the organisation shortly.

The unstructured interview

In an unstructured interview, make sure that you get across to the interviewer your main skills, attributes and achievements.

Positive communications

Communicate positively with the interviewer at all times.

- Make eye contact.
- Speak clearly.
- Look and sound interested and enthusiastic and keen to get the job.
- Give full answers, not just 'yes' and 'no'.
- Sit up straight.
- Keep your hands in your lap – don't fiddle with your hair or jewellery.
- Keep personal problems to yourself.
- Never being negative, e.g. 'I think filing is boring'.
- Don't bluff if you can't answer a question – just say you are sorry, but you don't know.
- Never argue with or contradict the interviewer.
- Say thank you and goodbye at the end of the interview.
- Remember to take all your possessions with you.

Coping with problem areas

If you don't understand a question say so politely; for example, 'I'm sorry, I'm not sure I understand what you mean. Could you repeat the question, please?'

If you are asked what questions you would like to ask, remember your prepared list. If these have already been answered, simply say 'I did have some questions to ask but you've covered everything I wanted to know, thank you'.

You may be asked a hypothetical question; for example, 'What would you do if you were alone on reception and the phone rings as a visitor appears?' Think about a previous similar situation when you have had to cope with this. Otherwise, simply use your common sense!

The final touches

Finally, remember that the interviewer is trying to assess not only your qualifications but also:

- how keen and eager you are to work hard and get on
- how well you will get on with the people you will be working with
- how well you can express yourself.

Use the interview as an opportunity to prove this by using not just the information in your lists, but your own experiences – on work experience, in a part-time job, at school, doing voluntary work – to provide evidence to support what you claim.

Chapter review and practice questions

▶▶

1   Select one organisation in your own area. Assume you have applied for a job there and want to find out more about the work that they do.
    a   State how you would find out the information you need.
    b   Investigate the organisation and find out one fact you could refer to at interview.
    c   Plan a question based on that fact.

2   Prepare a key checklist of all the main items of information about yourself that you would:
    a   include in any written job application
    b   try to mention in an interview.

3   Identify four skills or abilities that you have and, in each case, provide evidence from your own experiences which you could mention to prove your claim.

4   You are asked the following questions at an interview. Prepare an answer that is more than just 'yes' or 'no'.
    a   What was your favourite subject at school?
    b   What was your best subject at school?
    c   Did you enjoy school?
    d   Do you like working with people?
    e   Are you good at figures?
    f   What type of work have you done on a computer?
    g   What would you like to be doing in two years' time?
    h   What skills do you want to develop in the future?

Chapter 15 Staff development and training

What you will learn

Ongoing training and development for staff
Appraisal or performance reviews
Retraining to use new technology or new working practices
Investors in People and National Training awards

Overview: development and training

Most businesses encourage their staff to continue training and to develop their skills and abilities. This benefits the organisation, because as staff increase their knowledge and skills they can do new and different tasks and take on more responsibility. This also motivates staff. Most people enjoy their job more if they are learning new things and feel they are achieving.

Most organisations provide a range of training opportunities. They will also expect staff to take an interest in self-development.

Fact file

Training refers to specific opportunities to develop skills and abilities such as learning a new software package or attending a health and safety course. Training is usually **job related**.

Development refers to any activities which increase knowledge, skills or experience whether job related or not. It could include working in a different department or learning a foreign language.

The main methods of training and development used in business include:

- the use of **ongoing training** for all employees – e.g. encouraging staff to take higher-level qualifications or to participate in training events organised in the company
- the use of **appraisal** or **performance reviews** – at which staff have the opportunity to discuss what they would like to learn and do in the future
- **retraining** to use new technology or to understand new working practices – e.g. training to use a new software package or email system
- the use of **national awards**, such as Investors in People and National Training Awards.

Ongoing training for staff

Ongoing training means that training is always available. There are several reasons for this.

- New staff need to learn about the company and the working methods used. These may be different from those used by their last employer. They also need to learn about health and safety requirements, which also may be slightly different. These aspects are covered in an **induction programme** which all new staff must attend. Holding regular induction programmes mean that new staff settle down more quickly, understand how the company operates and can do their jobs more effectively from the beginning.
- Newly promoted staff may need extra training, even though they already work in the company, because the new job is more complex. They may also be supervising staff for the first time and need to develop this skill.
- Jobs change and so do the skills people need. Training helps people to keep up to date.

Training and development can include many different activities

- People are normally more motivated and interested in their work if they continue to learn and develop.
- Learning new knowledge and skills means people can take on more varied work, which makes their jobs more interesting.

Fact file

Training opportunities can be provided **on the job**. This is 'learning while you work'. An example would be someone showing you how to use a photocopier or office telephone system.

Off-the-job training can take place within the organisation, but in a different location such as a training room, or outside the organisation at an FE college or specialist centre.

Types of training and the costs of training

There are many types of ongoing training in many different locations, as shown in the chart opposite. The type of training an organisation can offer will often depend on what it can afford. Even the most committed organisation will be restricted by its training budget – the amount of money allocated for training and development activities. External courses can be quite expensive – accommodation and travel add to the cost. Internal events are cheaper, especially if a number of staff are involved.

A large organisation may have its own training department with special facilities, such as a lecture theatre, IT workshop, resource centre and smaller rooms for group discussions. In a smaller organisation, specialist facilities are less likely to be available. Staff may be encouraged to benefit from e-learning (where they learn on a PC, either at work or at home) or to go on courses run locally or specially arranged by the company.

Sometimes more imaginative types of training can be virtually free! Often these are known as **peer-to-peer** training such as job swapping and skills exchange sessions.

Type of training	Example activities	Where undertaken	Cost
Induction	Familiarisation with company, workplace, methods of working and health and safety	In the workplace	Low
Short courses	Customer service skills, health and safety, IT training, using the Internet, first aid, telephone skills, presentation skills, team building, time management, coping with stress	In the workplace; by e-learning; at specialist centre or college	Low if in company or by e-learning; more expensive if elsewhere – cost depends upon number of days/travel involved
Work-related and professional qualifications	IT, e-commerce, business, management, marketing, personnel, National Vocational Qualifications (e.g. Administration or Accounting)	Usually on day-release or evening courses at college; some available by e-learning	NVQs are free for Modern Apprentices as part of scheme; course costs vary depending upon level and length of course
Academic development	A levels, foundation degrees, first degrees, MBA	Usually on day-release or evening course at college or university	Quite expensive, especially if high level

It makes you think!

1. Below are eight topics to be included in an induction programme. Within your group, put them into a logical order for the participants.
   a. Company IT network and computer systems (hands-on session)
   b. Introduction to the company, its structure and operations
   c. Transfer to own working area and introduction to colleagues
   d. Introduction and welcome by the managing director
   e. Health, safety and fire training
   f. Information on terms and conditions of employment
   g. Guided tour of buildings
   h. Information on training and staff development opportunities
   How long you would allow for each activity?

2. Many companies allocate a mentor to each new employee. A mentor is a colleague with more experience who knows the company well and can give friendly and useful advice. Within your group, discuss three benefits of having a mentor, and identify any disadvantages.

3. The training manager in a medium-sized firm is considering transferring induction information to computer so that new staff will learn online. At present, for cost reasons, induction programmes are held for only five staff or more. This has meant that sometimes staff have worked for two or three weeks before they attend an induction session. Within your group, discuss the following questions:
   a. Why is it cheaper to wait until five staff have started than to hold induction programmes every week?
   b. Why is the company concerned about the cost of induction programmes?
   c. What disadvantages do you think there will be for staff who do their induction by e-learning? (See Snapshot on page 262.)

Snapshot

E-learning

Electronic learning on the intranet is the latest way for companies to train their staff

Large organisations are starting to install e-learning computer networks and encouraging employees to access training packages stored on the company intranet. Imparta, a specialist in e-learning technology, estimates that although the initial costs can be £100 per employee, after that training can cost half as much as before, with no travel and accommodation to pay.

Employees gain the benefit of learning when and how they like – and at their own pace.

Those who enjoy being on a computer or playing computer games appear to enjoy it most of all, especially when there are good computer graphics and interactive tests.

The topics available can be tailored to suit the company. The House of Fraser, a large retailer, has linked its 50 stores electronically and includes customer services, telephone skills, finance and management training packages. The Nationwide Trust, part of the Nationwide building society, offers staff at 15 sites training in IT, health and safety, management and multimedia on laptops away from the main office.

Experts forecast that e-learning will almost double by 2006 as it is suitable for all types of organisations, both small and large. Others have their doubts. They say people prefer the social aspects of learning in a group and the exchange of ideas. They also think some employers may expect staff to 'learn' in their lunchtime or at home, and to forget it altogether on busy days.

E-learning is being strongly promoted in Britain through Learn Direct, which holds a database of hundreds of training and learning opportunities, some online and some delivered in class. You simply log on to find what you need.

Appraisal or performance reviews

Most employers expect their staff to take an active interest in their own training and self-development. This is usually a major part of an **appraisal scheme**. Under this scheme, each employee has a confidential interview with his or her manager, usually once a year. The discussion covers:

- the work the employee has done well during the year
- areas where the employee feels less confident or has performed less well
- types of work (or jobs) the employee would like to do in the future.

In some companies these are called **performance reviews** because the employee's performance since the last review is discussed.

Employees are expected to make a positive contribution to the discussion. A good manager will listen carefully and try to help with any concerns or worries. He or she will also want to link the employee's future ambitions to the overall aims of the company.

In this way everyone benefits. Employees benefit because they are involved in making decisions about their future. Employers benefit because they can plan staff training needs to meet current and future requirements. During these sessions, managers often identify staff who show potential to do well in the future.

Arranging training

Once a training need has been identified, arrangements need to be made for the employee to attend a suitable training event. The procedure usually includes:

- identifying suitable courses or opportunities and comparing costs
- agreeing whether the training will be carried out within working hours or whether the employee will be expected to give up some free time as well (e.g. for an afternoon and evening course)
- completing a training request form
- having this agreed by the manager.

Employees who are keen to do a particular course often research the opportunities available themselves *before* their appraisal interview or performance review, then they can suggest these to their manager.

Spot check

Write down your answers to the following questions:

1. What is the difference between training and development?
2. Identify three reasons why ongoing training for staff is necessary.
3. What is e-learning?
4. a Which is usually cheaper – a training course held in the company or a training course held elsewhere?
   b Explain why the cost is different.
5. State two topics which would be discussed during an appraisal interview.
6. a Identify one skill that would be easier to learn on the job.
   b Identify one skill that would be easier to learn off the job.

Snapshot

First find the learning rep!

For some time, unions have been involved in supporting and encouraging members to undergo training to upgrade their skills. The government has backed this and has funded various projects through a Union Learning Fund. This enabled more than 3,000 union learning representatives to be trained. The TUC estimates that they have encouraged nearly 50,000 employees to take up work-based training. Some unions, such as the Graphical Paper and Media Union (GPMU) received funding to introduce online courses for its members.

If passed, the Employment Bill introduced in November 2001 will give union learning reps legal rights. It will enable all learning reps to be recognised, even in small companies; enable them to have paid leave to train for their own role; give them paid leave for carrying out their role and allow employees to obtain advice and guidance from the learning rep. It is expected that by 2011 there will be 22,000 union learning reps.

You can find out more at the TUC website, which gives information on learning opportunities. See www.heinemann.co.uk/hotlinks.

Retraining to use new technology or new working practices

Technology is constantly changing – business software is regularly updated, computer operating systems are upgraded, the organisation may install new software. In all these cases, staff will be expected to learn how to use the new or updated facilities.

Hardware changes less rapidly, but is still developing. Most businesses operate a networked system, where computers are occasionally linked together, and the network will also be upgraded to make it faster. Individual users may be expected to use their PC, a scanner, CD-burner and a Zip drive (which backs up files quickly).

Technological developments don't just affect computers – they result in changes to many items of business equipment. Today, digital photocopiers are available which can be operated from a computer. These are very different from basic types of copiers.

The term 'working practices' relates to the way people do their jobs, and these also change regularly. Ten years ago, for instance, people within a company communicated mainly by telephone or memo, whereas now email is the most common method.

Legal changes frequently affect the way people work. New health and safety or employment legislation will affect many staff, not just those working in human resources. Environmental legislation and concerns can change the way goods must be packed or waste materials must be handled.

In all these cases, staff need to be trained so that they know how the change will affect their work. Normally, they will be trained in the company if the change or update is specific to that organisation and affects many staff. However, staff who will be involved in a new development such as exporting goods overseas or enhancing a company's website may be sent elsewhere for specialist training.

Case study

The right training for the job

Philip Kent has just started work in the sales and marketing office of Brown and Bennett. He loved IT at school but is struggling to understand the computer system here, which is very different. He also dislikes talking to customers over the telephone as the company has many overseas customers and he is worried that he will not be able to understand them. His line manager, Craig Jenkins, has told him that he wants Philip to continue his studies and work towards either a higher-level business or a marketing qualification.

A week earlier, Martine Jessop started in the same firm. She doesn't mind answering the phone but can't transfer callers without cutting them off. She is also worried that she cannot use the fax machine properly, and would like to improve her IT skills so that she could produce documents more quickly and accurately and understand spreadsheets.

Craig Jenkins also considers that all his staff could usefully benefit from a team-building course. He is thinking of taking them away for a day to an activity centre where they will have to solve problems and do various tasks together. He has three brochures on his desk. One is for a centre 50 miles away, which has an excellent range of facilities and specialist trainers, but is quite expensive. One is for a local centre, familiar to all the staff, but with only average facilities. The other is completely different. It is a paint-balling activity centre about 15 miles away.

1. Identify one reason why Philip's line manager wants him to continue his studies.
2. Identify one benefit to Philip of continuing his studies.
3. Martine wants to go on a word processing course. Do you think Craig will agree? Give a reason for your answer.
4. Craig suggests that both Philip and Martine should improve their telephone skills, and also Martine's fax skills, by watching other people and then trying

themselves under supervision. They will therefore learn on the job. Identify two benefits of learning to use the telephone this way.

5 Martine is shy and the thought of paint-balling horrifies her. She hates the idea of being part of a team and is thinking about refusing to go.
   a What do you think Martine would learn on a team-building course?
   b Do you think Craig should insist she attends? Give a reason for your answer.

6 Martine finds out she could do an IT course in an evening that covers both word processing and spreadsheet. Again she wonders whether to refuse unless she can go during the day.
   a What would be the benefits for Martine of doing the course?
   b What would be the benefits for her employer?
   c Why would it be unwise for her to refuse?

7 a Why is Craig concerned about the cost of team-building training?
   b To what extent do you think this should influence his choice?

1 Brown and Bennett doesn't run an induction course for staff. Identify three benefits of introducing such a course.

2 What type of training do you think is needed by Philip and Martine? Make a list of suggestions.

3 Which of Philip and Martine's training needs do you think could be covered by learning at work, and which would they need to learn off the job? Give a reason for your decision in each case.

4 Identify two benefits of agreeing to this training for:
   a Brown and Bennett
   b Philip and Martine.

5 a Assess the three choices of activity centre which Craig Jenkins is considering by listing the benefits and drawbacks of each one.
   b Explain why Craig would have to consider carefully the cost of each one.
   c Craig is considering asking the staff which one they would prefer. What advantages and disadvantages are there in doing this?
   d If you were Craig, which would you choose and why?

6 Evaluate Brown and Bennett's approach to training and explain how this should benefit both the company and its staff.

National awards

The government wants organisations to train their staff so that Britain has a highly skilled workforce. It has therefore introduced schemes to encourage this.

INVESTORS IN PEOPLE

NATIONAL TRAINING AWARDS

Investors in People and the National Training Awards encourage excellence in the workplace – check to see if the organisations you investigate have either of these

Investors in People

Organisations which achieve the Investors in People Standard have to prove that they are committed to the development of their staff to meet their business goals. They are allowed to identify themselves by the use of the Investors in People logo on their stationery and in their advertisements.

To achieve the Standard, an organisation must prove it has met the evidence rquired. It is based on four principles:

- **Commitment** – the organisation is fully committed to developing its staff in order to achieve its aims and objectives.
- **Planning** – the organisation has decided its aims and objectives and knows what the staff need to do to achieve these.
- **Action** – the organisation has a clear, continuing programme of staff training and development to achieve its plans.
- **Evaluating** – at regular intervals, the organisation reviews the success of its training and development programme and adjusts this as necessary.

Once an organisation has achieved the Standard, it must maintain these principles and is reviewed to check that it is succeeding. If not, the Standard can be withdrawn. During these reviews, both managers and staff are interviewed and employees have to confirm that any claims made by the company are true.

In 2001, Investors in People celebrated its tenth year. During that time, over 25,000 organisations have achieved the Standard, employing 24 per cent of the UK workforce. This includes 11,000 organisations with fewer than 50 employees. Generally, if you work for a company which has achieved Investors in People, or is working towards it, you can be confident that you will be expected to take an active part in your own development.

National Training Awards

National Training Awards started in 1987 and are awarded to both individuals and employers. The NTA is an annual competition, organised and managed by UK Skills, and entrants have to prove they have demonstrated excellence in their use of learning, training and development to achieve business and personal success. In 2000, there were 683 entries and 52 winners, with 15 entrants receiving special awards. In 2001, the number of entrants increased to nearly 800 from across the UK and a special category was introduced for companies which also had an Investors in People award. Eleven entrants received special awards.

Organisations that win the award can use a special logo on their stationery and literature for up to three years. Individuals benefit through improved career prospects. Both gain national publicity in December of each year when the awards are announced.

Snapshot

Newgate Kennels – trained for excellence

Newgate Kennels Ltd of Wilmslow, Cheshire, is only one of two kennels in the UK which has achieved Investors in People. In addition, in 2001, it was named a special awards winner at the National Training Awards ceremony in London.

Newgate, which operates both a kennels and a cattery, can board up to 200 pets. The 12 staff underwent training in animal care, dog grooming, customer care, woodwork construction and coaching and mentoring. Training has helped to increase facilities such as a new small-animal room and a computerised booking system. Additional income has been earned through the sale of pet accessories and this has provided funding to pay for the rebuilding of older accommodation.

The manager and director, Joel Millet, says that training has greatly improved team spirit among the staff and has provided a back-up team capable of running the business in his absence with no loss of the 'personal, family-run feeling' for which the kennels are renowned.

What can go wrong?

Problems can occur in each of the following areas:

- Some businesses – and managers – are more committed to training than others. Small businesses can find it very difficult to cope if staff are away on a course. They may not be able to afford to run courses themselves. Therefore, training opportunities may be more limited.
- If a business is facing financial problems, the training budget may be cut. This reduces opportunities for all staff.
- Not all staff are keen to be trained, which can present problems for managers. To avoid this, the requirement to undertake training may be included in the job description.
- Different people learn in different ways, so insisting that everyone does e-learning or joins a college course may be a mistake. What suits one person doesn't always suit another.
- Training events can be very successful. On other occasions they may not. The trainer could be boring or the subject matter might be covered at the wrong level. For this reason, training departments usually issue feedback forms to attendees on which they can state their views. This prevents a disastrous session from being repeated.

It makes you think!

You are about to attend an appraisal review. You know your company has just opened an office in Paris and you would love to work there, but you would need to speak French first.

1. Log on to www.heinemann.co.uk/hotlinks and search the database for French courses in your area. Find out what is available online (at a level of your choice).
2. Find out how much it would cost to attend a French course at your local college.
3. Decide which way you would prefer to learn. Give your reasons.
4. When you put your request to your manager, she says she would like to encourage you, but she would 'expect you to learn in your own time, too, as this isn't vital for her department's aims'.
   a. What does she mean by this?
   b. Do you think she is being fair? Give a reason for your opinion.

Over to you!

1. Find out more about IIP and NTAs by visiting their website at: www.heinemann.co.uk/hotlinks. Then give two benefits of having such National Award schemes.
2. Log on to the Campaign for Learning site at www.heinemann.co.uk/hotlinks and find out more about different types of learning opportunities. You can also find out about celebrities plans for learning, unusual places where people learn and check your own learning style.
3. a. Ask your teacher or tutor what training and development opportunities are available to the staff in your school or college and what people must do to obtain agreement to develop themselves.
   b. If you work part time, or go on work experience, find out the same information. Or ask your parents or other relatives what happens in the organisations where they work. Then compare your findings with other members of your group.

Chapter review and practice questions

▶

1. Ongoing training is provided for all staff in most organisations. Give two reasons why this is needed.

2. State one benefit to an employer of providing training opportunities for staff.

3. a What is a performance review?
   b State two topics which would be covered during such a review.

4. Give two examples of training activities which might be held to update staff because of technological developments.

5. a What does the abbreviation IIP stand for?
   b What do organisations have to do to achieve this award?

▶

1. Give three reasons why training and development are required for staff after they have started working in a company.

2. Give two benefits of training and development for:
   a employees who participate
   b employers who arrange this.

3. An employee wishes to learn about e-commerce. He does not work in this area even though his company has a website. A training course is being held 200 miles away, which lasts a week and costs £2,000. He asks his employer if he can attend.
   a Identify three reasons why his employer might refuse this request.
   b Identify two arguments the employee could put forward to try to persuade his manager to agree.

4. Explain the main reasons why schemes such as Investors in People and National Training Awards have been introduced.

5. a Why are training and development needs usually discussed at an appraisal interview?
   b Why do managers try to link such the training needs of individuals to organisational aims?

Chapter 16 Customer service

What you will learn

- Why customers are important
- Customers and their expectations
- Customer satisfaction
- Investigating customer service
- Protecting the customer

Overview: customer service

The importance of customer services

Much of this unit has concentrated on the importance of employees to a business. However, another group of people – customers – are just as important. Indeed, without customers it is unlikely any business would need employees for very long! It is therefore in the interests of all businesses and their staff to attract new customers and to encourage existing customers to stay loyal to the organisation.

In Unit 1 you learned that attracting new customers is the job of the marketing and sales function. Making sure that customers receive the type of service they expect whenever they contact the organisation is the job of customer services. This may be a separate function, as you saw on pages 88–92, or it may be part of marketing and sales. Wherever it is located, its importance should not be underestimated. It is pointless spending money on advertising or special offers to attract customers, and then losing them because the service is dreadful.

Studies have shown that it costs five times as much to attract a new customer as to keep an existing customer. It has also been proved that if customers have a good experience they may tell one or two people about it, but if customers have a bad experience they will tell eight other people how awful something is!

Understanding the scope of customer services

You may think that customer service simply means being helpful and polite to all customers. While good service includes staff behaviour, it goes far beyond this. If you constantly have to apologise for a lack of stock, a poor delivery service or shoddy goods, it is doubtful any customer would stay with you for very long, no matter how pleasant you are!

In this chapter you will learn about the following aspects of customer service activities and why they are so important to businesses:

- **The benefits of customer service** – all staff need to understand that being committed to helping customers and providing an effective service benefits the business and therefore their own job security.
- **Customer expectations** – different types of customers have different expectations. Knowing about these can help a business to be more competitive by offering a range of services to meet these expectations.
- **Customer satisfaction** – it is essential to know whether existing customers are satisfied both with their purchases and the service they have received. Businesses can use this information to improve their products or services.
- **Features of customer service** – these vary from one business to another depending upon the product or service which is offered and the type of customer. However, there are many similar features, too. These features play a part in keeping customers satisfied.
- **Protecting the customer** – customers have legal rights. As a part of customer service, staff should know the main rights and how the business must conform to these.

It makes you think!

Before you begin to study this chapter in depth, refresh your memory on customer services by re-reading pages 88–92. Then try the quiz below to see how much you can remember. Check your answers with your teacher or tutor.

Customer service refresher quiz

1. Identify two types of information which customer services staff may have to provide.
2. Briefly, what is the difference between giving information and giving advice?
3. Identify one type of organisation where qualified staff may be employed to give specific advice to customers.
4. State two items of information you would expect to find stored on a customer database.
5. Identify two payment methods which may be used by a private individual when buying goods.
6. Identify two types of businesses which would offer a delivery service.
7. What is after-sales service?
8. Identify one product you might buy when you would expect to find good after-sales service.
9. Identify one type of product where a customer might have a technical query after taking delivery.
10. Give one reason why a customer may want to return an item after purchasing it.

Customers provide information as well as buying goods

Why customers are important

Every customer is valuable to a business – in the 'real' sense of being worth money! Each purchase made by a customer directly increases the sales revenue of the business which normally increases the overall profit. Customers are also a useful source of information. Wise businesses listen to their customers and then take action.

Offering good, effective customer services provides several benefits. It enables the business to do the following:

- **Gain and retain customers.** A satisfied customer is more likely to make another purchase and to tell his or her friends and relatives about the experience. This is a much cheaper way of attracting new customers than advertising. Therefore, good customer service can gain *and* retain customers at the same time!
- **Gain customer satisfaction and loyalty.** If customers continue to receive good service and attention and are always satisfied with the experience, they are far more likely to buy regularly from the organisation. They start to develop customer loyalty and may remain customers for many years.
- **Improve the image and reputation of the business.** Word soon gets around if a business offers excellent service. This may also be substantiated by the media or consumer reports in newspapers and magazines. Customer confidence increases and trust develops – the customer starts to rely on the staff and the service they provide.
- **Provide information about the products.** Information becomes a two-way process if customer service is good:
  - The business may provide customers with additional information on new or different products which may suit their needs.

- Sales information gives feedback to the business about the products which are most popular. Customer surveys add to this information and can be used to help improve future services.
- **Help a business to keep market share.** Most businesses operate in a competitive environment and aim to keep or increase their share of the market (see Unit 1, Chapter 7). Because customer service helps to retain customers, this means that the business has a much better chance of keeping its market share. If customer service attracts new customers, then this helps the business to increase its market share.
- **Increase sales revenue and profits.** Customer spending becomes sales revenue. This is directly affected by the number of items customers buy and the number of times they make a purchase. Unless the costs of buying the goods and running the business are increasing as fast as sales, the increased sales revenue will result in higher profits for the business.

Fact file

In business, there are two types of customers:

- **External customers** are all the other businesses or private individuals who contact or visit an organisation because they want to buy a product or service.
- **Internal customers** are people who work in the *same* organisation who need another member of staff to provide a service for them, for example a customer services assistant requesting information on delivery dates from the distribution team.

It makes you think!

Customers have a five-stage relationship with businesses:

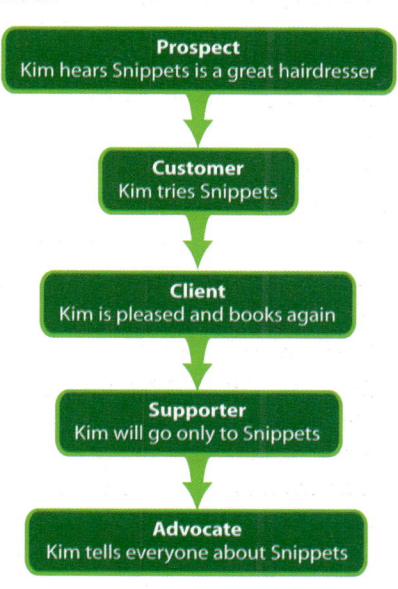

Prospect — Kim hears Snippets is a great hairdresser
↓
Customer — Kim tries Snippets
↓
Client — Kim is pleased and books again
↓
Supporter — Kim will go only to Snippets
↓
Advocate — Kim tells everyone about Snippets

At the stage of advocate, Kim is doing Snippets' marketing for them! If she becomes dissatisfied, or if the staff start taking her business for granted and paying less attention to her, the business not only loses a customer, but also loses all Kim's free advertising. The consequences of something going wrong, for example a delay for which no one apologises, could be serious for the business.

1. Try to decide one business for which you (or one of your relatives) is:
   - a. a prospect
   - b. a customer
   - c. a client
   - d. a supporter
   - e. an advocate.
2. In each case decide (or find out) what influenced you or your relative in moving up from one stage to the next.
3. Think of two events which might occur which could make you decide to change your loyalties.
4. Try to identify one occasion when you had a good experience and told other people about it and one occasion when you had a poor experience and warned other people away from the business.

Compare your answers with other members of your group.

Customers and their expectations

Types of customers

All customers have expectations. You already know the benefits of keeping external customers satisfied, but internal customers are important too. This is because in every transaction *someone* is trying to provide a service for an external customer. In the example above, unless the customer service assistant receives good service from the distribution team, she cannot answer the customer's query. So everyone in the 'customer service chain' is equally important.

The customer service chain

Customer expectations

The expectations of customers vary, depending upon what they are buying and, often, on how much they are paying. There are certain basic expectations which all customers have whenever they are dealing with an organisation. In each case, it is important to think how these may change slightly, depending upon the reason for the purchase and the amount paid.

Good value products

Good value means that the product is worth what it costs. This is a minimum expectation. Therefore, you expect a superior quality the more you pay for a product or a service. For example, you would have different expectations of a jacket costing £20 than one costing £200. The best experience of all for a customer is to buy a product or service and obtain *better* value than expected!

Rapid response to enquiries

You can reasonably expect an organisation's staff to be able to answer basic enquiries immediately. Customer service staff normally receive training about the type of enquiries they will be asked. However, it is quite possible that a customer may ask a different member of staff whom they just happen to see at the time they have a query. In this case, it is important that this person can either answer the query personally *or* knows to direct the customer immediately to the correct person. Customers can also expect more complex enquiries to be answered correctly, even if these take a little longer.

Clear and honest information

Ethical organisations are keen to ensure that their staff do not mislead customers. A common tactic by less ethical companies may be to promise deliveries which are unachievable, simply to obtain the order. However, if the goods do not arrive on time, the customer may cancel and go elsewhere. If the delivery date was specifically stated on the contract of sale, then the customer has a legal right to cancel (see page 281). Misleading a customer over the price of an item is illegal, as you will see on page 282.

Information about suitable products

There are many products bought by a customer where specialist advice is required, such as audio systems and digital cameras. An effective salesperson or customer services assistant:

- identifies the needs of the customer first
- has excellent knowledge of all the products stocked
- matches the needs of the customer to the product to assess the ones which would be the most suitable
- talks through the advantages and disadvantages of each one with the customer
- allows the customer to make the final decision, once he or she knows all the facts.

This strategy is far more likely to result in a return visit by the same customer for a different product or service!

Help with individual or general issues

Often customers have special, individual needs. These may relate to physical abilities or disabilities, age, technical information, methods of payment or time of delivery. An example is a customer who works full time and needs a product delivered or serviced outside working hours.

Dealing effectively with these requests depends upon:

- the policies of the organisation (e.g. its flexibility over delivery times and dates)
- the experience and knowledge of customer service staff of the products and services available
- the systems in the organisation to cope with 'one-off' problems and queries. Some firms pride themselves on their responsiveness, others are less good in this area.

Care and attention

Most people associate 'care and attention' with the type of service they receive, that is dealing with a person who understands and helps to advise them. The more complex their requirements, the more they welcome this assistance. For example, if you wanted to buy a mobile phone, and were not sure which one to buy, you would prefer to talk about your needs to someone who knows more than you do. This is sometimes called direct person-to-person contact and can either be in person or over the phone.

After-sales service

After-sales service is the service customers receive if they return to the organisation after making a purchase (see Unit 1, page 91). This may be:

- to return an item
- to have something repaired
- to order a spare part
- to make a complaint
- because they have a technical query.

It also refers to ongoing service provided to maintain or repair products such as photocopiers to washing machines.

After-sales service may involve the regular servicing of a product or its repair

It makes you think!

In an electrical superstore:

- customer A asks where to find sandwich toasters
- customer B asks which type of microwave oven would be best for her father, who is virtually blind
- customer C wants to know about DVD players and their features
- customers D and E want to know about freezers – one has a large family, the other is a single person who lives in a flat.

Within your group, decide which services each of these customers would expect. Note that you can select any service more than once.

a   A rapid response to a basic enquiry
b   Information about suitable products
c   Help with an individual issue
d   Direct person-to-person contact
e   Information about after-sales service (in this case, identify the type of after-sales service the customer would most likely to be interested in).

Spot check

Write down your answers to the following questions:

1. Identify two benefits to businesses of providing good customer services.
2. Explain how customer service can help businesses to keep their market share.
3. Ben receives a call from Jan Morris querying an invoice she recently received. She thinks an item has been overcharged. Ben tells her that he will investigate the matter and call her back promptly. Ben checks his computer – the selling price listed is the same as he quoted. He then phones Shelley in finance who says she will find out what has happened and ring him back.
   a. Who is the external customer?
   b. Who is Shelley's internal customer?
   c. Draw a customer service chain to illustrate this query, with the customer at the end.
   d. Identify the possible consequences of Shelley:
      i. forgetting to do what she says
      ii. giving Ben the wrong information.
4. a. What is meant by a 'good value product'?
   b. How might a customer's expectations of value change in relation to the price? Give an example.
5. Identify two basic expectations of all customers, besides obtaining good value for money.

Customer satisfaction

Customers are satisfied when they can rely on a business to meet their basic expectations. But how do businesses know when customers are satisfied? Also, is 'satisfaction' enough? If every business simply 'satisfied' its customers, then there would be no opportunity to increase market share. Some experts believe that customers should be 'delighted' with the service they receive and/or the product they buy. Only this will guarantee customers will stay loyal to the organisation.

Measuring customer satisfaction

Most of us take good customer service experiences for granted. It's the bad ones we remember! Satisfied customers usually don't say anything. Dissatisfied customers complain, but they may do this to friends and relatives rather than to staff – and go somewhere else next time. For these reasons, businesses should not assume that all is fine, simply because no one is saying very much. By the time they realise the mistake, there may be very few customers left! Generally, therefore, businesses use a number of different methods to assess customer satisfaction.

Analysing sales performance

This means obtaining a range of data on several aspects of sales, for example:

- the number of customers who visit the business or make enquiries
- the number of customers who make a purchase
- the number of purchases they make
- the type of purchases they make
- the amount they spend.

Many large stores have electronic point of sale (EPOS) systems (see page 97) which automatically analyse all sales. If the store also operates a customer loyalty scheme or has a store credit card, it can match the sales to the particular customer. This enables it to track how much individual customers are spending as well as when and what they are buying. If sales are falling, then this needs to be investigated. It makes a difference, obviously, whether this is happening only in one or two stores or across the whole organisation and whether only certain products are being rejected or whether customers are clearly buying elsewhere.

Recording the number of complaints/returned goods

When people complain or return goods they may be slightly dissatisfied or very dissatisfied. Their attitude will depend upon the reason for the complaint or return and the way they are dealt with at the time.

Complaints can range from the trivial to the very serious. If you were annoyed because a shop was out of stock of something you wanted and you complained, this isn't as serious as buying a chicken and finding when you get home that it is past its sell-by date. In the first case, you have suffered a minor irritation. In the second, you could have fallen very ill if you had eaten the food. You would expect the shop to take far more action in response to your second complaint. However, from a business point of view, *all* complaints are serious. The customer who regularly finds that products are out of stock could decide to shop elsewhere. For this reason, in most organisations *all* complaints are recorded. They are then analysed to identify the issues which are annoying customers so that action can be taken to prevent these occurring.

Customers return goods for many reasons. They may regret the purchase, even though there is nothing wrong with the item, or the goods may be faulty. Legally, a business has no obligation to accept goods simply because the buyer has changed his or her mind, but many do. This is another way in which they can gain an edge over their competitors. They may insist that a receipt is kept and the goods are returned within a specified time limit, but they will accept the return to encourage customers to shop there again and to buy an item even if they are unsure, on the basis they can 'always take it back'.

In the case of faulty goods a business has a legal obligation to accept these and give a full refund to the purchaser (see page 282).

Fact file

Businesses need to keep records of all **returns** for two reasons:

- A return is the opposite of a sale so the sales records have to be adjusted. These may show that some products are less popular once the number of returns is calculated.
- Faulty or unsatisfactory products may need to be referred back to the manufacturer, particularly if they are unsafe.

It's got a wicked picture, but we paid for the sound too!

SOUND & VISION

Buyers of faulty goods have a legal right to a refund

Making comparisons with competitors

It is important to identify which problems are common to the industry and which problems are being experienced only by an individual business. This is because identifying the best solution is only possible if the reason is known. For example, if a travel agency knew it was selling fewer holidays this year, it would take a different approach to solving the problem if it knew other travel agencies in the area were doing well. In this case, it needs to investigate what it is doing wrong or what they are doing better! If, however, demand for travel in that area is lower, say because of local redundancies, and all travel agencies are affected, the agency may concentrate on offering cheaper, bargain holidays to tempt customers into the shop.

Large businesses can find out about their competitors in several ways. They may pay for specialist market research reports or obtain the company report and accounts of their competitors. These are published for all public limited companies.

Smaller businesses will often receive guidance from their accountants who will know the average sales turnover and profit levels of similar businesses in the area.

Snapshot

Turning problems into opportunities

Modern thinking is to convert possible disasters into opportunities for greater profit! The jargon for this is to identify 'service recovery moments'. This can be done in several ways:

- Complaints are used to analyse the number of problems which customer service staff can deal with promptly and immediately. The aim is to improve 'first contact success' as much as possible. British Gas completely redesigned their complaints handling process to achieve this, including setting up expert teams to handle complex and difficult complaints quickly. The aim was to turn a negative experience into a positive one for the customer.

- Customers can be encouraged to make suggestions, which can often replace a complaint. Some supermarkets, such as Tesco, have suggestion boxes in every store as well as a customer service desk. Every customer who completes a suggestion form can opt for a telephone or written reply. Suggestions which are acted upon are posted up in the store. This means that customers with a minor complaint are encouraged to make a positive contribution to future store developments.

- Some organisations focus on a potential problem, solve it and then make it a key selling point, such as Disneyland which had a litter problem. It trained all staff to become litter conscious so that it had the best-kept theme parks in the world. It then advertised this fact.

- At a basic level, staff are trained to treat immediate disasters as a 'service recovery moment'. So the person in the store who slips on some water near the flower display is given such fantastic attention that she tells everyone she knows about it!

Feedback from customers

Feedback from existing customers can be obtained either by marketing staff (see Unit 1, Chapter 5) or by customer service staff. Ideally, the two should be complementary so that whereas a formal market research study may be undertaken by marketing, this will be supplemented by information from 'front-line staff' who have direct experience of dealing with customers and responding to problems. Various methods can be used.

'On the spot' questions from staff

In many restaurants, waiters are trained to ask customers if they are satisfied with their meal once they have started eating. Their reactions to a negative reply, however, can differ considerably! An excellent restaurant will immediately take action, a poor one will not. Ideally, if many customers complain about a particular dish, the chef or manager will make sure that something is done about it – and quickly.

Sales staff, too, are often trained to check if a customer has any further requirements, for example 'Would you like help with packing your shopping?' Notices are also placed at checkouts of large stores 'Forgotten anything? Let us get it for you?' All these questions help to provide additional customer service as well as checking that the customer is satisfied.

Observation

Managers and senior staff often observe customers so that they can assess customer behaviour. This is how they know where to place 'special offer' baskets and why they know to stock the products they want to promote at eye level. Customers always look there first, before looking at the top and bottom of a shelf! A manager who sees customers regularly leaving the shop empty-handed, or looking annoyed, would be concerned. He or she may stop some customers to ask them if there was a problem and add to observation by on-the-spot questioning.

Another type of observation is the 'mystery shopper.' In this case, independent researchers are recruited to visit the store (or contact the business by telephone) and assess the result. Their findings are then sent to the client company for analysis. At Dixons, the managing director used to do this personally, and report his findings to senior managers immediately afterwards. This may sound drastic, but it provided instant feedback about any problems and kept all store staff on their toes!

Questionnaires

A common method of finding out what customers think is to ask them to complete a questionnaire immediately after they have completed a transaction with a business. Examples include questionnaires which are:

- given to returning travellers on an airplane to ask them about their holiday experience
- left in hotel rooms to find out what guests think of their stay
- sent to mail order customers asking them to comment on the service they have received
- included in newspapers and magazines asking readers for their opinions.

Companies often offer incentives to encourage people to complete and return questionnaires such as entry in a prize draw. This increases the overall response rate.

Customer panels and interviews

A meeting or an interview with customers allows more discussion than a simple 'tick box' questionnaire. Boots is an example of an organisation which has had customer panels, made up of local customers, for many years. **Focus groups** are similar. They are formed to represent the general public and give their opinions on issues relating to government policies, television programmes and other general issues. Focus groups are interviewed by researchers to find out members' reactions to different ideas.

Some companies 'target interview' customers, usually over the telephone. They may do this for specific reasons, such as when customers cancel a subscription, reduce their spending or change their supplier, to find out why.

A website

A website can be used to find out customer opinions, either of the service itself or about the website. This is done by producing a short questionnaire. At a certain point in the transaction, a 'pop-up' screen appears asking users if they will answer a few short questions or provide feedback. Examples include:

- a recently restructured website, which asked users to comment on its user friendliness
- a website offering a service, which asked users to comment on whether they had found the website information comprehensive and easy to understand
- a website offering products, which asked users who completed a transaction to comment on whether the ordering system was easy or not.

There are some disadvantages with this method. Pop-up windows may irritate users and some may refuse to give feedback. For those who do, the questionnaire will normally be short and be designed for 'yes' or 'no' answers so that responses can be analysed quickly by computer. However, this prevents customers from giving individual replies or additional comments which may be useful.

Email

Many organisations use email to ask for feedback from their customers and contacts. This may be:

- by a general email, sent to all customers, asking for general comments
- by a specific email, sent to targeted customers, asking for individual comments
- by an email with a hyperlink which asks customers to complete a short questionnaire online.

Many organisations use a combination of these methods which helps to provide a more representative range of opinions.

Snapshot

What price loyalty schemes?

Loyalty cards enable supermarkets to find out about the shopping habits of their customers

More than half of British shoppers have loyalty cards, yet a recent survey by Mori for the Black Sun consultancy found that nearly 70 per cent of people said this did not make them stick to one chain. Nearly nine out of ten shoppers said they were more concerned about price and value for money than collecting loyalty points. In addition, more than 25 per cent said they rarely bothered to redeem their points.

Stores have mixed views and policies on this. Tesco runs a Clubcard scheme, Sainsbury's has its Reward Card and Marks & Spencer launched its loyalty card in 2002. But Safeway dropped its scheme in 2000 and Waitrose has never had one. The benefit for stores who operate these schemes is not just customer loyalty but also the information they obtain on regular shoppers. When sales fall, they can send out special vouchers to tempt them to return and buy again. They can also rely on inertia – many customers can't be bothered to shop around when they know the layout of one store, because shopping is so much easier and quicker.

Investigating customer service

There are three important points to remember when you are investigating customer service in an organisation:

- All organisations are different. Although there are standard areas of 'good practice' in customer service, there are other factors, including the type of product or service, the size and scale of the business, its resources and the cost-effectiveness of providing additional services. For example, a local grocer would not be able to operate the range of customer services you would find in a large supermarket.
- Most organisations would like to be in a situation where customers never complained or returned goods and where every customer was delighted with every aspect of their service. This is normally both unrealistic and unachievable. Everyone is different so what pleases one person will not suit another. In addition, all organisations have 'difficult' customers who are never pleased, no matter what they are offered!
- When carrying out your investigation, if you are thinking about how customer service could be developed and improved, then you must keep in mind the two points above. You should also be aware that most staff in an organisation work hard to provide a good customer service.

Specific features and factors to consider

As you have seen, the type of customer service features vary from one organisation to another. The most important features you need to investigate and the factors you should bear in mind are summarised in the chart opposite.

Customer service features

Features	Points to consider
Products	
Quality	All goods must be of 'satisfactory' quality, but premium quality is often linked to price
Safety	All goods must be safe, by law
Packaging	Packaging should be safe and not excessive
Clarity of information	Information must be clear and appropriate to the average customer
Staff	
Helpfulness	Staff should be helpful at all times
Dress	Dress will depend upon whether there is face-to-face contact with the customer
Accuracy of information	Information must be accurate, but is more critical in certain situations (e.g. medical information)
Communication skills and telephone manner	Staff must be able to explain facts clearly and concisely in a friendly manner either face to face or over the telephone
Managing a telephone conversation	'Managing' a telephone conversation involves being able to end a call without causing offence if the caller is talkative!
Premises	
Clean	All premises must be clean – scrupulously so where food is handled
Well signposted	Signposting will depend on number/type of visitors/callers, as will access for disabled people. Buildings open to the public are particularly important
Accessible for disabled	
Range of facilities	The range of facilities should be appropriate – these depend on the type of callers/length of average stay
Delivery	
Availability	Routine goods should be available at all times or staff should have information on supply. This is different if goods are 'one-off' or special items
Speed	Speed of delivery should be appropriate for item/service
Reliability	Reliability includes keeping the customer informed of any delays
After-sales care	
Dealing with complaints	Complaints should be dealt with courteously and logged. All may not be valid
Exchanging goods	Exchange policy can vary, but customers with faulty goods should be offered a full refund
Guarantees and repairs	Guarantees/repairs are most important for technical, complex or expensive goods
	After-sales care should be prompt and reasonably priced
Other features	
Range of payment methods	Payment methods should be appropriate to the goods/service and type of customers
Customer care telephone lines	Customer care telephone lines are normally a feature of large companies or those that regularly deal with customers by telephone or mail order
Staff training	Staff training is important. All staff should know how to deal with routine enquiries and who to contact if an enquiry or complaint is more complex.

New technology and customer service

The use of business websites and email has enabled many organisations to offer more comprehensive customer service. Many websites contain a specific customer service area where frequently asked questions (FAQs) are answered. This helps customers as they don't have to contact the company about routine queries and also reduces the number of calls to the organisation.

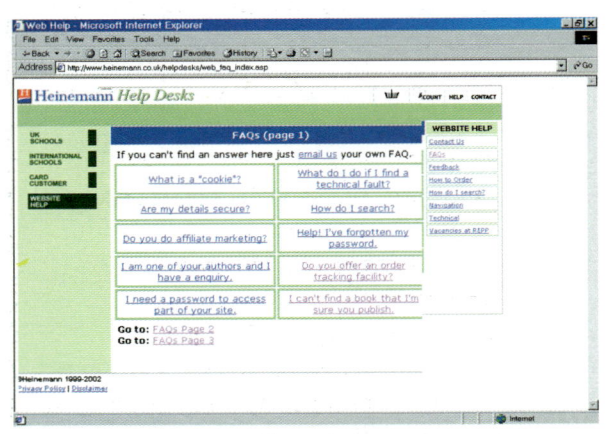

Business websites often have customer service pages where FAQs are answered

Email is useful for customers to be able to send any specific queries which are not answered on a FAQs page. Ideally, the website will provide a link to email so that all the customer needs to do is to click on the link and write the email. It is then important that someone answers this promptly! Many sites contain information about the method of response and the usual time taken. This reduces the need for the customer to have to follow up the email if a reply isn't received.

Such services are more appropriate for some companies than others; for example, an online stationery store may offer a comprehensive online customer service facility. Where staff usually deal with customers face to face, you are less likely to find this type of service.

It makes you think!

Within your group, identify the key customer service features you would expect to find in each of the following types of organisations:

a a large department store
b a furniture manufacturer
c a book club
d a greetings card shop
e a garden centre
f a theme park.

Remember that some will deal mainly with business customers, rather than individuals. Use the customer service features chart above to help you. Compare your answers with other groups.

Protecting the customer

All customers are protected in law from being misled by sellers or being sold faulty or unsafe goods. They are also protected from unsafe practices which would affect their health and safety.

Customers and health and safety

Customers are protected by the Health and Safety at Work Act (see page 213). An organisation must be safe for its employees, and also for visitors. Any customer who is injured or who has an accident while on the premises can take legal action if this occurs because of negligence on the part of the organisation itself; for example, if a customer breaks an ankle as a result of tripping on worn flooring. It is the responsibility of the organisation to make sure that its premises and facilities are safe for users.

Case study

The modern way

Dell makes computer equipment. Its customers can choose the specification of the computer that they want and then order it online. Dell has received much praise for its customer service and the fact that it doesn't ignore customers after a sale is made.

One of Dell's key features is its website. This concentrates not only on advertising the products and enabling customers to order online but also on its service. Customers who have ordered a machine can track every stage of delivery – from the warehouse to their home. They can check the status of their account, obtain product support or obtain the answers to common questions quite easily. Dell advertises its customer services as 'only a click away'.

If customers have more specific questions, they can email Dell with just one click of the mouse or find out other ways of contacting Dell quickly. This is particularly helpful for customers who buy a machine with a support package. If the machine is faulty, they can contact a technician to visit them to put matters right.

Find out more about Dell and its customer service facility by clicking first the Support heading and then the Customer Care heading at www.heinemann.co.uk/hotlinks. Finally, you will find it useful to explore the information on Dell's data protection and privacy policies (see also page 283).

▷ 1 What business is Dell in?
  2 How do customers buy goods from Dell?
  3 You are thinking of buying from Dell. Identify three expectations you are likely to have.
  4 Suggest one reason why Dell believes that it needs to provide excellent customer service on line.
  5 Suggest two queries a Dell customer may have after making a purchase.
  6 Suggest one method by which Dell could obtain feedback from customers to measure customer satisfaction.
  7 If you were investigating Dell's customer service, identify three main features you would look at, and give reasons for your choice.

▷ 1 Identify three products a customer could buy from Dell.
  2 In what way is Dell different from standard retailers such as PC World?
  3 Suggest two reasons why it is appropriate for Dell to provide its customer service online.
  4 Identify four expectations of a prospective Dell customer.
  5 What type of support do you think a Dell customer might need:
      a immediately after agreeing a purchase
      b after several months.
  6 a Suggest two types of information Dell will be able to obtain from its website to help it to continually improve its customer service.
      b How could Dell supplement this with direct customer feedback?
  7 Select four features you would study if you were investigating and evaluating Dell's customer service and give a reason for each of your choices.

Customers and the sale of products

A customer who buys a product or service enters into a contract of sale with the supplier. Like a contract of employment, a contract of sale has express and implied terms. In this case:

- an **express term** is something specifically stated at the time of purchase, preferably in writing, e.g. a customer stating that an item *must* be delivered by a specific date
- an **implied term** refers to an intention which is not specifically stated because it is obvious, e.g. the buyer must be prepared to pay a reasonable price for the item.

Terms are categorised in two further, important ways:

- A **condition** is very important. If this is not met, the contract is invalid. If you bought a computer, a condition would be that it has a processor and memory, so it works. If not, you could reject the computer.
- A **warranty** is less important. If you asked for a modem to be fitted and it wasn't, you could not reject the contract, but could take action so that you paid a lower price for the computer.

In addition, buyers are also protected by specific consumer laws. These are summarised in the box below. The first two relate to the sale and supply of goods and services, the third relates to product safety.

Important points to note about the sale of goods

It is helpful to remember the following points:

- A buyer makes a contract with the seller, who in turn makes a contract with his or her supplier. For example, if a jug kettle was faulty, your claim would be against the shop that sold it to you. The shop assistant should not tell you to claim against the manufacturer.
- If an item is faulty, the buyer has the right to a full refund. He or she does not have to accept a credit note. A buyer who agrees to a free repair instead does not lose the right to a refund if the repair is unsatisfactory.
- Notices, or clauses in a contract, which try to restrict consumer rights are unlawful unless they are 'fair and reasonable'. For example, a jeweller cannot say that all watches left for repair are at the owner's own risk. If the watch was lost or damaged, the jeweller would have to prove reasonable care was taken and the shop could not be held responsible for what happened.
- The recipient of a gift can return a faulty item, not just the person who made the actual purchase.
- Someone who buys an item on credit in their own home must be allowed a 'cooling off' period of five days, during which time the agreement can be cancelled without any penalties.
- Items sold on credit must clearly show the total charge for credit and the annual percentage rate of interest.

Sale of Goods Act 1979 and 1995

All goods sold must be:

- **as described** and conform to their description, e.g. waterproof boots must not leak
- **of satisfactory quality** in relation to the price paid, the description and the age of the item
- **fit for the purpose for which they are intended**, e.g. an umbrella must keep off the rain.

In addition, goods must be fit for any *specific* purpose the buyer made clear at the time of the sale; for example, the umbrella must be collapsible and fit in a bag.

Both second-hand and sale goods are covered by this Act, but if the price of an item has been reduced *specifically* because of a fault pointed out to the buyer at the time, the buyer cannot later complain about this particular problem.

Supply of Goods and Services Act 1982

Service standards are covered by this Act, such as hiring a plumber to mend a leak or taking a car to a garage for service. Buyers are protected against shoddy workmanship, delays and excessive charges.

The service provider must charge a reasonable price, do the work within a reasonable time, use reasonable care and skill and satisfactory materials.

Consumer Protection Act 1987

This Act relates to price and safety and states that it is an offence to:

- mislead consumers about the price (e.g. by not including VAT)
- mislead consumers over sale prices and claim exaggerated reductions
- supply goods which are not reasonably safe.

Customers and the labelling of products

It is clear from the Sale of Goods Act and the Consumer Protection Act that consumers must not be misled. Descriptions and prices must be absolutely clear, as must any credit charges. In addition, the Trade Descriptions Act covers other types of descriptions, including assurances by a salesperson – see the box below.

> **Trade Descriptions Act 1968**
>
> This Act is designed to prevent the false or misleading description of goods, for example:
>
> - selling goods which are wrongly described by the manufacturer
> - implied descriptions, such as a picture on a box which gives a false impression
> - other aspects of the goods, including quantity, size, composition, method of manufacture.
>
> Usually, the spoken word of the seller overrides a written description as the buyer will expect to rely on the expertise of the salesperson. However, this can be hard to prove in a dispute unless the statement is in writing.

Customers and misuse of information

The Data Protection Act limits the ways in which companies can use the information they obtain from their customers (see pages 217–219). Many organisations make this clear in their documentation and on their websites. For example, if you accessed the Dell site in the case study on page 281, you will have seen Dell's assurances on this. Companies which trade on the Internet are keen to give assurance that any information about credit card details will be kept confidential. Unless prospective buyers are confident about this, they will be unlikely to make a purchase.

Some organisations guarantee that any personal information volunteered by its customers will be kept confidential and will not be passed to other companies. Other organisations say that they *do* pass on information unless a customer 'ticks' a box requesting them not to do this.

> **Snapshot**
>
> *The power of the email people!*
>
> *Organisations which advertise products on a website must still comply with consumer law – and also need to reckon on the power of consumers. Kodak discovered this to its cost when it advertised a digital camera on its website at £100 and later notified customers who ordered one that this was an error and the price should have been £330.*
>
> *Angry customers set up their own website to record their protest and pressurised Kodak into honouring the original agreement. Under the Consumer Protection Act, Kodak may have been committing an offence by misleading buyers about the true price.*
>
> *Kodak agreed to reimburse all the customers who had bought the camera when it was priced at £100 and who were then sent a confirmatory email. Now, needless to say, the camera is advertised at the correct price!*

> **Over to you!**
>
> The website of the Office of Fair Trading gives advice on consumer rights, including the action to take if you have a problem yourself. There is also a student section.
>
> 1. Access the site at www.heinemann.co.uk/hotlinks and click the section which will give you advice on your rights. Then read the screen carefully to find the student section and click this option.
> 2. Use the information to write a brief instruction sheet to a friend who has recently bought a hairdryer which overheated and caught fire the first time she used it.

Spot check

Write down your answers to the following questions:

1. State two ways in which customer satisfaction can be measured.
2. Give one reason why it is important to keep records of returned goods.
3. Identify two methods which can be used to obtain feedback from customers.
4. Briefly explain how the use of email and business websites can be used to improve and develop customer service.
5. a Identify three features of customer service you would want to look at if you were investigating this area.
   b Give two examples of features which may be different depending upon the size of organisation and its business activities.
6. a Explain why it is important that customers are not misled about a product or its price.
   b Give an example of one law which protects the customer in this situation.

2. You have decided to buy a mobile phone.
   a As a customer, identify four expectations you will have when you visit the mobile phone shop.
   b Two days after buying the phone it stops working. What are your legal rights in this situation?
3. Marsha is always honest with customers, but Sean will do anything to make a sale. Yesterday Marsha overheard him promise a customer the goods would be delivered within two days even though she knew this was impossible.
   a What are the dangers of making promises like Sean does?
   b Identify two items of information on which it is illegal to mislead customers.

Chapter review and practice questions

1. Your sister is starting her own hairdressing business but says she's not worried about customer service because she is excellent at her job and has modern premises. Customer service, she says, applies only to people who sell goods and isn't important for her business.
   a To change her mind, summarise three benefits of customer service to a business.
   b Suggest two customer service features she could introduce into her business to impress customers.

1. One benefit to businesses of providing good customer service is to provide information about new or different products.
   a Explain three additional benefits to a business organisation.
   b Explain why a business will want information about the sales levels of products and the number of returns.
   c Identify one way in which a business can use this information to improve its level of service.
2. Your friend has recently started work at a hire shop which hires out home improvement and garden equipment. He had to attend a training course about product information and using items safely. He has also been instructed that any complaints or reports of faults must be logged carefully.
   a Explain why the shop insists that all staff must know about safety.
   b Give two reasons why complaints and faults are logged carefully.
   c Identify four additional customer service features that would be useful in this type of business.
3. The manager of a store wants to obtain feedback from customers. Explain four ways in which this information could be obtained. At least one of your suggestions should relate to the use of ICT.

Portfolio evidence for Unit 2

Overview: portfolio evidence

What is a portfolio?

Like Unit 1, Unit 2 is assessed through a portfolio of evidence. Your portfolio must contain specific information and be structured and organised so that the information is grouped together logically.

What type of information do I need?

OCR has stated the information you must obtain as you investigate *one* business (see pages 288–292). The different ways in which you can obtain it are listed below.

You must use the information to write about the business. Once again, it is *how* you use the information that determines the grade you will receive. This is also explained on pages 288–292.

Investigating a suitable business

You need to investigate *one* business only for this Unit. To obtain the right type of information it will need to be a medium-sized or large organisation that has:

- a range of different stakeholders
- a well-established, specific, human resources department
- a specific customer service department which has a stated customer service policy.

You will also find it helpful if the business is committed to staff development and training (and perhaps has, or is working towards IIP).

Where to find your information

You should discuss possible options with your tutor. You may decide to use one of the businesses you studied for Unit 1, or you could select an entirely different organisation. You could choose:

- an organisation you know, e.g.
  - where you go on work experience (see Appendix 1 on work experience, page 408)
  - where you work part time
- an organisation which is familiar to someone you know, e.g.
  - where a member of your family works
  - where a friend of your family works
  - where your tutor has a contact.

If obtaining information direct from an organisation proves to be difficult, your tutor may arrange:

- for you to supplement some of your information from a case study relating to another business
- for your class, as a whole, to obtain different types of information from different businesses and then share this. However, you must remember that your portfolio evidence must be *all your own work*!

Over to you!

1. Refer back to the portfolio notes on Unit 1 (pages 137–146) and check that you remember the key points on:
   - contacting an organisation and attending a meeting
   - obtaining help and guidance from your tutor
   - making out an action plan
   - referring to written sources of information
   - hints and tips for producing your portfolio.

2. On pages 288–292 you will find details of the information you need to obtain and the accounts you need to write to obtain different marks. These marks are then converted into your grade for the unit. The range of grades you can achieve is from A*A* to GG. Study this information now, and talk to your tutor about anything you do not understand.

3. Below is a checklist of questions you could ask when you visit the business. They cover all the main areas of Unit 2. Before your visit, do some research. Find out about the business and then try to add some of your own questions to the checklist. You may also be able to discuss certain topics more knowledgeably, such as stakeholders. If the business has a website, and uses this as a key part of its customer service provision, you should certainly know all about this before you meet anyone!

Business investigation questions checklist

- What is the name of the business?
- What activity does it undertake?
- Which groups of people are stakeholders in the business?
- What particular interest does each group have in the business?
- Which groups have the most power and influence? Why?
- Which groups have the least power and influence? Why?
- What different job roles are there in the business?
- Which three job roles have completely different responsibilities?
- What are these responsibilities, in each case, and how do they differ?
- Does the business issue contracts of employment to staff?
- What are the terms and conditions contained in a contract for a specific job role?
- How does the business ensure these terms and conditions meet its needs?
- How does the business ensure the terms and conditions meet the employee's needs?
- Is there any way that the contract could be changed to meet any needs better?
- Does the business have a policy for dealing with grievances and problems?
- What are the grievance procedures?
- What are the disciplinary procedures?
- If there was a disagreement with an employee over rights of employment or working conditions, what would happen?
- What would be the difference in the handling of a minor disagreement and a serious issue?
- How does the business promote and maintain good working relationships with employees?
- What is the process for recruiting and selecting staff?
- Is the process any different for internal staff who want to be promoted and external applicants?
- How does the company advertise for staff?
- Are job descriptions prepared?
- Are job descriptions sent to applicants?
- Is there a standard application form or do applicants apply by letter/CV?

- What happens if there are dozens of applicants for a job?
- Who interviews applicants? Does this change depending upon the vacancy?
- Who makes the final decision?
- Is the process very effective or are there occasional problems?
- Could any improvements be made to increase its effectiveness?
- What are the procedures for staff training?
- Is there an induction programme for new staff?
- Are staff encouraged to undertake training and development?
- Does the business hold, or is it working towards, Investors in People?
- Is the business involved in other national training initiatives, e.g. National Training Awards?
- Is there a training department?
- Do staff undergo training on the job, off the job, or both?
- Is there any appraisal or performance review scheme?
- How often are staff appraised?
- Is the appraisal scheme linked to staff development? If so, how?
- Have staff undergone training for new technology or new work practices?
- How are staff trained on health and safety requirements?
- How are they kept up to date with new developments?
- How effective are these procedures in enabling staff to perform well?
- How effective are these procedures in maintaining a safe and secure working environment?
- Could anything be done to improve training or development to improve effectiveness?
- Is there a separate customer service department?
- How are staff trained in customer service?
- How many ways can customers use to contact the business (e.g. visit, phone, email)?
- What are the customer service policies?
- How are complaints dealt with?
- How are complaints monitored?
- What would happen if complaints increased?
- Can customers return all goods or only faulty goods?
- How are customer service staff trained about consumer rights in law?
- Are questionnaires issued to find out customer views?
- How are these analysed?
- What other methods are used to find out about customer needs and expectations?
- Is there a suggestion scheme for improving customer service?
- How effective is customer service in meeting the needs and expectations of customers? How do you know this?
- Are there any ways in which customer service could be improved?

Unit 2 assessment evidence. Maximum marks = 50. Remember, each outcome builds on the last to achieve the maximum marks

Section	What you must find out	What you must then do	Points to consider
A	Who the stakeholders are in the business and the importance of each type of stakeholder	Write an account of the stakeholders in *one* business. • If you *identify* the stakeholders in the business, you can obtain up to **3 marks**. • If you *explain* the nature of the interest each stakeholder has in the business, then you can gain up to a further **2 marks**. • If you *evaluate* the extent to which each stakeholder has an influence on the business and how it operates, then you can gain an extra **2 marks**. **Total possible marks = 7**	Refer to the list on page 150 and identify which groups are relevant for the business you are investigating. Then find out more about each group – why do/would they contact the business? In which areas of the business are they most interested? Refer back to pages 151–161 for information. Be aware that you are likely to be able to find out more about customer or supplier interests than the interests of financiers if some aspects of this relationship are confidential. Different stakeholder groups have different types of influence – and those which are more powerful will be seen by the organisation as the most important. Find some specific examples of how the business has responded to requests (or demands!) by different groups. You could also try to 'rank' stakeholders in relation to their power. If there has ever been a conflict between two groups, the group that won was likely to be the more powerful. If there has been no conflict, you should think of a situation which might occur, and suggest how the business would be likely to respond.
B	The roles of *three* people who have different responsibilities within the business and the contracts of employment within the business	Write an account of this aspect of the business. • If you *describe* the roles of three people who have different responsibilities in the business, then you can gain up to **4 marks**. • If you explain the content of the contract of employment for one of these three people and describe the terms and conditions of employment and working arrangements,	You need to find out about people in three different roles. You can select from manager, supervisor, operative or support staff. If you have chosen a business where you work part time or are there on work experience as an 'operative', you could describe your own role. Make sure you identify the different responsibilities each person has. If you work part time, you could use your own contract of employment. You could ask a colleague if he or she would show you his or her contract

		then you can gain up to a further **2 marks**. • If you *evaluate*, using examples, how well the contract of employment you have just described meets the needs of the business and the employee *and* recommend and justify suitable changes to the contract of employment, then you can gain an extra **2 marks**. **Total possible marks = 8**	of employment, but be prepared to accept a refusal. Your colleague may prefer to keep this information confidential. In this case, you may be able to persuade the human resources department to show you a blank contract for an employee with a particular grade of responsibility or talk to your tutor about obtaining one from elsewhere (such as in a case study). Remember that when you evaluate the contract you need to look at the needs of *both* the employer and employee. Look for terms which help the employer to have a flexible workforce but which are fair to the employee. If you genuinely think the contract could not be improved, say why.
C	Employer and employee rights and responsibilities, including how the business deals with disputes	Write an account of this aspect of the business. • If you *describe*, using examples from the business, the rights of the employer and its employees you can gain up to **4 marks**. • If you *explain*, using examples, how the business resolves disagreements with its employees over rights of employment or working conditions, then you can gain up to a further **3 marks**. • If you *evaluate* the extent to which the business ensures that a good working relationship exists between the employer and its employees, then you can gain an extra **2 marks**. **Total possible marks = 9**	Remember that all employers and employees have *statutory rights* through legislation. A contract of employment can *add* to these, but cannot take them away. You should include examples. If you state that every employee has the legal right to an itemised pay slip, you could describe when these are issued and the information they contain (but don't ask anyone to tell you how much they are paid!). You also need to know how the grievance and disciplinary procedures operate. Since actual disputes will be confidential, instead give examples of problems which *might* occur and how these would then be resolved. Remember that a business will have both formal and informal ways of ensuring there are good working relationships. Keeping staff informed is one way and there may be a staff committee or regular team meetings. If you think that the atmosphere in the workplace is positive, you will need to identify the factors which contribute towards this. Focus on the business as a whole, not on individual concerns about minor issues.

Section	What you must find out	What you must then do	Points to consider
D	The employee recruitment process	Write an account about employee recruitment and selection in the business. • If you *describe* the recruitment and selection process that the business uses to meet its staffing needs, then you can gain up to **3 marks**. • If you *explain* why the business uses this particular processes, then you can gain up to a further **3 marks**. • If you *evaluate* the effectiveness of the process and suggest improvements to documentation and procedures, then you can gain an extra **2 marks**. **Total possible marks = 8**	Remember that the process will have different stages – from agreeing and advertising a vacancy, to dealing with applications and interviews and then appointing staff. Describe each stage fully. Now look at *why* this process is used. Why are vacancies advertised in the paper/Jobcentre/with an agency? Why is one method preferred to others? Are there application forms or do applicants apply with a letter and a CV? Why? Who is responsible for interviewing – one person or several? What differences are there and why? One way to tackle this is to identify possible problems. Is the application form easy to complete? What happens if an interviewer is ill? What happens if there are dozens of applications for one vacancy? If you think the process is *very* effective and cannot find any flaws, then say *why* you believe this to be so.

E	How the business trains its staff and encourages their further development. This includes finding out if the business either has, or is working towards, Investors in People	Write an account about staff training and development.
		
		• If you describe the procedures that the business follows for:
		  – staff training
		  – appraisal and performance review
		  – retraining for new technology or new work practices
		  – any national training initiatives
		  – health and safety training
		then you can gain up to **4 marks**.
		• If you then *analyse* how effectively these procedures enable people to perform their jobs well and maintain a safe and secure working environment, you can gain up to a further **3 marks**.
			If the business either has or is working towards IIP, this will be your starting point as the business is committed towards staff training and development. If there is a specific training section or training officer, try to talk to this person. Also find out if the business is involved in any National Training Award schemes (see page 266).
			
			Applications to attend training events (either internal or external) must usually be approved. There will be documentation for this. There will also be appraisal documents, but don't expect to see anyone's completed appraisal form as this information is confidential. Health and safety training is often the responsibility of the safety officer and is a legal requirement. Find out how new employees are instructed and how all employees are kept up to date.

- If you *extend* your analysis and suggest and justify alternative or additional procedures that might improve the effectiveness of employees and the safety of the working environment, you can gain up to a further **2 marks**.

Total possible marks = 9

Evidence of the effectiveness should be all around you! If people are using IT equipment and software competently and everyone is well aware of health and safety, this didn't happen by chance! Try to find specific examples of training that have taken place and how individuals feel it benefited them at work.

Most organisations (and many employees) would prefer to do more training and development but have to consider the costs carefully. If you suggest *more* training, it is advisable to add that this would cost more money and may not always be possible. You could suggest more (or less) off-the-job training, but remember that people who leave their desk must catch up later and other staff will have more to do while they are absent. If you do not think that any alternatives or additional procedures are necessary, say *why* you think this.

| F | How customer service and customer protection operates within the business | Write an account of these aspects of the business. <ul><li>If you *describe* the rights of customers under consumer law and identify the features within the business that contribute towards good customer service, you can gain up to **4 marks**.</li><li>If you then *analyse* how effectively the customer service provision of the business meets the needs and expectation of its customers, you can gain up to a further **3 marks**.</li><li>If you *extend* your analysis to suggest and justify ways in which customer service provision could be improved to further meet the needs and expectations of customers, you can gain up to a further **2 marks**.</li></ul> **Total possible marks = 9** | This is easier to do if you *start* by looking at the features of customer service – list them and then look at how they meet the needs of customers and their rights under consumer law. For example, the company 'returns' policy should cover faulty goods and the right of consumers to a refund. Remember that customer service may not be only face to face. Customers may make enquiries over the telephone or through a website.

All organisations measure customer satisfaction through surveys, questionnaires, monitoring complaints, and so on. Find out how this is done. If problems have been experienced (e.g. an increase in complaints), find out what was done to resolve these. Try to discover, too, how the business identifies the needs and expectations of its customers.

Try to find out what else the business would like to do (money permitting) |

Section	What you must find out	What you must then do	Points to consider
			to improve its service. This could include improving the speed of response or finding out more about customers' individual needs. There may be specific plans for the future which you could mention. If you feel that the customer service provision is excellent, you must be able to justify this opinion.

> **Special note**
>
> Readers of this book have the unique opportunity to use Richer Sounds, a national retailer of audio separates and related equipment, for their business investigations. Richer Sounds was voted the top British-owned company to work for by its employees in 2002. Information about Richer Sounds is given on the StudentZone on the Richer Sounds' website at www.richersounds.com – you will need the following password to access this zone: RICHERLEARNING.

Unit 3: Business finance

Introduction to Unit 3

Look around your local area and you'll see shops or small businesses which opened some time ago. Some will have been there for years and are successful, but from time to time you'll see others where 'Closing down sale' notices appear in the window, soon followed by an estate agent's 'For sale' or 'To let' board. In this case, the business was probably unprofitable and the owner could not afford to continue running it.

This unit explores what the words 'profitable' and 'unprofitable' mean. In broad terms, unprofitable businesses spend more money than they earn. You may have experienced this yourself when you want to go out with friends but don't have enough money to do so. This may sound simple, but even small businesses spend and earn money in many different ways. Because of this you will learn about the ways in which businesses need to check regularly whether or not they are operating profitably.

Businesses also need to think ahead. Will they be profitable in six months or a year? Will a plan for a new or improved product or service increase income enough to cover the extra costs involved? What would happen if an important customer or supplier closes down? This unit looks at ways in which businesses can think about the future to try to ensure that they remain profitable, or better still, become more profitable. There are two important documents which businesses produce to show whether or not they are profitable. These are the profit and loss account and the balance sheet. Both of these are looked at in some detail.

If a business wishes to expand or develop, it will need extra money (called **capital**) to finance its plans. This is also true if someone wants to start a new business. The unit explains different ways in which it could obtain this money and the advantages and disadvantages in each case.

All these issues are important if a business is to survive in the long term, but it would all be a waste of time if day-to-day activities were not carried out correctly. If customers failed to pay their bills or no one kept an eye on the amount of money in the bank account, a business could get into trouble and might even have to close. This unit therefore also looks at the documents used when businesses buy and sell goods or provide and use services. All of these documents need to be completed accurately.

Businesses provide products or a service for their customers and quite often both. For example, a business manufacturing baseball caps provides a product; a car wash provides a service; manufacturers of washing machines provide a product but normally provide a service by offering maintenance packages. In general, this unit deals with products, since the financial aspects are easier to explain. However, all the principles described still apply to the service sector.

Integrated computer technology (ICT) has many applications in business finance. As well as covering all the standard computer packages such as word processing, spreadsheets and databases, ICT is a general term which is used for all the things which can be done when computers store and process information. This includes facilities such as:

- computers sending information to each other
- bar code reading
- the Internet.

ICT systems can be applied to several business finance procedures. These applications will be explained at each stage. You also need to understand that using ICT can have disadvantages as well as advantages.

What you will learn

17 Investigating the flow of financial documents used to make a business purchase
18 Investigating methods of making and receiving payments
19 Covering the costs of a new product or service
20 Using a cash-flow forecast
21 Using a budget
22 Calculating the break-even point
23 Calculating the profit or loss of a business
24 Understanding a balance sheet
25 The importance of business accounts
26 Sources of business finance
27 Financial planning

Chapter 17: Investigating the flow of financial documents used to make a business purchase

What you will learn

Understanding financial documents
Financial documents and computerised accounting systems

Note: The blank forms required for the activities throughout this chapter can be found on pages 412–418.

Overview: financial documents used to make a business purchase

What is a purchase transaction?

When you buy a can of Coke from a shop, you pay cash for the drink and may receive a till receipt. When this happens you have completed a **financial transaction** because you have obtained goods and paid for them. More accurately, you have made a **purchase transaction**.

Millions of purchase transactions take place every day

Each day millions of purchase transactions take place between businesses. The main difference is that in business the process takes time and is carried out using a number of documents. At first sight, the different types of document and the amount of detailed information involved may seem complicated. However, every aspect of the process is important because:

- the time between an order being placed and the goods being delivered could be several weeks, or longer
- a lot of money may be involved
- several types of goods may be ordered at the same time
- records need to be available for inspection by the company's accountants, auditors or VAT officials who check they are accurate
- the records are used to produce summary documents such as profit and loss accounts and balance sheets (see Chapters 23 and 24)
- the information is used to look at trends, such as cash flow (see Chapter 20).

Financial documents and how they are used

Anna, an office manager at Daxo plc, is going to employ an extra member of staff who will need a desk, chair, filing cabinet and telephone. Anna has the authority to place orders for goods which cost up to £1000 so she can carry out the transaction herself. She gets out the catalogue of a regular supplier, Office Supplies Ltd. She is now starting a sequence of events which will result in the production of several financial documents.

1. **Purchase order**. When Anna has chosen the items she wants, she completes a purchase order form. Daxo has a standard form so that all she needs to do is fill in the information about the goods she

wants. She sends the form to the supplier by post.

2. **Delivery note**. A few days later, a van arrives and two men unload the desk and other items. Anna checks that they are the ones she ordered and that they are not damaged. One of the delivery men asks her to sign a delivery note, which has all the items listed on it, to confirm that she is happy with the items that have been delivered. The delivery note is one of Office Supplies' standard forms.

3. **Goods received note**. Anna also completes one of Daxo's goods received notes to confirm the delivery is complete and there is no damage. She sends a copy to Daxo's accounts department for its records.

4. **Invoice**. A week later, Daxo's accounts department receives an invoice from Office Supplies. It lists all the items that have been delivered, together with their price, and these are added up to show the total amount which must be paid.

5. **Credit note**. This is the opposite of an invoice because it shows money owed *to* the buyer. It would be issued if goods were returned. For example, Anna finds out that the new member of staff needs a special type of chair because he has a back problem. She has to obtain this from a specialist supplier. She contacts Office Supplies to see if she can return the other chair, which has never been used. Because she is a good customer, Office Supplies agree. It then sends a credit note to Daxo, rather than a refund.

6. **Statement of account**. If Daxo frequently places orders with the supplier, it will not pay for each order separately. Instead, Office Supplies will send a statement of account at the end of each month. This will list all the invoices which have been sent since the last payment was made, and any credit notes. Daxo will send a cheque for the total amount due as shown on the statement.

7. **Remittance advice slip**. This comes with the statement of account. It shows the amount owing and a reference number. Not all businesses send this, but its purpose is to make it easier for the customer to pay the bill.

8. **Cheque**. Daxo's accounts department sends a cheque to Office Supplies together with the remittance advice slip. Office Supplies' accounts department knows immediately what the cheque is for because the remittance advice slip provides this information.

9. **Receipt**. Office Supplies may send a receipt to Daxo, confirming that the cheque has been received, but this is unusual for a cheque payment. This is because once a cheque is paid into a bank account, this is confirmation that the bill has been paid. Receipts are important for cash transactions. If Anna's office needed a special item urgently, she could ask Ben to go to a local stationery shop. Anna may give Ben her own money to pay for the item and would tell him to get a receipt. The accounts office would need a receipt before they would repay Anna. The receipt is proof that the money has been spent.

The use of ICT

Most of this system is routine with many of the documents containing similar or identical information, so several IT packages have been produced to assist businesses to process this information efficiently. For example, once information from an order has been input into a computer, the delivery note and invoice can be produced automatically. In addition, the total from the invoice can be transferred to the statement of account. You will see more about the way ICT relates to financial transactions as you work through this unit.

Understanding financial documents

In addition to understanding the sequence of documents, you also need to be able to complete examples of each type of document

Over to you!

The sequence of documents used in a purchase transaction, such as the one Anna made, is shown below. Check that you understand this sequence and the reason why each document is used.

Issued by the purchaser

- **Order form** — describes order for goods or services with price
- **Goods received note** — is issued to record the actual items delivered
- Purchaser notifies seller if there are any shortages or damage
- **Cheque** — sent in settlement with remittance advice

Issued by the seller

- **Delivery note** — accompanies the goods and is signed by the customer as proof of delivery
- **Invoice** — gives full details of goods, price, discounts, VAT
- **Credit note** — issued if goods are returned or to adjust any over-charges on invoice
- **Statement of account** — summarises all transactions and shows the balance owing by the purchaser
- **Remittance advice slip** — summarises the account for return with payment
- **Receipt** — mainly issued to private customers or to confirm cash payment has been received

---

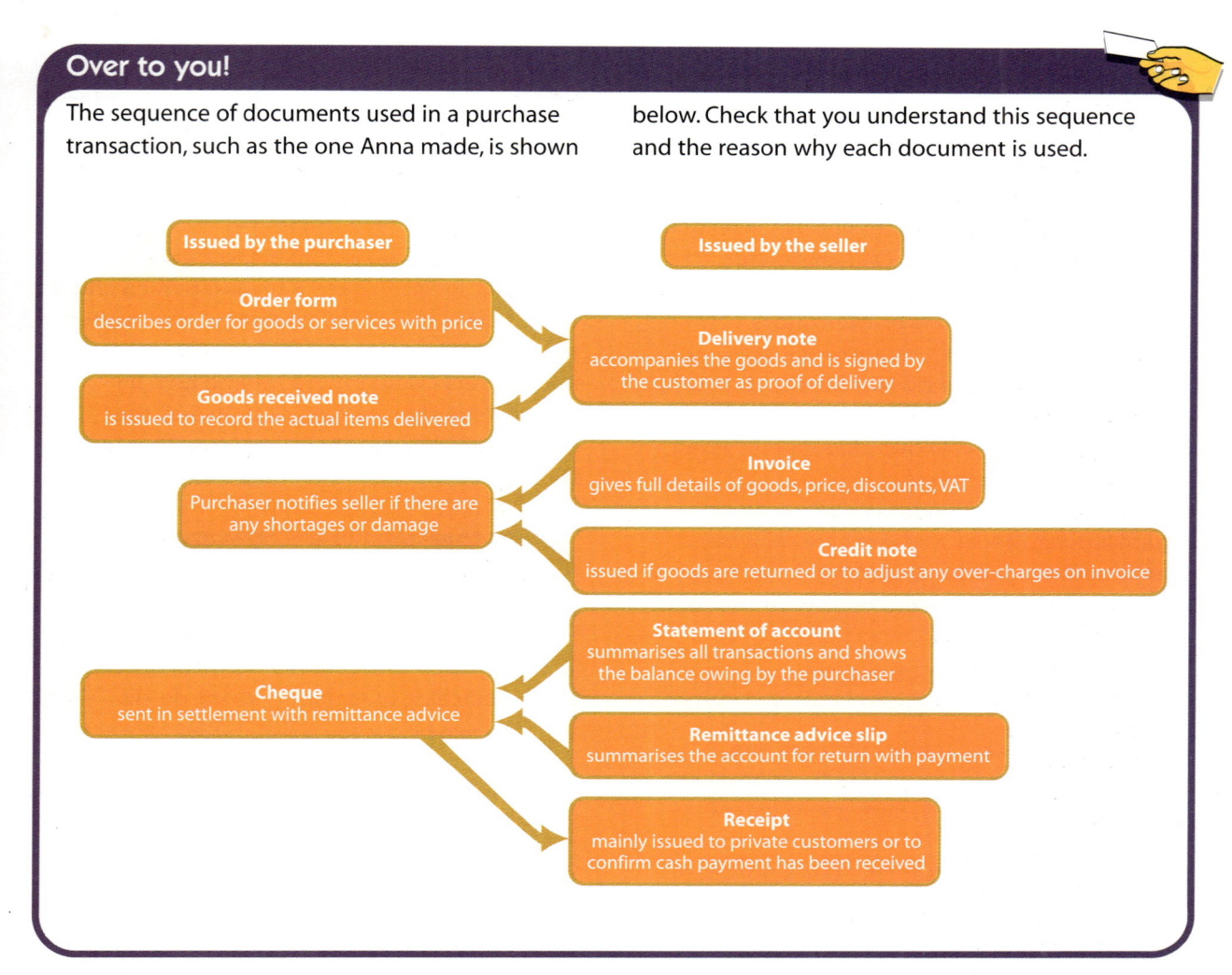

accurately. This is vital because any errors can have serious consequences. The following sections explain the purchasing documents in more detail. For this, we will look at a business called Mouse Matters which supplies computer mouse mats to retailers and business customers. Although it sells standard plain rectangular mats, its main activity is supplying specialised and customised mats.

Mouse Matters produces both a catalogue and price list. The price list is kept separate so that it can easily be updated without having to reprint the whole catalogue. Extracts from the catalogue and the price list are shown below.

Product List (non-standard range)

Standard mat – with Mouse Matters design (ref STM 1)

Ergonomic mat – with a soft gell pouch on which user can rest their wrist to reduce strain (ref ERM 3)

Photo mat – with customer's photograph (copies of photograph may be supplied by post or email) (ref PHM 5)

Animal mats – coloured in the shape of an animal (refs ADM 1, ACM 2 and AEM 3)

Perma mat – with special friction surface which does not wear and so does not 'clog up' the mouseball housing (ref PEM 2)

Customised mat – with customer's own design or company logo and advertising message (price on application)

All mats can be supplied with either a foam or vinyl base.

Item	Price per mat	Item code
Ergonomic Mat	£7.00	ERM 3
Photo Mat	£5.00	PHM 5
Dog Mat	£3.50	ADM 1
Cat Mat	£3.50	ACM 2
Elephant Mat	£3.50	AEM 3
Perma Mat	£9.50	PEM 2
Standard Mat	£1.50	STM 1

Chapter 17 Investigating financial documents

In business, the product list and the price list are very important. Customers will refer to a catalogue or product list *and* the price list when giving an order and will expect the invoice to show the same prices. Mouse Matters accounts staff will use these documents when they receive orders and issue invoices. On a computer system, all the prices are listed against the individual product codes or references.

Mouse Matters also requires supplies. To make the mats it uses raw materials, including foam, vinyl, cloth for the covering and glue. Mouse Matters uses its own documents when it is ordering these items.

Therefore, in common with all business organisations, Mouse Matters handles a large number of financial documents each day relating to all the purchases it makes *and* all the sales.

Purchase orders

Purchase orders are made out when one business buys goods or services from another. Sometimes, in an emergency, goods can be ordered by telephone. However, this verbal arrangement is then confirmed by a purchase order, usually sent by fax if the matter is urgent. Businesses have their own standard purchase order forms showing the company name, address, VAT (value added tax) registration number and other details. In many instances, a computer is used to produce the form, but it must be authorised (signed) afterwards. This confirms that the purchase order is official. Only authorised supervisors or managers will be allowed to sign an order and only senior managers if it is for a large amount of money.

On page 299 is an example of an order sent by Mouse Matters for some raw materials.

Checking the accuracy of completed purchase order forms

All purchase orders should be checked for accuracy by both the business sending the form and by the business receiving it. Mistakes can be costly or cause inconvenience.

The worst kind of problem can be caused by the figure '0'. For example, imagine a school wanted to order 10 computers to equip a classroom but because of a typing error the 10 became 100! Hopefully, the supplier would telephone to confirm that such a large order was correct. This type of error regularly occurs and results in businesses receiving goods they do not need – the supplier is not legally obliged to take back the items!

It makes sense for businesses which send out order forms to have a second person check them before they are despatched. Quite often, a junior member of staff will complete the form and the more senior person, who has the authority to sign, will check it. In addition, someone at the supplier's business should have the task of checking incoming forms for errors.

> ### It makes you think!
>
> 1 Imagine you are working for Mouse Matters and have been asked to send an order to Universal Fabrics. Fill in the blank purchase order form with the details given below. You will also need to refer to the completed purchase order form on page 299 for the other details.
>
>   The order number is 2003/707 and you should use today's date. The order is for 200 square metres of blue mouse cloth, 20 metres of black mouse cloth and 50 metres of 2 mm of vinyl sheet. Complete the correct item codes in each case and ask for delivery one week from today.
>
>   Check your completed form with someone else's in your class before showing it to your tutor. The two forms should be identical! If it is correct, your tutor will sign it as Purchasing Officer.
>
> 2 Decide what might happen if a purchase order contained one of the errors below. Within your group, decide how easy or difficult it might be to put things right.
>   a The supplier's post code is wrong.
>   b The supplier's name and address is wrong.
>   c The description of a material is right but the code is wrong.
>   d The price on the order is £2 less per item than that stated in the supplier's price list.
>   e The form is not signed.

Mouse Matters Ltd
Kellet Industrial Park
Erdington
BIRMINGHAM
B9 8KK

A

Tel: 0121 687 3610
Fax: 0121 123 4567
Website: www.mousematters.shop.uk

VAT Reg. No. 846/3822/98 **B**

Email: sales@mousematters.shop.uk

PURCHASE ORDER

To: **Universal Fabrics plc**
4–10 Dickinson Street
Battersea
LONDON
SW11 0RT

C

Supplier no.: 97 **D**

Official order no.: 2003/706 **E**

Date: 20 September 2003

Please supply:

F

Quantity	Description	Item code	Unit price
50 sq. metres	Mouse cloth (blue)	MC03	£5.50 per sq. metre
50 sq. metres	Mouse cloth (black)	MC04	£5.50 per sq. metre
100 sq. metres	2 mm vinyl sheet	V07	£6.60 per sq. metre

G (on Unit price column)

H

Delivery: 27 September 2003

I

Signed: _____

J

Designation: _____

Suppliers should note that orders are valid only if signed by a designated executive of the organisation

---

A The business details of Mouse Matters are given so that the seller is able to contact the company, if necessary, and also knows where the goods are to be delivered

B The VAT number is unique to the business and is allocated by HM Customs and Excise when the business registers for VAT (see page 304)

C Companies often store the names and addresses of suppliers on a database and only 'approved' suppliers who are on this list can be used

D When a business places regular orders with a supplier, the supplier is allocated a number. This will also be stored on the supplier database

E All orders are allocated a unique number. This enables orders stored in a manual file or on computer to be accessed quickly. Computer accounts software packages automatically give each purchase order the next number in the sequence

F The order information is a vital part of the form. Most businesses allocate each product an individual item code and this is listed in the catalogue and price list. It is repeated on the order form. A description of the product is also provided as a further check, e.g. if item code MC 03 actually identified green, not blue, mouse cloth, the customer could be contacted and asked to confirm which colour they wanted

G The unit price is the price for a specific quantity identified in a catalogue. This may be per item (e.g. for a computer) or per box (e.g. for floppy disks or envelopes)

H Some businesses quote a standard delivery time, e.g. 'within five working days'. This would then be the date quoted on the order form. If there is likely to be a problem, the supplier should contact the customer to give a delivery date

I Only authorised staff are allowed to sign orders

J This is the job title of the person signing the order

A purchase order

Spot check

Write down your answers to the following questions:

1. Why do businesses complete a purchase order?
2. State three items of information which need to be added to a blank purchase order.
3. Why is it important that a purchase order is signed only by an authorised person?
4. Why is it important that all purchase orders are checked carefully?
5. Mouse Matters has received an order from Colin's Computers this morning but it contains five errors. Look at it carefully and use the price list information on page 297 to help you identify some of the errors. For each error you find, say what you think might happen if the mistake was not found.

Colin's Computers
1 High Street
Selford
Norfolk
NR1 7BS

Tel: 0103 259136   Fax: 0103 308299
Contact us at: www.colincomp.co.uk

VAT Reg. 3672 3248 79

PURCHASE ORDER

Purchase order no: CC/2003/215

Mouse Matters Ltd
Kellett Industrial Park
Erdington
BRIGHTON

Date: 20 October 2003

Item code	Quantity	Description	Unit price
STM1	100	Standard mat	£1.50
ERN3	70	Ergonomic mat	£5.00
ADM1	100	Cat mat	£3.50
PEM2	50	Perma Mat	£9.50

Delivery: 26 October 2002

Authorised signatory: _____   Title: _____

Delivery notes

This is a document produced by the suppliers and sent to the customer with the goods. When the goods arrive, a member of staff will check the contents and sign two copies of the delivery note. One copy is kept by the customer and the other is returned to the supplier. Unless any problems have been identified, a signed delivery note tells the supplier that

- the goods have been delivered to the right place
- they have been delivered on time
- the customer is happy with the goods and that they are of right type, quality and quantity – and were not damaged.

When this has happened, the supplier can send the invoice.

If there are any problems with the delivery, such as an item missing or damaged, then this should be recorded on the delivery note so that the supplier will receive the information. However, goods cannot always be checked the moment they arrive, in which case the delivery note may be signed but marked 'goods not checked'. If a mistake is found when the goods are unpacked, the supplier must be notified immediately.

Large businesses tend to have their own vehicles and drivers to deliver to customers. However, some businesses use specialist haulage contractors to deliver goods. In this case, a different document may be produced, called an **advice note**. This is identical to a delivery note and may have the name and address of the haulage company at the top. A copy will be sent to the supplier by the haulage company as proof that the task has been carried out satisfactorily.

Universal Fabrics has now despatched the goods to Mouse Matters following receipt of its order number 2003/706 (see page 299). The delivery note which accompanied the goods is shown on page 302.

Checking completed delivery notes

Before a delivery note is sent with the goods, it should be checked for accuracy. The following are potentially the most serious errors:

- Mistakes copying the order number – the order number is needed by the customer to check the delivery against the original order.
- Mistakes in copying the customer number and/or the address – this may mean that the document will be filed in the wrong place and the goods and invoice will be sent to the wrong customer!
- Errors in copying the item code or quantity – the items on the delivery note will not match the goods delivered, leading to confusion.

Goods received notes

Goods are often delivered using the business's own vans or special carrier. At other times, they may be sent through the post. Unless the goods have been paid for in advance, an invoice will follow and the accounts staff responsible for paying the bill will need proof that the correct goods have been received and are in good condition. For this reason, many organisations complete a goods received note each time an order is unpacked and checked. This is a double check, especially for orders which could not be checked at the time of delivery or when a delivery note was signed by reception staff, rather than by staff in the warehouse.

The main reasons for having goods received notes are:

- to record what has been delivered
- to record when it was delivered
- to confirm who supplied the goods and their reference code.

This information is needed by the accounts staff so that when the invoice is received from the supplier it is simple to check that the details on the invoice match the goods received note. If there are any discrepancies or damage, the supplier would be contacted immediately.

The goods received note on page 303 was completed by Mouse Matters staff when they received the order from Universal Fabrics and the delivery note shown on page 302.

Mistakes which could be made on goods received notes

- On a manual system, details can be copied wrongly from the order form.
- If the goods are not checked properly, a missing item or a fault may go unnoticed.
- An incomplete description of any problems. A full explanation of the type of any damage or omission should be noted.

Universal Fabrics
4–10 Dickinson Street
Battersea
LONDON
SW11 0RT

Tel: 020 8123 4567   VAT Reg. No. 876/1882/99
Fax: 020 81236789
Website: www.unifab.shop.uk   Email: sales@unifab.shop.uk

DELIVERY NOTE

To: Mouse Matters Ltd   Delivery address (if different):
A   Kellet Industrial Park
         Erdington
         BIRMINGHAM   B9 8KK

Date: 27 September 2003

Your order no.	Customer account no.	Despatch date	Invoice no.	Delivery method
2003/706	147	27 September 2003	2003615	Own transport
B	**C**		**D**	

Item code	Quantity	Description	
MC03	50 sq. metres	Blue mouse cloth	**E**
MC04	50 sq. metres	Black mouse cloth	
V07	100 sq. metres	2 mm vinyl sheet	

Thank you for your order. Please retain this delivery note for your records

Received in good condition (or comment here)
Goods received but not checked

F

Signed: *JFinch*   Date: *27th Sept 2003*

Please print name: JOHN FINCH

White copy: customer
Pink copy: carrier
Yellow copy: Universal Fabrics

A The customer's name and the address to which the goods have to be delivered. This is normally the main address of the business but, in some cases, the order could be sent from head office for delivery to a branch office in a different town

B This repeats the order number from the Mouse Matters purchase order. This is important for Mouse Matters because some businesses receive hundreds of orders a week from different suppliers. It is important that they can quickly link the materials arriving to the order which was sent

C Just as Mouse Matters gives a special number to each of its suppliers, Universal Fabrics does the same for its customers. All the information about individual customers will be stored on a database

D An invoice to match this order will have already been prepared to send to Mouse Matters with a serial number allocated. It will not be sent until the returned delivery note confirms that the goods have been received

E This part repeats the information on the purchase order (see page 299) but *never* includes the price

F This part is completed by the person from Mouse Matters who receives and checks the goods. If this person is not satisfied that everything is correct, a comment should be made in the space provided before signing and dating the note

A delivery note

GOODS RECEIVED NOTE — Mouse Matters Ltd

Supplier:

Universal Fabrics
4–10 Dickinson Street
Battersea
LONDON   **A**
SW11 0RT

Supplier a/c no.: 97   **B**

Carrier: Universal Fabrics
D

GRN no.: 2003/1075   **C**

GRN date: 27 Sept 2003

Delivery note date: 27 Sept 2003

Checker: D Evans   **E**

Order no. **F**	Quantity ordered	Quantity delivered	Description of goods	Tick box or enter details if goods damaged or discrepancy identified
2003/706	50 sq m	50 sq m	Blue mouse cloth	✓
	50 sq m	50 sq m	Black mouse cloth	✓
	100 sq m	100 sq m	2 mm vinyl sheet	1 mm vinyl sheet sent in error

White copy: Purchases file
Pink copy: Accounts

A The supplier's name and address should match the one on the delivery note

B Each authorised supplier has an account number. All supplier records are filed under that number. On a computer system, once the number is keyed in, the address would automatically be displayed

C As with other documents, goods received notes have a serial number so that they can be easily traced. This is particularly easy on a computer system

D The name of the carrier is recorded so that if there is any damage during delivery, the carrier can be contacted

E The person who receives and checks the goods writes his or her name or initials on the form so that he or she can be contacted if there is a query

F The order number, order quantity and description are copied from the order form. Any differences between these details and what is delivered are noted in the third and fourth columns

A goods received note

It makes you think!

Within your group, discuss what action Office Supplies should take if each of these problems was experienced:

a Ten boxes of paper were crushed and damaged in transit. They are unusable.
b Pink paper was delivered instead of white.
c The order stated 50 folders but 500 folders were delivered.
d The order stated 20 cartridges but only 15 were delivered.

Later in this chapter, you will see how the paperwork is sorted out to resolve any problems like these.

Over to you!

So far, the financial documents shown have been set out so that they all look similar. This is to help you while you are learning about these documents.

In reality, the design of different documents varies from one company to another, but they still do the same job.

Ask your parents for examples of some routine bills you receive at home, such as your telephone or gas bill, and see if your tutor can show you some examples from the school or college office. You can then see how the design varies but the main information stays the same!

Chapter 17 Investigating financial documents

Spot check

Write down your answers to the following questions:

1. Who would sign a delivery note – the seller or the purchaser?
2. What would you write on a delivery note if you didn't have time to check the goods?
3. Why is it important that all goods are checked carefully before they are paid for?
4. Identify one mistake which could be made on a delivery note and state what the results might be.
5. Why do most organisations complete a goods received note when goods are delivered?
6. Why is it important for the checker to put his or her name on the goods received note?
7. In the case of the delivery from Universal Fabrics, the vinyl sheet was the wrong size. What action should now be taken?
8. Identify two mistakes which could be made when completing a goods received note and, in each case, state what the consequences might be.
9. Mouse Matters has received an order for mouse mats from Colin's Computers. The goods have been assembled and are ready to go on the company's own van for delivery. You have been asked to prepare a delivery note. Complete a Mouse Matters delivery note and use today's date. The order number was CC/2003/356. The customer number is 265. The invoice number will be 1792/04. The goods ordered were:

Item code	Quantity	Description	Unit price
ERM 3	50	Ergonomic Mat	£7.00
PHM 5	70	Photo Mat	£5.00
ADM 1	95	Dog Mat	£3.50

Remember that you must not complete the box at the bottom – this is for Colin's Computers' staff to complete. Check your completed form with your tutor.

10. Using a Mouse Matters goods received note, check and record a stationery delivery which has just arrived.

    Order number 2003/516 was sent to Office Supplies, 14 High Street, Erdington, Birmingham B9 3KP, and was delivered by Office Supplies' own van yesterday. The delivery note is also dated yesterday. The supplier number of Office Supplies is 61.

    The order was for 500 reams of white A4 paper and 20 black inkjet printer cartridges. The paper is fine but you can find only 19 cartridges. You are told to note this discrepancy on the goods received note.

    The next goods received note number is 2003/1085. Make this out with today's date and record the information given.

Invoices

An invoice is sent from a supplier to a customer requesting payment for goods which have been delivered. It gives details of the goods and their price. These prices are added together to give the total amount owing. If everything is in order, the customer sends payment to the supplier.

An example of an invoice is shown on page 305. This is the invoice which Universal Fabrics sent to Mouse Matters after they had delivered the goods requested (see pages 299 and 302).

Checking invoices

Invoices should be checked carefully before they are sent. If there are errors, this could cause payment to be delayed or, in an extreme case, not paid at all. Most invoices today are prepared on computer so the calculations will be correct *providing* all the entries are made correctly! If you are handwriting an invoice and using a calculator to work out the totals, it is very important to check that the figures are correct at every stage.

Universal Fabrics plc
4–10 Dickinson Street
Battersea
LONDON
SW11 0RT

Tel: 020 8123 4567   VAT Reg. No. 876/1882/99
Fax: 020 81236789   Email: sales@unifab.shop.uk
Website: www.unifab.shop.uk

INVOICE

To: Mouse Matters Ltd
      Kellet Industrial Park
      Erdington
      BIRMINGHAM
      B9 8KK

A

Your order no.	Customer account no.	Date/tax point	Invoice no.
2003/706	147	8 October 2003	2003615

B

Item code	Quantity	Description	Unit price £	Net value £
MC03	50 sq. metres	Blue mouse cloth	5.50	275.00
MC04	50 sq. metres	Black mouse cloth	5.50	275.00
V07	100 sq. metres	2 mm vinyl sheet	6.60	660.00
			TOTAL	£1210.00
			VAT 17.5%	£211.75
			TOTAL DUE	£1421.75

C
D
E

Terms: net 28 days   F   White copy: customer
Carriage paid   Pink copy: sales
E & OE   G   Yellow copy: accounts

A The order number was shown on the original purchase order and it also appears on the delivery note, as does the customer account number and invoice number. All these details should match

B The information about the goods should be the same as on the purchase order and confirmed on the delivery note. However, on the invoice the unit prices are multiplied by the quantity to give the value of each item

C The total amount for all the goods purchased is shown

D A further amount is then added for value added tax (VAT). The current rate is 17.5%. You calculate this by multiplying the total amount by 17.5%

E The total due is the total for the goods *plus* the amount for VAT

F The terms state when payment is due. In this case, the invoice must be paid within 28 days of issue

G E & OE stands for 'errors and omissions excepted'. This means that if Universal Fabrics made an error on the invoice, such as missing out an item, it could not be held to this in law. It could send a supplementary invoice for the additional amount due and it would still have to be paid

An invoice

Fact file

Value added tax, or **VAT**, is one of several taxes levied by the government. VAT works by charging a business a percentage of all the money it receives from selling services or products. The current rate of VAT is 17.5 per cent but the government could change this.

Businesses can claim back the VAT on things which they buy. For example, a car manufacturer charges VAT on the finished cars sold but claims back the VAT on all the parts which it buys to make the car.

HM Customs and Excise is the government agency which collects VAT. It can visit businesses and see financial documents to check that the figures are correct. This is a very good reason why all financial documents should be completed accurately.

Most businesses have to comply with this system. This is called being 'VAT registered'. Each has an individual VAT registration number which must appear on their invoices.

Small businesses, currently those with a turnover of less than £55,000, do not have to register, do not charge VAT on sales and cannot reclaim VAT paid to their suppliers.

VAT is not charged on all goods and services. Currently, these include food (but not meals in restaurants or takeaways), books, newspapers and children's clothing.

It makes you think!

1. Work through each of the sections of the invoice shown on page 305. If you do not understand any section, ask your tutor to explain it to you. Then check the invoice carefully. Items you must check are:
   a that the details from the order on page 299 have been completed correctly, especially the quantities and the prices
   b that all the calculations are correct.
2. Mouse Matters has received another order from Colin's Computers. This is shown on page 307. The order has been fulfilled and sent, and the delivery note has been returned signed as checked and correct.
   Make out an invoice to Colin's Computers using a blank Mouse Matters invoice. The invoice number is 604321. Check all your entries and all your calculations very carefully. Then ask your tutor to approve your invoice.
3. Some firms offer other businesses a discount (money off), especially for large orders. This amount is deducted *before* any VAT is added and is clearly shown on the invoice. Mouse Matters receives discount from Office Supplies. The calculations on an invoice it has received are shown below.
   a Check if the calculations are correct.
   b Calculate how much Mouse Matters would have paid *without* any discount. Remember you must start again because the VAT amount would be different. You cannot just subtract £12.46!

Extract from Office Supplies invoice

Item code	Quantity	Description	Unit price £	Net value £
203PP	25 reams	White A4 paper	3.79	94.75
200PF	10 packs	Square-cut folders	2.99	29.90
			Total for goods	124.65
			Less 10% discount	12.46
			Sub-total	112.19
			Plus VAT (17.5%)	19.63
			Total due	131.82

Colin's Computers
1 High Street
Selford
Norfolk
NR1 7BS

Tel: 0103 259136   Fax: 0103 308299
Contact us at: www.colincomp.shop.uk

VAT Reg. 3672 3248 79

PURCHASE ORDER

Purchase Order No: CC/2003/215

Mouse Matters Ltd
Kellett Industrial Park
Erdington
BRIGHTON   B9 8KK

Date: 7 October 2002

Item code	Quantity	Description	Unit price
STM1	40	Standard mat	£1.50
ERM3	50	Ergonomic mat	£7.00
PHM5	25	Photo Mat	£5.00
PEM2	50	Perma Mat	£9.50

Delivery: 10 January 2003

Authorised signatory: *J Smith*   Title: *Store Manager*

Credit notes

Sometimes the customer may be overcharged. This may be because:

- a mistake has been made on the invoice
- faulty or damaged goods have been returned – these should have been recorded on the delivery note and the goods received note
- the wrong goods have been sent and have to be returned
- the customer ordered more goods than were required and the supplier has agreed to take the extra ones back.

A simple solution to this problem would be for the supplier to send a cheque to the customer. However, when the two businesses deal regularly with each other, a credit note may be issued.

An example of a credit note is shown on page 308. Colin's Computers returned 10 Perma Mats because they were faulty. They cannot be charged for these mats so Mouse Matters has sent them a credit note. You will notice that the information in the boxes is very similar to an invoice – and so are the calculations. Check each entry in turn and make sure that you understand what they mean.

It makes you think!

Within your group, discuss what might happen if the following mistakes were made on a credit note.

a   The price quoted is from an out-of-date catalogue.
b   The invoice number is not quoted.
c   VAT has not been added.

Mouse Matters Ltd
Kellet Industrial Park
Erdington
BIRMINGHAM
B9 8KK

Tel: 0121 687 3610
Fax: 0121 123 4567
Website: www.mousematters.shop.uk

VAT Reg. No. 846/3822/98

Email: sales@mousematters.shop.uk

CREDIT NOTE

To: **Colin's Computers**
1 High Street
Selford
Norfolk
NR1 7BS

Your returns ref.	Customer account no.	Date/tax point	Invoice no.	Credit note no.
21	147	17 January 2002	2004321	20366

Item code	Quantity	Description	Unit price	Net value
PEM2	10	Perma Mats	£9.50	£95.00
			TOTAL	£95.00
			VAT 17.5%	£16.62
			REFUNDED CHARGE	£111.62

Reason for return:
Goods faulty

White copy: customer
Pink copy: carrier
Yellow copy: Universal Fabrics

A credit note

Statements of account

Businesses often deal with each other several times a month. For example, Colin's Computers could place two or three orders a week with Mouse Matters. Invoices would be sent after each order was delivered but to save time and effort, Colin's Computers would be allowed to pay a number of invoices at once. This means that they make only one payment.

Mouse Matters sends out statements of account at the end of each month, like most companies, to all the customers who owe it money. It would normally expect payment to be made within the following two weeks. On a computerised system, statements will be calculated and produced automatically.

Credit notes must also be included in the statement of account. The amount on each one must be *deducted* from the amount owing and so must any payments which have been made by the customer during the month.

On a statement, all the transactions during the month are listed in date order.

An example of a statement of account is shown on page 310. It is a statement that Mouse Matters is sending to its customer, Globe Computer Stores.

Fact file

A statement of account has three monetary columns. The first is the **debit** column which shows the amounts owed by the customer. The second is the **credit** column and shows amounts *paid* by the customer and owed by the supplier (and listed on credit notes).

It is sometimes easy to confuse credit and debit. One way is to think of debit as being similar to 'debt'. If you lend a friend £2, then he or she is in debt to you for this amount.

The third column shows a **running balance**. This means it is calculated after each transaction. The final amount is often repeated, this is the amount of money actually owed by the customer. Occasionally there may be a **credit balance** on a statement. This happens if the total of the credit notes and payments is greater than the amount owed. In this case the supplier owes the customer money.

Checking completed statements

On computerised statements, the information is transferred automatically for each transaction during the month and the balance is calculated. Most computer systems 'build up' a statement throughout the month. Only at the end of the month are they checked and printed out for every customer.

If the statement is produced manually, the most common types of error are:

- failing to carry the balance forward or carrying forward the wrong amount
- omitting a transaction
- failing to reorder the transactions into date order before entering them
- mixing up the debit and the credit columns
- forgetting that a debit item *increases* the balance, whereas a credit item *decreases* the balance
- miscalculating the running balance. If you do this wrong once, then all your totals will be wrong from then on! It is therefore a good idea to check each entry twice and then check the final calculation at the end.

Remittance advice slips

When customers receive their statements of account, they should send a cheque in payment to the supplier within a few days. As you can see in the statement sent by Mouse Matters on page 310, a remittance advice slip can be attached to the statement. This is often divided by a perforated line, so it can easily be separated and sent back with the cheque.

The customer must state the amount enclosed and the cheque number. The customer should make out a cheque for the same amount as the balance. If not, a note should be sent to explain why there is a difference. The date of payment is the date the remittance advice and cheque are sent to the supplier. Many suppliers put a reference code on the remittance advice, but this is optional.

Checking completed remittance advice slips

There are two main aspects which should be checked by the customer:

- that the details entered on the remittance advice match those on the statement
- that the final entries are accurate and the amount enclosed is the same as the amount written on the cheque.

Cheques

You buy two mouse mats for £5, using money you drew out of your bank account earlier that day. Later, the shop owner pays your money, together with his other takings, into his bank. So, eventually, your £5 is transferred from your bank account to the shop's bank account.

Business transactions may involve thousands of pounds a day. Imagine using cash for these! Quite apart from the weight of coins and the inconvenience, the security risks would be high. Cheques are one way of making this process simpler and less risky.

When Mouse Matters receives a cheque from a customer and pays it into the bank, the money will be transferred automatically from the customer's account to Mouse Matters' account. Because the bank records the transaction and shows the transfer on the bank statement, no receipt is necessary.

Mouse Matters Ltd
Kellet Industrial Park
Erdington
BIRMINGHAM
B9 8KK

Tel: 0121 687 3610
Fax: 0121 123 4567
Website: www.mousematters.shop.uk

VAT Reg. No. 846/3822/98

Email: sales@mousematters.shop.uk

STATEMENT OF ACCOUNT

To: Globe Computer Stores
Mira Way
NUNEATON
Warwickshire
CV10 0BJ

Customer a/c no: 5579

Credit limit: £10,000 **A**

Date: 31 May 2003

Date	Details	Debit (£)	Credit (£)	Balance (£)
1 May	**B** Balance owing			800.52
10 May	**C** Invoice 702348	3823.52		4624.04
15 May	**D** Cheque 5014		800.52	3823.52
27 May	**E** Credit note 20384		370.12	3453.40
			G AMOUNT NOW DUE:	**£3453.40**

F appears alongside the Balance column.

REMITTANCE ADVICE **H**

From: Globe Computer Stores
Mira Way
NUNEATON
Warwickshire
CV10 0BJ

Customer a/c no. 5579

Date of statement: 30 May 2003

AMOUNT ENCLOSED: _____   CHEQUE NO: _____

Your ref: _____   Date of payment: _____

All cheques should be made payable to Mouse Matters Ltd

A The credit limit shows the maximum value of goods that Mouse Matters is prepared to allow this customer to have without receiving a payment

B The opening balance is the 'amount now due' figure from the last statement. Notice that the third entry in the box, D, is a cheque received for this amount

C This entry summarises an invoice which has been sent on 10 May. The invoice serial number has been included for reference. The amount from the invoice is recorded in the debit column since this *increases* the money owed to the supplier, Mouse Matters

D This shows that a cheque has been received from Globe Computer Stores to pay for the amount given on the statement it received at the end of April. Remember that it is shown on the May statement as an opening balance, B. This figure is recorded in the credit column as it *reduces* the total amount owed by the customer

E This is money which Mouse Matters owes Globe Computer Stores so the amount is written in the credit column (see credit notes)

F The end column gives a running balance of the money owed. It is recalculated after each transaction. Remember, all debit entries *increase* the money owed and all credit entries *decrease* it

G The final part repeats the last entry of the running balance because is the amount which Mouse Matters expects to receive

H A remittance advice slip is often sent with a statement. This helps to make the payment process a little easier. Mouse Matters will send it ready completed with the customer's name, account number and the statement date

A statement of account

Spot check

Write down your answers to the following questions:

1. What is an invoice?
2. What item of information always appears on an invoice but never appears on a delivery note?
3. What is VAT?
4. You buy 17 mouse mats at £5 each + VAT. How much would you owe Mouse Matters?
5. Give two reasons why a company would need to send a credit note to a customer.
6. Explain whether a credit note *increases* or *decreases* the amount of money owed by a customer.
7. How often do companies usually send out statements of account?
8. What is meant by the 'credit limit'?
9. What is a 'running balance'?
10. Using a blank statement of account, complete Mouse Matters' June statement of account for Globe Computer Stores.

    - Start by dating it 30 June and copy the address, customer number, credit limit and opening balance from the May statement shown on page 310. Remember to carry forward the 'amount now due' on the May statement as the 'balance owing' figure for 1 June. Remember, too, to enter all the transactions in *date order* (sort them out first!) and to calculate the running balance *after each entry*.

    - The following invoices were sent:

      8 June £2,506.45, number 702449

      20 June £456.98, number 702883.

    - The previous month's balance was paid by cheque number 5056 on 15 June.

    - A credit note, number 20399, was issued for £201.22 on 22 June.

    - Finally, complete the name and address of Globe Computer Stores on the remittance advice form, the account number and the date of the statement.

Check your completed work carefully yourself and, when you are sure it is right, ask your tutor to approve it. Then keep it safely.

Snapshot

A cashless future?

Most people dislike taking large sums of money to the bank because of the security risk. Businesses that receive large amounts of cash, such as supermarkets, have this collected by special security firms in armoured vans. The security staff wear special helmets and clothing and there are very strict procedures for opening and closing the van. In addition, the driver is in constant radio contact with the base so that any attempted robbery or problem can be reported immediately.

In the future, these vans may be unnecessary! Today, fewer and fewer transactions are carried out with cash and even the use of cheques is declining. Bankers now predict that by 2008 only one payment in ten will be by cheque. Today, most people – and businesses – prefer to use credit or debit cards, or transfer money through BACS, the bank automated payments systems (for example direct debit or credit transfer). Cash is obtained from cash machines, whereas ten years ago people had to make out a cheque to themselves to withdraw money!

In the future, the use of new 'smart' cards using chip technology and developments in e-commerce and Internet banking are likely to make cheques obsolete. They may even make cash virtually obsolete for all but the smallest transactions.

The counterfoil, sometimes called the stub. It is joined to each cheque by a perforated line. When the cheque is removed the counterfoil remains in the cheque book. It provides a record of all the essential information relating to the cheque – the name of the person or organisation that the cheque is payable to, the date, why the money was paid and the amount.

The name and address of the business's bank branch. All bank accounts are held at a specific branch, normally one close to the business so that cash can be paid in and withdrawn easily

The words ACCOUNT PAYEE appear in vertical lines down the centre of all cheques today. This is for security as the cheque must be paid into the account of the person or organisation that is named to receive payment

The sort code of the bank. It is repeated at the bottom of the cheque. Every bank branch has its own sort code by which it is identified

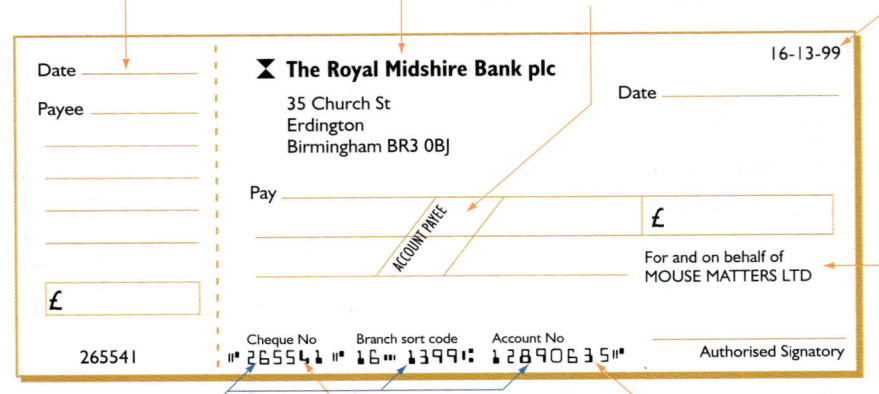

The account holder's name is printed on the cheque. In the case of a company, the words 'for and on behalf of' precede the name. This shows that the person is signing for the company, rather than on his or her own behalf. The authorised signatory is the person who signs the cheque. This is normally someone in authority

The bank branch's sort code, customer's bank account number and cheque number are printed in machine readable type. This enables vast quantities of cheques to be processed rapidly through the banking system

The cheque number. This number increases sequentially on each cheque and is shown on both the cheque and the counterfoil

Each bank account has a separate number. This speeds up the process of dealing with accounts and is more accurate than using names and addresses as some individuals or businesses may have several accounts

A blank cheque

Key parts of a cheque

There are two types of information on a cheque. Some is pre-printed by the bank. For a business, this can include a heading showing the name and address of the company.

Page 312 shows a pre-printed, blank cheque.

> **It makes you think!**
>
> The next section describes the parts of the cheque which have to be completed. Before you read this, suggest a logical order in which you would complete a cheque. There are no rules but one part should *always* be completed last. Which do you think it is?

Completing a cheque

Mouse Matters must pay Universal Fabrics to settle their account. On page 313 is the cheque made out in payment. Use this to identify each of the sections which was completed by Mouse Matters. Note that a written cheque must always be completed in ink (preferably black or blue) and *never* in pencil!

Large organisations usually have cheques made out to their own design which they have agreed with the bank. The cheques may be in continuous format, with perforations, or printed out attached to a remittance advice. They are printed automatically in batches, often called a cheque run. The signatures are stored in the system and added as the cheques are processed. Only certain individuals are allowed to carry out a 'cheque run' and, before this takes place, the computer system will already have calculated the total amount being paid and checked this against the current bank balance.

Checking the accuracy of a cheque

It is important that each cheque is checked carefully because if a mistake is made, then it is likely the bank will reject it and refer it back to the payee. The payee then has to contact the person who issued it and explain there is a problem.

The date is inserted on the counterfoil and on the cheque itself. This is usually the date on which the cheque is written. Sometimes a person may wish to make out a **post-dated** cheque. This means putting a future date on the cheque. Most companies will not allow this as it means the cheque cannot be paid into the bank until this date has passed.

The name of the business (or person) who is to receive the money is entered on the cheque. The name should be written carefully using the correct spelling. The correct term for this person is the **payee**. When cheques are sent to individuals, banks prefer the full name to be inserted, e.g. James Smith rather than J Smith. This name is also repeated on the counterfoil

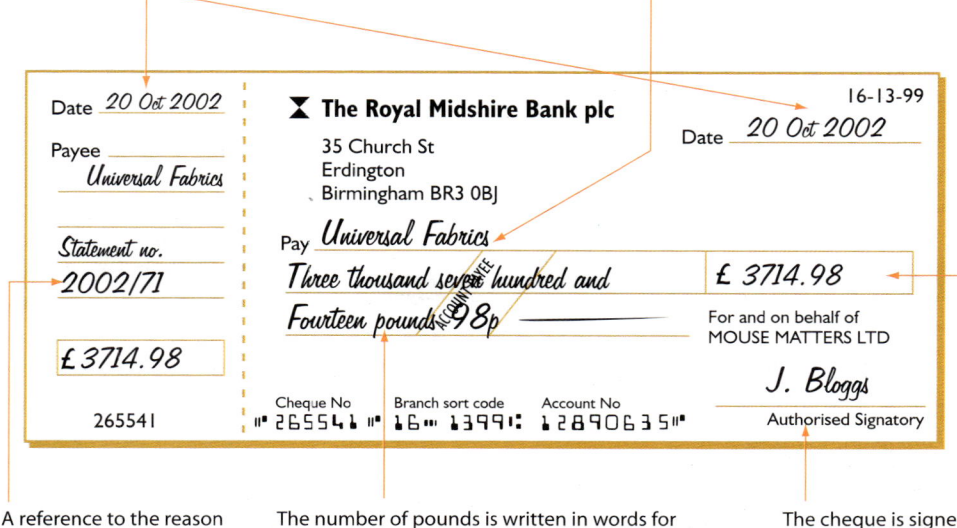

The amount is also written in figures in the box. The £ sign is already printed. The amount in this box must agree with the amount written in words. This figure is also copied onto the counterfoil

A reference to the reason for payment should be made on the counterfoil. In business, this is usually the invoice or statement number

The number of pounds is written in words for amounts in pounds and in figures for amounts in pence. Some people prefer to end with the word 'only', particularly if the amount is for pounds only. If this word is not written, then any spare spaces should be made unusable. This is normally done by drawing one or two horizontal lines. Banks also prefer the writing to start at the left-hand side so that nothing may be inserted in a blank space at the left

The cheque is signed by an authorised signatory. The official term for the account holder on whose name the cheque is drawn is rhe **drawer**. Sometimes, particularly in the case of a personal account, the name of the person is printed below. This is the last part of the cheque to be completed. If a business cheque is for a large amount of money, it is usual to have two or even three signatories, as a security measure. It is sensible for anyone signing a cheque to check the details first

A completed cheque

These are the most common problems:

- Information is missing. If any section is not completed, then the cheque is not valid and the bank will not accept it. A common mistake is when someone forgets to sign a cheque.
- The date is wrong. Banks will not accept cheques which are more than six months out of date or cheques made out for a future date. A common mistake is to write the 'old' year by mistake in January, which means the cheque is out of date immediately!
- There is a difference between the amount in words and the amount in figures. If the difference is small, the bank *may* ring the drawer to clarify the amount but does not have to do so. It may simply reject it, and certainly will do this if the difference is large.
- An alteration on a cheque. Banks don't like alterations on cheques because they cannot be sure that someone else hasn't tried to alter it – which would be forgery. If a mistake is made, it is often better to tear up the cheque, write on the counterfoil that the cheque has been cancelled and start again on a new blank one. If the mistake is minor, a bank *may* accept an alteration provided that the signature of the drawer is written alongside to verify the change.
- If the drawer does not have enough money in his or her bank account to cover the amount on the cheque, the cheque will be returned.

Fact file

If a cheque is not acceptable to a bank, it is sent back to the **payee** – the person or business which tried to pay it into their account. It will be stamped 'Return to drawer' or 'R/D' and there will often be a specified reason given as to why the cheque was rejected. A slang expression you may hear is that the cheque 'bounced', that is there wasn't enough money in the account to pay the cheque.

A cheque will also be rejected if it is 'stopped'. This means that the **drawer** has changed his or her mind about payment and told the bank not to honour the cheque. If you bought a car and it broke down a mile from the showroom, you might not be very happy about the garage cashing your cheque! You could ring the bank, give staff the account details, and ask them not to pay the cheque. A small fee will be charged for this. However, do remember that you cannot stop a cheque if you used a cheque guarantee card to guarantee that payment will be made.

Spot check

Write down your answers to the following questions:

1. Identify the advantage of issuing a remittance advice slip attached to a statement.
2. Identify the four items of information which are completed on a remittance advice slip by the person making the payment.
3. You are told to make out a remittance advice slip for less than the total payment shown on the statement. Can you think of one reason why you might be asked to do this?
4. What is the correct term for the:
   a. person who receives a cheque
   b. person who signs a cheque?
5. State three reasons why a cheque might be rejected by a bank.
6. What are the four items of information which should be written on a cheque counterfoil?
7. Why do the words 'for and on behalf of' appear above the signature on a business cheque?
8. a. What do the three sets of printed figures on the bottom of a cheque represent?
   b. Why are they unusual in appearance?
9. On page 311, you were asked to prepare a statement from Mouse Matters to send to Globe Computer Stores for June. You work for Globe and your manager has given you a cheque for the full amount in payment, the cheque number is 398831. He asks you to put the reference number 2019/4. Use today's date. Complete the remittance advice form attached to the Mouse Matters statement with this information.
10. You work for Mouse Matters and have been asked to make out three cheques. Using blank copies of Mouse Matters' cheque, complete them with the appropriate information. Remember to complete the counterfoils with this information. Do *not* sign them. Your tutor will do this if they are correct and clearly readable! Use today's date.
    a. A cheque to Office Supplies Ltd for £140 in payment of its statement 30019.
    b. A cheque to Universal Fabrics Ltd for £2,090.50 in payment of its statement 609192.
    c. A cheque to James Marshall for £452.70 for decorating Mouse Matters' offices.

Receipts

All payments through the banking system are recorded on a customer's bank statement. If something goes wrong with a transaction or if a business claims that it has not been paid, it is a simple matter to check the bank records to find out if its claim is correct. This is not the case with a cash transaction.

When you use cash to buy something you will normally receive a till receipt. This is so that you can prove you have paid for the goods if anyone, such as a member of the security staff, challenges you. If a printed receipt isn't issued automatically, and you wanted to prove you had paid in cash, you would need to ask for a written receipt. Tradespeople, such as service engineers, who do household repairs usually have a pre-printed receipt book to record payments. They enter the details of the work and payment and give a copy to the householder. For the person paying, the engineer and the engineer's employer, this is the proof that the transaction took place.

Businesses must have proof that *all* payments have been paid and received. This is why they insist that any staff who spend money on behalf of the business obtain a receipt. This could be a manager paying for a taxi when on a business trip or a junior employee asked to buy some magazines for reception. If either the manager or the junior employee loses the receipt, both could be refused **reimbursement** (the company will not refund their money).

An example of a handwritten receipt is shown below. This is an example of a receipt issued by Mouse Matters when it sells mouse mats to employees for cash. It sells these at a discount price. Two copies of the receipt are issued. One is given to the employee and one is kept as a record for the business.

Checking a receipt

How often do you check a receipt you are given in a shop? In business, you should check all receipts you make out, *before* you hand them over!

A receipt should contain the date, reference number, a list of items purchased, the amount paid for each and the total value.

Mouse Matters Ltd
Kellet Industrial Park
Erdington
BIRMINGHAM
B9 8KK

Tel: 0121 687 3610
Fax: 0121 123 4567
Website: www.mousematters.shop.uk

VAT Reg. No. 846/3822/98

Email: sales@mousematters.shop.uk

CASH SALE RECEIPT

Name: Jon Sumner

Address: 3 Nelson Street
Erdington
Birmingham

Receipt No: 29387

Date: 13 December 2003

Received by: Jan Nichols

Quantity	Description	Price	Total
3	Perma Mats (PEM2)	£8.00	£24.00
		Sub-total:	£24.00
		VAT at 17.5%:	£ 4.20
		Total paid:	£28.20

A cash sale receipt

If VAT must be added, this must also be shown separately. All calculations should be checked for accuracy.

A handwritten receipt should include the name of the person who paid and should be signed by the person who received the money. It should also be neat and easy to read!

It makes you think!

1. Alex buys a friend a CD as a Christmas present and pays by cheque. The CD costs £12.99 and he is given a receipt and throws it in the nearest waste bin. Unfortunately, the friend has already got the CD and Alex offers to take it back and exchange it. When he returns to the store, he finds that the CD is now on sale at a reduced price of £9.99. The shop says that it is only prepared to refund the reduced amount or give him this amount of credit towards another purchase. Within your group, discuss the following:
   a. How could Alex prove he paid £12.99?
   b. Could Alex prove he bought that particular CD?

   The next time you get a receipt, check the information that appears on it which would *not* be found on a cheque or cheque counterfoil. You should find several things!

2. Within your group, discuss the following:
   a. Staff who buy goods from their employer are never allowed to make out their own receipts. Suggest why.
   b. Staff are usually limited to the quantity of goods they can buy. At Mouse Matters, staff can purchase goods only up to a value of £20 at one time. Why do you think Mouse Matters has this rule?

Financial documents and computerised accounting systems

Most businesses, except perhaps very small ones, use computerised accounting systems.

This gives the business several advantages because the system will:

- record all credit sales to customers
- record all cash sales to customers
- produce invoices, credit notes and statements
- list all outstanding payments
- record all purchases made, both by supplier and type of goods
- record all accounts which have been paid or still have to be paid to suppliers
- record all bank transactions
- update the company's accounts every time a transaction takes place
- produce a variety of 'reports' such as balance sheets, VAT returns, bank balance analysis, profit and loss account. It also prints an 'audit report' which shows every single entry that has been made – this allows a check to be made in the event of a query.

Snapshot

Sage advice!

One of the best known accounts packages is called Sage. Sage offers different packages, designed for use by businesses of different sizes. The smallest package is for small firms which have 1–25 employees. The next size is for medium-sized companies with 25–100 employees. The final version is for larger companies which employ more than 100 staff.

All the packages can be adapted to suit particular needs. In addition to the normal accounts facilities, the system can include payroll, so that wages and salaries are recorded, e-business transactions and customer relations management (see page 118).

To find out more about Sage, visit its website at www.heinemann.co.uk/hotlinks

Advantages of computerised systems

- Many routine and tedious jobs are done automatically.
- Fewer mistakes are made. Computers calculate accurately provided the correct data is entered.
- Many kinds of up-to-date information are available instantly, e.g. which customers are late paying their bills, how much profit has been made so far that month.
- Accountants and auditors (who check the accounts of limited companies) prefer computerised account information as it can be checked more easily. This is because software packages include an audit report.
- The system can be linked to other systems e.g. payroll and e-commerce transactions.
- All customers can be listed at the touch of a few keys; address labels can be printed and used to send out mail shots.
- Customers who are slow in paying can be listed, allowing payments to be chased up more easily.
- Account numbers are allocated automatically, avoiding any problems of incorrect or inaccurate numbers being entered.
- In a paper system, documents may get lost or filed in the wrong place. Computers do not normally lose things!
- Access to parts of the computer package can be limited to certain people, e.g. the payroll list which stores confidential about how much people are paid.

Disadvantages of computerised systems

- The appropriate software and hardware have to be bought and set up. This can cost a considerable amount of money.
- All existing information on paper records has to be keyed in and carefully checked. This takes time and money. Often, the paper-based system has to be continued for a few weeks until everyone is happy that the computer system is working properly and people understand it!
- The existing manual system may have to be changed or adjusted to suit the way that the computer package works. Staff then have to learn how it works.
- Staff need to be trained to use the computer package. While this is happening, work may take longer.
- There is usually restricted access to some parts of the package which only one person can access at once. This can cause problems, unless a more expensive multi-user licence is purchased.
- If there is a computer failure, no work can be carried out.
- A mistake can be difficult to correct. On many packages, it is impossible to correct a wrong entry. For example, if five products have been ordered and someone keys in 15, another entry may have to be made to subtract the 15 before the correct figure is entered. This is so that audit checks can be made to track everything which has happened.
- The computer package may insist that every customer has a reference number. This can be tedious if a business has thousands of casual or 'one-off' customers.
- Although some controls will be included in the software to prevent mistakes (such as not allowing a letter to be entered in a number box), the computer cannot check the actual figures keyed in. Numerical mistakes in particular (such as transposed figures) may not be noticed.
- Printing out large numbers of documents such as monthly statements can tie up the printer for several hours. Other people cannot use it during this period.
- Computers often carry out routine, repetitive tasks. If the wrong instruction is given (like two copies of every statement, rather than one copy), the mistake will be repeated over and over again until someone spots it!

Snapshot

Fast reactions = better business

The mail order business is growing rapidly. Today, many goods can be ordered by phone, from companies like Next Direct, or over the Internet from organisations like Amazon. Many businesses pride themselves on their speedy and efficient responses which have been helped by advances in computerised systems.

If you phone one of these companies, you may first hear a computerised voice giving you a range of options. You select the one you want by pressing a key. If you have an account with the company, you can obtain up-to-date information by selecting certain keys. Or you can make contact with a sales operator who is equipped with a telephone and a computer.

You are asked for either your customer account number or your name and postcode. From this, the computer automatically generates your full address which is then checked with you. If you have used the business before, your customer account number automatically appears on screen. As each item code is entered, the description appears on screen together with the unit price, total cost and when it is available for delivery. The sales person will check the order details with you and confirm the total amount, including any delivery charges. You are then asked how you wish to pay. Once these details have been entered and verified, the order is then 'live'. Finally, the delivery date will be checked with you. If there are any special instructions, such as 'leave goods next door at number 35', these will be entered too.

Computerisation has meant that items can be 'picked' automatically from warehouse shelves and the stock figures adjusted. These details will be passed to sales and production operations. The distribution section will automatically print out the delivery note from the details which have already been entered against your name. This is how the delivery person knows where to deliver the goods.

Invoices are often printed in large batches overnight from the previous day's transactions. Statements are generated at the end of each month. At the same time, the company's accounts are adjusted. Sales and bank accounts are adjusted every time a customer places an order and pays an account.

Purchases are handled in the same way. Purchase orders generate goods received notes which are matched against incoming invoices and the purchases account is updated. When invoices are paid, the money is automatically deducted from the bank account. The accountants can see the daily financial position at the touch of a key.

The next time you place an order for an item from a mail order company, you may like to consider all the systems busily at work, automatically processing it!

Chapter review and practice questions

▷ ▷

1. Put the following documents into the sequence in which they are used in a purchase transaction:

   Invoice   Cheque
   Goods received note   Delivery note
   Purchase order   Statement of account

2. The following items appear on financial documents. Identify which five items would appear on a purchase order and which five would not. Copy out the chart opposite and complete it with your answer.

Supplier's name and address	Description of goods
VAT	Receipt number
A note that goods are damaged	Quantity ordered
Delivery date	Signature of authorised person
Date of payment	Bank sort code

Items found on a purchase order	Items not on a purchase order

3 You have two invoices to pay. One includes VAT, the other does not mention VAT. Explain this difference.

4 Suggest the consequences of a new employee making each of the following mistakes:
- **a** posting an unsigned cheque
- **b** ticking off items received on a goods received note without checking them properly
- **c** losing an invoice
- **d** sending out a statement containing inaccurate calculations
- **e** writing the wrong address on a delivery note.

Integrated activity

You work in the accounts department at Mouse Matters. Your supervisor is Alex Bennett. She has asked you to do the following tasks today and to pass all the documents to her for her approval. Use copies of the blank forms provided and pass them to your tutor once you have finished. Do *not* rush. Accuracy is more important than speed at this stage!

1. Make out an order to Swift Computer Supplies at 23 Musgrove Hill, Fairfields, Berkshire RG8 4ML for an Omega inkjet printer. The catalogue reference is 920-KP and the price is £130. Alex also wants 6 boxes of 650 MB Rewritable CD-ROMs, reference 820-CD-RW. These are priced per box at £4.99.
The next order number is 2003/1092, the order should be dated today and delivery should be one week from today. The supplier number of Swift Computers is 159.

2. An order from Jackson College, Railway Road, Beddington, BD4 9SP has been received by fax. It urgently wants 50 Photo Mats, ref. PHM 5 at £5 each and 20 Ergonomic Mats, ref. ERM 3 at £7 each. Their order number is 208399 and their customer account number is 3408. It will be delivered tomorrow by Mouse Matters' own transport. The invoice number allocated is 807293.
Make out a delivery note to accompany the order.

3. Prepare the invoice ready to send to Jackson College. Date it today.

4. Jackson College telephones to say 10 Photo Mats were damaged and these have been returned with the driver. The college's returns reference is 50.
Make out a credit note – number 20380 – for this return.

5. The goods have now arrived from Swift Computer Supplies. You are asked to check them and complete a goods received note (GRN). Your next GRN number is 2003/2080. The delivery note is dated today.
When you unpack the order you find that only 5 boxes of CD-ROMs have been included. The printer is fine.

6. At the end of the month you are asked to prepare a statement for Jackson College. Its opening balance at the start of this month was £240.00. A cheque for this amount was received two days ago. You must also include the invoice and the credit note you made out earlier and calculate the balance. The credit limit for Jackson College is £5,000.

7. Alex telephones you to say she has received an invoice from Swift Computer Supplies for £187.93 and a credit note for £5.86. She asks you to confirm, in writing, whether these amounts are correct.

8. For your final total owing to Swift Computer Supplies, Alex asks you to make out a cheque, against its statement 2930, but not to sign it. She will do that.

9. Alex's daughter works at Mouse Matters and wants to buy two Cat Mats as presents. The staff price for these is £3 each + VAT. She pays cash and you are asked to make out a receipt. Alex's daughter is called Sarah and she lives at 10 Farmers Lane, Marshampton, MR7 2PL. Your next receipt number is 30293.

10. Alex is thinking about changing over the manual accounts system to a computerised one. She wants your opinion on whether this will save you work or be more complicated. Write her a brief note summarising three advantages and three disadvantages of her idea.

Chapter 18: Investigating methods of making and receiving payments

> **What you will learn**
> Understanding payment methods

Overview: payment methods

The choice of payment methods

Chapter 17 looked at two methods of payment:

- cash payments
- cheque payments.

This chapter looks at these methods in more detail and describes three more types of payment:

- credit card
- debit card
- credit transfer/direct debit.

What is the difference?

Each payment method has its advantages and disadvantages, both from the customer's and the supplier's point of view.

- **Cash** is normally used for small value transactions such as buying a magazine from a newsagent. This is a face-to-face transaction because the customer and supplier meet.
- **Cheques** can also be used in face-to-face transactions, but may also be sent through the post. They allow money to be transferred from the customer's bank account to the supplier's bank account.
- **Credit cards** are normally used by private individuals when buying something from a shop or by telephone or over the Internet. The person using the card is sent a statement listing the transactions he or she has made in a month and has the option of paying the amount in full or paying part of the total and being charged interest on the rest. The fact that payment takes place some time after the actual transaction and interest can be charged is the reason they are called credit cards.
- **Debit cards** are issued by banks. When customers use the card to make a purchase, the money is automatically taken from their bank account. The money is transferred quite quickly and there is no interest charge. Most businesses allow customers to pay by debit card over the phone or over the Internet.
- **Credit transfer/direct debit** systems allow money to be transferred from one bank account to another automatically, for example most businesses pay employees' salaries directly into their bank accounts using credit transfer.

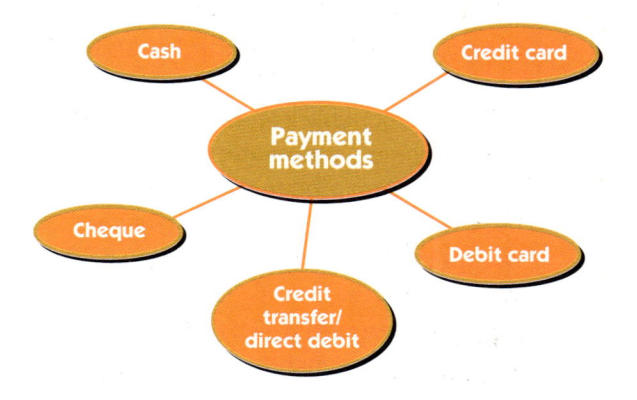

Payment methods

Which one to choose?

You need to know how each of these methods of payment works and why a particular method may be preferred over another.

A customer who wants to buy something from a shop may have to decide whether to pay by cash, use a cheque, pay by credit card or debit card. The retailer may also wish to have a choice and may offer a discount for certain methods of payment. These choices may be influenced by:

- the costs involved – to both buyer and seller
- the time taken for the transfer of money to take place.

It makes you think!

1. Your aunt is opening a shop and has to decide which payment methods to offer her customers:
   - She wants to accept cash but is concerned about the security aspects – the money will need to be taken regularly to the bank.
   - She can accept cheques but is concerned that some may 'bounce' unless she knows the person giving the cheque.
   - She wonders whether to accept credit cards and debit cards – it would mean setting up the service and having a special 'swipe' machine. In addition, there is a charge to the retailer for every transaction made this way.

   Advise your aunt on which methods she should choose. Write down your conclusions.

2. A customer asks for discount. Write down which payment methods would be most acceptable in this situation.

After you have completed the chapter, look back at your answers and see if you reach the same conclusions.

Fact file

Both individuals and businesses can open **bank accounts**. The money in a bank account is called a **credit balance**. Banks accept deposits into an account and will increase the balance. They also allow **withdrawals** of money from the account. Private customers often make withdrawals by using a cash machine located outside the bank and in many other public places. The official term for a cash machine is **automatic teller machine**. 'Teller' is an old term used to describe the people who dealt with customers at a bank counter.

When a bank account is opened, the bank will give the new customer a cheque book and a **cheque guarantee card** which also serves as a debit card. It will send monthly statements listing deposits and withdrawals. Virtually all banks now offer Internet banking so that account details and transactions can be done over the Internet. Additional services and facilities are available for business customers such as access to a business adviser.

When businesses deal with each other, deposits and withdrawals can both be made by any of the five methods listed on page 321.

Details of deposits, withdrawals and the balance are entered and stored on the bank's computer system. This makes it easy to carry out changes to accounts electronically. For example, a direct debit transaction will automatically transfer money from a customer's to a supplier's account. Each account is located at a particular branch of a bank and it has a unique number. Each branch has a sort code which is a special kind of address in the banking system.

Understanding payment methods

Cash payments

This is the most straightforward way of making and receiving a payment. A customer hands over the money and normally receives the goods at the same time. A receipt is provided by the seller as proof that the money has been received (see pages 314–316).

The advantages of cash payments are as follows:

- Full payment is received immediately.
- There is minimal risk of fraud.

There are, however, some disadvantages in cash transactions:

- They are not suitable when a very large amount of money is involved. It is unwise for individuals to carry large amounts of money which could be stolen.
- It is not easy to get hold of large amounts of cash. Each customer is limited as to how much can be withdrawn from a cash machine on any given day, typically £200. If a customer wishes to draw a large amount of money from a bank, he or she has to make a special arrangement and give notice.
- Retailers and suppliers do not like storing and transporting large amounts of cash. If they have to store money overnight, a safe is needed. An alternative is to take cash to the bank at the end of the day. This is a security risk and many businesses insist that two members of staff make the journey.

Snapshot

Another type of cash limit!

The amount of money on a banknote is called its <u>denomination</u>. The highest denomination note in England and Wales is £50. In Scotland, it is £100. Fewer notes are printed now because there are no notes printed for values less than £5. This is threatening jobs at the company which prints banknotes in England because there is less work to do. The official term for all the notes and coins which can be accepted in payment is <u>legal tender</u>.

However, there is a limit to the quantity of some types of legal tender which may be accepted in payment. Legally, businesses can refuse to accept a large number of coins. For example, if you try to buy a bar of chocolate with 35 one-penny pieces, the shopkeeper can refuse them because the limit is 20p. Normally, traders do not stick to this rule because they still want the money. However, if you regularly save all your spare change in a large bottle, you may be wiser to have this changed by a bank, rather than ask a local shop to accept it!

Cheque payments

Cheques allow payments to be made for large amounts of money without the risks involved in handling large amounts of cash. (Turn back to page 309 if you need to remind yourself how the cheque system works.)

Other advantages of using cheques are as follows:

- The system is efficient and rarely goes wrong.
- A receipt is not needed since the transaction is shown on both bank statements.
- Cheques can be safely sent through the post since they can be paid only into the payee's bank account.
- A cheque payment can be guaranteed if it is supported by a cheque guarantee card. The number on the card is written on the back of the cheque. Banks will then guarantee to pay the money even if there is a problem with the drawer's account. However, there is a limit to the amount which can be guaranteed, and this is printed on the guarantee card.

The disadvantages of using cheques are as follows:

- It can take several days for the money to arrive in the payee's account. The bank will not show the money as a credit into the account until after the cheque has cleared. This means that the funds have been taken out of the drawer's account and there are no problems.
- If there is a mistake on a cheque and the bank will not accept it, the payee receives it back. He or she then has to contact the drawer to sort things out. This is tedious and time consuming.
- If a cheque book and a cheque guarantee card are stolen, the thief could spend quite a lot of money before the theft is discovered.
- Banks charge a fee for business accounts, often related to the number of transactions. Many cheque transactions can result in higher fees.

Spot check

Write down your answers to the following questions:

1. State two advantages and one disadvantage for a business which receives many cash payments.
2. What does the term 'legal tender' mean?
3. You try to pay your bus fare in 1p pieces and the driver refuses to take your money. Can he or she do this? Give a reason for your answer.
4. a What is a cheque guarantee card?
   b Why will many businesses accept a cheque payment only if it is supported by a guarantee card?
5. Identify two advantages and two disadvantages for a business that accepts cheque payments.

Credit card payments

Many shops and businesses acccept payment from customers using a variety of credit cards

Many shops, restaurants and hotels display a number of small stickers on the window or door saying 'Mastercard' or 'Visa'. These are the two most popular types of credit card and the sticker means that the business accepts payments using either type of card.

When a payment is made by credit card, the amount is automatically listed on the customer's account and added to the supplier's account balance.

Once a month, the customer receives a statement of all the transactions since the last statement. This statement includes the total outstanding balance and the minimum payment required that month.

The statement will also remind the card holder of the maximum amount he or she is allowed to spend, called the **credit limit**. If the card holder pays the full amount on the statement by the due date, there is no charge. This payment could be made several weeks after the original transaction and during that period the card holder has had free credit.

If only part of the balance is paid off, the customer is charged interest. Many cards charge quite a high rate of interest for this. This is one of the ways in which credit card companies make their money.

The card companies also make money by charging businesses between 1 and 4 per cent of the transaction amount.

Processing a credit card payment

Originally, retailers inserted a special voucher into a machine and then placed the card on top. The machine made an impression of the card on the voucher, which the customer then signed. A copy was given to the customer, a second was sent to the credit card handler and the third was kept by the business. In this system, each business is allocated a **floor limit**. This is the maximum amount which can be accepted on a credit card payment. Obviously, Sainsbury's limit is far higher than a local grocer's! Above the limit, the card company must be contacted to check it will accept payment. If so, the supplier is given an authorisation number to record on the voucher.

Today, virtually all businesses have electronic links to card services – known as **merchant services** – such as Streamline or Barclays. An electronic terminal is installed and each credit card is 'swiped' through the machine. The details are sent electronically to the merchant service which checks that the credit card company will allow the transaction to go ahead and notifies them how much must be debited to the customer's account. A voucher is printed by the terminal which the customer signs, in duplicate. One copy is kept by the supplier to check against the merchant statement. The second copy is kept by the customer to check against the credit card statement. Each terminal is normally rented by the business and a typical charge would be about £15 per month.

Corporate credit cards

Most credit cards are owned by private individuals who use them to pay for food, clothing, holidays, and so on. Some businesses give corporate credit cards to employees. They are used by employees who need to make purchases or pay bills when they are away from the business premises, such as sales representatives who travel around the UK or abroad and need to pay for hotel accommodation and other expenses. In this case, the account is sent to the employer. The company's accountants will check the statements carefully to make sure that everything which has been spent is an acceptable business expense.

Owners of small businesses could also use a corporate credit card in their first few months of trading. Suppliers may be reluctant to give credit until they have got to know the customer and are sure that they can pay their bills. A credit card would enable the owner to make essential purchases without any problems.

Snapshot

When a card knows who you are!

In 2002, the Department of Trade and Industry, reported that 5 per cent of people had experienced some form of credit card fraud. This was mainly due to cards being stolen and used by the thief. It is estimated that £400 million is lost each year because of this problem.

There are also concerns that security problems related to Internet payments may deter people from buying from web stores, and this will prevent the growth of e-commerce in Britain. In fact, so far, this has been found to be less of a problem than card theft, and website designers now have secure areas on the site (identified by a padlock) and give customers reassurance through their published security and privacy policies.

Changes are now on the way to make credit cards safer by removing the need for customers to hand their card to someone else and/or sign to validate the transaction. Because the details on a card and a signature can be easily copied, this part of the transaction puts customers at risk of fraud. To prevent this, British banks are introducing a new type of card called 'chip and pin'. Each new card will have an electronic chip inserted in it. The customer (not the sales assistant) will swipe the card through the terminal and then enter a PIN (personal identification number). The chip in the card will match this number to the one stored in its memory to validate the transaction. This will mean that customers can keep the details on their card to themselves and will not need to sign the voucher as proof of their identity. The total cost of this new system to banks and businesses is likely to be about £1 billion, but it is forecast to substantially lower the cost of fraudulent transactions.

It makes you think!

1. The advantages and disadvantages of credit cards are listed in the chart on page 326. Within your group, decide which of these applies *only* to the supplier, *only* to the customer or to both of them.

2. Legally, a business has the right to charge an extra fee to customers who use a credit card to cover the cost of the handling fee. In reality, very few do this. Within your group, discuss why you think this is the case.

Advantages and disadvantages of credit cards

	Advantages		Disadvantages
a	Money from transactions credited into supplier's account within 2–4 days	a	Risk of fraud, through the use of stolen cards. However, these are normally borne by the credit card company, particularly if the owner has card protection insurance
b	No cash involved	b	Cost of installing and paying for an electronic terminal
c	Enable customers to buy expensive products immediately and make 'impulse' purchases	c	Cost of processing the transactions
d	Enable customers to make a payment over the telephone or over the Internet	d	Card holders may spend more than they can afford
e	Once transaction confirmed, payment to supplier guaranteed	e	Interest can be high if card isn't paid off in full each month – and cash withdrawals are expensive
f	Credit card holders can use card to obtain cash from a cash machine – although they pay interest on withdrawals from the moment they make the transaction	f	Because the method of calculating interest is complicated, people may find the interest charges higher than they first thought
g	Credit card holders have additional protection if goods are faulty, provided each item cost over a minimum amount (normally £50)		

Debit card payments

Apart from cash, debit cards are now the most popular method people use to pay for goods and services, with over 42 million in use. Debit cards work in a similar way to cheques because money is transferred directly from the customer's bank account to the supplier's account. The main types of cards available in the UK are Connect and Switch (soon to be renamed Maestro).

In order to accept debit card payments, businesses require a terminal which is connected by telephone line to a system called EFTPOS (electronic funds transfer at point of sale) (see Unit 1, page 97). Most electronic terminals nowadays are dual purpose so the same one is used to process both credit and debit card transactions.

Most people who have a bank account are issued with a debit card as it can also be used to withdraw cash from a cash machine and as a cheque guarantee card.

The way debit cards work is shown in the illustration on page 327.

- The system checks straight away that the card is valid, and has not been reported stolen, for example.
- It also checks that the customer has enough money in his or her account to pay the bill. This is one of the main differences between a credit card and a debit card.
- The customer's signature is required which should match the sample signature on the back of the card.
- The money is taken from the customer's account within 24 hours.
- The money is not transferred into the supplier's account for two to three days.

The advantages of debit cards are that:

- the customer has no need to carry around large amounts of cash on shopping trips
- transactions are quicker to process than waiting for customers to write out a cheque
- payment is guaranteed once the transaction has been validated
- debit cards are less vulnerable to fraud. This is because the card is valid only as long as there is enough money in a

customer's current account. In contrast, a credit card may have a limit of several thousand pounds and so is far more valuable to a thief.

The disadvantages are few. However, some retailers may be concerned that:

- there is the cost of installing a terminal (particularly if the outlet doesn't accept credit cards)
- there is a further charge for processing debit card transactions – but this is much cheaper than the handling charge for credit cards
- a rejected debit card transaction (because the customer has insufficient money in their bank account) may need to be tactfully handled, particularly if a 'regular' customer could be embarrassed in front of other shoppers.

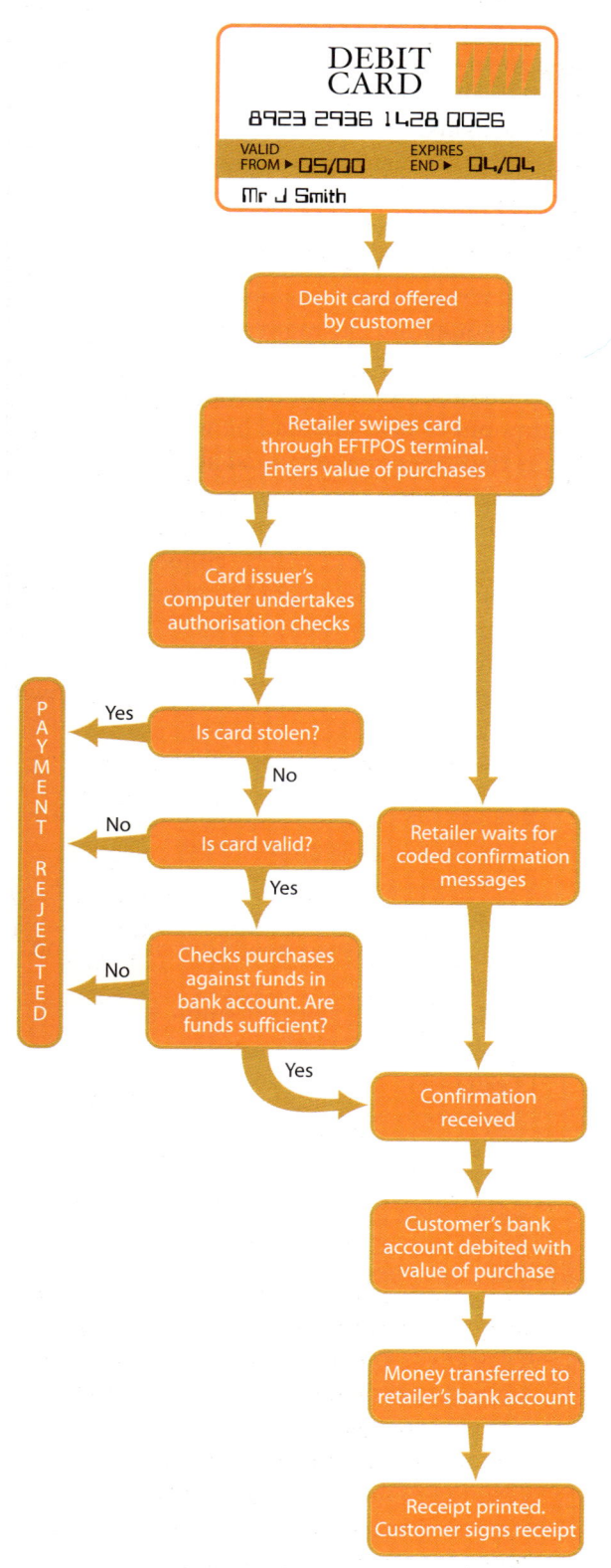

How debit cards work

Debit card offered by customer
↓
Retailer swipes card through EFTPOS terminal. Enters value of purchases
↓
Card issuer's computer undertakes authorisation checks
↓
Is card stolen? — Yes → PAYMENT REJECTED
↓ No
Is card valid? — No → PAYMENT REJECTED
↓ Yes
Checks purchases against funds in bank account. Are funds sufficient? — No → PAYMENT REJECTED
↓ Yes
Retailer waits for coded confirmation messages
↓
Confirmation received
↓
Customer's bank account debited with value of purchase
↓
Money transferred to retailer's bank account
↓
Receipt printed. Customer signs receipt

Over to you!

1. Within your group, discuss what you would do if you were processing a card transaction for a customer and it was rejected by the terminal because:
   a. the debit card holder appeared to have insufficient funds in his or her account
   b. the credit card was logged as stolen.
2. Find out more about merchant services which handle credit and debit card transactions at www.heinemann.co.uk/hotlinks. On the Barclays site, you can see a copy of a merchant invoice and compare the handling costs for both credit and debit cards.

Credit transfer/direct debit payments

All the methods of payment described above have needed the customer to give something to the retailer – either cash, a cheque or a credit/debit card. However, it is also possible to transfer money between bank accounts without any of these. This system is known as the **Bank Automated Clearing System (BACS)** which offers two main services, **direct credit** and **direct debit**.

Direct credit (or credit transfer)

Direct credit takes place when a business pays money directly from its bank account to one or more other bank accounts using electronic transfer.

Most wages and salaries are paid by this method. When you start work, your employer will ask for your bank account details, that is the name of the account, the account number and the name, address and sort code of your bank. This information will be recorded in the payroll system. When the salaries are calculated each month, the business will send a list of the payments to be made to the bank. This can be done electronically. The bank will then automatically credit each employee with his or her salary and debit the employer's account for the total sum. Each pay slip will confirm details of the transaction.

Other common uses of credit transfer include: payment of housing benefit by local authorities, payment of company dividends to shareholders and pension payments. Increasingly, businesses are paying their suppliers by this method. In all of these cases, a document is sent through the post confirming that the transfer will take place. In the case of suppliers, this is a remittance advice slip.

Advantages of this system include:

- fewer security problems because no cash is involved
- accurate records of all transactions through bank statements and other bank documents
- cheaper to administer than numerous cheque payments.

Disadvantages are few for a well-organised business:

- The bank will need advance notification when a large number of payments must be processed, e.g. a payroll of several thousand people. Missing the deadline would result in late payments.
- Credit transfer payments need checking carefully before they are processed. A minor error across several thousand payments could result in serious problems!

Direct debit payments

Many people pay electricity bills, telephone bills and even their car insurance by direct debit. Most businesses have a special direct debit form which they ask customers to complete. This form will record the customer's bank account details and must be signed by the customer to authorise the payments. The business then contacts the customer's bank which accepts the direct debit arrangement.

The arrangement enables the company to send a request for payment to the customer's bank at regular intervals. However, under the direct debit system, both the time periods *and* the amount of payment can be varied. The one rule is that the company *must* send notification to the customer in advance of a payment that is due, and the amount and date on which the payment will be collected. The customer also has the right to cancel the arrangement at any time.

Businesses may receive many payments by direct debit and also make several of their own payments this way.

Direct debits have several advantages:

- Businesses like this method because they know payment is guaranteed.
- Customers do not have to remember to pay bills on a certain date.
- Customers have no need to write out and post cheques.
- Because the system is flexible, the business can vary the amount and the date of payment.
- Only reputable businesses are authorised to use this system, to prevent fraud.
- The customer always receives written notification of payments.

Disadvantages are few, but may include the following:

- Customers run the risk of setting up so many direct debit payments to different companies that they run short of money during some months.
- Customers may fail to check bank statements against the notifications sent by the company, or to check any price increases that have taken place.

A variation on the direct debit system is the **standing order**. This is also used to pay another person or business a certain amount of money, but here payments are made at pre-arranged intervals, such as monthly or quarterly, and cannot be varied. The amount of money is also fixed. A standing order is set up by the customer, not the business, and is far less flexible than a direct debit. It is therefore becoming less popular. It can also only be changed by the customer. A standing order is a direct arrangement between two banks and does not involve BACS.

Spot check

Write down your answers to the following questions:

1. Give two advantages to a business of accepting credit card payments.
2. Identify the major difference for the customer between paying for an item by debit card and by credit card.
3. Briefly explain how a credit or debit card transaction is processed by a retailer.
4. Identify the major benefit of 'chip and pin' credit cards.
5. State three types of payment for which the credit transfer (or direct credit) system is used.
6. Identify one advantage to the customer and one advantage to a business of direct debit payments.

Snapshot!

Upwards and onwards!

BACS considers that direct credit and direct debit are much better than other methods of payment and is confident that these facilities will be used more and more. Today, there are more than three billion direct credit and debit transactions each year. Over 70 per cent of the UK workforce is paid by credit transfer and over 70 per cent of mortgages are paid by direct debit.

More than 40,000 companies deal directly with BACS and it is estimated there are savings of up to 85 per cent using these payment methods rather than cheques or cash.

Find out more by accessing www.heinemann.co.uk/hotlinks.

Chapter review and practice questions

1. A new employee has started work for an organisation and is asked for details about his bank account.
   a. Why does the employer want this information?
   b. What details will the employee have to provide?

2. A friend is thinking of setting up a direct debit to pay her regular bills but has a few concerns.
   a. She is concerned that all these companies will just be able to 'help themselves' to her money. Is this true? Give a reason for your answer.
   b. What advice could you give her on checks that she should make regularly?

3. James is starting at university soon, about 100 miles away from home. He has been fortunate to book accommodation in a hall of residence for the first year. His mother has agreed to pay his accommodation fees, which must be paid quarterly.
   a. James' mother cannot decide whether to set up a direct debit with the university accommodation office to pay these costs or to send a cheque. Which method would you advise, and why?
   b. James has suggested that he should have a credit card and use this to buy anything he needs at university – with his mother paying the bill! James' mother refuses point blank! Explain why.

4. Carmen has recently taken over her father's small garden centre. She wants to modernise it to attract new customers and stock more expensive items such as greenhouses. Her father only ever accepted cash or cheques from customers, which Carmen thinks has held the business back.
   a. Give two reasons why Carmen's father probably preferred cash or cheques to other forms of payment.
   b. Identify two other payment methods Carmen could offer customers and, in each case, state why these could improve her trade.

5. Three customers buy products from a shop on the same day. One pays by cash, another by cheque and a third by credit card. In each case, describe what happens before the money is credited to the retailer's bank account.

Integrated activity

Credit cards can tempt people to spend too much

The government and many other organisations are becoming increasingly worried about the number of people who run up large debts on credit cards. In some instances, they cannot afford to pay the interest charges, let alone the outstanding debt. At the end of 2001 an amazing £40 billion was owed to credit card companies in the UK. Some people argue that it is too easy to obtain credit in this way.

As an experiment, a 23-year-old journalist, who had just left university and was paid £20,000 year, approached several organisations for loans and credit. Even though she still owed money for her student loan, within two days she had been offered credit of over £130,000! This included the total credit limit on three credit cards. Had she spent all this money, it would have taken her years and years to repay it.

Credit card companies offer many 'deals' to persuade people to switch to their cards. These include 'teaser' low rates of interest for a few months – sometimes even 0 per cent – if a credit card holder transfers an existing balance to their card. However, the low rate often applies only to the transferred balance, not to any new purchases.

Your friend's brother Nick has problems managing his money. He has two credit cards, which he got when he started work, but he now owes the companies over £4,000 – and interest is added every month. He went rather wild with the cards at the start, buying clothes, CDs and computer games, plus a football season ticket. But Nick is lucky. He recently won some money which you think he should use to pay off his debts and then get rid of his cards until he learns how to cope. Nick has recently moved into a flat, though, and says he can't manage his life without his cards.

1. Why do some people get into financial difficulties when they have credit cards?
2. How do credit card companies try to persuade people to use their particular card?
3. Nick likes his credit cards. Identify three reasons why he finds them so useful.
4. What system could Nick use to pay regular bills, such as electricity, gas and his mobile phone bill?
5. Nick is paid his salary by credit transfer. What does this mean?
6. Identify two safer methods for Nick to use to pay for items he wants to buy, such as CDs.
7. Many people think the government should do something to restrict the amount of credit people are offered, to prevent them having money problems. Others think this is unnecessary and people should be allowed to choose for themselves. Decide your own view, and why, and then compare your ideas with other members of your group.

Chapter 18 Investigating methods of payment

- Lee has bought his new van and started his pizza delivery service. The running costs of offering this service include petrol, road tax and insurance for the delivery van. The largest running cost would probably be the driver's wages.
- The new car factory would involve many different kinds of running costs. The wage bill would probably be hundreds of thousands of pounds each month. The bill would be not only for production workers but also for office staff and managers. Another major running cost would be the materials needed to build the cars, such as engines, body panels and seats. Other costs would include power to drive the machines and for lighting, fuel for heating, advertising . . . and food for the canteen!

It makes you think!

In the last section, you were asked to think of start-up costs if your school or college decided to build an eight-classroom teaching block to provide extra ICT facilities. Within your group, think of as many running costs as you can which would be needed if the plans went ahead.

When you have completed the activity, compare your ideas with the costs shown in the box on page 336. Again, try not to look at this until you have finished!

ICT and costs

In Chapter 1 you learned that the use of ICT can reduce administrative costs when processing financial transactions. ICT can also reduce *both* start-up and running costs.

Some ways in which ICT can reduce start-up costs

- Spreadsheet packages can be used to list and analyse all costs, e.g. through break-even analysis (see Chapter 22). Spreadsheets are ideal because they enable 'What if?' calculations to be undertaken quickly and easily, e.g. 'What will be the effect on our start-up costs if we buy this van?'
- Packages such as network analysis can be used to plan the sequence of tasks which have to done to make sure that the project is completed on time, and this helps to minimise hold-ups and delays.
- A project team planning a major development can communicate using ICT quickly and easily. Documents can be sent electronically for comparison and all the team can contribute, no matter where they are physically located. Good ideas can be shared easily.

Some ways in which ICT can reduce running costs

- Using bar codes in retail stores and warehouses reduces the time needed to enter stock details on the system and stock can be tracked more quickly so that people do not have to spend time counting items.
- Stock control packages and spreadsheets can identify items which need re-ordering automatically.
- Electronic ordering means that items can be delivered as and when they are needed. This reduces warehouse space. (To refresh your memory, look back at the JIT system described on page 77).
- Staff records can be stored on a computer database. They can be updated when salaries change or people receive training. This can reduce administrative costs.
- If a delivery firm has lorries which have to go to several customers in a day, an ICT system can be used to plan the most efficient route.

What can go wrong?

As you saw in the Snapshot on page 333, the main problem is that costs may be inaccurate or may increase so that the final cost is much higher than first estimated. This can happen for several reasons:

- The original estimates were incorrect.
- It took a long time to take the decision to proceed and costs have gone up in the meantime.
- Delays and hold-ups occurred which added to the costs.
- Too little time was spent monitoring costs – which is why ICT is so useful!

Chapter review and practice questions

1. Describe the difference between start-up costs and running costs.

2. A school decides to build a sports pavilion. Identify two start-up costs and two running costs.

3. A business estimates the start-up costs for a new product to be £5 million. The actual cost is £8 million. Suggest one reason why this might have happened.

4. A fitness centre is thinking of extending the business by opening a retail section to sell home exercise equipment such as exercise bikes and running machines. The building next door is for sale and would be ideal for the purpose. Make a list of all the start-up costs the business may need to consider. Use the box on page 336 to help you. Then compare your ideas with other members of your group and with your tutor.

Integrated activity

Joanna wants to open a shop selling CDs and computer games and has made a list of the costs she thinks she will incur. She has found a shop, but needs to have it refurbished. She has also arranged an appointment to discuss her ideas with her accountant and with her bank manager.

1. Joanna's bank manager tells her to divide her costs into start-up and running costs. Her costs are listed below. Divide them for her.
   a. Wages for staff
   b. CDs and games for the initial stock
   c. Shelves, racks and other shop fittings
   d. Electricity for lighting and power for equipment
   e. CDs and games to replace stock sold
   f. A cash till.

2. Joanna is keen to use ICT to reduce her running costs. Suggest two ways in which this would help her.

3. Joanna's bank manager tells her the sooner she is 'up and running' the better. The bank manager doesn't think it will take two months to refurbish and stock the shop if Joanna organises it properly. Joanna hasn't got an IT package to help her do this so must do it herself. Below are the tasks she must do and the time each will take her:
   - Install furniture and stock fittings (5 days)
   - Paint and decorate shop (5 days)
   - Do window display (1 day)
   - Take out old fittings (2 days)
   - Put in new wiring for decks and CD players (2 days)
   - Store new stock (2 days).

   a. Start by putting the list of jobs she must do into a sensible order.
   b. Calculate how many days it will take to complete the project.
   c. Suggest how Joanna can keep any delays to a minimum.
   d. For a very large project, suggest why this type of scheduling is better done on a computer.

4. Joanna's accountant tells her that stock can be both a start-up cost and a running cost. Why is this?

Business start-up and running costs

These are very comprehensive lists – very few businesses would need all these items.

Start-up costs

Market research
Premises (purchase price or rent deposit or lease premium)
Any building alterations required
Fixtures and fittings
Legal/professional fees
Furniture
Equipment
Communications equipment, e.g. computer, phone, fax
Advertising/promotional materials
Initial stock supplies or raw materials
Utilities and power, e.g. electricity, gas, heating, water, telephone (if not already installed/connected)
Insurance (first premium)
Production machinery and tools
Protective clothing and equipment
Transport/delivery vehicles
Packaging materials
Business stationery
Licences/permits (required by certain businesses such as pubs, children's nurseries, nursing homes, pet shops, gambling establishments)
Interest on any loans

Running costs

Owner's salary
Staff salaries
Insurance premiums
Rent or lease payments
Business rates
Advertising and promotions
Accountancy fees
Raw materials or stocks for resale
Utility payments, e.g. gas, electricity, water rates
Communication charges – for telephone, fax, Internet links
Vehicle running costs (tax, insurance, fuel)
Depreciation on vehicles and equipment
Repairs and maintenance
Loan repayments
Interest on loans
Business stationery
Packaging materials
Postal and distribution charges
Miscellaneous supplies (e.g. cleaning materials, magazines for reception)
Miscellaneous expenses (e.g. window cleaning, printing, photocopying)
Professional subscriptions and fees
Tax

Chapter 20: Using a cash-flow forecast

What you will learn
- Understanding cash flow
- Spreadsheets and cash-flow forecasts

Overview: using a cash-flow forecast

What is cash flow?

In previous chapters you learned that businesses receive money from customers and spend money on materials and other items. Money going into a business is known as **inflow** or **income** or **revenue**. Money which a business spends is called **outflow** or **expenditure** or **payments**. Cash flow is a way of analysing both of these at the same time to look at the combined effect.

Fact file

The word 'cash' can be very misleading for two reasons.

- In Chapter 18 you looked at various types of payment methods, only one of which was cash. Yet cash flow looks at *all* the money entering and leaving a business – no matter what type of payment method is used.
- In business, **cash transactions** are those which are paid for at the time the purchase is made so they include payments in cash, by cheque, by credit card or debit card. This is because the seller receives the money almost immediately. These contrast with **credit transactions** when a business allows another company a few weeks to pay its bills, and issues invoices and other purchase documents which you looked at in Chapter 17.

How does cash flow work?

Consider these two examples:

1. A sandwich shop receives fresh supplies of cooked meat, seafood, salad items, cheese and bread each morning and pays the suppliers at the end of each week. The shop accepts only cash transactions and so receives payment each time a sale is made. The cash takings are paid into the bank each evening. By the end of the week, there is plenty of money in the bank to pay the suppliers (unless the shop is selling the sandwiches far too cheaply!). This type of situation is known as **positive cash flow** because income is always higher than expenditure.

2. A farmer who grows potatoes plants them in March. The potatoes are harvested in September when he sells them to the wholesaler and receives payment. Between March and September he has to pay for fertiliser, diesel for his tractor, and several other items. During this period he has a **negative cash flow** since he is paying out money and receiving none. Hopefully, he received enough money from last September's sales to keep him going.

Problems and cash flow

The above example of the farmer shows how important it is that businesses monitor cash flow. If the farmer runs out of cash before September, he has a problem. Even if a business is profitable but runs out of cash, it could get into trouble and may have to close.

In this chapter, you will learn about different kinds of income and expenditure. You will also learn how to build a cash-flow forecast and explain what it means. Cash-flow forecasts predict how much income and expenditure there will be over a certain length of time and highlight any potential problems.

You will learn about the problems businesses experience in relation to cash flow. For instance:

- when expenditure is higher than income, a business could get into difficulties – this could happen if an unexpected bill arrives or the expenditure on a particular item is higher than expected
- even if income is a lot higher than expenditure, there could still be a problem. Having too much cash sounds fine, but if it is not invested properly, money from interest could be lost.

The principle of cash flow and the effect of different levels of cash is shown in the illustration below.

Other uses of cash-flow forecasts

Cash-flow forecasts are also useful when deciding whether to:

- produce new goods or services
- invest in new resources
- carry out new activities
- expand or reduce existing activities.

Spreadsheets and cash flow

Spreadsheets are ideal for building cash-flow forecasts. They allow businesses to test out what would happen if different events took place, for example if electricity prices increased by a large amount. This is known as a 'What if?' assessment, which you first met in Chapter 19, page 334. You need to understand how spreadsheets are used in cash-flow forecasting and, hopefully, will be able to practise using them in class. You will not be asked to use a spreadsheet in the examination, but you could be asked to explain why they are used. You also need to know the advantages and disadvantages of using them in this way.

Snapshot

Too little, too late

A recent survey has shown that half of all new businesses fail within two years. Many of them had good-quality products or services, hardworking and talented people, and worked hard at advertising and promoting their business.

The reason they failed is that they simply ran out of money – they had negative cash flow. A common problem was customers who were allowed to buy goods on credit who paid their bills late, or not at all. Yet, at the same time, the business had to pay its own suppliers.

Small businesses have the legal right to charge customers interest if they are late paying their bills, but many do not. Why? Because they are worried that the customer will go somewhere else if they do this and they cannot afford to lose their custom. In many cases, it is large powerful businesses which make small firms wait for their money.

Cash in bank

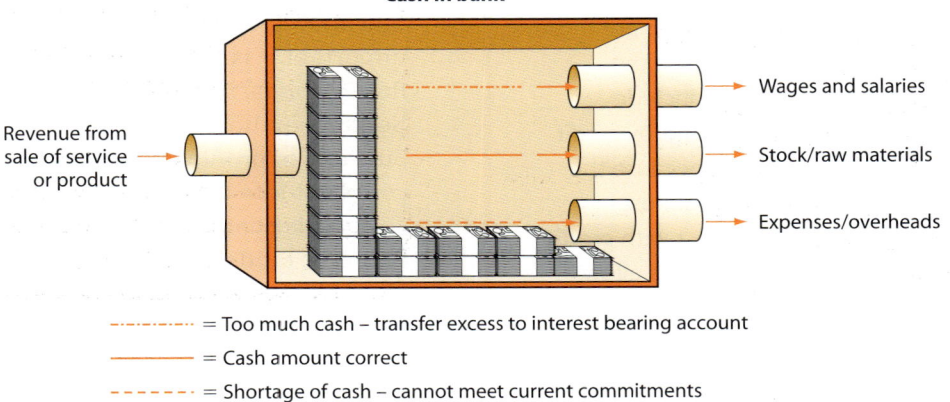

Revenue from sale of service or product → → Wages and salaries
→ Stock/raw materials
→ Expenses/overheads

- - - - - = Too much cash – transfer excess to interest bearing account
———— = Cash amount correct
- - - - - = Shortage of cash – cannot meet current commitments

The principle of cash flow

Understanding cash flow

Inflows of money

Remember that inflows can also be called income or revenue. The most obvious kind of income for a business is from customers who buy goods or use services. Money is received from them almost immediately if it is a cash transaction, or several weeks later if another business is allowed credit and pays after a statement of account has been received.

Businesses can also receive income in other ways:

- They can borrow money from a bank or other source.
- Local and national government grants could be available.
- They may rent out part of their property to another business or individual.

From a cash-flow point of view, some of this money, such as payments from customers and rent, will arrive regularly. Other amounts of money, such as a government grant, will be paid only once.

Outflows of money

This is also called expenditure or payments. Large businesses can have thousands of different kinds of expenditure. They have many people in the accounts department checking invoices and statements of account and then arranging for payments to be made. A few examples of more common forms of expenditure are:

- business rates paid to the local authority (see also page 31)
- staff wages and salaries
- raw materials for production
- electricity, gas, water and telephone bills
- rent, if the business does not own the premises it uses
- advertising costs
- VAT payments
- insurance premiums
- equipment purchases
- stationery and other consumable items such as printer cartridges, floppy disks and cleaning materials.

Spot check

Write down your answers to the following questions:

1. State whether each of the following is true or false.
   a. Cash flow relates to all of the money going into the business, no matter what method of payment is used.
   b. A positive cash flow is when income is greater than expenditure.
   c. A negative cash flow is when income is greater than expenditure.
   d. Businesses that have a negative cash flow are in danger of not being able to pay their bills.
   e. It doesn't matter whether businesses receive money they are owed promptly.
2. Give two reasons why businesses prepare cash-flow forecasts.
3. Give two examples of inflows or income to a business.
4. Give two examples of outflows or payments by a business.
5. Explain why spreadsheets are often used to prepare cash-flow forecasts.

It makes you think!

You have a friend who runs his own business. He is preparing a cash-flow forecast and has to state his expenditure over the next six months.

Within your group, and for *each* of the items listed above, decide whether your friend would know the exact amount he had to pay or would have to estimate it.

A basic cash-flow forecast

Look at the simple cash-flow forecast for a business shown below.

Work through the cash-flow forecast carefully, noting the following points:

- The headings of the six columns are the first six months of a year. Cash-flow forecasts are normally done on a monthly basis for either six or twelve months ahead.
- Each column starts with an **opening balance**. The first one shows how much money is expected to be in the bank at the beginning of January. In the example, this is £5,000.
- The next row in the column shows the amount of money the business expects to receive during January – its inflows. In the example, this is £20,000.
- The third row of figures is the sum of the opening balance and the inflows. For January the total amount is £5,000 + £20,000 = £25,000.
- The next row gives the amount of money the business expects to spend during January – its outflows. In the example, this is £18,000.
- The final figure in the column is the 'total' amount *minus* the outflows. This is the amount of money which should be in the bank on 31 January. In the example, once the business has paid its January bills, it will have £7,000 left. This is the **closing balance** for that month.
- The closing balance figure for January is transferred to the top of the next column since it is also the opening balance for February.
- The most important figures are in the last row, the closing balance. If this figure becomes too low, then the business will have a cash flow problem. In the example, the closing balance for June is zero. This would be very serious, since the bank may not allow the business to pay out even a small cheque to settle any of its bills, including wages.

	Jan. £	Feb. £	March £	April £	May £	June £
Opening balance	5,000	7,000	4,000	6,000	12,000	15,000
Add inflows	20,000	22,000	18,000	20,000	23,000	18,000
Total	25,000	29,000	22,000	26,000	35,000	33,000
Less outflows	18,000	25,000	16,000	14,000	20,000	33,000
Closing balance	7,000	4,000	6,000	12,000	15,000	0

A simple cash-flow forecast

It makes you think!

Tom wants to go on holiday in July and is trying to work out if he will be able to afford it. He reckons that he will need £400, including spending money. At the start of January he has £100 in his bank account from the money he received for Christmas. He earns £60 a month from a part-time job, and thinks that he will get £100 for his birthday in April. He is going to try to keep his spending on entertainment down to £20 a month.

1. Make out a blank grid for a cash-flow forecast by copying the coloured headings in the forecast above.
2. Complete the cash-flow forecast with the information about Tom and decide whether he can afford his holiday.

More complicated cash-flow forecasts

Now look at the cash-flow forecast shown below. It may look complicated, but the basic layout is the same as the one you have just done! It just includes more detail, particularly in the outflows section. The secret of understanding cash-flow forecasts is to examine them stage by stage – they fit together a bit like a jigsaw.

Understanding the headings

The column headings show the months of the forecast, just like the last example.

The row headings are divided into the same type of sections:

- inflows or receipts
- outflows or payments
- a monthly summary.

The inflows or receipts section now shows two different types of income, rather than one. These are added together to give the **sub-total of inflows**. This is represented by the letter **A** in the table.

The outflows includes many types of payments. All these are added together to give a **sub-total of outflows**, represented by the letter **B** in the table.

Calculate the **net cash flow** by subtracting **B** from **A**. This gives figure **C** which is all the inflows less all the outflows.

The monthly summary shows the opening bank balance – figure **D**. As you will see below, the net cash flow is either added to or subtracted from this figure to give the final closing bank balance **E**.

Check *now* with your tutor if you don't understand any of these explanations.

	July £	August £	Sept. £	Oct. £	Nov. £	Dec. £
INFLOWS/RECEIPTS						
Sales	200,000	190,000	210,000	210,000	210,000	200,000
Loans received	0	0	0	0	0	0
Sub-total of inflows (A)	200,000	190,000	210,000	210,000	210,000	200,000
OUTFLOWS AND PAYMENTS						
Materials purchased	70,000	70,000	70,000	70,000	70,000	70,000
Wages/salaries	120,000	105,000	105,000	115,000	115,000	115,000
Capital items	0	0	10,000	0	0	0
Rent and rates	700	700	700	700	700	700
Electricity	650	650	650	650	650	650
Stationery	100	100	100	100	100	100
Telephone	200	200	200	200	200	200
Advertising	2,000	2,000	2,000	2,000	2,000	2,000
Insurance	250	250	250	250	250	250
Loan repayment	12,000	12,000	12,000	12,000	12,000	12,000
Sub-total of outflows (B)	205,900	190,900	200,900	200,900	200,900	200,900
Net cashflow, A-B (C)	−5,900	−900	9,100	9,100	9,100	−900
MONTHLY SUMMARY						
Opening bank balance (D)	10,000	4,100	3,200	12,300	21,400	30,500
Net cashflow (C)	−5,900	−900	9,100	9,100	9,100	−900
Closing bank balance (E)	4,100	3,200	12,300	21,400	30,500	29,600

Fact file

Businesses separate their payments into different groups.

- **Materials purchased** are raw materials used in the production of goods to be sold – or are stock which will be resold in a retail business.
- **Expenses** are payments for all the other items needed to run the business – rent, advertising, and so on. These can also be sub-divided into:
  a **capital items** – items which will last for some time, such as a vehicle, computer or other equipment
  b **consumable items** – items which are used up quickly, such as stationery or floppy disks.

Preparing a forecast

The forecast that you have just looked at was drawn up by Alison Pettigrew who runs a printing business. At Easter, she decided to carry out a cash flow analysis for the second half of the year. In doing this, she had the following things in mind:

- Sales have been growing in recent years and she can forecast for the July to December period by adding a percentage increase on to last year's results.
  She knows that sales revenue drops in the summer and before Christmas.
- Her 'materials purchased' figure – which is how much Alison spends on raw materials – is fairly static.
- Alison has agreed to reward her staff with a pay rise in October and she wants to honour this promise.
- She is also thinking about taking out a loan of £50,000 and spending it in June to upgrade her main printing machine. When she does this, she will need one fewer member of staff. This will not be a problem since one of the machine operators is due to retire at the end of July.
- Alison wants to pay off her loan, including interest, over the six months. All the other figures are easy to estimate from her records.
- Finally, all her computers and software are out of date. Her supplier has offered to replace the system in September for £10,000.

Alison is concerned whether her overall cash flow will be sufficient, particularly if she upgrades the company's IT system.

Over to you!

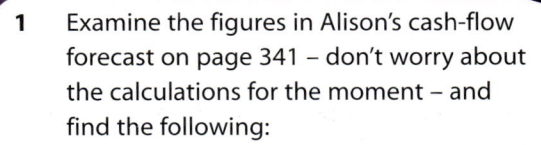

1. Examine the figures in Alison's cash-flow forecast on page 341 – don't worry about the calculations for the moment – and find the following:
   a the changes in sales which Alison thinks will happen in the summer and before Christmas
   b the changes in the wages bill when a member of staff retires
   c the effect of the pay rise – work out the overall percentage rise if you can
   d the cost of replacing the IT system
   e the loan repayment.

2. Finally, make sure you can tell the difference between the figures Alison has entered, and those which are 'calculation' lines. The calculation lines in the example all have a letter beside them, A–E. These are completed only *after* the entries have been made.

Calculating the cash-flow forecast

Once Alison had entered all the figures in the forecast, she used her calculator to work out the inflow and outflow sub-totals (A and B). She then worked out the difference between A and B to find the net cash flow (C). This is the overall amount of cash which would enter or leave her bank account in that particular month.

- If her net cash flow is **positive** that month, she *adds* this figure to her opening bank balance.
- If her net cash flow is **negative** that month, she must *subtract* it from her closing bank balance.

Note that a negative number is shown by a minus sign, that is –£5,000 or by writing the number in brackets, that is (£5,000).

Analysing the results

Once she had completed the forecast, Alison noted the following:

- At the start of July, the balance in her bank account is £10,000 but it falls to £4,100 at the end of July and £3,200 by the end of August before steadily climbing to £29,600 at the end of December. Alison is happy with this because she knew that things would get worse before they got better and by December she has £19,600 more than when she started.
- Alison was concerned that for one or two months her forecast might have shown a **negative** bank balance. In this case, she would have had to tell the bank and arrange an overdraft facility (see below). The bank would probably have agreed to this providing it was only for a few months and Alison could project a positive balance soon. (Overdrafts are explained in full in Chapter 26.)
- The business can afford the computer system upgrade in September.

Alison's main concern, by far, is the *last line* of the cash-flow forecast – the closing bank balance. If it were to be negative at the end of any month, she would have to think carefully about what she should do. For example, if the forecast sales in August were £10,000 lower, she would have a difficult decision to make. She could increase her marketing costs to try to increase sales, but if this failed her cash-flow forecast would be even worse!

Fact file

You may have heard the expression, in business, 'But what's the **bottom line**?' In a cash-flow forecast the key information is actually on the bottom line, but this has now become a general expression for the most important figure, or set of figures. If you wanted to go on holiday and your parents asked for the bottom line, they want to know how much it will cost them!

Banks, too, are very interested in the bottom line and normally don't like this to be a negative! If you had £10 in your account and gave a friend a cheque for £20, the bank could refuse to accept the cheque, as you saw in the last chapter. Or it could allow you an **unauthorised overdraft** – a loan of the money – on which you will pay a very high rate of interest.

Businesses (and individuals) should warn the bank if this situation could occur and obtain an **arranged overdraft** on which interest is lower. The bank would agree an **overdraft limit** which is the maximum amount allowed before cheques are rejected. Having an overdraft used to be known as being 'in the red' because, before computers, banks printed negative figures in red on a bank statement.

It makes you think!

Alison examines her cash-flow forecast and wonders what would happen if things don't quite work out the way she expects. She decides to be pessimistic and changes her figures as follows:

- She assumes sales will be £10,000 less in November.
- She assumes material costs increase by £10,000 from October onwards.

Doing this shows her that her final bank balance in December would now be −£10,400!

	July £	Aug. £	Sept. £	Oct. £	Nov. £	Dec. £
INFLOWS/RECEIPTS						
Sales	200,000	190,000	210,000	210,000	200,000	200,000
Loans received	0	0	0	0	0	0
Sub-total of inflows (A)	200,000	190,000	210,000	210,000	200,000	200,000
OUTFLOWS AND PAYMENTS						
Materials purchased	70,000	70,000	70,000	80,000	80,000	80,000
Wages/salaries	120,000	105,000	105,000	115,000	115,000	115,000
Capital items	0	0	10,000	0	0	0
Rent and rates	700	700	700	700	700	700
Electricity	650	650	650	650	650	650
Stationery	100	100	100	100	100	100
Telephone	200	200	200	200	200	200
Advertising	2,000	2,000	2,000	2,000	2,000	2,000
Insurance	250	250	250	250	250	250
Loan repayment	12,000	12,000	12,000	12,000	12,000	12,000
Sub-total of outflows (B)	205,900	190,900	200,900	210,900	210,900	210,900
Net cashflow, A−B (C)	−5,900	−900	9,100	−900	−10,900	−10,900
MONTHLY SUMMARY						
Opening bank balance (D)	10,000	4,100	3,200	12,300	11,400	500
Net cashflow (C)	−5,900	−900	9,100	−900	−10,900	−10,900
Closing bank balance (E)	4,100	3,200	12,300	11,400	500	−10,400

Alison has several choices. She could spend more on marketing, cancel her IT upgrade or forget the pay rise. Alternatively, she could arrange an overdraft, but this would depend upon the situation being better in January.

1. Check that you can see the *alterations* Alison has made to her forecast – and that you understand them.

2. Within your group, discuss Alison's choices – and the consequences. See if you can identify any other ways in which Alison could increase income or reduce her costs – and the results. Then decide what you would do, if you were running Alison's business.

Spreadsheets and cash-flow forecasts

Cash-flow forecasts can be carried out far more easily using a spreadsheet. You will *not* have to use them in the examination, but you should know how they can be used. Ideally, you should practise using spreadsheets to work out cash-flow forecasts. This is because there are several advantages to using a spreadsheet package, but also some disadvantages!

Advantages of spreadsheets

- Spreadsheets allow you to calculate large amounts of numeric data easily. For example, rows or columns on spreadsheets can be added or subtracted from each other easily.
- Lengthy and tedious manual calculations, with figures having to be changed and re-calculated, are avoided.
- Spreadsheets have a wide variety of uses. As well as producing cash-flow forecasts, they are ideal for analysing budgets and forecasting sales, calculating profits and identifying stock shortages.
- There are no errors in calculations, *provided* that the figures *and* the formulae have been entered correctly.
- Recalculations are carried out automatically when data is changed.
- The user can spend more time analysing the results of the spreadsheet, rather than doing the actual calculations.
- Spreadsheets give an accurate financial picture so that problems can be identified, solutions considered and the best decision made.
- Spreadsheets can be used to produce line graphs, bar charts and pie charts. These help patterns and trends to be identified.
- Spreadsheets can be 'cut' and 'pasted' into other packages so they can be included in a word-processed document or a PowerPoint presentation, for example.

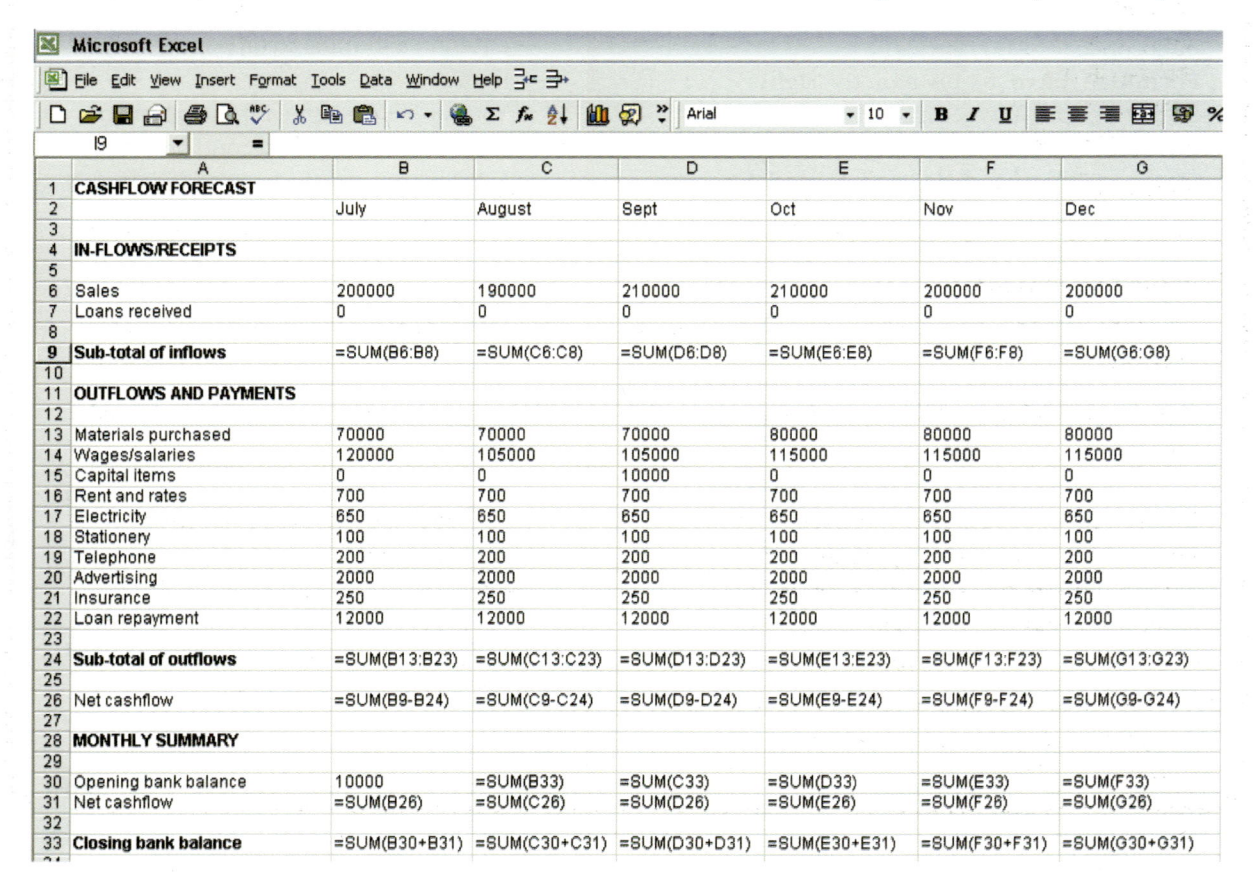

	A	B	C	D	E	F	G
1	CASHFLOW FORECAST						
2		July	August	Sept	Oct	Nov	Dec
3							
4	IN-FLOWS/RECEIPTS						
5							
6	Sales	200000	190000	210000	210000	200000	200000
7	Loans received	0	0	0	0	0	0
8							
9	Sub-total of inflows	=SUM(B6:B8)	=SUM(C6:C8)	=SUM(D6:D8)	=SUM(E6:E8)	=SUM(F6:F8)	=SUM(G6:G8)
10							
11	OUTFLOWS AND PAYMENTS						
12							
13	Materials purchased	70000	70000	70000	80000	80000	80000
14	Wages/salaries	120000	105000	105000	115000	115000	115000
15	Capital items	0	0	10000	0	0	0
16	Rent and rates	700	700	700	700	700	700
17	Electricity	650	650	650	650	650	650
18	Stationery	100	100	100	100	100	100
19	Telephone	200	200	200	200	200	200
20	Advertising	2000	2000	2000	2000	2000	2000
21	Insurance	250	250	250	250	250	250
22	Loan repayment	12000	12000	12000	12000	12000	12000
23							
24	Sub-total of outflows	=SUM(B13:B23)	=SUM(C13:C23)	=SUM(D13:D23)	=SUM(E13:E23)	=SUM(F13:F23)	=SUM(G13:G23)
25							
26	Net cashflow	=SUM(B9-B24)	=SUM(C9-C24)	=SUM(D9-D24)	=SUM(E9-E24)	=SUM(F9-F24)	=SUM(G9-G24)
27							
28	MONTHLY SUMMARY						
29							
30	Opening bank balance	10000	=SUM(B33)	=SUM(C33)	=SUM(D33)	=SUM(E33)	=SUM(F33)
31	Net cashflow	=SUM(B26)	=SUM(C26)	=SUM(D26)	=SUM(E26)	=SUM(F26)	=SUM(G26)
32							
33	Closing bank balance	=SUM(B30+B31)	=SUM(C30+C31)	=SUM(D30+D31)	=SUM(E30+E31)	=SUM(F30+F31)	=SUM(G30+G31)

Spreadsheets may be used to work out cash-flow forecasts

Disadvantages of spreadsheets

- If a spreadsheet is very large, it is difficult to print out on A4 paper without reducing the type size to the point where a magnifying glass is needed to read it! Similarly, a spreadsheet can be too large to be seen on one screen, which can make working on it tedious.
- A small mistake can lead to a major problem, e.g. if a formula affects several cells.
- On some packages there is no facility for attaching notes to explain a cell entry.
- Layout is important if a spreadsheet is to be easy to understand. New users may have difficulties in planning how to set out a new spreadsheet.
- Changing data on a spreadsheet may mean that there is no historic record of adjustments which have been made. Saving each version of the change is possible, but if this happens several times, it may be difficult to keep track of each one.
- Formulae have to be exactly right. Some people have difficulty in using formulae.
- Copying formulae from one spreadsheet to another is easy, but this may not be possible if a formula depends upon figures in the first spreadsheet. This is called a derived formula. In this case, the figures may have to be re-entered.
- There is a limit to the number of variables that can be entered on one spreadsheet, which works on the basis of rows and columns. Sometimes several spreadsheets have to be prepared to analyse the same data in different ways.
- Errors may be made if you enter a cell reference in a calculation as an absolute reference when it should be a relative reference, and vice versa. (If you do not understand this point, your IT tutor will explain it to you.)
- Spreadsheets take time to set up. Sometimes it is easier to use a calculator. However, if the calculation is going to be part of longer report, a spreadsheet should be used. In addition, it looks more professional.
- As with all IT work, it is possible to lose a file or corrupt it and lose hours of work. Remember to save your work regularly and to keep a backup copy.

Fact file

If you have a problem entering formulae in a cash flow spreadsheet, use the following to help. You may find it useful to refer to the cash-flow forecast on page 345 while you work through this.

- Total A is found by doing the 'sum' of all the receipt rows.
- Total B is found by doing the 'sum' of all the payment rows.
- Net cash flow C is found by deducting the cell containing total B from the cell containing total A.
- You can repeat the net cash flow figure C again in the monthly summary simply by entering a formula to repeat the cell number.
- You can do the same for the opening bank balance on the second and subsequent months by entering the cell number of the *previous* bank balance.
- The formula for the closing balance will always be a *plus* – whether or not you are dealing with a positive or negative amount – providing you precede the negative amount with a minus sign. This is because the spreadsheet will understand that a plus formula with a negative number equals minus. A useful check, if you are unsure, is to work out this number on your calculator to see you get the same total!

If you have any problems replicating formula across columns, talk to your tutor.

Finally, whether you prepare forecasts on paper or on a spreadsheet, you may find it useful to enter a zero if there is no entry, rather than leave a cell blank. This way, you are less likely to enter the wrong information.

Over to you!

1. Use the information from the forecast below to prepare a spreadsheet. Use formulae to instruct the package to fill in the boxes marked *. If you complete it correctly, the bank balance for September should be £9,850.
2. Use the spreadsheet to try out some 'What if?' analysis. For example:

   a. There is a strike of delivery drivers in August and sales fall to £2,000.
   b. Because of a temporary shortage, material prices double in July.

   When you have entered this new information, find out the final bank balance for each month and explain the difference these changes have made.

	July £	Aug. £	Sept. £
INFLOWS/RECEIPTS			
Sales	11,000	11,000	11,500
Other receipts	0	500	0
Sub-total of inflows	*	*	*
OUTFLOWS AND PAYMENTS			
Materials purchased	5,500	6,000	5,500
Wages/salaries	2,200	2,200	2,200
Capital items	100	100	100
Rent	500	500	500
Rates	600	700	700
Electricity	2000	250	250
Sub-total of outflows	*	*	*
Net cashflow	*	*	*
MONTHLY SUMMARY			
Opening bank balance	4,000	*	*
Net cashflow	*	*	*
Closing bank balance	*	*	*

Telephone charges are a business outflow

Chapter review and practice questions

1. Rearrange the words below into two groups of three words. In each group the words should mean the same thing.

Income	Inflow
Outflow	Revenue
Expenditure	Payments

2. State whether each of the following is an example of inflow or outflow to a business:
   a. Insurance
   b. Government grants
   c. Salaries and wages
   d. Sales
   e. Production material purchases
   f. Properties rented to other businesses
   g. Electricity supply
   h. Manufacturing equipment.

3. Identify three advantages and three disadvantages of using a spreadsheet for cash-flow forecasting.

4. A business is predicting a negative cash flow for the next two months. Suggest what action it could take to cope with the problem.

Integrated activity

Matt Kent runs Apex Photographic Services. He wants to work out his cash flow for July, August and September. He has predicted the following:

- His sales receipts will be £9,000 each month.
- In August, he will buy new photographic equipment. This will cost £8,000. This is a capital item of expenditure.
- Wages and salaries are £3,500, £4,000 and £3,500.
- The following payments will be the same each month. Telephone £120, rent £200, rates £110, electricity £230, stationery £400, insurance £50.
- Matt will spend £500 on materials each month.
- Matt wants to promote the business after the summer holidays and will spend £2,000 on advertising in September.
- Matt's opening bank balance is £7,000.

Either copy the following grid to produce the forecast on paper, *or* copy it into a spreadsheet.

	July £	Aug. £	Sept. £
INFLOWS/RECEIPTS			
Sales			
Sub-total of inflows (A)			
OUTFLOWS AND PAYMENTS			
Materials purchased			
Wages/salaries			
Capital items			
Rent			
Rates			
Electricity			
Repairs			
Stationery			
Telephone			
Advertising			
Insurance			
Loan repayment			
Other			
Sub-total of outflows (B)			
Net cashflow, A–B (C)			
MONTHLY SUMMARY			
Opening bank balance (D)			
Net cashflow (C)			
Closing bank balance (E)			

1. Work out Matt's closing bank balance for each month.
2. Identify the month in which Matt has a negative cash flow situation, and say whether this matters.
3. Matt is contacted by a local business in August and offered the opportunity to do a lot of work for it from September. This will be worth an additional £2,000 a month. Matt knows he would have to take on an additional member of staff to cope with the extra work. He would want the new person to start in August and would pay £1,200 a month. Can Matt afford this? Rework your forecast to give Matt advice.
4. State your overall opinion of the way Matt manages the business and its financial 'health'

Chapter 20 Using a cash-flow forecast

Chapter 21: Using a budget

What you will learn
Understanding budgets

Overview: using a budget

What is a budget?

Most people have some kind of budgeting system. Your parents know how much money they earn each month and what the household bills are for food, electricity, and so on. They can then plan what to do with their money. After paying for everyday living expenses, most people want to know how much is left for entertainment such as holidays. This may not be written down on paper, but the figures will be in their head. If things go according to plan, most people hope to have a little money left at the end of each month and perhaps transfer some into a savings account for a holiday. Some people are more organised and write down their predicted income and expenditure on paper, especially if they want to save for a special event.

Budgets and businesses

Most organisations have budgets and a specific budget procedure. Budgets are a type of plan used to predict expenditure, usually over a year. The budget is detailed so that *types* of expenditure and the *amounts* planned to be spent are listed individually.

Anyone who plans a budget normally wants to keep to it. This can be harder than the actual planning! In an organisation, throughout the year, financial information is used to work out how much has actually been spent each week or each month. This expenditure is then compared with the amount planned in the budget.

Sometimes there may be an underspend, when less money has been spent than planned. There may also be an overspend, when more money has been spent than planned. The difference between the actual result and the planned budget figure is called a **variance**. If there is quite a difference for any item, particularly an overspend, then managers will investigate the problem and try to put it right. Otherwise, by the end of the year, the business would be spending far more money than it intended to, or could afford.

In this chapter you will learn how businesses prepare and use a budget. You will find out how this helps the business to both plan its expenditure and check on its performance.

It makes you think!

Jon and Chris are planning to go on holiday next summer. Neither are very good at managing their money so they decide to 'budget' for their holiday. Both write down all their income and predicted expenditure for each month, with the aim of having money to save each month.

Jon is an optimist. He earns £30 a week in a part-time job and decides to try to save £100 a month. This, he thinks, will give him plenty of spending money, but it will mean staying in most evenings for the next few months. Chris, too, earns £30 a week. He decides he can save £70 a month without too much trouble.

1. Who do you think is most likely to keep to his plan, and why?
2. What does this tell you about realistic planning in relation to budgets?

Understanding budgets

The budget process

The diagram below shows an example of the budget process for one department. In January, the overall budget for the business is agreed. This is usually divided into departmental budgets. In March, the first month of the budget year, expenditure for each department is recorded.

	Budget period starts ↓	Budget report for March includes variances ↓	Budget report for April includes variances ↓	Budget report for May includes variances ↓
Annual budgets agreed for all departments		Expenditure on materials and other items required	Further expenditure Problems causing variances investigated	Further expenditure Problems causing new variances investigated
Jan.	**Feb.**	**March**	**April**	**May**

The budget process for one department

Shortly after the end of the month, this information is given to each manager so that he or she can see how much has actually been spent compared with the amount scheduled in the budget. Any major differences can be investigated and, hopefully, corrected. When each manager receives the next report, soon after the end of April, the results of the action taken can be checked.

The purposes of budgets

- To give information in detail so that problems can be identified precisely.
- To give feedback frequently and quickly so that speedy action can be taken.
- To give individual managers the authority and responsibility to control their own area. This means that they can authorise expenditure, but have to prove to senior managers that the money has been spent wisely. For example, a production manager could authorise that portable fans could be bought if the operators were complaining about the heat from the machines.
- To enable senior managers to quickly judge the performance of the business by looking at the individual budget reports and combining them to see the overall effect. It also allows them to discuss each budget holder's performance with him or her individually.

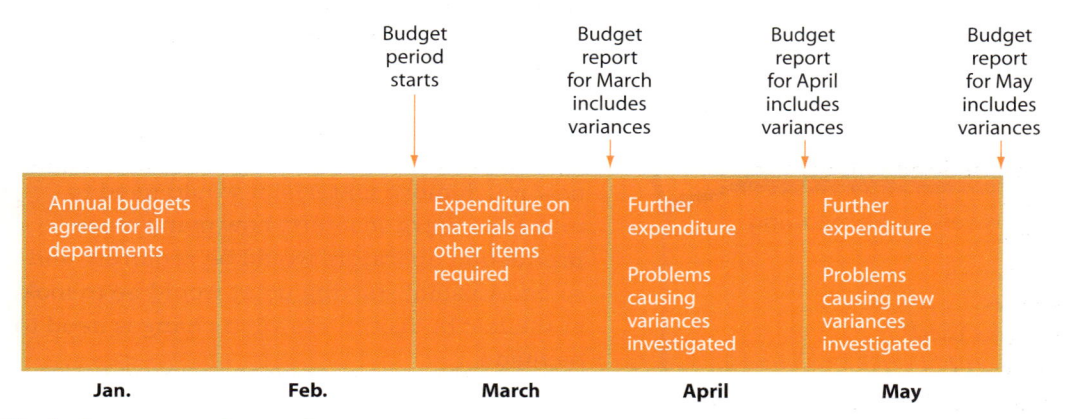

Fact file

Because the budget process continually repeats itself, it is sometimes called the **budget cycle**. Each manager responsible for a budget is called a **budget holder**.

In many organisations, budgets are set for each department. However, a term you may hear on work experience is **cost centre**. This is simply another way of dividing up a budget into different areas.

Budgets versus cash-flow forecasts

You may have already noticed that there are some similarities between budgets and cash-flow forecasts. However, there are also some differences.

Similarities

- They both forecast estimated expenditure over a future period of time.
- They are normally broken down into monthly intervals.
- What actually happens can be checked against the plan.

Differences

- Budgets are produced for individual departments, whereas cash-flow forecasts are for the business as a whole.
- Budgets have one person who is responsible, whereas cash-flow forecasts are monitored by the finance department.
- Budgets are not concerned with money entering and leaving the bank account. For example, when materials are used by a particular department, the money is charged to that department's budget. The supplier may have already been paid.

> **Spot check**
>
> Write down your answers to the following questions:
> 1. What is a budget?
> 2. Why are budgets used?
> 3. What is a variance?
> 4. What is a person called who is responsible for a budget?
> 5. Why are variances investigated?
> 6. What do you think would happen if budget reports were given only at the end of the budget year instead of at the end of each month?

Setting a budget

The process of setting a budget often begins several months before the start of the budget year and is carried out in stages.

Stage one

The starting point in a manufacturing business is forecasting how many goods will be sold over the budget year. This is multiplied by the selling prices of the goods to give the total expected income. In a business providing a service, this would mean forecasting how many customers are expected and how much they would pay in total.

Forecasting the number of goods which could be sold or the number of customers is called the **level of activity**. For example, if a business which made and sold 10,000 mini-scooters in a year thought that it could sell 12,000 in the next year, then the level of activity would be forecast to increase by 20 per cent. This task is usually carried out by the marketing department.

Stage two

This involves telling all the organisation's departments about the change in the level of activity. They are then asked to make proposals for their budget for next year. For example, the production department in the mini-scooter business would have to work out how much more material it would need to make the extra scooters, how many more production operators would be required, and so on. A useful starting point would be to look at the last budget to see what changes need to be made.

Stage three

This involves departmental managers discussing their planned budgets with senior managers. The discussion is really a sort of negotiation since the aim of setting a new budget is not just to meet changes in the level of activity but to reduce costs wherever possible. In the case of the mini-scooter business, 20 production workers are needed to manufacture 10,000 scooters a year. The 20 per cent increase in demand would logically mean that four more operators would be needed. The production manager would be asked if the target could be met if only two or three extra operators were employed.

Stage four

This occurs when all the departmental budgets have been agreed and are combined into a **master budget** which summarises the planned income and expenditure of the whole business over the next 12 months.

This process is shown in the diagram opposite.

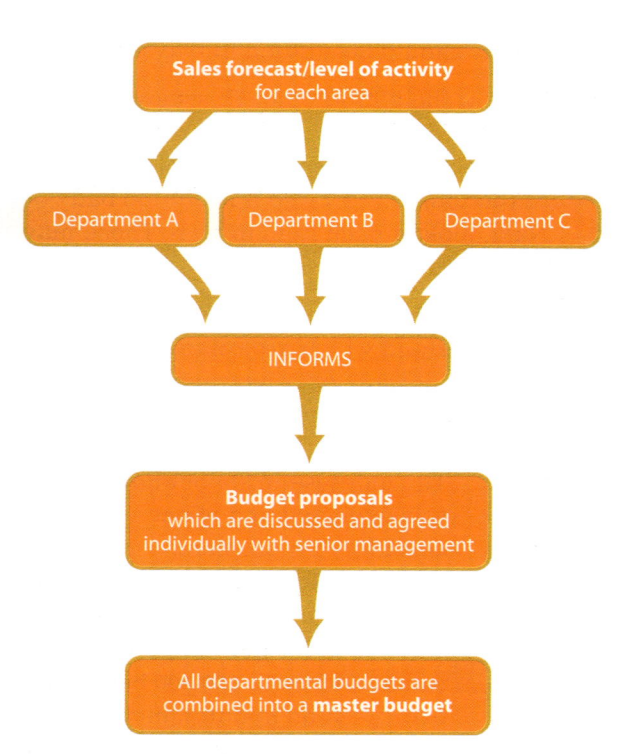

```
Sales forecast/level of activity
         for each area
    ↙        ↓        ↘
Department A  Department B  Department C
              ↓
           INFORMS
              ↓
       Budget proposals
  which are discussed and agreed
  individually with senior management
              ↓
   All departmental budgets are
   combined into a master budget
```

The process of setting a budget

Fact file

A budget which gives details of expenditure is called an **operating budget**. This is the most common type of budget, but there are others.

A **capital budget** is often drawn up separately. It is a list of large expensive items which are planned to be bought over the year.

Sales budgets are sales targets which the marketing and sales department should meet. They are used to predict income.

It makes you think!

Miniscoot is the business which produces the mini-scooters. The scooters are made by buying in sheets of aluminium and moulding them into the shapes of the scooter parts. The wheels and tyres are bought in from other manufacturers. The components are then assembled into the final product before being sent to the next department which packs them and sends them to toy wholesalers.

The budget for the production department has been agreed and is shown in the chart below. Use this to answer the questions that follow.

Miniscoot production department budget, March 2003–February 2004

Item	Monthly expenditure (£)
Sheet aluminium	12,000
Wheels	8,900
Tyres	9,500
Wages	16,500
Maintenance	4,000
Electricity	1,750
Moulds	850
Total	**53,500**

1. How many items are concerned with:
   a. materials required to manufacture the mini-scooters
   b. expenses incurred in running the department (often known as **overheads**)?
2. Identify two items of information the production manager would need in order to calculate the cost of wheels next year.
3. Why do you think each raw material item has been listed separately?
4. Suggest the likely effect on the budget of each of the following events:
   a. The price of aluminium falls.
   b. Electricity prices increase.
   c. An old machine continually breaks down.
   d. The operatives are asked to work overtime so that production targets will be met.

Budget reports

Once a budget has been agreed, each department will receive a regular report on the money it has spent. Some businesses produce these every week, but the most common reporting period is once a month. Below is the budget report for production at Miniscoot in March.

If you compare this with the budget shown on page 353, you will see that part of it is the same – the heading, the list of items and the first column of figures. Only the second column of figures is new. This shows the *actual* amount of money spent on the items listed during March.

The third column is a very important one for the business, and the department's manager will look at this one very carefully. It identifies the *difference* between the expenditure forecast in the budget and the actual amount spent.

- Any entry preceded with a minus sign in the last column identifies an overspend – more money has been spent than planned. For example, the report states that £12,250 has been spent on sheet aluminium whereas the amount budgeted was £12,000. The difference is calculated by:

  £12,000 − £12,250 = −£250

  The figure is negative since £250 more has been spent than was planned.
  Any entry *without* a minus sign shows an underspend. In this case, money has been saved. For example, expenditure on moulds was planned to be £850, but only £800 was spent.

The report should be studied in two stages:

1. Look at the bottom line. This shows that the spending *in total* is £350 more than planned. This is a small amount in relation to the total budget – so it is not too bad.
2. Next, look at each item in turn. These may be separated into:

   - small differences, which are bound to occur and which are relatively unimportant, e.g. electricity and moulds
   - larger differences, which could be important:
     - The increase in sheet aluminium was expected and is not considered a problem.
     - However, the £2,500 extra spent on maintenance is worrying as if this carried on for the full year it would add up to £30,000 being overspent on maintenance.
     - The department's manager would be pleased with the £2,500 underspend on wages, but he knows that it is only temporary. One of his skilled operators left in February and will be replaced in April. In March, other staff managed to do his work, knowing that it would be for only a few weeks.

The manager will need to take action about the most important problem he identified – the costs of maintenance. He arranges a meeting with the maintenance manager – to try to prevent this happening again.

Miniscoot production department budget report, March 2003

Item	Monthly expenditure (£)	Actual expenditure (£)	Variance (£)
Sheet aluminium	12,000	12,250	−250
Wheels	8,900	9,000	−100
Tyres	9,500	9,500	0
Wages	16,500	14,000	2,500
Maintenance	4,000	6,500	−2,500
Electricity	1,750	1,800	−50
Moulds	850	800	50
Total	**53,500**	**53,850**	**−350**

Changing a budget

Budgets are normally designed to have a certain degree of flexibility, to cope with minor changes that can occur. However, during a year, something could happen which would make it impossible for the budget to work at all. For example, material prices could increase due to a world shortage or sales could fall dramatically, reducing income. Both are outside the control of the business and, in this situation, the budgets should be changed to take account of the new circumstances. Budgets are rarely changed because income has increased! It is more likely to be the case that the department now has less money to spend (see also Chapter 27).

Snapshot

Green = target met!

Today, virtually all companies produce and monitor budgets on computer. Computers are ideal for producing these documents because all the data related to income from sales and spending on purchases can be input and automatically allocated to the right budget heading. Managers are used to receiving regular computer reports which list target expenditure, actual expenditure and variances. In some organisations, these are produced weekly or even daily!

The disadvantage is that senior managers may have to plough through dozens of pages of information each month to identify key items and assess how this is affecting company performance.

A new system has been developed by management consultancy KPMG to help make life simpler. This shows on a single page whether sales, expenses, stock control and cash flow are on target or not. Each month, a coloured square indicates if key targets are being met. Green says 'yes', amber indicates concern, whereas red indicates a problem. KPMG calls its new system an 'early warning dashboard' as it gives companies the ability to take instant action if they perceive a serious problem.

Chapter review and practice questions

1 Which of the following could be said to be the main purposes of a budget? Identify all those that apply:
   a To check on the bank balance
   b To give frequent feedback to managers
   c To give detailed information on performance
   d To explain what has happened at the end of a year
   e To identify customers who do not pay bills
   f To give individual managers more control over their department.

2 The stages of setting a budget are listed below. Re-arrange them into the correct order.
   a Preparation of master budget
   b Forecasting the level of activity
   c Negotiation with senior managers
   d Departments put forward proposals for their budget
   e Preparation of departmental budgets

3 Mark is trying to save to buy a new car. He lives in a flat with two friends and although he earns enough to save, he seems to find it impossible! You have offered to help him. He tells you that he takes home £1,450 a month in salary and, each month, spends £250 on rent, £50 on council tax, £20 each on electricity and gas, £70 on travel, £50 on lunches, £35 on his mobile phone and £130 on food and household items. He has a gym membership which costs him £25 a month and he spends £100 a month on clothes and £100 on entertainment. He also budgets £200 a month for existing car expenses. He estimated he could save £400 a month without any problem, but something has gone wrong!
   a Make out a budget sheet listing Mark's expenditure. Calculate how much he *planned* to spend each month.

b Mark's actual bills last month were as follows:
- Rent, council tax, electricity and gas were on target, as were car expenses and travel and his gym membership.
- He spent an extra £30 on lunches because of birthday celebrations at work.
- His mobile phone bill was £55.
- He saved on food and household items by spending only £110.
- He spent £150 on clothes because of some bargains he saw in a sale.
- He spent £90 on entertainment but also had to buy two birthday presents which cost him £40 in total.
- He booked a holiday and had to pay £150 deposit.

Enter these amounts in an 'actual' column and, for each item, calculate the variance.

c What advice would you give Mark after completing his budget analysis?

Integrated activity

You are working in the production department at Miniscoot on work experience. Because the production manager knows you are learning about budgets, she involves you in the process. She asks you to help her work out the budget for April. The expenditure figures are:

Sheet aluminium – £14,750
Wheels – £8,800
Tyres – £11,500
Wages – £16,750
Maintenance – £3,900
Electricity – £1,770
Moulds – £900

She also explains that some problems had occurred during the month. Several scooters had been rejected at final inspection. The fault was eventually traced to a machine, which had not been set up correctly. More scooters had been produced to replace the faulty ones. Another problem arose when there was a two-week strike at the factory, which supplied tyres. An alternative source of supply was found but the tyres were more expensive.

You are asked to undertake the following tasks:

1. Copy out the headings from the Miniscoot production department budget report for March, shown on page 354. Remember to change your main heading to say 'April'.
2. Copy out the item list from the March report *and* the figures listed as 'Allowed monthly expenditure' – as these are the same each month.
3. Use the information above to put figures in the Actual expenditure column.
4. Calculate the figures in the variance column.
5. Calculate the totals of the Actual expenditure and Variance columns.
6. Identify the two items where the variance is very high and write notes under each heading explaining what has caused the problem.

Chapter 22: Calculating the break-even point

What you will learn

Understanding break-even analysis
Using a chart to show a break-even analysis
More about costs and revenue
Using a formula to calculate the break-even point

Overview: break-even point

What is the break-even point?

A local council decided that it would allow two people to open their own hot-dog stands in its two main parks. Within six months, the two businesses developed in completely different ways. One had very few customers and the owner had nothing to do for most of the time while the other was kept very busy and had a part-time assistant. Eventually, the first business proved to be unprofitable and had to close while the owner of the second could afford to buy a new car.

The key factor in this type of business is the number of customers which it attracts. People can normally eat only one hot-dog at once! Compare this with a shop which sells pet food in bulk at discount prices. It may need only a few customers a day to do well.

In the case of the hot-dog stands, a key question is how many customers a day does it take to make the business profitable? Fifty? Two hundred? The answer to this question – the point at which the number of customers makes the business profitable – is the **break-even point**.

This chapter explains how to work out this figure using two methods: by drawing a chart and using a formula. It also describes how businesses can use **break-even analysis** to make decisions about investing for future activities.

Fact file

In any organisation which aims to make a profit, an important feature is the **level** or **volume** of activity – whether this is measured by sales or customers. In other words, how many products are sold or how many customers use a service.

Break-even analysis is a key way of helping a business to understand what this level needs to be. Normally, this technique is used to assess an idea for a particular project such as a new product or an improvement to an existing product.

Understanding break-even analysis

Costs and revenue

Three sets of figures are needed to carry out a break-even analysis.

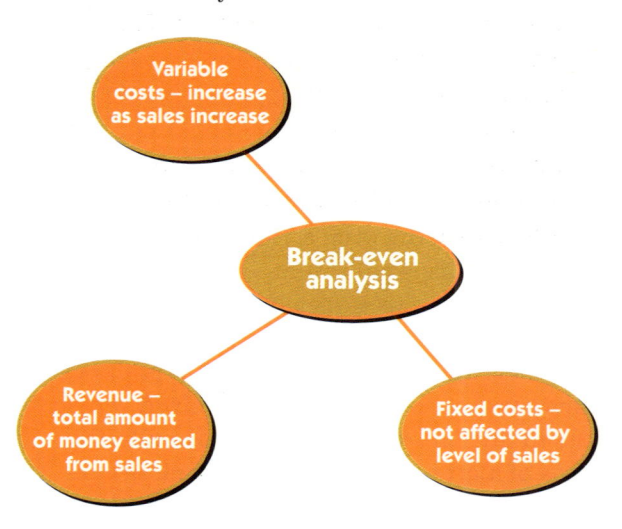

- Variable costs – increase as sales increase
- Break-even analysis
- Revenue – total amount of money earned from sales
- Fixed costs – not affected by level of sales

A break-even analysis requires three sets of figures

Variable costs

These are sometimes called direct costs because they are *directly affected* by the level of activity. For example, for every car Ford produces, it will have to buy five tyres (don't forget the spare!). Therefore, the number of tyres can easily be calculated by multiplying five by the number of cars made. If the number of cars decreased, so would the number of tyres.

Fixed costs

Fixed costs are *not* affected by the level of activity. For example, if a newsagent does not sell a single newspaper, magazine or chocolate bar, he or she still has to pay rent, business rates, telephone rental, and so on. These are all fixed costs because they must be paid, whether or not any customers buy any products.

Revenue

Revenue or **sales income** is the total amount received by the business from customers. It is probably the easiest of the three items to calculate. In the case of a shop, it would be the total till receipts. Most tills calculate this automatically. Larger businesses keep their sales records in a sales account and a simple calculation will give the total. Businesses which have a computerised accounts system can obtain this figure instantly, at any time.

Using a chart to show a break-even analysis

There are two ways in which the above figures can be used to carry out a break-even analysis. The first is by drawing a chart or graph and the second uses a formula.

There are five stages in the process of drawing a break-even chart. The chart is a type of graph where the vertical axis shows the amount of money spent and received, which is called 'income/expenditure'. Normally, the axes of a graph have only one label. Break-even charts are an exception to this rule and the reason for this will soon become clear. The horizontal axis shows the level of activity, for example the number of products sold.

To construct a break-even chart, let's look at Jack, who is thinking of selling Christmas trees to earn some extra money.

Jack has a permanent, but seasonal, job working at a leisure park during the summer. In the winter he does casual work. This year he is thinking about selling small Christmas trees for three weeks in December. There is a spare plot of land in the town centre which he thinks would be better than an out-of-town site since he would attract more customers. The rent would be quite high, costing £1,000 for the three weeks.

Jack can buy trees for an average price of £15 and sell them for £20. In addition, he will have to hire a truck to collect the trees and to operate his free delivery service. The truck rental is £200 for the three-week period.

Jack has listed his costs and revenue as follows:

- Variable costs = the price of the trees, £15. The total variable cost is the number of trees he buys, multiplied by £15.
- Fixed costs = the rent for the land and the cost of the van hire. These amount to £1,200 and Jack will have to pay for these regardless of how many trees he sells.
- Revenue = the total amount of money Jack will receive from selling trees at £20 each. If he sold 100 trees, he would receive £2,000.

Jack's major concern is whether he will make a profit. If he doesn't sell a single tree, he will be out of pocket by £1,200.

Creating a break-even chart
Stage one

Jack needs the above information to draw his chart. Next he needs to decide on the scales to use.

For the horizontal scale, he needs to decide what is the highest number of trees he is likely to sell. He estimates this to be 500 so he makes sure that the scale he draws can cope with this amount.

The highest figure on the vertical scale is the maximum amount of money likely to be received. In this case, it is the maximum number of trees likely to be sold multiplied by the selling price:

500 × £20 = £10,000.

Below you can see the first stage of Jack's chart.

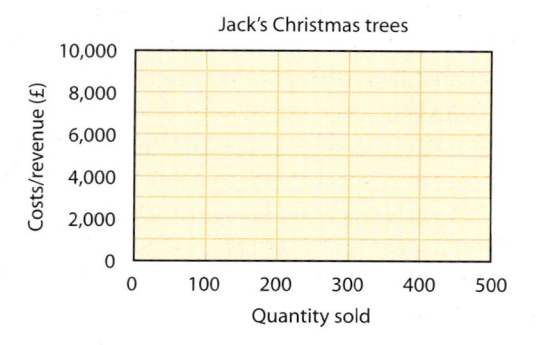

Jack's break-even analysis chart: stage 1

Stage two

Jack needs to draw three lines on his chart. The first will represent his fixed costs. It is a horizontal line starting at the £1,200 mark. It is a straight horizontal line because his fixed costs *never change* – no matter what his sales are.

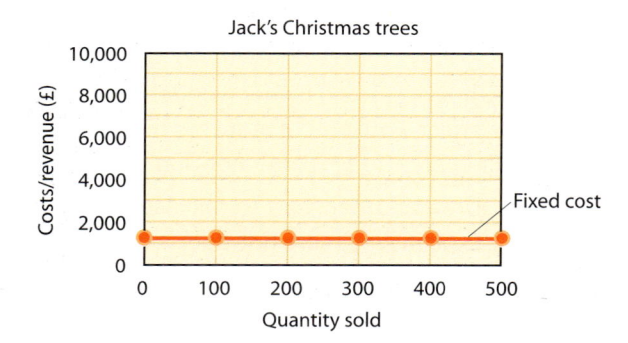

Jack's break-even analysis chart: stage 2

Stage three

Jack next needs to include his variable costs. If Jack sells no trees, he will have no variable costs. If he buys 500 trees, these will cost him £15 × 500 = £7,500. His variable costs may therefore be as low as zero or as high as £7,500.

However, these costs are *on top of* his fixed costs. He must therefore start this second line at the point where the fixed cost line meets the vertical axis. Because this line actually shows *both* sets of costs, it shows the **total costs** of his enterprise.

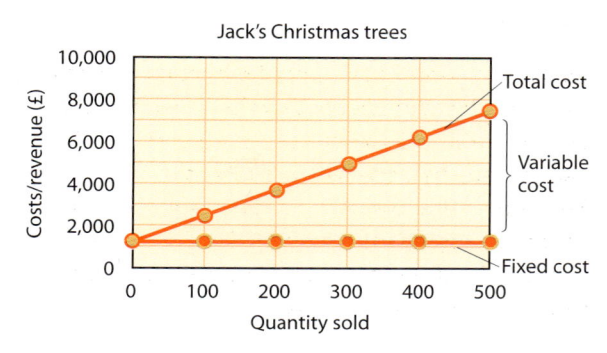

Jack's break-even analysis chart: stage 3

Stage four

Jack's third line represents his income from sales. If Jack sells no trees, he will receive no income, so this line must *start* at zero. If Jack sells his maximum number (500), his total revenue would be 500 × £20 = £10,000 so this is where his line will end.

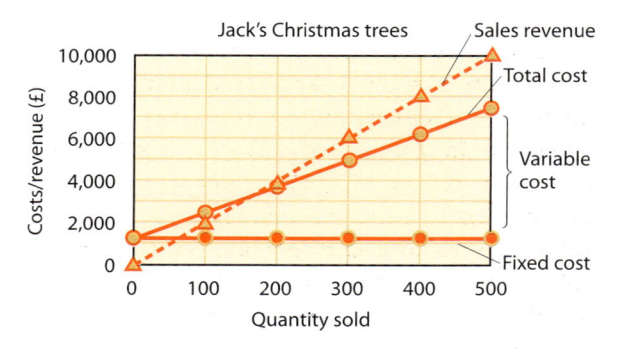

Jack's break-even analysis chart: stage 4

Stage five

The position on the chart where the revenue line crosses the total cost line is the **break-even point**. Jack now draws a vertical line down to the number sold and reads off the number. The line meets the horizontal axis at the number 240. This means that Jack needs to sell 240 trees before he starts to make a profit.

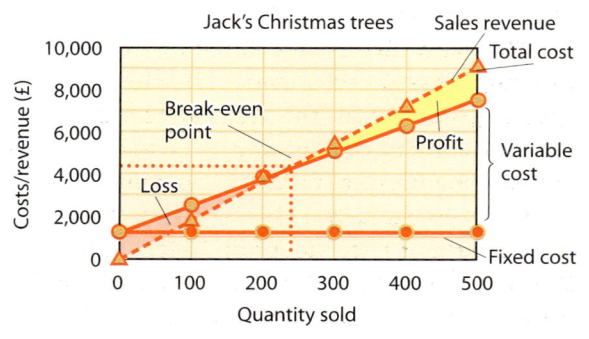

Jack's break-even analysis chart: stage 5

Chapter 22 Calculating the break-even point

Spot check

Write down your answers to the following questions:

1.
   a. What are fixed costs?
   b. Your school or college has fixed costs. Identify three of these.
2.
   a. What are variable costs?
   b. Neriman runs a taxi firm. Identify one major variable cost for her business.
3. The fixed costs of a fitness centre are £2,500 a month and its variable costs this month were £3,000. Calculate its total costs.
4. What does the break-even point tell you about a business?
5.
   a. Explain why the data used to create a break-even chart must be accurate.
   b. If Jack suddenly found the cost price of Christmas trees had increased to £16, how would this affect his break-even chart? Would he have to sell more trees or fewer to break even?

It makes you think!

For the hot-dog stand described at the beginning of the chapter, the cost and revenue figures are as follows:

- Variable costs, such as bread rolls and sausages, cost 70p per hot-dog.
- Fixed costs, such as vehicle maintenance and petrol, are £100 per week.
- The selling price of one hot-dog is £1.20.
- The most hot-dogs likely to be sold in a week are 400.

Use this information to create a break-even chart, by carrying out the following tasks:

a. On graph paper, draw and label the two break-even chart axes.
b. Draw the fixed, variable and total cost lines and label them.
c. Draw in the revenue line and identify the number of hot-dogs which need to be sold in a week to break even.
d. From the chart, estimate the profit or loss if:
   i. 100 hot-dogs were sold
   ii. 300 hot-dogs were sold
e. The hot-dog stand owner wonders what the effect would be of reducing his selling price to £1.10 per hot-dog.
   i. Draw another chart to calculate this.
   ii. Explain why more hot-dogs would need to be sold to break even.

Snapshot

Cooking up a profit!

Promoter Tim Etchells organised a UK tour for Jamie Oliver, the famous TV chef, giving cookery demonstrations. Most of the costs were fixed, consisting of hiring theatres, a director, roadies and Jamie's fee. The total amounted to £4 million and had to be paid even if not one seat ticket – costing £18 each –. was sold.

In the past, Tim has made profits of up to £500,000 from similar events. On others, he has lost large amounts of money.

At Jamie's demonstration events, copies of his latest book were sold at a profit of £10 each. This added to the income from the sale of seats and improved the chances of breaking even. The books were sold at a relatively high price because Jamie signed them. No doubt his wrist ached by the end of the tour!

This is an unusual example of break-even where there are very few variable costs.

Final note: Jamie may like to consider a career change. A Rolling Stones world tour in 1994 earned about £80 million!

What can go wrong?

A break-even analysis will not show the correct break-even point if any of the data are wrong. Equally, if the situation changed, a new break-even chart would have to be produced.

For instance, if Jack underestimated the number of collections and deliveries he had to make and had to hire another truck, this would *increase* his fixed costs.

More about costs and revenue

You have already read that three groups of figures are required to carry out a break-even analysis – variable costs, fixed costs and revenue. The types of costs and source of revenue involved will be different for various kinds of business. This section describes the most common forms in each category.

Variable costs

What makes up the variable costs

Materials

All businesses which make products have to buy materials. Shoe manufacturers have to buy leather or plastic in sheet form. CD manufacturers buy plastic in pellet form for moulding; they also need labels and packaging. Even businesses in the service sector may have materials to buy which are a variable cost. For example, dentists buy mouthwash for their patients to use and hairdressers buy shampoo. As you saw in Unit 1, environmentalists argue that, even though products can be sold at a profit, manufacturers should try to cut down the quantity of materials they use because the earth's resources are limited. A good example of this is any packaging which cannot be recycled.

Labour

This comprises the total salaries of the people required to carry out the operations involved. Fast-food chain McDonald's uses mainly part-time staff whose working hours are varied to meet the level of sales. In this situation, the cost is easy to calculate since people are paid on an hourly basis. Where people are paid on a weekly or monthly basis, the main factors are the number of people employed and how much they are paid. There may be other costs associated with employing people such as paying into pension schemes, providing office space and equipment and protective clothing.

Energy

This can be a variable cost when industrial processes use a large amount of energy. For example, in the steel industry, furnaces use enormous amounts of electricity to melt iron ore to turn it into steel. Energy comes mainly in the form of gas, oil or electricity. Note that energy can also be a fixed cost when used for things such as heating and lighting (see below).

Fixed costs

Rent

Many businesses do not own the premises in which they operate and so they pay rent to the landlord, normally monthly. Quite often, rent is based on the floor area and this can vary depending on the district (see page 31).

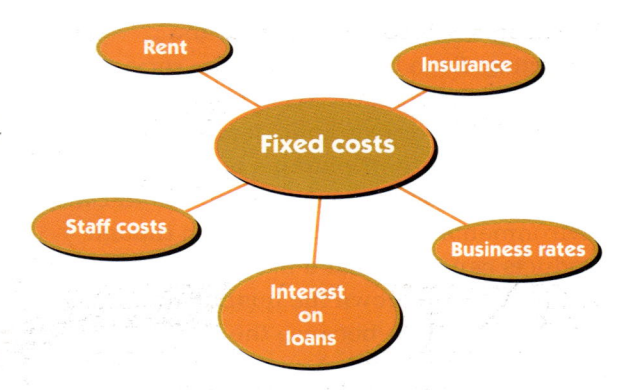

What makes up the fixed costs

Sometimes, businesses rent only part of a building, for example one floor.

Business rates

As you learned in Unit 1, business rates are paid on all business properties and the amount depends upon various factors, including the size and location of the buildings.

Interest on loans

If the business borrows money to fund a new venture, it will have to pay interest as well as paying back the capital (see pages 381 and 387).

Insurance

By law, employers have to pay employee liability insurance so that any employees who are injured can be compensated. In addition, it is advisable to insure property such as buildings and equipment against damage or loss – by unexpected events such as fire, flood or theft. Businesses normally insure against the *additional* losses they would incur in a major disaster, such as finding new premises and relocating.

Staff costs

This is the salary bill for people who are employed in the business but who do not contribute directly to making the product or delivering the service. They could include cleaners, receptionists, managers and accountants.

Revenue

This is the easiest part of the break-even chart to calculate. It is simply the income which the business expects to receive from customers for the goods or service provided. It does not matter how or when customers are expected to pay – for a break-even chart, it is the total amount received which is important.

Snapshot

Going down – at a cost!

In 2002, Jean-Bernard Bros, the deputy mayor of Paris, put forward a plan to build a large underground complex directly under the Eiffel Tower to a depth of 30 metres. This would include shops, restaurants, a cinema, museum and a car park. The idea was to persuade the six million tourists a year who visit the tower to spend more money.

The estimated cost of building the complex will be almost £50 million and the construction will take four years. The construction cost is a fixed cost which will have to be spread over several years when calculating how much visitors must spend for the project to break even. The construction cost will be approximately £47.5 million pounds.

Although many Parisians are keen to have a new tourist attraction, others are doubtful. Some say that the work will weaken the foundations and the tower will fall over. Others point out that the area sometimes floods when the river Seine is high.

While local people argue, work has started to repaint the 1,063-foot tower. This will take 25 specially trained workers two years to complete and will use 50,000 tonnes of lead-free, brown paint – an example of a rather unusual variable cost!

Using a formula to calculate the break-even point

An alternative way of finding the break-even point is to use the formula:

$$\text{Break-even point} = \frac{\text{Fixed costs}}{(\text{Selling price} - \text{Variable cost per unit})}$$

While you don't need to memorise this formula – it will be printed for you in the external test – you do have to know how to apply it!

Applying the formula

You may remember that the figures for the hot-dog stand were as follows:

- Variable costs per unit = 70p
- Fixed costs = £100
- Selling price per unit = £1.20.

The task now is to put these figures into the formula, that is:

$$\text{Break-even point} = \frac{£100}{£1.20 - 70p}$$

$$= \frac{100}{0.5} = 200$$

It makes you think!

Try to apply the formula to Jack's plan to sell Christmas trees. The trees will cost him £15 each, he aims to sell them for £20 and his fixed costs would be £1,200.

Use the formula to see if you obtain the same break-even point answer you found by using the chart. (If not, talk to your tutor to find out what has gone wrong!)

Chapter review and practice questions

1. The chart below gives various types of expenses. Your task is to decide which would be incurred by three different businesses:

   a a bank
   b a garage
   c a CD manufacturer.

   Note that some items could apply to two businesses or all three.

Expense/cost
Production machinery
Engine oil
Office stationery
Buildings
Packaging
Telephone bill
Power for equipment
Counter staff
Plastic granules
Supervisors' salaries
Photocopier rental
Production operators' wages, paid as piecework
Heating
Tea bags
Spark plugs
Receptionist
Computer software
Security staff
Lighting

2. Four friends want to make some money for a children's charity. They decide to make plaster models of famous footballers, paint them and sell them to friends and relatives. Because the plaster will take a few hours to dry, they decide that they will need several of the rubber moulds if they are to produce a reasonable quantity. They do some calculations and arrive at the following figures:

   - cost of plaster and paint for each figure = 20p
   - cost of 10 rubber moulds = £30
   - predicted selling price of each figure = 75p.

   a Draw a chart to find the number of figures they have to sell to break even. Assume that they will sell a maximum of 150.
   b From the chart, estimate the profit the group will make if they sell 120 figures.
   c Use the formula to check the break-even point.
   d Use the formula to calculate the new break-even point if the cost of the rubber moulds is increased from £30 to £50.

Integrated activity

Ben runs a business which offers a service to traders in a town. For a fee, he will arrange for leaflets to be delivered to every home in agreed districts, or around the whole town if required. He also prints leaflets if customers require this. The people he uses to distribute the leaflets are employed on a casual basis. The amount they are paid depends on the number of leaflets they deliver.

Ben has a small factory and warehouse for producing and storing leaflets. He also has a van and a driver to collect the leaflets from his customers and deliver them to the distribution staff. His office is in one corner of the warehouse which is also occupied by Javed who looks after the administration and accounts. Both the van driver and Javed are permanent staff.

Leaflets are produced by Andrea and Ken on the printing press. Andrea is employed full time while Ken, who is semi-retired, helps out when the print shop is busy.

1. The chart opposite lists Ben's expenses in one month. Divide these into two lists, one headed 'fixed costs', the other headed 'variable costs'.

2. Ben is approached by a marketing agency which asks him if he can produce 500 posters a month. It is prepared to pay £1.50 for each poster. Ben does some calculations.

   He will have to modify a printing machine and will need a bank loan to pay for this. The repayment on the loan will be £100 a month. He will also have to ask Ken to work extra hours and buy extra materials such as ink and paper. The total variable cost will be £1.20 per poster.

   After doing these calculations, Ben decides to accept the order. Use either the chart method or formula to discover why he came to this conclusion.

3. Ben's biggest worry about the plan to produce posters is that the interest on the bank loan is variable. He decides to carry out a 'What if?' analysis. He thinks the worst that could happen is that he will have to repay £130 a month.

   Use the formula to recalculate the break-even point. Should Ben still accept the order?

4. Ben decides to accept the order to produce posters. After two months, the marketing agency tells him it may want to increase the number of posters to 1,000 a month. It asks Ben to quote for the price he would charge. All Ben's costs have stayed the same as in his original calculations.

   Ben decides to recalculate the break-even point if the price he quotes the agency is:

   a £1.40
   b £1.30.

Use the formula to produce the break-even point for each of these and decide which selling price Ben should suggest.

Cost

Van MOT
Javed's salary
Petrol for van
New photocopier
Andrea's salary
Blank paper
Electricity for the printing press
Ken's wages
Fax machine
The driver's salary
Telephone bill
Printing ink
Distribution staff wages
Heating
Lighting
Stationery
New office carpet
Tea bags

Chapter 23: Calculating the profit or loss of a business

What you will learn
Understanding profit and loss accounts

Overview: calculating profit or loss

The importance of profit or loss

All businesses aim to make a profit so finding out whether they have actually done so is very important. The Inland Revenue thinks so, too, as tax is calculated on the profits of a business.

In the last four chapters, you have learned about:

- the costs of a new product or service
- cash-flow forecasts
- budgets
- break-even analysis.

These all have one thing in common. They help a business to *plan for the future*. They enable businesses to make decisions about what activities may, or may not, be profitable.

However, all these techniques result in **forecasts** which are never perfect because all the figures they contain are estimates.

The topics in this chapter and the next one, which describes balance sheets, are different because they show *what has actually happened*. Both of these financial statements – the profit and loss account and the balance sheet – are produced after a year of trading.

A summary of the different kinds of financial events and how these link together is shown below.

Key features of a profit and loss account

A profit and loss account summarises all the income and expenditure of a business for a year. You already know about the ways in which a business makes and receives payments. This information is used in a profit and loss account by adding up all the money received from customers. Then all the payments on wages, rent, electricity and other items are added together. The difference between these two totals is either a profit or a loss.

Financial events and how they link together

	Start of year ⇓		End of year ⇓
Planning		**Activity**	**Summary of financial performance for year**
Estimating cost of new product or service + Cash-flow forecasting + Break-even analysis + Budget setting		The business buys materials, makes and sells products. Customers are provided with a service + Payments made and received + Regular budget reports produced	Profit and loss account + Balance sheet

The diagram below shows the difference. A company has the same expenditure in both years. In the first year, its income is higher than its expenditure and it makes a profit. In the second year, the income falls considerably and it makes a loss.

The link between income, expenditure, profit and loss

Profit and loss accounts are presented in a standard way. You need to learn what this is and to understand how the calculations are made. Computers can carry out these calculations accurately and quickly. Because of this, some large businesses produce summaries of their profit and loss statements half-way through the year or even every three months.

However, the main reason why businesses produce profit and loss accounts is because it is a legal requirement. The government asks businesses to pay tax on their profits. Limited companies pay corporation tax which is based on the profit they earn. Sole traders and partners pay income tax on the profit. Public limited companies must publish their profit and loss accounts and balance sheets and make these available to shareholders and the public.

Fact file

'Profit *and* loss' is not a very good title to give this kind of financial report! Businesses can make *either* a profit *or* a loss, not both at the same time. A better heading would be 'profit or loss account' but the word 'and' has been used for a long time and everyone is used to it.

However, instead of writing 'profit and loss account' every time, you may find it referred to as the 'P and L account' in business.

Understanding profit and loss accounts

The purpose of producing profit and loss accounts

In Chapter 25 you will learn that financial statements, such as profit and loss accounts and balance sheets, give information about the business to different types of people such as shareholders, customers and employees. In addition, senior managers find them useful to look at the overall performance of the business. It is similar to having a car MOT tested or an individual having a health check.

The financial statements can also be compared with the previous year's performance and with the performance of other similar businesses.

A financial year

You should already know that there are different kinds of 'year'. The calendar year starts on 1 January and ends on 31 December, whereas your school or college works on an academic year which starts in September. In addition, the government has a 'fiscal year' – fiscal means tax – which starts on 6 April one year and ends on 5 April the following year. This is the period over which tax liabilities are calculated.

Businesses have their own individual 'financial year' which can start and end at any time. Not many companies start and end their financial year at the same time as the calendar year because producing the financial statements is a busy time for the accounts department. They would not really want to give up their Christmas and New Year holidays to meet the deadline. Many, however, link their financial year to the fiscal year and aim to complete their accounts at the end of March each year.

COMFYSEAT LTD
PROFIT AND LOSS ACCOUNT
FOR YEAR ENDING 16 MARCH 2003

Sales		107,000
Cost of sales		13,750
Gross profit		
Expenses		
Wages/salaries	57,420	
Electricity	900	
Insurance	1,700	
Rent	2,400	
Advertising	1,200	
Other	400	
Total expenses		
NET PROFIT		

Integrated activity

On 30 March 1999 priceline.com was floated on the US stock exchange. The shares were offered for sale at $16 each and by the end of the first day's trading, they were selling for over $60 each. Its business was selling airline tickets by allowing customers to name the price they wanted to pay. It was a kind of auction system.

By the end of 1999, priceline.com had sold tickets worth $35 million to customers and had paid the airlines $36.5 million for the tickets. The cost of running the business over this time had been $52.5 million.

Make out a simple profit and loss account for priceline.com, using the format shown above and use your calculations to answer the following questions:

a What is the gross profit figure for priceline.com?
b What is the net profit? (Bear in mind you have only one entry to insert in the expenses section.)
c If you had bought some shares, as an investor, what would you think of the net profit figure you have produced?
d If all other costs remained the same, what sales revenue would priceline.com have needed to break even?

Chapter 24: Understanding a balance sheet

What you will learn

Understanding balance sheets
Computers and balance sheets

Overview: balance sheets

Money owed and money owned

Almost all businesses are run by using other people's money. This could be called 'money owed', but the correct term is **liabilities**, sometimes known as **source of funds**. Businesses can obtain money from several different kinds of sources, as you will see in the next chapter. The most common are:

- shareholders who have invested in the business by buying shares
- loans from banks and other kinds of financial institution
- creditors who have not been paid.

In small businesses, the main source of funding is the owner's own money. Some people sell their house or extend their mortgage to find the money to start up or expand their business.

'Money *owned*' (note the difference!) is a list of things which the business is doing or has done with the money it received from other people or institutions. This may have been invested in buildings, equipment or stocks of materials. These are called **assets**, sometimes described as **use of funds**.

What is a balance sheet?

A balance sheet is a list of all the assets and all the liabilities. The reason for the term **balance sheet** is that the *total* amount of assets *must* equal the liabilities. In other words, the figures must 'balance'. The business has to account for every penny that it has borrowed and explain how it has been used.

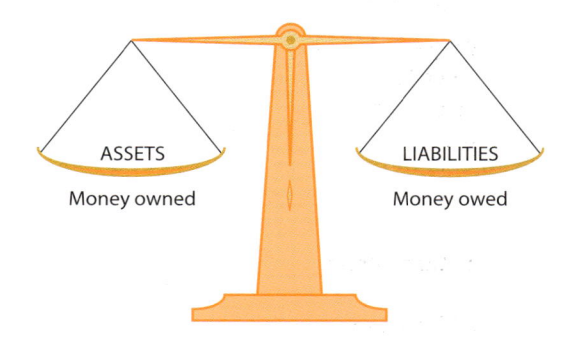

The reason for the term 'balance sheet'

A balance sheet is produced by all but the smallest businesses at the end of the financial year. This is also the last day of the year for which the profit and loss account is calculated. You may wish to look back at the diagram on page 366 to refresh your memory on how the various financial events fit together.

A key point about balance sheets is that they are a snapshot. In other words, they are a list of all the assets and liabilities on *one particular day*. If a company's financial year ends on 31 May, then the balance sheet is only true on that day. If, for some reason, a balance sheet were to be produced on 1 June, it would tell a slightly different story. In contrast, profit and loss accounts summarise activities over the whole financial year.

The purpose of a balance sheet

The main purpose of a balance sheet is to provide financial information, particularly to those who have lent money to the business. The balance sheet shows how this money has been used, and whether it has been spent on buildings, equipment, stock or other items. It is also of interest to:

- anyone who is thinking of investing in the business by buying shares
- banks and other institutions who have lent money already, or who may be asked to lend money to the business in the future
- customers who want to know if they can rely on the business in future years
- suppliers who want to know if the company can pay its bills.

Finally, the current balance sheet can be compared with those from previous years to look for trends. It can also be compared with those of businesses which are in similar markets to see, for example, if some are more profitable than others.

In this chapter you will learn how to understand the format of a balance sheet and how assets and liabilities are calculated.

It makes you think!

When a business wants to raise money, it must state how this money will be used. There are legal issues if a business raises money for a stated purpose and uses it for something completely different. Investors will therefore look for relevant items on the balance sheet. For instance, investors in a car manufacturer would expect to see large entries on the balance sheet for buildings and specialised equipment. On the other hand, a retailer of high-quality musical instruments may rent the premises it uses and, in this case, a major asset on the balance sheet would be the stock of instruments.

Within your group, decide the main items on which each of the following businesses would spend their money:

a a pharmaceutical company which is trying to find a cure for arthritis
b a mail order company which sells gifts and clothing by post
c a property development company which buys and renovates shopping centres
d an airline
e your school or college.

Understanding balance sheets

The design of a balance sheet

All balance sheets are designed in the same way. They have two main headings – assets and liabilities – and each of these headings has two sub-headings. Overall, you will see four sub-headings. These are:

(**Assets**)
    Fixed assets
    Current assets
(**Liabilities**)
    Current liabilities
    Capital and reserves.

The headings on a balance sheet

Each heading has a particular meaning. These are summarised below.

Assets are all the items *owned* by the business, and liabilities relate to money *owed* by the company.

Fixed assets

These are assets which the organisation owns and which it will probably keep for several years so they are *fixed* in the company. This section of the balance sheet will include the value of buildings and their fittings such as heating equipment, machinery, vehicles, office furniture and computers. The main points about fixed assets are:

- they last for several years
- they normally cost a lot of money and are not bought very often
- they have a resale value.

This part of the balance sheet changes dramatically only when there is a major purchase or when a capital item is sold.

Current assets

The use of the word 'current' means that the assets will not stay in the business for long. For example, a car showroom could take delivery of five cars and have sold them within a week. More cars will arrive to be sold and so on. In this case, the balance sheet would show the value of the number of cars in the showroom on the last day of the financial year.

Another kind of current assets is **debtors**. Debtors are people who owe the business money. They have received goods or services and have not yet paid for them. This process could take a month or more. Debtors are classed as an asset because the money they owe belongs to the company.

The final main type of asset is the amount of money in the bank on the last day of the financial year. If the business was overdrawn, the figure would be negative.

Current liabilities

The word 'current' is used for the same reason as it was used in current assets. The value is temporary and may change every day. Current liabilities are the amount of money which the company owes other businesses or people, known as **creditors**. The money may still be in the business's bank account but it will have to be paid soon. Some of it will leave the bank account shortly after the day the balance sheet is compiled, when the business next pays its bills.

Capital and reserves

This section records the amount of money which the business has borrowed on a long-term basis to start up and fund its operation. It includes three main items – **share capital**, **reserves** and **profit and loss account**.

- Share capital is the original amount of money paid to the business in return for shares. The business pays dividends to the shareholders each year from the profit it makes.
- Businesses do not give all of their profits back to shareholders. They retain some to re-invest in the business and help it to grow. This money still belongs to the shareholders and is called reserves.
- The net profit from the **profit and loss account** for the financial year just ended is transferred into the balance sheet. In the next year's balance sheet, this amount will be added to the reserves. Really, it would make more sense if the heading was '*from* profit and loss account'!

Fact file

Many people confuse **debtors** (those who owe money) and **creditors** (those who are owed money). Use the illustration below to help you to remember the difference!

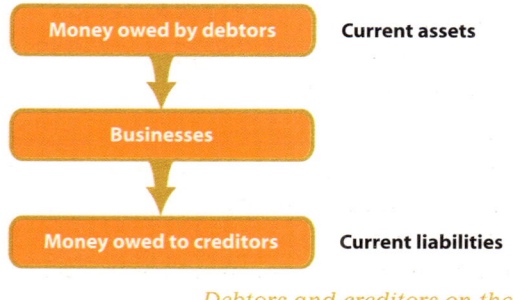

Money owed by debtors → **Current assets**

↓

Businesses

↓

Money owed to creditors → **Current liabilities**

Debtors and creditors on the balance sheet

Spot check

Write down your answers to the following questions:

1. Why is a 'balance' sheet so called?
2. What is an asset?
3. What is a liability?
4. A balance sheet is often called a 'snapshot'. Why is this?
5. What is the key point to remember about the relationship between total assets and total liabilities on a balance sheet?
6. State the main difference between a fixed asset and a current asset.
7. Are debtors an asset or a liability? Explain your answer.
8. What are current liabilities?

It makes you think!

Within your group, divide the following list of items into two columns, one headed 'assets' and the other headed 'liabilities':

- Stock
- Equipment
- Premises
- Share capital
- Creditors
- Money in bank
- Debtors
- Computers
- Reserves

Fact file

After the 'creditors' heading on the balance sheet, you will sometimes see the words **amounts falling due within one year**. Businesses sometimes borrow money which does not have to be paid back for several years. If this is the case, the money owed to this type of creditor would *not* be included under current liabilities.

The calculations on a balance sheet

Study the balance sheet shown below. Most of the headings and other items on the left-hand side have already been described. The new ones are the calculations which have to be done to make the balance sheet complete:

Total fixed assets – this is the sum of all the fixed assets. In the balance sheet below it is the total of the two figures for buildings and equipment.

Total current assets – this is calculated by adding up the figures for stock, debtors and cash in bank.

Net current assets/liabilities – this is found by adding the *total* current assets to the creditors' figure. Note that the creditors' figure is negative so that adding them together subtracts the second from the first. This figure is an indication of the business's ability to meet its short-term debts. If it is positive, the business should be able to pay off all its creditors and still have money left over.

Total assets less current liabilities – this is found by adding the totals for the fixed and the current assets together and then subtracting the amount owed to creditors, or, strictly speaking, adding the last figure since it is already negative! This figure should equal the one on the last line, shareholders' funds.

Shareholders' funds – this is simply the last entries for share capital, reserves and profit and loss account added together. It should be equal to the 'Total assets minus current liabilities' figure. This is the amount of money

BALANCE SHEET	
ASSETS	**£**
Fixed assets	
Buildings	50,000
Equipment	25,000
Total fixed assets	75,000
Current assets	
Stock	30,000
Debtors	20,000
Cash at bank	10,000
Total current assets	60,000
LIABILITIES	
Current liabilities	
Creditors: amounts falling due within one year	−15,000
Net current assets/liabilities	45,000
Total assets less current liabilities	120,000
Capital and reserves	
Share capital	80,000
Reserves	30,000
Profit and loss account	10,000
Shareholders' funds	120,000

which belongs to the shareholders. It is made up of the original amount the shareholders invested by buying shares plus the profits which the business has made by using the money to run the business since the investment was made.

Over to you!

The layout of a balance sheet is fairly standard and many public limited companies make their financial reports available on their website. For example, if you log on to Marks & Spencer's site – wwwheinemann.co.uk/hotlinks – you will find its financial reports under the heading 'Investor relations'.

1. Access the company's balance sheet and check its design and layout. You will find a few minor headings added, but the overall structure is the same as the ones in this section.
2. Why has Marks & Spencer put its balance sheet in the section headed 'Investor relations'? Compare your ideas with other students in your group.

Fact file

When a negative figure appears on a financial statement, it normally has a negative sign in front of it, e.g. –£500. Sometimes negative numbers are put in brackets with no negative sign, e.g. (500). The reason for this is that some people argue that a minus sign is easy to miss. If you checked out Marks & Spencer's balance sheet, you would have found that brackets are used. When you are next working on spreadsheets, try putting a figure in brackets, but beware! Some spreadsheet packages automatically remove the brackets and insert a minus sign.

Public limited companies, such as Marks and Spencer, are required to publish their accounts

Computers and balance sheets

Spreadsheets can be used to produce balance sheets. Large organisations such as Marks & Spencer use sophisticated accounting software to produce their balance sheet. Even small businesses can buy 'off-the-shelf' accounting software packages which will automatically produce their balance sheet at the end of each financial year.

Try setting up a balance sheet using a spreadsheet package, but be aware that the formulae used are a little more complicated than you may normally insert and one simple error will throw the calculations out. However, once you know the formulae are correct, you can be certain that all your calculations will be correct as well!

Chapter review and practice questions

1. Decide whether each of the following statements is true or false:
   a. Balance sheets summarise a year's transactions.
   b. The only people interested in a balance sheet are the business's accountants.
   c. In a balance sheet, the total assets should be the same as the total liabilities.
   d. Current assets is a term used to describe 'temporary' assets which may change soon.
   e. The main purpose of a balance sheet is to show what has happened to the money invested in a business.
   f. Items are called fixed assets because they are bolted to the floor.
   g. Balance sheets are normally produced once a year, at the end of the financial year.

2. Identify the items on a balance sheet which show money that belongs to the shareholders.

3. Below is shown a balance sheet for Superfit plc, a national chain of leisure centres. All the figures have been entered but none of the calculations have been carried out.
   a. Copy out and complete the balance sheet. There is an '*' in each space you need to complete.
   b. Which two figures do you need to check to show that your calculations are correct?

SUPERFIT PLC BALANCE SHEET	£
ASSETS	
Fixed assets	
Buildings	100,000
Equipment	45,000
Total fixed assets	*
Current assets	
Stock	30,000
Debtors	40,000
Cash at bank	15,000
Total current assets	*
LIABILITIES	
Current liabilities	
Creditors: amounts falling due within one year	−25,000
Net current assets/liabilities	*
Total assets less current liabilities	*
Capital and reserves	
Share capital	150,000
Reserves	45,000
Profit and loss account	10,000
Shareholders' funds	*

Integrated activity

You work for Kenware Motors Ltd and have been asked to help to prepare their balance sheet for the year. The finance manager, Paula Prescot, has given you the following information and has asked you to prepare a draft version which she will check later today.

Buildings	£37,000
Equipment	£21,000
Debtors	£17,000
Creditors	£16,000
Share capital	£63,000
Cash in bank	£12,000
Profit and loss account	£10,000
Stock	£32,000
Reserves	£30,000

1. Make all the entries and carry out the calculations required. Use the correct format (as shown on the page opposite). Note that, in agreement with your tutor, you could produce this on a spreadsheet.
2. When you take the balance sheet back to Paula for checking she apologises to you. By mistake, she gave you outdated information. She asks you to:
   a. increase the debtors by £10,000
   b. increase the value of the buildings by £20,000
   c. change the share capital to £100,000
   d. change the transfer from the profit and loss account to −£6,000
   e. change the amount owed by creditors to £25,000.

   Make out a revised balance sheet with the new financial information.

suppliers and wages *and* to cope with minor emergencies. Anyone looking at this figure would be concerned if the account was overdrawn. It could mean that the business is not making enough money to cover its expenses.

Creditors

A high figure for current liabilities could mean that the business is not paying its bills reasonably quickly. This could mean that the business is in trouble and, in any event, it would be upsetting suppliers. A high figure for other types of loans would be examined carefully, in case the business was borrowing too much money and might struggle to repay the loan. If interest rates increased unexpectedly, the company would have increased payments to make.

Share capital, reserves, profit and loss account

The money listed under these headings all belongs to the shareholders – see also pages 374–375.

Shareholders' funds

This figure is the total amount of money which 'belongs' to all the shareholders. Unless something unusual happens, they cannot actually have this money. If a business goes into liquidation, shareholders receive only any money left over after other debtors such as the Inland Revenue and employees' salaries have been paid. In practice, this may mean that they receive very little, or even nothing at all. As you learned in Unit 2, page 152, most shareholders will sell their shares if they are unhappy with the performance of the company.

Combining figures

As well as looking at individual items, stakeholders may also look at combinations of figures. For example:

- **Sales and profit.** At first sight, a large increase in sales looks good. However, if the profit has gone down, then the efficiency of the business has fallen. Many businesses fail by over-trading, in other words they try to grow too rapidly. An increase in profits, even if sales have gone down, is probably a healthier sign.
- **Cash at bank and creditors**. If the cash figure is higher than the amount listed against creditors, the business could pay all of its bills immediately. If the figures were reversed, creditors could become nervous and stop supplying goods.
- **Cash at bank and debtors**. At first sight, a low amount of money in the bank could spell trouble. However, if the debtors' figure is high, this simply means that the business is not good at collecting its debts.

Snapshot

Going for broke!

Until the early 1990s, a company called GEC had performed well over many years. It ran a variety of businesses making traditional goods such as washing machines and railway locomotives. It had paid good dividends and the share price increased steadily. It also had £3 billion in reserves. Some people called this a 'cash mountain'.

By the end of the 1990s the company had changed its name to Marconi. It then changed its strategy and sold off many of its original businesses and used its reserves to invest heavily in the high-tech sector. Several of these new businesses got into trouble and, by the end of 2001, Marconi was also in real danger of going bankrupt.

One of Marconi's managers was encouraged to buy shares and, at one time, when the price was over £15, his holding was worth £350,000. When the business got into trouble, the share price fell to below £1 and the total value of his holding fell to £16,000.

Marconi has now changed its strategy again. It is trying to get rid of many businesses in which it invested earlier, and to build up its business again. You may find it interesting to see if it succeeds!

Stakeholders interested in business accounts

Stakeholders interested in business accounts

Shareholders

Shareholders can be private individuals who buy shares hoping to make money out of them. It is an alternative to investing in a bank's savings account to earn interest. Investing in shares is more risky than using a savings account since the value of the shares can fall as well as rise. However, on average the returns are usually greater over a long period of time.

Most shares are owned by other businesses, such as insurance companies. These are called **institutional shareholders**. They invest for the same reason as private individuals. Quite often, senior managers and directors have shares in their own business. Employees may also own shares and some businesses encourage employees to do this through a share option scheme (see Snapshot on page 153).

Shareholders have only one decision to make, whether to keep their shares or sell them. If sales and profit are both increasing, they will probably decide to hold on to them.

Managers

In large businesses there may be several levels of managers, as you saw in Unit 2, Chapter 9. Senior managers and directors decide on the strategy of the business. In other words, they try to make the business more profitable, or at least keep things on an even keel. Some businesses offer senior managers annual bonuses based on the performance of the business as a whole. Different senior managers will also have particular interests. For example, the sales director will look at the sales figure, the finance director will wonder if the debtors' figure could be reduced while the managing director will be interested in (among other things) the overall net profit. All the managers will be interested in the overall performance of the company because serious problems could mean their jobs are threatened. In addition, it is quite common for senior managers to hold shares in their company.

Employees

Employees do not normally have much influence in how the business as a whole is run, unless they belong to a workers' co-operative. However, all employees have an interest in how well the business is doing. If business is good, they can expect reasonable pay rises each year and job security. If a business gets into trouble, there could be no pay rise (a pay freeze) or, even worse, redundancies. In addition, employees can hold shares and some businesses pay all their employees a bonus if it performs well. Employees would therefore probably look at the sales and profit figures first.

Banks

All businesses have a bank account so the bank can see each day the 'cash at bank' figure which appears on the balance sheet once a year. If the account becomes overdrawn, the bank will know immediately and will ask some serious questions unless it has been warned! Other than this, the bank has no particular interest in how well the business is performing, provided that it is happy that any overdraft can be paid off as agreed.

However, banks *also* lend money to businesses over a period which can be several years, as you will see in the next chapter.

In this case, the bank will want to be sure that the loan can be repaid. It may insist that the loan is repaid immediately if the business seems to be in trouble. A low profit figure would worry the bank.

Customers

When you buy a pair of shoes from a shop, you are a retail customer. If the shoes develop a fault, you would expect to be able to take them back to the shop and get your money back. If, when you returned to the shop, you found it closed with a big notice in the window saying 'Business closed due to bankruptcy' you would have a problem. Had you known that the business was having problems, you might not have risked buying the shoes. Even so, you do not usually find customers asking to see the shop's business accounts to make sure that the business is being run well! This is because, if one shop closed down, you would normally have others to choose from, so you may not be very concerned.

The situation can be very different, however, for business customers. For example, an aircraft manufacturer such as Airbus would probably buy many engines from Rolls-Royce. This is a very big commitment. The engines take a long time to produce, cost a lot of money and spare parts are needed for many years after the engines have been delivered. In other words, the customer (Airbus) has a large and long-term relationship with its supplier. If Rolls-Royce got into financial difficulties and went out of business, Airbus would have a major problem. So, Airbus has a keen interest in Rolls-Royce's

The interests of stakeholders in the profit and loss account and balance sheet

Stakeholder	Profit and loss account	Balance sheet
Shareholders	Sales – are they increasing year by year? Profit – this money 'belongs' to the shareholders. In practice only some of it is given to them as dividends. The rest is re-invested in the business which will affect future profits	Probably the first figure shareholders look at is the 'Shareholders' funds' figure. This influences the share price. If it keeps increasing, the share price will rise They may also be interested in the general health of the business by looking at cash at bank, and creditors and debtors
Managers	Similar to shareholders In addition they may be shareholders in their own right. If they have made good business decisions, sales should have increased as well as profits There may also be a bonus system linked to profits But if sales and profits are down, managers could lose their jobs!	Senior managers will be interested in all major aspects of the balance sheet, e.g. is the figure for debtors increasing? They will be more interested in the current health of the business which is given by the assets and creditors' figures
Employees	Increased sales and profits means that the business is healthy and jobs and wage increases are secure	Employees will be more interested in the balance sheet if they own shares (see Shareholders above)
Banks	Good profits mean that any loans can be repaid	Banks should already know the 'cash at bank figure'!
Customers	Healthy sales and profits indicate that the business is being well managed and should be able to supply goods or services in the future	The creditors' figure suggests how quickly or otherwise the business pays its debts

financial situation. There are many other examples of situations where business customers are very interested in the financial health of their suppliers.

Such customers would also want to know that the supplier pays its debts regularly and if sales and profits show that the business has a healthy future.

The chart on page 382 summarises the interests of different stakeholders in relation to both the profit and loss account and the balance sheet.

It makes you think!

Within your group, read the following and then answer the questions below.

You may remember that suppliers are another important type of business stakeholder. Imagine you supply office furniture to businesses. You allow all your customers to buy on credit, that is buy now, pay later.

You are approached by a large organisation to refurbish all their offices. The contract is worth £2 million! You will have to buy all the supplies and fit the furniture *before* you are paid yourself.

1. How interested would you be in the financial 'health' of your customer?
2. What figures on the profit and loss account and the balance sheet would you most like to see? Explain the reasons for your choice.
3. Would you still go ahead with the 'deal' if the company was private and refused to let you see its accounts?

Chapter review and practice questions

1 Decide whether each of the following statements is true or false:
   a If a business makes a profit, no one is interested in the rest of the accounts.
   b The creditors' figure shows how much the business owes.
   c If the cash at bank figure is much higher than the creditors' figure, the business could pay off all of its debts instantly.
   d Private customers are usually more interested in the financial health of a supplier than business customers are.
   e Almost all stakeholders are interested in the net profit figure.
   f The sales director is responsible mainly for the sales figure on the balance sheet.
   g Only public limited companies have shareholders.

2 Identify the main interest of each of the following groups of stakeholders when examining a company's financial accounts:
   a a shareholder
   b a business customer who is interested in buying an expensive machine from the company
   c an employee who works for the company
   d a senior manager in the company
   e the manager of a rival company.

3 A private limited company wants to take out a bank loan to finance an expansion programme. The managing director visits the bank with this year's accounts.
   a The bank manager asks for the accounts for three previous years as well. Suggest one reason why these are needed.
   b The bank manager points out that the debtors' figure is very high. What does this mean, and why is the manager concerned?
   c The bank manager then studies the net profit figure carefully for each year. Explain the importance of this information and how it would affect the bank's decision.

Integrated activity

This activity is rather different from the others in this unit. Start by dividing into four groups:

Group A – shareholders with a substantial investment in the company

Group B – senior managers who are responsible for the company's performance. They include the managing director, the financial manager and the sales manager

Group C – a group of employees who work for the company and also own a few shares each through the company share scheme

Group D – represents a large business organisation which is considering giving a major contract to the company.

Scenario: P & J Systems is a specialist computer supplier to business. It gives advice on computer network systems (where all the computers are linked) and IT equipment. It will advise on and install IT equipment, business software and IT security systems and upgrade these as required. It also has a new media department which designs and maintains websites, including web stores, for clients. P & J employs 80 staff who all work on the same site. It has been in business for three years and the latest financial figures have just been released.

1. Study the figures carefully and decide:
    a. the key items in which you are interested
    b. what the figures tell you about the 'financial health' of the company.
2. List any concerns you have and compare these with those raised by other groups.
3. Finally, decide what action you think P & J senior managers should take, if any.

Extracts from P & J Systems accounts

	May 2002 £	May 2003 £
Sales	1,350,000	1,470,000
Net profit	254,000	173,000
Debtors	121,000	187,000
Cash at bank	87,000	23,000
Creditors	64,000	97,000
Reserves	894,000	1,149,000
Shareholders' funds	2,708,000	2,881,000

Chapter 26: Sources of business finance

What you will learn

Understanding sources of finance
A summary of factors affecting the choice of funding sources

Overview: sources of finance

The need for money!

Many of the companies which are household names were founded by one or a few people who used their own money to start and run a business. For example, Carphone Warehouse was started by Charles Dunstone in 1989 using £6,000 of his own money. He had decided that there was a gap in the mobile phone market, selling to private customers and small businesses. Most firms in the market were concentrating on big businesses. He felt that private individuals needed careful advice, and a high level of customer care was his main aim. He quickly linked up with two partners who also invested in the business.

The business grew by re-investing profits and by June 2000, Charles Dunstone had over 1,000 shops and the business was said to be worth £2 billion. Because Charles and his partners wanted to expand even further, they decided to float the business on the stock exchange by selling shares. This was the first time that they had needed other people's money.

From 1989 to 2000, Charles Dunstone and his partners had made some deliberate decisions about finance. They decided not to ask for a bank loan or any other type of money. Then they decided to raise money by selling shares on the stock market, instead of choosing any other method. In this chapter you will learn about the different options available to business and will see why managers often make specific choices, as Charles Dunstone did.

All businesses need money to survive

Businesses need money:

- when they first **start up**
- to **expand** and **grow**.

The options available

There are several ways that businesses can obtain money, including:

- **owners' funds** – when the owner puts his or her own money into the business
- **profits** – when the owner 'ploughs' back profits to help the business to grow
- **loans** – when the owner decides to borrow money
- **government grants** – which are available for specific reasons
- **hiring and leasing** – which give options when obtaining new machinery or equipment
- **issuing shares** – as Charles Dunstone did
- **selling assets** – such as selling spare land to raise money
- **venture capital** – when the investor often takes a 'stake' in the business.

Each of these has its advantages and disadvantages. This chapter looks at these and

Differences between a bank loan and an overdraft

Bank loan	Bank overdraft
The money is paid back over an agreed period, e.g. three or five years	Overdrafts are temporary (e.g. for a few months) and for relatively small amounts of money for day-to-day expenses. They are not normally used for capital investment
The interest rates are quite high	They are part of a current account arrangement so that money can be borrowed or repaid on a daily daily basis
The interest rate can be fixed for the whole period or can vary depending on the general rise and fall of interest rates	Interest is paid only on the amount outstanding each day
If repayments are not kept up, the bank can ask for the total amount of money to be repaid	The interest rate is quite high in comparison with other forms of loan
Loans are often 'secured' against a fixed asset such as a building. If the business defaults on the loan (does not repay it), the secured item belongs to the bank	There is usually no requirement to provide security

Government grants

The government department which aims to improve the performance of business in the United Kingdom is the Department of Trade and Industry (DTI). If you undertook the activity on page 156, and researched the DTI yourself, you should already know quite a lot about its work. Its main aims are to:

- encourage business start-ups
- help small and medium-sized businesses to grow
- promote best practice
- encourage unemployed people to start a business
- promote businesses in disadvantaged areas
- encourage the development of new technology
- encourage businesses to adopt computer-based technology

The following are some of the types of grants and assistance available:

- **Assisted areas** – these are areas of the country which have been identified as needing extra help because unemployment is high and the economy is poor. There are several types of help available. One example is Regional Selective Assistance where grants are offered for projects of over £500,000 if jobs would be created or preserved. In a similar way, businesses employing fewer than 250 employees may be able to receive grants for projects under £50,000.
- **Small Firms Loan Guarantee** – guarantees are made to help small businesses obtain a bank loan. This happens when there is a viable proposal but the bank is unwilling to lend the money because the business cannot offer security against the loan.
- **UK online for business** – this helps businesses exploit the benefits of computer technologies to improve competitiveness.

There are several government departments which deal with specific kinds of grants and advice. The easiest way for businesses to find out what is available is to contact a local office of one of the following organisations, which are part-funded by the DTI: Business Link in England, Small Business Gateway in Scotland, Business Connect in Wales and Ednet in Northern Ireland.

Grants and advice for small and medium-sized businesses are available through Business Link offices in England

In addition to assistance from national government sources, help is also available from the following:

- **Local authorities** are keen to attract businesses to their area and help existing businesses to develop. The department responsible for this is the Economic Development office. The types of assistance available include help with finding premises, financial assistance, job creation grants and rent-free periods.
- The **European Union** (EU) provides help for disadvantaged areas (see page 32).

Snapshot

Financial help for young entrepreneurs

There are two non-government bodies which support young people who are starting their own business:

- Shell LiveWIRE is aimed at people aged between 16 and 30 years who are thinking of starting a business or who are in their first 18 months of trading. Individuals who contact LiveWIRE receive information and support from one of their advisers. In addition, there is an annual competition with cash prizes as high as £10,000.
- The Prince's Trust also supports 18–30-year-olds who have a business idea. It is aimed at people who are unemployed or disadvantaged. Applicants have to produce a viable business plan and, if successful, can receive a loan of up to £5,000. The loan is interest-free for the first six months and after this, a low level of interest is charged. Repayment is after four years. Volunteer business mentors give encouragement and support. The trust operates in England, Wales and Northern Ireland. The Prince's Scottish Youth Business Trust offers a similar scheme in Scotland.

The Prince's Trust has helped many young people to set up in business

Spot check

Write down your answers to the following questions:

1. State two reasons why additional business finance may be required.

2.
   a. Briefly explain the term 'owners' funds'.
   b. Why might an entrepreneur prefer to use only his or her own money to start a business?

3. Identify two differences between a bank loan and an overdraft.

4. Identify one advantage and one disadvantage of reinvesting the profits from a business to finance its expansion.

5. Identify the major drawback of a small business owner remortgaging his or her house for capital.

6. State two types of grants available from the government for business.

Over to you!

Divide into six groups. Each group is responsible for one of the following tasks:

Group 1: Visit your local Economic Development office to find out about sources of business finance for your area.

Group 2: Visit your local Business Link office and find out about government grants for businesses in your region.

Groups 3–6: Visit four major banks in your area and obtain leaflets on sources of finance available to businesses.

Then prepare a summary page which can be photocopied and given to other members of the class. Your tutor may also want you to make a short presentation to summarise your findings.

You can also find out this information on the websites of these organisations, but this time it is your job to find the website yourself! You may also wish to supplement your information with that obtained from the DTI on business support (see page 156).

Hiring and leasing

You already know that businesses need to spend money on fixed or capital assets such as buildings, machinery, computers and vehicles. Purchases can be made when a business starts up or when it has been running for some time. In the second case, this may be because of expansion or because out-of-date equipment needs replacing. The business may have to take out a loan to cover the cost or fund it from retained profits.

An alternative to buying an asset outright is to **hire** or **lease** it. This happens when another specialist finance company pays for the asset at the start and then hires or leases it back to the business which needs the asset.

Hiring

Some people hire a car when they go abroad on holiday. They do this because it is not possible to take their car with them if they are flying. The cost of renting is high, compared with owning a car at home, but it is worth it for the short period.

Businesses occasionally hire things for a short period for similar reasons. Executives travelling on business frequently hire a car. A firm will hire a hotel conference suite which will hold a large number of delegates for a sales promotion. A factory may hire large portable heaters until a faulty heating system is repaired. However, in general, businesses do not hire things for short periods on a regular basis. If they need to use something often, they buy it outright or lease it.

Leasing

This works in a similar way to hiring. The leasing company (known as the **lessor**) owns the property and reclaims it at the end of the leasing period. Regular instalments are paid, either every month or every year. Some leasing agreements allow the business which has been using the asset (known as the **lessee**) to buy it at the end of the leasing period. Leasing is often used for cars, photocopiers and transport vehicles. Aircraft are also often leased to airlines.

The following are the main advantages of leasing:

- The assets can be used immediately while allowing repayments to be staggered. This helps the company's cash flow (see Chapter 20).
- The most up-to-date technology can be obtained which increases productivity and efficiency.
- The finance company may take responsibility for repairs, servicing and even insuring the asset.
- The asset can be reclaimed by the finance company only if the business defaults on its payments.

The following are the main disadvantages of leasing:

- The total amount paid is more than the actual cost of the asset because of the interest paid.
- The business must keep the asset until the lease agreement expires, even if it finds that it does not need it before that time. It cannot send it back earlier than expected to save money!

Issuing shares

Shares can be issued by private limited companies and public limited companies (plcs), but only shares issued by plcs can be bought by the public (see Unit 1, Chapter 2, pages 18–19).

A successful private company may decide to 'float' the company – and become a plc – to raise more capital. This is what Carphone Warehouse decided to do.

Public limited companies can also issue additional shares to finance expansion at a later date. This is known as a **rights issue**. They offer extra shares to existing shareholders at a reduced price to tempt them to buy.

Many plcs offer two types of shares: **ordinary shares** and **preference shares**. Preference shares are slightly different because shareholders who own them are paid a *fixed* dividend. In addition, these shareholders take preference if the company experiences financial difficulties. Preference shareholders would be paid out first, hence the name.

The problem for many plcs is that the value of their shares can fluctuate for other reasons besides company performance. Institutional

Snapshot

Hire and hire!

Although the last thing on your mind at a school speech night may have been your surroundings, if you had been observant, you would have probably seen potted plants all around the entrance or stage. The same type of plants are to be found in the reception areas of many companies and are hired from specialist horticultural firms who both provide and maintain the plants on either a short- or long-term basis.

On a larger scale, if you visited Wimbledon or Henley out of season, or if you live near a golf course which hosts the British Open, then you will see hiring firms completely transform the area when an event is scheduled. Marquees, tables, chairs, catering equipment, gas cookers, fridges and dozens of other supplies are moved in, set up and then dismantled at the end. Specialist firms work to a strict schedule and must prove they can stick to this to win the next contract.

Whereas hiring is big business for sporting events, in other areas leasing is more popular and is growing in popularity for IT installations. Some computer manufacturers, such as Dell and IBM, now set up their own leasing agreements with customers which includes IT support. Their aim is to increase sales.

The Finance and Leasing Association estimates that a quarter of all fixed capital investment is now done by leasing or hiring. You can find out more from its website at www.heinemann.co.uk/hotlinks

shareholders normally want rapid and constant returns on their investment and may take a dim view of plans to reinvest profits or continually expand. Richard Branson became so weary of interference from the City in the way he ran his business that he bought the shares for Virgin back again!

However, life may not always be wonderful for shareholders, either. Between 2000 and 2002, the value of shares fell in the UK and in January 2002, the seventh largest business in the USA, Enron, collapsed. Many Enron employees had been considerably encouraged to buy shares and, in addition, the company pension fund held shares in the business. These employees suffered enormously after the collapse – not only did they lose jobs, but their savings and pension as well.

> **Snapshot**
>
> *Aiming to encourage business!*
>
> The London Stock Exchange was founded in 1760. Its task is to process the buying and selling of shares in public limited companies. The people who do this are called members. Most companies are quoted on the main market listing, but in 1995 another option became available. AIM – the Alternative Investment Market – was launched to encourage small but growing companies to become plcs.
>
> To gain some idea of the size of the operation:
>
> - In 2001, £125 billion pounds was raised by UK companies
> - On an average day, 6 billion shares are bought or sold.
> - There were about 2,500 companies registered on the main market and 500 on AIM in 2002.
>
> The cost of registering is as little as £5,000.
>
> Shares can be bought and sold on the Internet.
>
> Over 70 per cent of shares are owned by institutional investors such as insurance companies and pension funds.

Selling assets

At first sight, this may seem like a backward step – just like someone selling their home because they can't afford the mortgage. However, on some occasions a business may have sound reasons for selling assets as part of its long-term development plan. This would be the case if the business plans to use the money raised to fund a project which would make *more* money than could be made by keeping the asset. The main examples of this are listed below.

Sell/lease-back

On pages 390–391, you saw how companies can hire or lease buildings or equipment to save having to find the cost of purchasing them. If a business owns an asset such as a building, and needs to raise capital, it can sell the building to a specialist finance company. Both businesses will agree a contract which states that the original owner will be able to use the premises and pay rent. The company selling the property hopes to make enough money by investing the capital released to more than cover the rent.

Old equipment

A business could have a three-year-old black and white photocopier and need a colour copier. A less advanced business might be happy to buy the second-hand copier. The selling business could use the proceeds of the sale towards buying a new copier. Alternatively, a company upgrading its IT provision could sell off its old computers cheaply to staff.

Relocation

Businesses sometimes decide that it would be cheaper to run their operation in another location and move from an expensive town centre site to cheaper premises on the outskirts. A more drastic example would be where a business moves from the southeast of England to a deprived area such as the North East or Scotland where wages and premises are much less costly. In addition, there may be grants available in the new location (see also Unit 1, Chapter 3, page 32).

Sub-contracting

This is when a business arranges for another company to carry out some of its work. Usually, the sub-contracting company is specialised in a particular area and can do the work more cheaply. Where a business sub-contracts work, it may sell its surplus buildings and machinery as these are no longer needed. Sub-contracting is quite common in the aircraft manufacturing industry.

Selling a business

This is an extreme case of selling assets. Some very large businesses, called holding companies, own several smaller businesses, called subsidiaries. A holding company may sell a subsidiary if it finds a buyer who will pay a good price or if it decides just to concentrate on its core business operations (see Unit 1, Chapter 4, page 39). It may do this if it is having financial problems, such as Marconi, which you read about on page 380. Usually, the business is sold for more than the price paid originally, but not always. When McDonald's bought its 35 Aroma coffee shops, it paid £10.5 million, but when it sold 26 of them to Caffé Nero in 2002, it received less than £5.5 million (see page 369).

Venture capital

There are over 100 venture capital firms in the UK. This type of company specialises in investing money in businesses which are not listed on the stock exchange. They are interested in businesses which have the potential to grow rapidly and have good management. The following are the main aspects of the investment:

- The venture capital company becomes a shareholder in the business so that, although they may receive dividends, their main aim is for the businesses to grow rapidly so that share prices increase.
- Many venture capital companies play an active role in the business by sitting on the board of directors and even becoming involved in the day-to-day management. They can be a source of expert advice.
- Venture capital companies normally keep the shares for between three and seven years.
- They make most of their money by selling their shares when the business has grown. They may sell their shares back to the management or when the business is floated on the stock market.
- They can often be helpful for business start-ups.

As an example, Focus DIY began as a small chain of stores assisted by a bank loan of £300,000. A venture capital company, Duke Street Capital, took a 50 per cent share in the business and helped it to grow. By 2002, Focus had 428 outlets and was worth £1.2 billion. It was expected to be floated on the stock exchange within two years. Along the way, it had also bought Wickes DIY chain.

> **It makes you think!**
>
> Manchester United football club had a problem in 2002. David Beckham's contract was about to expire. If this had been allowed to happen, Beckham could have moved to another club without Manchester United receiving any transfer fee! The club had to decide whether to put Beckham on the transfer list or to renew his contract – and increase his salary to meet his demands.
>
> Within your group, imagine that you are running a football club which isn't doing too well. You have three choices:
>
> - To sell your star player – an excellent goal scorer – and buy three promising young players with the money you obtain.
> - To sell two average players and buy one promising young player.
> - Continue with the current team.
>
> 1. Decide the advantages and disadvantages of each option.
> 2. Agree what you would do.
> 3. Would your decision be any different if your star player was demanding a huge increase in salary next year?

Fact file

Two other sources of funds are useful to business. The first are **business angels** (see page 160).

The second are called **incubators** (after the machines used to help premature babies in their first weeks of life). They are useful for IT businesses in their early days. They offer premises, management advice, contacts with potential customers, funding, accountancy packages and companionship! Starting a business can be a lonely experience for a new entrepreneur.

A summary of factors affecting the choice of funding sources

As you saw on page 386, a business will consider various factors when deciding which source of funding to obtain. The chart on page 395 summarises these and compares them with each funding source for easy reference.

Chapter review and practice questions

1. Identify four major factors businesses must consider when deciding how to raise finance.

2. Decide whether each of the following statements is true or false:

   a. Owners never need external funding to start a business.
   b. Owners of businesses prefer to use their own money and retained profits because they can make their own decisions about what they do.
   c. Banks often ask for security when agreeing to a loan.
   d. Reinvesting the profits is the best way of raising large amounts of money.
   e. Loans have to be repaid after an agreed time.
   f. Banks always agree to a business having an overdraft.
   g. Grants from the government often depend on where the business is located.
   h. The Prince's Trust lends money only to people who are aged 35 and over.

3. Vision Cruise Lines plc is organising an event to promote its cruises. It intends to set up a large exhibition hall to look like various sections of a cruise ship. The company will invite previous and potential customers listed on its database, as well as all its shareholders. The following day is the annual general meeting and the chairman wants to persuade the shareholders that it will make financial sense for the company to expand by buying another cruise ship next year.

   a. What source of finance will Vision use to obtain use of the exhibition hall?
   b. Suggest three ways in which money could be raised to pay for the new cruise ship.
   c. Suggest one reason why shareholders will be concerned about the source of finance used.

Factors affecting choice of funding

Type of funding	Amount	Cost	Risk	Permanent or temporary	Influence/control	Advice
Owners' funds	Limited by the amount of cash the owner can obtain. Limited by profit made after start-up	No interest to pay. Limited by how much the owners can afford to leave in the business. Loss of interest on savings	Owners take their own risks with their own money. If they have borrowed money by mortgaging their house, they could lose their home	Permanent investment – hopefully, the benefits are growth in the value of the business	Owner retains complete control over the business	No formal advice available
Profits	Variable, depends on the success of the business	None – but depends on size of profit and how much is retained to fund growth	Owners take their own risk about how much profit to reinvest	Varies from year to year, but success breeds success!	It is the business's own money – it can spend it how it likes	No formal advice available
Loans	Depends on the bank's judgement of the business plan and/or business accounts	Interest rate normally quite high. Loan has to be repaid in full	Bank may demand all the money back if repayments are not made. Loans often secured against an asset which could be lost	Temporary – the loan must be repaid by the end of the agreed time	Bank checks the original proposal and may want updates. It will specify what can and cannot be done with the money	Specialist advisers available at bank
Government grants	Depends on the terms of the grant	None	Grant may be recalled if conditions are not fulfilled	A 'one-off' payment which does not have to be paid back	Probably none, after the initial approval process	Probably none
Hiring and leasing	Depends on the value of the item	Initial deposit for hiring, then fixed monthly payments. Leasing is similar but no initial deposit required	Item will be reclaimed if the payments are not kept up	Lasts for the duration of agreement	None	None
Issuing shares	No fixed limit	Dividends decided by the business, depending on the profit	Risk taken by the shareholder	Permanent, unless the business closes	Private shareholders have little practical influence. Institutional shareholders can have a powerful influence	Institutional shareholders don't usually offer advice, but views would be important to company
Selling assets	Depends on the market value of the asset	None	None, unless a buyer cannot be found	Permanent	Not applicable	None
Venture capital	Depends on the amount requested. Must be justified by the business plan	Dividends paid on shareholding	Shared by the owner and the venture capitalist	Temporary – normally 3–5 years	Varies, but normally the venture capitalist has a say in how things are run	Experienced advice available

Integrated activity

You are working at Business Link on work experience. One of the managers suggests you might be interested in suggesting the best source of finance for some of the enquiries she has just received.

In each case, suggest the funding source which might be the most appropriate and give a reason for your answer.

1. Bob is an electrician. He carries out domestic work such as rewiring houses. He has an old van which keeps breaking down and he is fed up with the repair bills. He does not want to take out a bank loan to buy a new van.
2. Imran has built up a successful business selling office stationery and equipment to local firms. It is extremely profitable. He has found out that a competitor is due to retire and wants to sell his business.
3. Louise is very artistic and did well at college. She is 20 years old and wants to set up a small business making silver jewellery.
4. Tinycraft produces high quality wooden toys for children. Most of the work is done by hand using a few simple power tools. A machine run by a computer has just been developed which would speed up production and reduce labour costs. It should pay for itself in three years. The business is healthy at present, but the profits have only just been enough to pay the owner's salary.
5. Cleanup Ltd makes a range of plastic domestic items such as nail brushes and washing-up brushes. Its machines are quite old and the company needs to replace them if it is to remain competitive. The business owns a plot of land next to the factory which it does not need.
6. Fitfreak Ltd has grown steadily over ten years and now runs over 100 fitness centres in central England. So far, it has used venture capital and retained profits to grow. The owners want to spread rapidly into the rest of the country.
7. Rashid and Shahida have worked together to develop a revolutionary new IT security system. They would welcome professional advice, although they know their business plan is excellent and the potential for their system is tremendous. They need substantial funding to launch their system, but would not object to losing some control over the business.
8. Kath was made redundant last year and received £20,000. She is interested in setting up a small business restoring antique furniture, which she has done as a hobby for many years.

Chapter 27 Financial planning

What you will learn

Understanding financial planning

Overview: financial planning

Financial planning and flexibility

You have already seen that businesses make financial plans using techniques such as cash-flow forecasting and budgeting. Many businesses carry out their activities from year to year without changing a great deal. They have several regular customers and the product or service does not change very quickly.

If they wish to introduce a new product or service, then this must be incorporated into their financial plans. In some industries, the process of planning and developing new products and services is methodical and part of the overall financial planning process. However, some types of businesses need to be able to change far more quickly. This may be:

- because the owner or senior managers are very ambitious and want to take advantage of every possible opportunity, e.g. Carphone Warehouse (see page 385).
- because of external events which affect the business and its financial plans.

Coping with the unexpected

British Airways is one business that was severely affected by external events on 11 September 2001. Following the terrorist attacks on the USA, demand for transatlantic air travel fell dramatically and BA's European operations were also severely affected because the public preferred cheaper services such as easyJet and Ryanair. Its forecast profits were no longer feasible and all the financial plans had to be revised very quickly.

These types of problems are not just confined to large businesses. For example, Phil Jobson ran a family business in Cumbria selling pharmaceutical products to vets. The business had been in the family for decades and, through continued hard work, had remained profitable and successful. Early in 2001, the foot-and-mouth epidemic in sheep and cattle occurred. Many thousands of animals were killed and Phil's business was in trouble since there were far fewer animals for the vets to attend to. He quickly decided to supply disinfectant which farmers were using to try to keep the disease at bay. It cost quite a lot of money to do this and he had to borrow money from the bank to cover the extra costs involved.

Coping with financial crises

Even the soundest of businesses has to take emergency action occasionally to cope with the unexpected. This chapter looks at how the financial procedures listed above can be used to help a business through a major change such as:

- an expansion of a business
- the cost of unexpected events
- a reduction in the costs of the business.

All of these situations would mean that financial plans would have to be changed. The revised plans would be needed by:

- business departments
- the business as a whole
- investors in the business
- creditors who might lend money to the business.

The main features of this chapter are illustrated using an ongoing case study, rather than a final integrated activity. It is recommended that you undertake each task as it occurs. This will also provide useful revision for many of the previous chapters you have studied.

Understanding financial planning

Case study scenario

Chris Thomas, managing director, Finefigs Ltd

Finefigs Ltd is a family business which was established in 1963 by John Thomas. It produces and sells plastic figures (such as soldiers from different armies and eras, for collectors) and small toys for Christmas crackers. It also has a contract to produce parts for children's dolls for a large toy manufacturer.

John borrowed money from his father to start the business and paid it back in three years. Since then, the business has been funded by retained profits. Recently, John has retired and the business has been taken over by his daughter, Chris, who is keen to expand it.

Chris had been running the business for six months when she read in the newspaper of a blockbuster animated children's film, *Greenworld*, which was being produced. The film tells the story of the animals and insects which live in a suburban garden. Unknown to the human owners, the various creatures have a society all of their own.

Chris realised that there would be a market for plastic models of the animals. She knew that other, larger manufacturers would have the same idea. However, after much travelling and several meetings, she was able to negotiate a contract to make the models. She was particularly pleased that the contract would not require any royalty payments to the film company in advance. However, after production had started, Finefigs would have to pay 5 per cent of the sales price in royalties for each figure produced, for permission to use the names from the film.

Cost of a new product

Chris calls a meeting of her senior managers to discuss the contract. She has 24 hours to decide whether or not to sign it. She has already asked her marketing and sales managers to forecast sales for the next 12 months. The answer was sales of 400,000 models based on a selling price of £2.50.

Using this figure as a target sales figure, Chris asked her other managers to think of all the other additional types of costs which would be incurred. She asked them to estimate each cost and split it into start-up and running costs. The information they provided is shown in the chart below.

It makes you think!

Study the information in the chart below and answer the following questions:

1. Why do you think the production section and the packaging section need extra members of staff?
2. How have the royalty payments been calculated? Check the figure to see if you agree with it.
3. To work out the break-even figure, Chris needs the costs divided into fixed costs and variable costs. She would prefer to pay for the new machine in the first year and therefore has called this a fixed cost. Decide under which heading you would put all the remaining costs, and in each case give a reason for your decision.

Chart showing start-up and running costs for Greenworld models

Department	Start-up costs	Running costs
Sales and marketing	None	Advertising – £30,000 Royalty payments to film company – £50,000
Production	New moulding machine – £82,000	Power – £500 Extra machine operator – £12,000
Purchasing	None	Additional raw plastic – £510,000
Finance	None	None
Packaging and transport	None	Extra packing operator – £12,000 Packing materials – £240,000

Break-even analysis

Chris has now worked out the figures she will use for her break-even analysis. This will help her to decide whether to sign the contract.

Chris's list is shown on page 404. Check if your answers to the questions below match hers!

Snapshot

No trains today courtesy of copyright!

All famous names are copyright – including the fictional character Harry Potter and the name of his creator, author J K Rowling. This means they must not be used on products or in promotions without special permission. Warner Brothers, the makers of the film Harry Potter and the Philosopher's Stone, *were keen to ensure this – so much so that companies involved in the film or the production of characters from the film had to sign special agreements.*

This meant, for instance, that the Hogwarts train, which is stored in a railway shed in the north of England, cannot be displayed as a tourist attraction despite the fact that many people would pay to see it.

It makes you think!

Chris has asked you to find out the break-even point for her. You can do this *either* by drawing a chart or by using the formula

$$\text{Break-even point} = \frac{\text{Fixed costs}}{\text{Selling price} - \text{Variable cost per unit}}$$

She reminds you of the information you need:

- the total fixed costs – which you have just calculated
- the selling price per unit – which Chris wants to be £2.50
- the variable cost per unit – this is the total variable costs (which you have just calculated) divided by the total number of units sold, which is predicted to be 400,000.

Chris has already decided that she will go ahead if she would make a profit on sales of over 300,000 figures.

What is your result? Will she go ahead?

Sources of business finance

While you are working, Chris and her financial manager are having a meeting. The financial manager is against the idea of paying for the machine in one year because this could affect the business's cash flow. It would be better, he argues, to pay for it over several years, out of earnings. In this case, they will need to find a suitable source of finance. Chris and her finance manager draw up a list of possibilities and make notes against each heading – see the chart below.

It makes you think!

1. Study Chris's financial options carefully. There are four possibilities. Identify these.
2. Within your group, decide the strengths and weaknesses of each possibility.
3. Put the possibilities in order of choice, with number one your preferred choice down to number four.

Chris and her finance manager work out how the project is to be funded

Chris's financial options

Funding	Comments
Owners' funds	The business is a private limited company. The shares are owned by Chris, her father and other family members. They are happy with the dividends they receive and do not want to invest any more money in the business. Chris has just bought a house and can only just afford the mortgage repayments
Profits	These have been healthy, but the retained profit will be needed to cover the extra running costs in the first 12 months
Loans	Chris's bank manager is quite interested in the idea. She says that she may be able to offer a loan but needs more information
Government grants	Chris contacts the local Business Links office. She is told that her business is not in an Assisted Area and that no grants are available
Hiring and leasing	Leasing the machine could be another option, but Chris would prefer to buy it outright as then she may be able to obtain a discount on the purchase price
Issuing shares	The family already owns shares. A possibility would be to offer shares to employees. Alternatively, Chris could plan to float the business on the stock market. This would be a major step and would take time to arrange. Chris is also concerned she could lose control of running the business
Selling assets	The business needs everything that it owns. Chris knows that she could probably sell the building on a sale/lease-back basis
Venture capital	This is a possibility, but Chris does not want to have anyone else having a say in the running of the business. She is also aware that venture capitalists prefer new, fast-growing enterprises. Chris's business is relatively unexciting and growing steadily, rather than rapidly

Making decisions

Chris now has some choices to make. She is able to make better decisions, because having updated financial information means she isn't guessing what to do! She is aware of the *consequences* of each decision, and that is important.

She has also involved her other managers at each stage, and will ask for their agreement about the eventual course of action. This is also important. If all the managers are fully aware of future plans and committed to the overall success of the business, they will ensure their departments work together to achieve their targets.

Following your information on break-even (see the key on page 404), Chris decides to go ahead. The project will start in April. She now has to decide about finance. As a first step, she wants to talk further to her bank manager to see whether a loan is a possibility, and what sort of terms and conditions would apply.

It makes you think!

Help Chris to prepare for the meeting with the bank manager.

1. What financial information will she require? List all the documents and *new* financial plans the bank manager will want to see.
2. The bank manager may ask for security against the loan. Suggest *one* type of security Chris could offer.
3. Chris thinks an overdraft would also be useful for the next few months until she starts receiving income from sales. What is the main difference between a loan and an overdraft?

Cash-flow forecast

The meeting at the bank goes well. The bank manager agrees to lend the money to purchase the new machine. Only interest will be paid for the first year, but the whole loan will have to be repaid by the end of three

Chris discusses the project with her managers. If the project is to be a success, she will need their commitment to it.

years, starting with repayments as well as the interest payments in the second year.

The bank manager says she will agree to an overdraft facility only once she has seen Chris's new cash-flow forecast. That afternoon the finance manager and the marketing and sales manager recalculate the company's cash flow to include the new contract work. The finance manager projects monthly income and expenditure while the sales director enters forecast sales.

The finance manager also suggests that cash flow would improve if the company could negotiate an agreement with Plastico, the suppliers of the raw plastic, to buy the plastic but pay for it only two or three months later. He agrees to find out if this would be a possibility.

It makes you think!

The bottom line of the cash-flow forecast is shown below. This is the line Chris studies, as it tells her how much money she will have in the bank each month. Study this yourself and answer the following:

1. For how many months is there a negative balance?
2. Why does the situation get worse before it gets better?
3. What is the maximum overdraft Chris would require in any month?
4. Given the figures and the overall trend, is the bank manager likely to agree to Chris's request? Give a reason for your decision.
5. Plastico is a supplier to Finefigs. Finefigs buys and pays its bills at the end of the following month.
   a. Is Plastico a debtor or a creditor?
   b. Explain why it would be helpful to Finefigs to negotiate a new agreement for a few months to delay payments.
   c. What would be the danger in Finefigs simply deciding not to pay Plastico for a few months without consulting it?

Month	April	May	June	July	Aug.	Sept.
Cash at bank (£)	50,000	5,000	(25,000)	(53,000)	(48,000)	(19,000)

Month	Oct.	Nov.	Dec.	Jan.	Feb.	March
Cash at bank (£)	(3,000)	12,000	19,000	57,000	72,000	98,000

Keeping up the good work – and budgeting

The bank manager agrees to the request for an overdraft facility. Chris signs the contract. Now work must start. The purchasing manager orders the new machine and increases the orders for raw plastic and packing materials. The human resources section recruits the new staff and sales and marketing starts planning its advertising campaign. The financial manager says that Plastico may be prepared to negotiate a better price for bulk orders but cannot give extended credit. Chris is pleased with progress so far but also knows that everything done relates to plans for the future. Now she must make sure that the company follows these plans.

Chris knows that the way to do this is to revise the departmental budgets and then monitor expenditure carefully and check any variances.

It makes you think!

The old and revised budgets for production for April are shown below. Study these and decide your answers to the following:

1. Why has the figure for raw plastic increased?
2. Why has the figure for labour increased?
3. At the end of May, the following occurred:

- Raw plastic cost only £98,000 because Plastico reduced its price.
- The production operative had to work overtime to meet the first month's target and the wage bill was £5,800.
- Power used also increased because of this and the bill was £225.
- There were a few teething problems with the new machine and maintenance increased to £2,250.

Calculate the total variance for the production department for that month.

Budget before new contract

PRODUCTION DEPARTMENT BUDGET PLAN – APRIL 2003

Item	Monthly expenditure (£)	Actual expenditure (£)	Variance (£)
Materials (raw plastic)	50,000		
Labour	4,000		
Power	150		
Maintenance	2,000		
Total	56,150		

Budget after new contract

PRODUCTION DEPARTMENT BUDGET PLAN – APRIL 2003

Item	Monthly expenditure (£)	Actual expenditure (£)	Variance (£)
Materials (raw plastic)	100,000		
Labour	5,000		
Power	200		
Maintenance	2,000		
Total	107,200		

Final accounts

At the end of the first year of the project, Finefigs produced their profit and loss account and balance sheet. Sales have been higher than the sales manager's predictions and the overdraft facility hasn't been used for several months. The profit figure is higher than in the previous year and Chris is pleased with progress. Predicted sales are good, so that even though she will have to start paying off the loan capital, future profits will continue to rise.

The effect of external changes

The case study of Finefigs shows what might happen when a business decides to expand its operations and introduce a new product or service. This is one example of a major change, but at least it was a deliberate choice of the owners. Sometimes a business has to change because of things which happen outside the company – such as affected British Airways and the pharmaceutical firm in Cumbria. Other examples of external events which could affect a business are:

- a change in government policy
- a sudden increase in the price of raw materials
- a strike either within the business or at a major suppliers
- a fire or flood at the factory
- the entry of a new aggressive competitor into the market
- actions by a competitor that affect business operations.

In each of these situations, the business would have to go through a similar procedure to Finefigs. In an emergency, cash flow would probably be examined *first* because this would be affected immediately if sales or costs changed. New plans would have to be made to overcome the problem and break-even forecasts and budgets would have to be revised. If extra money was needed, then sources of funding would have to be explored.

Not all changes which happen to a business are bad. A competitor may go out of business or the sales of a product may increase dramatically. Although these are good for business prospects, they still need to be analysed carefully so that the business can use the situation to best advantage.

The end of the story?

If you think that this is the end of the story, you have forgotten one important thing! Each business monitors budget performance all year before next year's budgets are prepared. In addition, all the ongoing financial figures are examined carefully by the management accountant who is keen to keep costs as low as possible all the time. This directly affects the business's profitability. Chris, like other business owners, is also constantly looking at ways to improve business performance.

At a Finefigs management meeting:

- the marketing and sales manager says sales would increase substantially if the selling price of the figures was reduced to £2.30
- the production manager is concerned that 10 per cent of figures are being rejected because they are not up to standard
- the management accountant thinks the amount paid for packaging is too high, and believes that various other costs could be cut by up to 10 per cent
- the human resources manager warns Chris that staff are expecting a 3 per cent pay rise this year
- Chris tells the managers that she has spotted a new business opportunity with the closure of a competitor's business.

All this information needs to be incorporated into future financial plans. So, really, the story never ends. Financial plans are not prepared once, placed in a drawer and forgotten. They need to be constantly adjusted to take advantage of opportunities and cope with unforeseen events. That is the only way to try to ensure that the business will stay profitable in the years to come.

> **Chris's list of costs**
>
> *Fixed costs:* new moulding machine + additional staff + advertising + power = £136,500.
> *Variable costs:* royalty payments, additional raw plastic, packing materials = £800,000
> *Key to break even:*
> 136,500/2.5 − 2.0 = 136,500/0.5 = 273,000

The external test for Unit 3

Unit 3, on business finance, is assessed by an externally set test. You need to pass this to obtain your GCSE in Applied Business. This section gives hints on how to prepare and revise for the test. It also explains what the test paper looks like and gives you hints and tips about what to do during the test itself to get the best result you can.

Preparation and revision

There are 11 sections in Unit 3, and you may have been learning these topics for some time before you take the test. It is normal to feel happier about some more than others. These are likely to be:

- those you found the easiest
- those you did recently.

It is tempting to ignore those you never really understood, the ones you found boring or which you did ages ago! *Don't!* This is because the test covers virtually all of the topics, even though there may not be exactly 11 questions on the paper. If you understand only a few topics, then you won't be able to attempt all the questions and this will affect your marks.

What you need to know

To pass the test you need to:

- understand each topic
- apply your knowledge to practical situations described in case studies. This includes completing business documents, creating break-even charts and completing a cash-flow forecast.

Try to be methodical about your preparation and practise the topics you feel least confident about. Use the spot checks and the section reviews throughout the unit to help you.

Checklist

On page 406 is a list of activities you must be able to do and topics you must understand. Identify each one when you feel you are confident in this area – with the agreement of your tutor!

The test itself

The structure of the test

- The time allowed for the test is 1½ hours.
- There will be several questions and the maximum mark for each question will be given in brackets at the end of each question.
- The total mark you could achieve is 100. This means that you have about one minute to attempt to achieve one mark.
- If the answer to a question is in three parts and the total marks allocated for the question is six, each answer will be for two marks. The paper will have spaces for you to fill when answering the questions.
- The question paper will normally begin with some information about a fictitious organisation. It may include financial details such as a cash flow diagram. You will need this information to answer the questions which will be based on the case study.

Checklist

I know and understand:	I can:
1 Financial documents – purchase orders, delivery notes, GRNs, invoices, credit notes, statements of account, remittance advice slips, cheques and receipts • Why each one is used • The sequence in which they are used • The main headings on each • The benefit of using IT to produce these	Complete financial documents Make calculations on financial documents
2 The following methods of payment – cash, cheque, credit card, debit card, credit/transfer and direct debit • Why and when each one is used • The costs of each one • How long each one takes	Identify the circumstances under which different methods of payment would be used
3 The difference between start-up and running costs • How IT can be used to help reduce costs	Identify typical start-up and running costs
4 Cash-flow forecasts • Why they are prepared and used • The advantages and disadvntages of using a spreadsheet to prepare a forecast	Identify inflows and outflows Complete a cash-flow forecast Make calculations on a cash-flow forecast Identify problems on a cash-flow forecast Use a spreadsheet to predict the impact of changes
5 Why budgets are prepared and how they are monitored	Complete a simple budget Calculate variances on a budget
6 Why break-even points are calculated and how they are affected by changing costs and revenues	Create a break-even chart Calculate the break-even point using the formula
7 The reason for producing a profit and loss statement and how computers can be used to create these	Complete a profit and loss statement Make calculations on a profit and loss statement
8 Why a balance sheet is prepared and how assets and liabilities are calculated	Complete a balance sheet Make calculations on a balance sheet
9 Which stakeholders are interested in business documents and why	Identify the main aspects of financial documents in which stakeholders are interested
10 The different sources of business finance and the circumstances under which a business may choose a particular source	Identify the source of finance which would be chosen in a given situation
11 Why businesses need to prepare and change financial plans and how they are used	Identify the changes which would have to be made to cope with an unexpected development

Types of questions

- The *key word* helps you to understand what you are supposed to be doing.
- If you are asked to identify or describe something, then a fairly brief description is needed.
- If the question asks you to explain something, then you should also give reasons.
- If the word 'evaluate' is included, you are being asked to give a reasoned opinion on the information.
- The use of the word 'suggest' means that you are being asked to give a solution to a problem or situation.

Practice makes perfect!

You should have the opportunity to take practice papers, perhaps under test conditions in class. These help you to become familiar with the structure and layout of the question paper. If there are any questions you do not understand, or any answers you get wrong, then do talk about these to your tutor, especially if you do not understand *why* you had a problem.

The day before

Check that you know:

- the materials you can take into the test (calculator, pens and so on) and the items you cannot
- whether you need to take any ID with you, to prove who you are
- the room in which the test is being held
- the time it starts
- what to do if you are delayed getting to the test because of major transport problems. Although this is unlikely to occur, it is worth knowing what you would have to do. The usual rule is ring your tutor immediately and get there as quickly as possible! But do check for your own school or college.

Strategies in the test

Students with 'good examination technique' can usually gain a higher grade simply because of the way they approach a test paper, not because they have more knowledge.

Golden rules

- Don't be in a hurry to start writing
- Read each question carefully at least *twice* to make sure that you understand what is being asked.
- Note the marks allowed. This will tell you how much time you can spend on the question (remember, roughly one minute for one mark!).
- Ignore questions you don't understand or can't do. Work through the paper doing all the questions you *can* do first.
- Go back to the questions you found hard the first time through. Hopefully, you will have gained some time if you found some questions quite easy. On your 'second run' through the paper you may be able to do all the rest. Otherwise, do those you can and at least attempt those you think you can't.
- Fill in the blanks even if you have to guess! You don't get a mark for a blank line, but you *may* get lucky, and get a mark for the right guess!
- If you have time left, check and check again. Don't try to escape the test room as soon as possible! Use every second wisely.
- A final tip, some students write a sensible answer and then, in a panic near the end, go back and change it! Be careful about doing this, especially if you are impulsive.
- Lastly, don't worry about the result. If you have done the best you can, then worrying won't help. If you haven't, then you know what to do for the resit, don't you!

The external test for unit 3

Appendix 1: Getting the most out of work experience

Overview: work experience

The benefits of work experience

As part of your Applied Business course you may visit one or more businesses on work experience where you will work as an employee either for one or two weeks, or perhaps on a different basis, such as one day a week for a number of weeks.

This is an ideal opportunity to:

- find out what it is like to work in business
- find out more about businesses and the way they operate – you should be able to see *why* you are learning many of the topics you are covering *and* how they apply in practice
- find out information for your portfolio evidence *either* for Unit 1 *or* for Unit 2, or perhaps for both.

Before you go

It is important to find out as much as you can about the business before you go and how you will have to alter your routine. This includes finding out:

- where the business is
- how long it will take to travel there
- what time you will have to get up
- what you should wear
- who you must report to
- the working hours
- what the business does
- what section you will be working in (then you can think about likely jobs you will be given to do).

What can go wrong?

Some students go on work experience and return feeling positive, having learned a great deal. A few return despondent. The experience has been disappointing. Either they didn't like the place, the work or the people (or all three!). In one or two unfortunate cases, students are actually sent back to school or college as 'unsuitable' or 'trouble makers'.

Why do these differences occur and what can *you* do to try to ensure that you have a successful time? Problems are most likely to occur when there is a major difference between what an employer expects, and what the student on work experience might expect!

It makes you think!

Do the quiz opposite to assess your own expectations and attitude to work experience.

Then look at the key on page 411 and see how you score!

Work experience quiz

For each question, choose the answer that most closely reflects your feelings.

1. I think work experience is likely to be:
   a. useful and interesting
   b. a change from school or college
   c. boring
   d. a complete waste of time

2. On the first day, I think:
   a. I will be told all about the business and the work I will be expected to do
   b. I will be given a tour and introduced to everyone
   c. Both of these
   d. None of these

3. I expect people I work with:
   a. to be friendly and chatty
   b. to tell me all about their jobs
   c. to tell me what they want me to do
   d. to ignore me

4. If I am working in an office, I would expect to have:
   a. my own desk and computer
   b. a chair and a space to work
   c. all of these
   d. none of these

5. If I have nothing to do, I think that:
   a. someone will tell me what to do
   b. I will be able to go home early
   c. I should ask what I can do to be helpful
   d. I can surf the Internet

6. If I want to obtain information for my portfolio, I must:
   a. search the business files to find what I need
   b. make proper arrangements to talk to someone who knows about the business and prepare first
   c. ask all the staff for their opinions
   d. walk around the business and watch what is going on

7. I think that employers who offer students work experience:
   a. are just after unpaid help
   b. expect students to know more than they do
   c. are doing students a big favour
   d. only do it because they think it will make them look good

8. I expect to work:
   a. the same hours as full-time employees
   b. school or college hours
   c. hours that suit me
   d. late, perhaps, if there was an emergency

9. If I was regularly asked to do repetitive, boring jobs, I would:
   a. do it slowly and take a lot of breaks
   b. refuse
   c. make mistakes and hope I'd be given something else to do
   d. say that I wouldn't mind doing it some of the time but ask if I could be shown how to do other things as well

10. If I woke up feeling ill one morning, I would:
    a. simply stay in bed
    b. ring up and talk to my supervisor
    c. ring up my tutor
    d. ask my parents to ring up my tutor

Expectations of employers and students

Employer expectations

You may remember from Unit 1 that the main purpose of most businesses is to make a profit. To do this successfully, everyone needs to work hard to fulfil the needs and expectations of customers.

The main purpose of business organisations is not to give placements to students on work experience! For that reason, most businesses consider that they are doing schools or colleges a *favour* when they agree to have a student on work experience.

This is because the student normally has:

- no previous experience of business
- limited skills and abilities for working in business
- no knowledge of the business itself.

There is, therefore, a limit to the type of jobs work experience students can be asked to do. If the staff are very busy, this creates a double problem. Someone has to make time to explain what is needed and check it is done correctly.

Employers want work experience students who are keen, eager, pleasant and can use their initiative to make *suggestions* as to what they can do.

Student expectations

Most students have a realistic attitude to work experience. If they have a part-time job, then this helps. They realise how they must act and behave and are more used to dealing with people at work. They realise that the harder they try and the more they put into the experience, the more they are likely to get out of it.

A few, unfortunately, have other ideas. They expect to be treated as a 'guest' or 'visitor' all the time. They don't expect to 'muck in' and go on errands or fetch coffee. A few don't even expect to be told what to do!

At the other extreme, some students are so nervous they are overwhelmed. They are scared to ask about anything and worried about having to talk to people. They want simply to sit in a corner and be virtually ignored all the time! Yet if this was to happen they would have an unsatisfactory experience and learn very little.

Golden rules on work experience

The best approach is a calm, pleasant business-like attitude. Then remember the following:

- If you are pleasant to people, they are usually pleasant in return. However, don't expect everyone at work to be the same. It won't be your fault. Some people may just be very busy or under a lot of pressure.
- Hopefully, on your first day, you will be told about the business and what you will be expected to do. However, if a crisis has just occurred, this may be skimped. Try to stay positive and 'learn as you go'. Sometimes being thrown in at the deep end can be quite challenging! Don't make *any* judgements after just one day!
- Don't expect staff to have time to chat with you when they are working.
- If you are given an instruction you don't understand, then ask for it to be repeated. This is far better than making a mess of a job because you 'guessed' what to do.
- If you have nothing to do, then look around. Offer to help someone who is busy or to do a routine job (like collecting the post or making coffee) – and keep offering, all week if necessary!
- If you are obtaining information for your portfolio, then make arrangements to talk to someone, and prepare for the meeting properly (see page 142).
- *Never* breach any company policies in relation to the use of IT equipment or access to confidential information. Remember, you have the same legal responsibilities as other employees!

- Make sure you listen carefully to health and safety information you are given, and always follow specific procedures.
- Make sure you are *always* punctual and don't rush off first at the end of the day. If you are likely to be late one morning through no fault of your own, e.g. if you have transport difficulties, ring in and speak to your supervisor, then get there as soon as you can!
- Make certain you know *exactly* what you should do if you are genuinely ill during the time you are on work experience.
- Finally, just in case, make sure you know what to do if you had a *serious* problem, e.g. no work to do at all or someone treating you very unfairly. Normally, the first step would be to talk to your supervisor at work. However, you may in this situation prefer to speak to your tutor.

It makes you think!

Caroline has her own hairdressing salon. She regularly allows students from a local school to spend a week there on work experience. These are usually girls who want to become hairdressers themselves. Both she and her staff do their best to show the students as much as they can about the business, but may struggle to do this later in the week when they are very busy themselves.

The staff actually 'grade' each student from A to E. The students never know their grade, although Caroline does give each student feedback at the end of the week. Normally, she likes to be kind, even if a student hasn't been particularly good.

Within your group, try to decide what characteristics would determine each grade of student. To start, think about some of the routine jobs which go on in a hairdressers' business. Remember that these students actually want to be hairdressers so presumably want to work there!

Then think of good and bad points different students may have and how you would classify these. Finally, compare your ideas with other members of your group.

Key to work experience quiz

Mark yourself as follows:
1. a = 2, b = 1, c = 0, d = 0
2. a = 2, b = 1, c = 1, d = 0
3. a = 1, b = 1, c = 2, d = 0
4. a = 1, b = 2, c = 1, d = 0
5. a = 1, b = 0, c = 2, d = 0
6. a = 0, b = 2, c = 0, d = 0
7. a = 0, b = 1, c = 2, d = 0
8. a = 2, b = 0, c = 0, d = 1
9. a = 0, b = 0, c = 0, d = 2
10. a = 0, b = 2, c = 1, d = 0

16–20 = Good score! You have a positive but realistic attitude and should do well. Remember that even if you have one or two disappointments, such as being thrown in at the deep end on the first day, this doesn't mean you will have a bad experience overall.

11–16 = Look at the questions where you scored badly and see why. Do you need to adjust your attitude and expectations in one or two areas? Remember that the more you put into anything, the more you are likely to gain yourself!

6–10 = You have some ideas which need adjusting or you will be disappointed, and you will annoy and disappoint your colleagues. Remember, they are the ones doing you the favour, not vice versa!

Under 6 = Do everyone a favour. Don't go!

Appendix 2

Photocopiable documents for use with activities in Unit 3 Chapter 17

Mouse Matters Ltd
Kellet Industrial Park
Erdington
BIRMINGHAM
BR9 8KK

Tel: 0121 687 3610
Fax: 0121 123 4567
Website: www.mousematters.shop.uk

VAT Reg. No. 846/3822/98

Email: sales@mousematters.shop.uk

PURCHASE ORDER

To:

Supplier no.:

Official order no.:

Date:

Please supply:

Quantity	Description	Item code	Unit price

Delivery: _____

Signed: _____   Designation: _____

Suppliers should note that orders are valid only if signed by a designated executive of the organisation

Mouse Matters Ltd
Kellett Industrial Park
Erdington
BIRMINGHAM
BR9 8KK

Tel: 0121 687 3610
Fax: 0121 123 4567
Website: www.mousematters.shop.uk

VAT Reg. No. 846/3822/98

Email: sales@mousematters.shop.uk

DELIVERY NOTE

To:

Delivery address (if different):

Your order no.	Customer account no.	Despatch date	Invoice no.	Delivery method

Item code	Quantity	Description

Thank you for your order. Please retain this delivery note for your records

Received in good condition (or comment here)
_____
_____

Signed: _____   Date: _____

Please print name: _____

White copy: customer
Yellow copy: driver
Pink copy: Mouse Matters

GOODS RECEIVED NOTE

Mouse Matters Ltd

Supplier:

GRN no.:

GRN date:

Supplier a/c no.:

Delivery note date:

Carrier:

Checker:

Order no.	Quantity ordered	Quantity delivered	Description of goods	Tick box or enter details if goods damaged or discrepancy identified

White copy: Purchases file
Pink copy: Accounts

Mouse Matters Ltd

Kellett Industrial Park
Erdington
BIRMINGHAM
BR9 8KK

Tel: 0121 687 3610
Fax: 0121 123 4567
Website: www.mousematters.shop.uk

VAT Reg. No. 846/3822/98
Email: sales@mousematters.shop.uk

INVOICE

To:

Your order no.	Customer account no.	Date/tax point	Invoice no.

Item code	Quantity	Description	Unit price £	Net value £
			TOTAL	
			VAT 17.5%	
			TOTAL DUE	

Terms:
Carriage paid
E & OE

White copy: customer
Pink copy: sales
Yellow copy: accounts

Mouse Matters Ltd
Kellet Industrial Park
Erdington
BIRMINGHAM
BR9 8KK

Tel: 0121 687 3610
Fax: 0121 123 4567
Website: www.mousematters.shop.uk

VAT Reg. No. 846/3822/98

Email: sales@mousematters.shop.uk

CREDIT NOTE

To:

Your returns ref.	Customer account no.	Date/tax point	Invoice no.	Credit note no.

Item code	Quantity	Description	Unit price	Net value
			TOTAL	
			VAT 17.5%	
			REFUNDED CHARGE	

Reason for return:

White copy: customer
Pink copy: sales
Yellow copy: accounts

Mouse Matters Ltd
Kellet Industrial Park
Erdington
BIRMINGHAM
BR9 8KK

Tel: 0121 687 3610
Fax: 0121 123 4567
Website: www.mousematters.shop.uk

VAT Reg. No. 846/3822/98

Email: sales@mousematters.shop.uk

STATEMENT OF ACCOUNT

To:

Customer a/c no.:

Credit limit:

Date:

Date	Details	Debit (£)	Credit (£)	Balance (£)

AMOUNT NOW DUE:

REMITTANCE ADVICE

From:

Customer a/c no.:

Date of statement:

AMOUNT ENCLOSED: _____

CHEQUE NO: _____

Your ref: _____

Date of payment: _____

All cheques should be made payable to Mouse Matters Ltd

Date _____

Payee _____

_____

_____

_____

£ _____

265541

✗ The Royal Midshire Bank plc

35 Church St
Erdington
Birmingham BR3 0BJ

Pay _____ ACCOUNT PAYEE _____

£ _____

For and on behalf of
MOUSE MATTERS LTD

16-13-99

Date _____

Cheque No Branch sort code Account No
⑈265541⑈ 16⎓1399⁚ 12890635⑈

_____
Authorised Signatory

Mouse Matters Ltd
Kellett Industrial Park
Erdington
BIRMINGHAM
BR9 8KK

Tel: 0121 687 3610
Fax: 0121 123 4567
Website: www.mousematters.shop.uk

VAT Reg. No. 846/3822/98
Email: sales@mousematters.shop.uk

CASH SALE RECEIPT

Name: Receipt no.:

Address: Date:

                                    Received by:

Quantity	Description	Price	Total
		SUBTOTAL	
		VAT 17.5%	
		TOTAL PAID	

APPENDIX 2

Index

A

Accounts
  business 378–384, 403
  preparing 64
Administration 54, 67, 68, 180
Advertisements, job 236, 238, 247, 251
Advertising 84
Advice note 301
Advisory, Conciliation and Arbitration Service (ACAS) 229
After sales services 91, 273
Agriculture, forestry and fishing 43
Aims and objectives of business 2–20
Application forms – for jobs 247
Appraisal interviews 57, 262
Assets 371, 372, 374, 379
  selling 392
Assisted areas 32

B

Balance sheet
  calculations on 374
  understanding 371–377, 379
Bank accounts 322
Bank loans and overdrafts 343, 387, 388
Bank Automated Payment System (BACS) 311, 327, 329
Banks, as stakeholders 381
Benefits for staff 177
Board of directors 171
Break-even point 357–365, 399
  analysis 357
  chart 358
  formula 363
Breaks from work 190
Budgets 350–356, 402
  process 351
  reports 354
  setting 352
Business accounts
  importance of 378–384
  key items in 379
Business activity 37–53
  and trends 40, 42, 43, 45, 47
  manufacturing 43
  producing raw goods 42
  sales of goods 45
  service activities 47
Business aims 2
Business angel 160, 394
Business communications 101–111
Business investigation checklists
  meetings checklist 142
  Unit 1 questions 142
  Unit 2 questions 28
Business Link 32, 389
Business location 29–36
Business objectives 3
  and employer rights 205
Business organisations
  investigating 137, 285
Business ownership 11–28
Business rates 32

C

Call centres 35
Capital 13, 65, 293, 373
Cartel 113
Cash 321, 322
  at bank 379
Cashflow forecasts 337–348
Casual workers 189
Central Government *see* Government
Certificate of Incorporation 17
Charities 6, 156, 157
Cheque guarantee card 322
Cheques 296, 309, 321, 323
Cleaning 67, 69
Clerical work 67, 68
Client services 38
Communications 101–111
  and feedback 107
  at interviews 257
  electronic 94, 103
  methods of 104
  selecting best method 105
Communications industries 49
Community *see* Local community
Companies
  private limited 16
  public limited 18
Competitiveness 5, 196
Competitors 112, 114, 275
  location of 118
Computer-aided manufacturing (CAM) 75
Computer-assisted design (CAD) 75
Computer security 95
Computerised accounting systems 316
Construction, trends in 45
Consumer Protection Act 282
Contract of Employment 186, 188, 204
Contract of Sale 281
Control of Substances Hazardous to Health Regulations (COSHH) 213
Co-operatives 20
Core business activity 39
Corporation tax 18
Cost of sales 368
Costs
  fixed 358, 361
  running 333
  start-up 333
  variable 358, 361

Covering the costs of a new product or service 332–336
Credit cards 321, 324
Credit facilities 90
Credit note 296, 307
Credit transfer 321, 327, 328
Creditors 373, 380
Curriculum vitae (CV) 248
Customer profiles 117
Customer service 54, 88–92, 269–284
  and on-line support 92, 96
  and technology 280
  features of 279
  investigating 278
Customers 82, 151
  and health and safety 280
  and location of businesss 33
  and sale of products 281
  as stakeholders 382
  expectations of 272
  feedback 276
  importance of 270
  satisfaction 274

D

Data Protection Act 207, 217, 219, 283
Databases 95
Debit cards 321, 326
Debtors 373, 379
Deed of Partnership 14
Delivery Note 296, 300
Demand, consumer 40, 116, 125
Department of Trade and Industry (DTI) 156, 388
Design of goods 93
Development and training, of staff 259–268
Direct credit 328
Direct debit 321, 327, 328
Disability Discrimination Act 209
Disagreements, resolving 224–234
Disciplinary procedures 226
Discrimination 208, 209, 236
Dismissal 227
Display Screen Equipment Regulations 214
Documents, financial 295–320

E

E-commerce *see* Internet companies
Economic conditions 112, 122
Education, trends in 50
E-learning 262
Electricity at Work Regulations 213
Electronic Data Interchange (EDI) 77, 97
Electronic Funds Transfer (EFT) 97
Electronic Point of Sale systems (EPOS) 97
E-marketing 98
Employee organisations 59
Employee rights 206, 207
Employees, as stakeholders 151, 381
Employee's Liability (Compulsory Insurance) Regulations 214
Employer rights 204, 205
Employment
  sector trends 40, 42, 43, 45, 47
  terms and conditions of 57
  see also Working arrangements
Employment Bill 210
Employment law 208
Employment Relations Act 210
Employment Rights Act 210
Employment tribunals 229
Energy production 43
Entrepreneurs 11, 12
Environmental constraints on business 112, 127–133
Environmental groups 156, 157
Environmental objectives 6
Equal opportunities 208
Equal Opportunities Commission 231
Equal Pay Act 208, 211
Ethics, in recruitment 236

European Court of Justice 230
European funds for business 32
Exchange rates 125
Expenses 342, 368
External influences on business 112–136
External test for Unit 3 405

F

Franchises 22
Finance
  factors affecting 395
  function 54, 62
  sources of 32, 66, 160, 385–396
Financial documents 295–320
Financial institutions 160
Financial planning 397–404
Financial services, trends in 48, 198
Financial year 367
Financiers, as stakeholders 158
Fire Precautions Regulations 214
Fixed costs 358, 361
Flexibility, need for 195
Flexitime 190
Functional areas 54–100
  communications between 101, 102

G

Goods received note 296, 301
Government
  and economy 122, 126
  and environment 128
  as stakeholder 155
  departments 24
Grants to business 32, 160, 388
Graphical communications 105
Grievance procedures 225
Gross profit 13, 368

H

Harassment 210
Health and safety 60, 67, 70, 212–216

and customers 280
Health and Safety at Work
    Act 60, 212, 213
Health and Safety Executive
    (HSE) 212
Health care, trends in 50
Hiring and leasing 390
Holiday entitlement 193
Home based working 192
Hot desking 192
Hotels and restaurants,
    trends in 48
Human resources 54, 56

I
ICT 51, 94, 103, 107, 197, 218,
    262, 264, 280, 194, 195, 334
Induction programmes 57, 259
Inflation 123
Information and advice 89
    see also Customer service
Inland Revenue 14, 63
Insurance 214, 362
Interest rates 122, 362, 386
Internet companies 35, 46,
    72, 161, 277
Interviews 241, 256
Investors in People (IIP) 266
Invoices 296, 304
IT in business 94, 316, 338,
    345, 375
IT support 54, 67, 71, 180

J
Job advertisements 236, 238,
    247, 251
Job applications 246
    and CVs 248
    and forms 247
    and letters 249
Job descriptions 163, 169, 238
Job interviews 241, 256
Job roles 163–185
Job security 172, 176, 178, 181
Job sharing 198
Job skills audit 254
Job titles 167

L
Labour, cost and skills 30
Learning reps 163

Letters, job application 249
Liabilities 371, 372, 373
Limited companies
    private 16
    public 18
Limited liability 12, 17
Loans, from bank 387, 388
Local authorities 25, 31, 389
Local community, as
    stakeholder 153
Location of business 29–36

M
Mail order companies 35, 318
Maintenance
    of buildings 67, 69
    of equipment 78
Making and receiving
    payments 321–331
Management of Health and
    Safety at Work
    Regulations 214
Managers
    and job roles 171–174
    as stakeholders 381
Managing the economy 126
Manual Handling Operations
    Regulations 214
Manufacturing, trends in 44
Market research 82
Market share 114
Marketing and sales 54, 81
Marketing mix 83
Mergers 5
Methods of communication
    104
Mining and quarrying, trends
    in 43
Mobile working 191
Monitoring
    performance against
        objectives 7
    use of resources 77, 78
Monopoly 26, 113
Motivation 58
Multinational companies 119

N
National Minimum Wage 179
National Training Awards
    266

National Vocational
    Qualifications 180
Net profit 13, 368, 379
Noise at Work Regulations
    213

O
Objectives, business 3, 6
Office for National Statistics
    (ONS) 42
Office of Fair Trading (OFT)
    113, 283
Operations function 54, 73–81
Operatives, and job roles
    178, 179
Oral communications 104
Organisation charts 163,
    164–168
Outflows 337, 339
Output, sector trends 40, 42,
    43, 45, 47
Outsourcing 65
Overdrafts, bank 343, 388
Overtime 190

P
Packaging (Essential
    Requirements)
    Regulations 131
Partnership Act 15
Partnerships 14
Part-time Workers
    (Prevention of Less
    Favourable Treatment)
    Regulations 190
Payments 64, 321–331, 337,
    339
Performance reviews 262
Person specification 238
Personal job applications
    246–258
Personal services, trends in
    50
Personal skills audit 255
Pollution 113, 128, 129
Portfolio evidence
    for Unit 1 137
    for Unit 2 285
Presentations, giving 107
Pressure groups, as
    stakeholders 156

Index 421

Prices 5, 113, 114, 115, 123
Primary sector 38
Prince's Trust (The) 160, 389
Private limited companies 16
Private sector/ownership 2, 11
Privatisation 25
Production 73
Productivity 195
Profit 4, 13, 368, 386
Profit and loss
   accounts 366, 379
   calculating 366–370
   and layout 368
Promotion
   of goods and services 85
   of staff 57, 58
Provision and Use of Work Equipment Regulations (PUWER) 214
Public administration and defence, trends in 50
Public corporations 25
Public limited companies 18
Public ownership 12, 24
Public sector 1, 12, 24
Publicity campaigns 85
Purchase orders 295, 298
Purchasing function 75

Q
Quality 5, 78
   improving 196

R
Race Relations Act 209
Real estate, renting and business activities, trends in 50
Receipts 64, 296, 315
Recruitment 235–245
   and retention 56
Recycling 131
Redundancy
References (job) 242, 248
Regulation of Investigatory Powers Act 218
Remittance advice slips 296, 309
Reporting of Injuries, Diseases and Dangerous Occurrences Regulations (RIDDOR) 213
Research and Development function 54, 93
Reserves 19, 65, 373
Resolving disagreements 224–234
Resources 74–78
Retail Prices Index (RPI) 124
Retailing, trends in 46
Revenue 337, 358, 362
Rights of employers and employees 203–223
Risk assessment 70, 214, 215
Running costs 333

S
Safety
   committee 215
   officer 215
   policy 215
   representatives 62, 212, 215
Safety Signs and Signals Regulations 214
Sale of Goods Act 282
Sales
   cost of 368
   promotions 85
   revenue 368, 379
   staff 86
   techniques 35
Sectors
   primary 38
   private 2, 11
   public 2, 12, 24
   secondary 38
   services 38, 48
   trends in 40
Security 67, 70
   for computers 95
   staff 180
Sex Discrimination Act 208, 209
Share capital 373
Shareholders 17, 19
   as stakeholders 152, 381
   funds in balance sheet 374, 380
Shares, issuing 391
Shell LiveWIRE 160, 389
Shortlisting (for jobs) 240
Sick leave/pay 194
SMART objectives 6
Sole traders 13
Sources of business finance 32, 66, 160, 385–396
Spreadsheets 338, 345, 375
Staff
   associations 59, 206, 228
   benefits 177
   costs 362
   development and training 57, 58, 259–268
   retention 56
Stakeholders 149–162,
   and business accounts 381–383
   and influence 149, 160
Start-up costs 333
Statement of account 296, 308
Stock control 78
Stock Exchange 19, 392
Suggestion schemes 152
Supervisors, and job roles 174–176
Suppliers, as stakeholders 158
Supply of Goods and Services Act 282
Support staff, and job roles 180–182

T
Takeovers 5
Team working 197
Teleworking 191
Trade Descriptions Act 283
Trade Unions 59–61, 156, 157, 228, 263
Training
   and development 57, 58, 259–268
   and employment 206
   types of 261
Transport and storage, trends in 49
Transport links, and location 32
Trends
   in service activities 58
   sector 40

U
Unlimited liability 12, 14, 16

V
Value added tax (VAT) 306
Variable costs 358, 361
Venture capital 160, 393
Victimisation 210
Video communications 104

W
Wages and salaries 65
Waste minimisation 130
Wholesaling, trends in 46
Work experience, hints and tips 408
Working arrangements 186–202
   changing 195, 200
   different types of 189
Working conditions 57
Working Time Regulations 203, 209
Workplace (Health, Safety and Welfare) Regulations 92, 212, 213
Written communications 105

Y
Young Workers' Directive 210